W9-BLX-975

STAGING

THE WAR

STAGING
THE WAR

American Drama and World War II

ALBERT WERTHEIM

INDIANA
University Press
Bloomington & Indianapolis

This book is a publication of

Indiana University Press
601 North Morton Street
Bloomington, IN 47404-3797 USA

http://iupress.indiana.edu

Telephone orders   800-842-6796
Fax orders   812-855-7931
Orders by e-mail   iuporder@indiana.edu

The paper used in this publication meets the minimum requirements of American National Standard for Information Sciences—Permanence of Paper for Printed Library Materials, ANSI Z39.48-1984.

Manufactured in the United States of America

Library of Congress Cataloging-in-Publication Data

Wertheim, Albert.
    Staging the war : American drama and World War II /
Albert Wertheim.
        p. cm.
    Includes bibliographical references (p.   ) and index.
    ISBN 0-253-34310-0 (alk. paper)
    1. American drama—20th century—History and criticism.
    2. World War, 1939–1945—Literature and the war.
    3. Theater—United States—History—20th century. 4. War in literature. I. Title.
PS338.W67W47 2004
812'.5409358—dc21

                            2003006845

    1   2   3   4   5   09   08   07   06   05   04

For Judy, Lewis and Ellie, Gerald and Raluca, and Benjamin

CONTENTS

INTRODUCTION

What happened in American drama in the years between the Depression and the conclusion of World War II? How did the war make its impact on the drama? And more important, how was the drama used during the war years to shape American attitudes about U.S. participation in the combat, who the enemy was, and the proper role of citizens both at home and in the service? Studies of American drama and anthologies of American plays for the most part skip cavalierly from the 1930s Depression-era plays of Clifford Odets and the Group Theatre to Tennessee Williams's *The Glass Menagerie*, which opened six weeks before V-E Day in 1945, or to Arthur Miller's *All My Sons* in 1947. With the exception of Thornton Wilder's *Our Town*, and perhaps Robert Sherwood's *Abe Lincoln in Illinois* and Lillian Hellman's *Watch on the Rhine*, little is said about the decade between the heyday of Odets and the first successes of Miller and Williams. Yet that very decade is the decade of World War II, arguably the most important of the twentieth century. Although there are studies of wartime film, like the two books both called *Hollywood Goes to War*, inexplicably, no one has paid much attention to the playwriting and theatre of the period.[1]

From the period of Hitler's rise in the 1930s to the decade following the end of World War II, there are many fine plays about the war and the issues surrounding it. Some of these plays were later made into films. But the films, often made months or years after the Broadway production, usually lacked the currency and immediacy of the plays, which had been staged at a particular moment in the war era. The plays examined in this study deserve close attention both for their excellence as works of drama and for the things they reveal about American society during the war. Many of the plays are still vibrant and stage-worthy, but there is much to learn as well about wartime issues from other plays that now seem dated, and from those that did not have long runs on Broadway either because they were not well crafted or because they were raising issues that audiences would rather not have had raised. With great perspicacity, Hamlet instructs the actors who have come to Elsinore Castle that "the purpose of playing, whose end, both at the first and now, was and is, to hold, as 'twere, the mirror up to nature." And so it is that the drama during the World War II period holds the mirror up to life and thought in America, registering the dominant feelings of its citizens as well as the social changes that were occurring.

The years covered by this study, approximately 1934 to 1955, are among the most critical years of the twentieth century. Certainly the combat across the Atlantic and the Pacific as well as the political issues that sparked that combat are at the vibrant heart of those years, but just as important are the changes in the American way of life. These include a renewed endorsement for the freedoms Americans had come to take for granted, for these were suddenly under attack from fascist ideologies abroad and fascist subversives at home. The war brought with it a change in the American economic picture. Big business garnered new profits from wartime industry, and business moved from the slump of the Depression to new prosperity. The unemployment of the 1930s began to be reversed by the war of the 1940s. And wartime brought with it important changes as well for the civic and ethical responsibilities of American businessmen, who were often producing goods that would be used by the armed forces and by the fighting men overseas. World War II saw new roles for women in the workplace. As able-bodied men went overseas to serve their country, women left their traditional places at the kitchen sink and scrubbing board to take over the jobs men had left behind. They worked on assembly lines and even in heavy industry, revising a nation's idea of what roles women could assume in the work force. These things the plays of the period register.

The plays register, too, a variety of American demographic dislocations. Servicemen from around the country found themselves in boot camps far away from home, often in small towns and in new geographies. There they met, as their fathers had before them in World War I, other men from every corner of the nation. The small-town boy from Iowa became friends with the urban recruit from New York, the Southerner from North Carolina with the erstwhile logger from Oregon. Protestants mingled with Jews and Catholics, Italian Americans with Swedish Americans, the rich with the poor, the educated with the undereducated. Hitler had cited the weakness of America because it was a nation of mongrel races. Americans were themselves learning and then proving to the world that the United States embodies a strength that emanates from diversity united, even though that diversity did not extend to America's populations of color: African Americans, Asian Americans, Hispanics, and Native Americans.

As several wartime dramas reflect, a mingling of another kind took place in the towns and port cities where army and naval bases were located. Small towns found themselves changed overnight when they became the sites of sizable army camps containing a multitude of servicemen. The flood of those young men coming to town on their weekend passes radically changed the life of once conservative communities. Liquor flowed, and recruits who had lived under the military strictures for weeks came in search of pleasure. Local young women forged relationships, licit and illicit, with the GIs stationed nearby. Josephine

Bentham and Herschel Williams's 1942 play, *Janie,* projects the change in comic terms. Shortly after the war, Tennessee Williams, by contrast, in *A Streetcar Named Desire,* remembers the influx of troops to the army camp near Belle Reve as a wellspring of debauchery and a major contributor to the tragic ruin of Blanche Dubois. Furthermore, as the plays show—for example, Maxwell Anderson's *The Eve of St. Mark*—men who were leaving home to serve their country often hastily married women they had but recently met, or simply short-circuited the usual courtship ritual with a girl back home. Men on leave also came to new cities, usually port cities, and before a week was up had sexual experiences and sometimes married women they had just met. The musical *On the Town,* which Leonard Bernstein wrote with Betty Comden, Adolph Green, and Jerome Robbins, offers a lighthearted insight into that situation. Edward Chodorov's important comedy *Those Endearing Young Charms* looks at the situation in thoughtful and incisive ways. Not only did the press of war give little time for extended romance, courtship, and engagements, but men died, leaving behind grieving parents, young wives suddenly made widows, and children who never would see their fathers. Lads who had lustily gone off to war saw terrible things in combat or were themselves wounded, returning home to wives and families as scarred men, physically crippled and psychologically damaged. Plays such as Lillian Hellman's *The Searching Wind,* Arthur Laurents's *Home of the Brave,* and Elsa Shelly's *Foxhole in the Parlor* made Broadway audiences aware of the war's casualties among its survivors.

Before Pearl Harbor, American plays provide eloquent evidence for the national conflict between American post–World War I isolationism and the voices of those warning that the U.S. must take a stand to stem the aggression and the ideologies of Hitler and Mussolini. And after Pearl Harbor, the drama cues the nation about the nature of American patriotism, why the United States is at war and over what issues. It speaks as well about the lives of servicemen and the lives of their families, and the need for all Americans, in the military or at home, to pull their individual oars so the war can be concluded quickly, with victory for the Allies and for the survival of (American) democracy.

During the 1930s and in the years immediately after Pearl Harbor, almost every American playwright of any note addressed the war and its issues. Some of these playwrights were more eloquent and adept at writing about political topics than others. Wartime dramatic contributions of much interest emerged from the pens of Clifford Odets, Thornton Wilder, William Saroyan, Claire Boothe, Robert Sherwood, S. N. Behrman, Sidney Kingsley, Sidney Howard, Maxwell Anderson, Lillian Hellman, George S. Kaufman, Moss Hart, Howard Lindsay and Russel Crouse, Rose Franken, Robert Ardrey, Archibald MacLeish, Philip Barry, and Elmer Rice. The one playwright notable for his absence and silence during this period is Eugene O'Neill, who had received the Nobel Prize for literature in 1936 and who remains the only American playwright ever to be awarded that honor. Nobel Prize in hand, O'Neill was ideally situated to pen an attention-getting drama or statement about World War II issues. What

O'Neill produced, however, was the curiously irrelevant *The Iceman Cometh*, certainly one of his masterpieces but one that closed quickly, probably because it was so vastly removed from the concerns of the day. Why was O'Neill so remarkably silent about the war and the burning issues of the time? Was he uninterested in the world events or incapable of writing about them, beset by illness or obsessed with his own demons? Whatever the answer, his is the one voice glaringly absent from this study.

But not every American playwright was writing for the Broadway stage. Indeed, although this study considers in some detail war issues and American plays presented in the New York theatres, other important developments using drama and dramatic material were taking place in other venues. Perhaps the most illuminating and original material discussed in this study is the wealth of dramatic material issued by and performed under the auspices of the U.S. government. During the Depression the successes and strong audience effect of the Federal Theatre Project and the Group Theatre and of playwrights like Clifford Odets, John Howard Lawson, or George Sklar had shown how theatre could pack a political punch and serve to rally audiences behind causes—often leftist causes—or to support social issues. After the U.S. declared war and entered the fray, Washington seemed to remember how those very dramaturgical techniques used so effectively by the Group Theatre and its playwrights could productively be used in the service of wartime patriotic, pro-government propaganda.

The U.S. military found itself after Pearl Harbor fighting in what were called the European and the Pacific theatres of the war. But it became engaged as well in the more traditional definition of theatre, in the production of dramatic material for the stage. The U.S. Army conducted, of all things, a playwriting competition among the troops and selected, for production in New York and around the country, the five best one-act play submissions. The Air Forces (as that division of the military was then called) for its part commissioned distinguished playwright Moss Hart to write *Winged Victory*, a dramatic production that employed scores of servicemen as actors and musicians in an extraordinarily extravagant production that touted the excellence of the Air Forces, promoted the desirability of enlisting in that branch of the military, and inspired audience confidence in American air power. The U.S.O. disseminated to American military bases at home and abroad scripts of skits, entertainments, and musicals, including three written largely by Pvt. Frank Loesser. The Military Training Division also took to playwriting. It issued didactic dramas to training sites. These were largely aimed at alerting recruits to good eating habits, personal hygiene, and the insidiousness of the enemy.

An unlikely theatrical "angel" and artistic sponsor, the Treasury Department during the war issued scores of play scripts for schoolchildren, young adults, college students, and community groups. The aim of those scripts was twofold. Americans were urged to support the war effort by purchasing War Bonds and War Stamps: not an easy sell immediately after the Depression, which had so seriously compromised American faith in financial instruments. The Treasury plays also sought to address economists' concerns that wartime prosperity, coming as it did on the heels of the Depression, would encourage reckless spending on the part of American consumers. The danger the Treasury Department envisioned was that while the U.S. was fighting a war across both the Atlantic and the Pacific, it would have to fight another war against black-market buying and runaway inflation at home. The Treasury plays sought to teach citizens, from schoolchildren to adults, that if America was to win the war, its citizens would have to play their part in the war effort by curbing wayward spending, stemming inflation, and investing in the government through the purchase of War Bonds and War Stamps.

The theatrical stage was not the only dramatic vehicle that played a role in wartime awareness and propaganda efforts. Every evening during the war, Americans were tuned to their radios for the latest battlefront reports. And when they weren't hearing those, they could listen to some truly remarkable wartime drama. Even before the United States entered the war, radio was discovered as not merely a conveyor of news and light entertainment but as a powerful medium—political and otherwise—that could create a drama of words and sounds to sway audiences. Perhaps the most persuasive testimony to the power of radio, particularly in a time of global uncertainty, was Orson Welles's famous 30 October 1938 radio dramatization of *The War of the Worlds.* The success of Archibald MacLeish's two brilliant, poetic, immediately prewar radio plays, *The Fall of the City* and *Air Raid,* was likewise remarkable and eye-opening about the power of radio as a medium for drama. Not only individual plays but also drama series began to appear on radio. In the months before Pearl Harbor, a radio drama series called *The Free Company* and using playwrights like William Saroyan, Marc Connelly, Paul Green, Stephen Vincent Benét, and Maxwell Anderson bolstered American morale and helped Americans get their patriotic priorities in order in the face of the inevitable American entry into the war. Within eight days after the U.S. entered the war, radio playwright Norman Corwin aired his now famous *We Hold These Truths,* a play about the Bill of Rights and the freedoms American troops were being called on to protect. An estimated sixty million people, nearly half the American population, listened to that broadcast.

Almost immediately after Corwin's broadcast, playwrights, producers, and the government all realized that America had a whole new and incredibly vast audience for theatre: the American radio public, which numbered literally in the millions. A plethora of patriotic radio dramas and drama series resulted. And with scripts needed on a weekly basis, able playwrights were in demand. Both aspiring and seasoned playwrights were snapped up and employed by the radio networks. Those playwrights—such as Arthur Laurents, Arthur Miller, Maxwell Anderson, Morton Wishengrad, Stephen Vincent Benét, and Archibald MacLeish—wrote a spate of effective thirty-minute plays about war. Those plays were often acted by the greatest talents from Broadway and Hollywood who performed pro bono as their contribution to the war effort. Radio theatre during the war years was an often fruitful, though sometimes contentious, ménage à trois composed of talented playwrights, major radio broadcasting companies, and the U.S. government. For the playwrights, this provided the unusual job opportunity not only of writing scripts on a regular or frequent basis but of writing scripts that would be heard by an audience vastly greater than any Broadway theatre could ever deliver, and acted by the most celebrated performers. For example, a then completely unknown playwright named Arthur Miller, who wrote radio scripts during the war for the *Cavalcade of America* series, had his scripts performed by such stars as Jean Hersholt, Orson Welles, Madeleine Carroll, and Paul Muni.

Once the war was over and victory attained, once the confetti of V-E Day and V-J Day had been swept aside, drama was employed to help Americans understand what had happened and why and, more important, to script what winning the war should mean for the American future. The plays of the postwar period move Americans boldly forward toward a new era of internationalism and toward a recognition that America—which had rejected membership in the League of Nations after World War I—must now not merely become a member of the United Nations but take on a leadership role in that body. Plays like Howard Lindsay and Russel Crouse's *State of the Union* and Robert Sherwood's *The Rugged Path* were among those making an eloquent case for a new American international presence.

While the war was being waged, little was known of what was taking place in the Nazi death camps. Only when those camps were liberated at the close of the war did the full horror come into view. The postwar plays begin to help Americans come to grips with the unspeakable, with what has since come to be known as the Holocaust. Postwar dramas such as Frances Goodrich and Albert Hackett's *The Diary of Anne Frank* and Ben Hecht's *A Flag Is Born* were the first steps in helping Americans face and understand the human tragedy that was the war in Europe. And the racial matters so central to the Holocaust and the German ideals of racial purity also play themselves out in other important ways on the American postwar stage. How could Americans damn Hitler's master race politics that sent Jews and other minorities to the gas chambers and ovens, yet continue in good conscience to practice and affirm racism at home? Should Negro servicemen, who had served the U.S. so loyally during the war, albeit in segregated units, return home to be second-class citizens confined in the future to service in segregated military units, and should they continue to have racial segregation imposed upon them in their hometowns? Groundbreaking postwar plays by white playwrights depicting African-American soldiers returning home, such as Arnaud d'Usseau and James Gow's *Deep Are the Roots,* Robert Ardrey's *Jeb,* and Maxine Wood's *On Whitman Avenue,* poignantly raise the issues of racial discrimination even as they seem to prepare the way for African-American playwrights like Lorraine Hansberry, LeRoi Jones, Ed Bullins, and Loften Mitchell to soar into flight a decade later.

This study is, in part, an attempt to fill in a very significant gap in the history of American drama. More important, however, it seeks to explore the complex interrelationship between the drama and the most central and significant historical, political, and social event of the twentieth century. How did the prewar events in Europe, American participation in the war, and war's aftermath make their indelible mark on American playwriting? And how, at the same time, did playwrights use the drama and dramaturgy as an effective means for shaping the American public's understanding of why the U.S. should enter the conflict in Europe? And later, why the war was being fought? What basic freedoms had American troops committed themselves to protect? And what responsibilities were required of the American populace, first during the war and then after victory? When one examines over 150 plays in the course of a twenty-year period, as this study does, repeated patterns, central issues, and reiterated messages begin lucidly to emerge. Indeed, this study has both the advantages and disadvantages inherent in a macroproject: it shows clearly and vividly the shape of the connection between the drama and World War II, even as it will seem to some to be a discussion of too many plays. Writing this study has, however, for me been a personal pleasure because as I explored the drama from the mid-1930s to the mid-1950s, the face of the war became increasingly clear as did the power of theatre to "hold, as 'twere, the mirror up to nature."

When I began to undertake this study, I had a sketchy idea about which well-known plays I ought to examine, but I quickly discovered scores of plays—some of them quite wonderful—about which I had no previous knowledge. In unexpected ways, writing this book proved an adventure that led to the discovery of hitherto almost unrecognized dramatic material. I was amazed to discover three U.S.O. musicals written primarily by Pvt. Frank Loesser before he became famous for *Guys and Dolls, Where's Charley, Most Happy Fella,* and *How to Succeed in Business.* Even his biography, written by his daughter, fails to mention the U.S.O. musicals, one of which is graced with a cover drawn by Al Hirschfeld and another of which contains choreography notations by Pvt. José Limon.

Likewise, I happened on one treasure trove of dramatic materials issued by the U.S. Treasury Department, and another issued by the Military Training Division of the Second Service Command. In the course of writing the chapter on wartime radio plays, I was pleased to discover the almost unknown and largely unpublished radio drama that Arthur Miller wrote before his postwar Broadway success, *All My Sons,* skyrocketed him to fame. It was also a pleasure to read and discuss illuminating but now nearly unremembered plays such as Maxine Woods's *On Whitman Avenue,* Elsa Shelley's *Foxhole in the Parlor,* Dan James's *Winter Soldiers,* Ben Hecht's *We Will Never Die* and *A Flag Is Born,* and Rose Franken's *Soldier's Wife.* I was gratified, too, to discover the largely unrecognized playwriting excellence of Edward Chodorov, whose plays have never received the attention they justly deserve. If this study restores some of these plays and playwrights to life and brings them to the attention of readers, I shall be very pleased.

A discovery of another kind that I made came from reading dramas that did not seem at first glance to be about World War II. Reading those dramas in a wartime context, however, nuanced them in unanticipated ways. Suddenly Thornton Wilder's *Our Town,* William Saroyan's *The Time of Your Life,* Sidney Kingsley's *Patriots,* and Tennessee Williams's *A Streetcar Named Desire* showed new facets of meaning that I had missed when I saw or read them without the date of their original performance in mind. In short, writing this book was something of an education for me and may be one, I trust, for readers as well.

On a more personal level, writing this study has been an unusually satisfying and even sometimes cathartic experience for me. I am a child of World War II and my life was markedly shaped by its events. The plays I discuss were written and performed in the years just prior to my birth and during those of my very early childhood. In a sense, they articulate the tensions and events going on around me in the 1940s, the meaning of which I was not capable of understanding at the time. The legacy of the war and the uncertainties of wartime were already mine at my birth. My parents, both born and raised in Germany, came to America as refugees in 1937, fleeing from Nazi persecution. They arrived speaking German and brought with them little in the way of worldly possessions. Even as a toddler during the war, I sensed their feelings of profound hatred for the Third Reich as well as their enormous feelings of patriotism and love for the country that had succored them. With some strain on a meager family budget, I was proudly dressed in a child's Sunday best of the day: a wartime child-sized sailor suit. Before I was two years old, I was taught by my father and mother to recognize the photos of Hitler, Mussolini, and Hirohito in the newspapers and to spit at them. I remember the snatches of adult conversation etched with names and words like Roosevelt, Theresienstadt, sugar ration, *Judenstern,* Himmler, and later *umgekommen* (killed). And there were those two oft-repeated words, *ausgewandert nach,* which means "emigrated to," followed such words as *Brasilien, Süd Afrika, Australien, Palestina, Kuba, Bolivien, Kanada, Argentinien, England, Shanghai,* and *Nyassaland.* Those sounds of wartime diaspora were among the first I knew.

At the war's end, I found myself, then a five-year old, swept along by the crowds on a New York pier. My mother's seventy-year-old aunt was about to disembark from a ship containing one of the first boatloads of prisoners released from Theresienstadt concentration camp, where she had spent most the war. The look of the gaunt and frightened people who emerged from that ship haunts me to this day. In subsequent years, I was—and continue to be—stunned by the realization that had I been born in Germany instead of in New York, my parents and I would surely have died in Theresienstadt, Auschwitz, Gurz, Riga, or one of the other camps to which relatives were sent and from which they never returned. I understand, too, the depth of my parents' feelings of love for America. In what other land could they have arrived with no English and few belongings, and twenty years later been able to see their son attend Columbia and Yale or to have him become a university professor? If there are strains of my own patriotism in this study, they are ones that come to me naturally. In many ways, writing this study has meant for me writing the history of my origins and of my childhood and giving thanks that I was born in the U.S. and survived the war.

No study like this ever gets written without the help and encouragement of others. I am pleased, therefore, to acknowledge here those who have been such a great help and support as I did the research and composed the text. I am especially grateful to those stalwart and dear friends who read my manuscript chapter by chapter as I wrote it. John Barlow, Joseph Kissane, Larry Kallenberg, Jeffrey Spielberger, and Leah Strassman are the angels who read closely and saved me from numerous errors and infelicities as well as from sheer blindness. They each gave generous and meticulous attention to the manuscript, making a great many extremely valuable suggestions about style and content and catching an embarrassing number of lapses. I incorporated their suggestions thankfully and shamelessly. Richard Fish of LodeStone Audio Theatre, who is a font of knowledge about radio drama and about Norman Corwin, kindly read and provided valuable advice about the radio drama chapter. Howard Blue was kind enough to share with me his prepublication galleys for his useful and well-researched *Words at War: World War II Era Radio Drama and the Postwar Broadcasting Industry Blacklist.*

I was fortunate to have been aided in ways large and small by the exemplary staff of the Indiana University Library. Lisa Browar was especially helpful as I tracked down recondite material. Most of all, however, I know I can never adequately repay Lou Malcomb, the Indiana University librarian for government documents. Without her tireless efforts on behalf of this project, the chapter on government-sponsored drama would never have been written. I am also most grateful for the kindness of the consistently helpful staff at the New York Public Library's Center for the Performing Arts, and in particular to Rod Bladell, Louise Martzinek, Jeremy Megraw, and Kevin Winkler. Thanks are likewise due to the staff of the Museum of Radio and Television in New York and of the Library of Congress. Anne Guernsey at the Museum of the City of New York was unusually helpful in helping me get a release to use photo materials.

Much of this study was written with the help of a generous grant from the President's Arts and Humanities Initiative at Indiana University. I am also greatly indebted to my Indiana colleagues James H. Madison and Stephen Watt, who were good enough warmly to endorse my project at its earliest stages and encourage me while I was writing it. I have also been unusually blessed with Michael Lundell, my fabulous editor at Indiana University Press. He has made the publication of this book a virtually wrinkle-free experience. My colleagues and friends at Indiana University and in Bloomington have been a great support to me both as I wrote this study and in other ways that they will know. I want especially to thank Lillian Barr, Budd Stalnaker, Henry Cooper, Peter Slemon, Carole Holton and Jeff Alberts, Anne and Jan Gardner, Vincent Liotta, Jeanne Madison, Mary McGann and Tim Wiles, Lewis H. Miller, Keith and Marion Michael, Alvin and Erna Rosenfeld, John Eakin, Brian Winchester, Howard Jensen, Pat Barlow, Susan and Jim Jensen, Harry Geduld, Donald J. Gray, and

Justin Foster. My great thanks as well to other colleagues and friends: Nancy T. Bazin (Old Dominion University), Ann Fox (Davidson College), C. J. Gianakaris (Western Michigan University), Glenda E. Gill (Michigan Technical University), Anthony Heilbut, Chris Hudgins (University of Nevada, Las Vegas), Norma Jenckes (University of Cincinnati), Al LaValley (Dartmouth), Kyung-won Lee (Yonsei University), Suk-koo Rhee (Yonsei University), and Tony Stafford (University of Texas, El Paso).

The support over the years from my mentor at Yale, Eugene M. Waith, has meant a great deal to me. The debt to my late father and to my mother will never be repaid. Nor will that to my wife, Judy, who has lived with the project day by day. To her; to my children, Lewis and Ellie, and Gerald and Raluca; and to my grandson, Benjamin, this book is dedicated with love.

STAGING

THE WAR

ONE

Getting Involved: American Drama on the Eve of World War II

I

During the years when the Depression was taking its toll on this country, the storm clouds of war were rapidly gathering over Europe and Asia. Preoccupied with domestic labor and unemployment problems and still recovering from the scars of World War I, a war in which it seemed to many the U.S. had paid a price for allowing itself to be involved in the disputes of other countries, Americans seemed eager in the 1930s to cling to pacifism and splendid isolation and to avert their eyes from events beyond American shores. They turned away from the quarrels in Europe to laugh instead over the quarrels between Fibber McGee and Molly or the antics of Edgar Bergen and Charlie McCarthy. Looking back on that period, Tennessee Williams in *The Glass Menagerie* (31 March 1945) has his narrator, Tom Wingfield, brilliantly capture the tenor of the times in a lyrical comment:

> Adventure and change were imminent in this year. They were waiting around the corner for all these kids. Suspended in the mist over Berchtesgaden, caught in the folds of Chamberlain's umbrella—In Spain there was Guernica! But here there was only hot swing music and liquor, dance halls, bars, and movies, and sex that hung in the gloom like a chandelier and flooded the world with brief, deceptive rainbows. . . . All the world was waiting for bombardments![1]

The last sentence, moreover, sardonically references the optimistic 1930s hit song "The World Is Waiting for the Sunrise." A half-century after World War II,

America's willful denial of events in Europe was likewise movingly captured in Arthur Miller's *Broken Glass* (1994). And in the Broadway theatres of the late 1930s, there was certainly much on the boards to take the public's mind off the hardships of the Depression and off the initial acts of the tragic drama then unfolding in Europe. The period from 1938 to 1941 saw the popular productions of such lighthearted fare as *Hellzapoppin* (1938), *The Philadelphia Story* (1939), *The Man Who Came to Dinner* (1939), *Life with Father* (1939), *My Sister Eileen* (1940), and *Arsenic and Old Lace* (1941). Eventually, however, not even such Broadway delights could provide sufficient diversion from the terrible activities already in progress in Europe, from the horror of *Kristallnacht* and rampant anti-Semitism, the invasion of Poland, the German takeover of Paris, and the bombing of Coventry, to Hitler's strikes against Greece and Russia. Increasingly, war-related plays took their place on Broadway alongside the comic and more usual dramatic fare.

But in the 1930s, many Americans simply tried to avert their gaze from Europe; others, imbued with post–World War I pacifism, urged American neutrality on ideological grounds; still others felt that the U.S. needed to address the problems of the Depression at home before addressing those across the ocean. Splendid isolation and pacifism were, for many, desirable goals for the United States. Indeed, possibly the most widely read novel of the 1930s was Margaret Mitchell's subversively pacifist *Gone with the Wind* (1936), which pointedly presented the destruction and loss of human life that inevitably accompany war. And when that novel was made into the famous 1939 epic motion picture, Mitchell's pacifist message was italicized by the new process of Technicolor, which could display wartime bloodletting with new vividness. In the theatre of the mid-1930s, the pacifism of the day found voice in several plays, including three notable new offerings of the 1936 New York season: Irwin Shaw's *Bury the Dead*, Paul Green and Kurt Weill's *Johnny Johnson*, and Robert Sherwood's *Idiot's Delight*. The previous year had seen the production of a dramatic paradox: Albert Maltz's militantly pacifist one-act play *Private Hicks*, about a national guardsman who refuses to shoot at industrial strikers. But the clouds over Europe grew increasingly dark. The abuse of Jews and dissidents and the existence of concentration camps (though not what was happening in them) became known through the media and through the poignant accounts of the increasing number of refugees escaping to American shores from Germany and Nazi-occupied countries. As a result, some pacifists and some who had turned a blind eye began to rethink their stances; playwrights like Irwin Shaw and Robert Sherwood, who had written pacifist plays, found themselves doing a one-hundred-and-eighty-degree turn.

Although theatre can serve as diverting, escapist entertainment, theatre can also be a vehicle for reaching a large and popular audience, alerting them to pressing political and social issues. And who better in the 1930s to know the power of theatre than those playwrights connected with the Group Theatre or Federal Theatre Project? The political engagement and pugnacity of those playwrights can be felt by the very titles of the books written about Depression-era theatre: *Real Life Drama, The Fervent Years, The Drama of Attack, Drama Was a Weapon, Drama and Commitment,* and *The Political Stage.*[2] Thus, even as madcap comedies of *diversion* were being mounted in the late 1930s by Kaufman, Hart, and others, a new drama of *conversion* was also finding its way onto the stage and into the minds of Americans, shaping their attitudes toward the events brewing in Europe and turning their fear, indifference, and avoidance into concern and involvement. Many of the writers who had written the politically engaged dramas of the Depression years now turned their attention to the dire events in Europe and to America's foreseeable involvement in another global war. And other playwrights joined them. Some of these conversion plays have become classics of the American theatre: Thornton Wilder's *Our Town* (5 February 1938), Robert Sherwood's *Abe Lincoln in Illinois* (15 October 1938), William Saroyan's *The Time of Your Life* (25 October 1939), Sherwood's *There Shall Be No Night* (29 March 1940), and Lillian Hellman's *Watch on the Rhine* (1 April 1941). These plays and others written during the period immediately prior to the bombing of Pearl Harbor use the strategies of drama to raise the consciousness of their American audiences, encouraging them to take an active stand in stemming the tide of fascism in Europe. They tell us much not only about American society and attitudes during those tense years before the American declaration of war on 7 December 1941 but also about the effective uses of drama during a period of crisis.

It is not surprising that one of the first playwrights to use drama to warn Americans about the dangerous nature of European totalitarianism is Elmer Rice, a writer particularly sensitive to political and social change. In September 1934, when Rice's *Judgment Day* opened at the Belasco Theatre in New York, Mussolini's dictatorship in Italy was already firmly established and Hitler had been named chancellor and given dictatorial power in Germany twenty-one months earlier. Trained as a lawyer, Rice found courtrooms and law offices congenial settings for his plays. His *Judgment Day,* like his *Counsellor-at-Law* and *On Trial,* is a courtroom drama. Set in an anonymous Eastern European country, *Judgment Day* is obviously inspired by the much-publicized trial of Bulgarian communist leader Georgi Dimitrov, who, living in exile in Germany, was arrested along with other communists on 27 February 1933 and subsequently put on trial in Leipzig by the newly elected Adolf Hitler. Charged with setting fire to the German Reichstag building, Dimitrov was eventually deemed not guilty and subsequently released, largely as a result of a strong defense and the worldwide attention given to his trial. Notwithstanding Georgi Dimitrov's acquittal, Rice saw the handwriting on the German wall, and in *Judgment Day* directed the American gaze to read that handwriting.[3] In Rice's play, the defendants in a rigged trial are accused of an assassination attempt on the country's dictator, and in the course of the play, the brutalities of dictatorship are powerfully exposed. The courtroom setting is at once *Judgment Day*'s asset and liability. It allows the many outrages of dictatorship to be recounted through courtroom testimony, yet, by withholding the actual stage presentation of violence, Rice's play is hindered from moving the audience in emotional, visceral ways. As the trial in *Judgment Day* comes to its conclusion, Rice's defense lawyer, pointedly cast as an American, pleads emotionally:

> To adjudge these defendants innocent is to proclaim to the world that we take our place among those nations who put justice and honor above political considerations; that in our land, truth and right still prevail. To condemn them, to find them guilty, is to acknowledge that justice is dead, that liberty no longer exists; it is to invite the indignation and the opprobrium of the civilized world. (192)[4]

The appeal here is clearly to American democratic values and the concern for the preservation of American civil liberties. Nevertheless, in Rice's 1934 drama, dictatorship, set as it is in some anonymous corner of Eastern Europe, still seems a relatively remote threat for Americans, who can enjoy the luxury of being outraged and condemning but who need not worry that dictatorship might take root and flourish on American soil.[5]

Even more remote is the fascism that is portrayed rather vaguely in S. N. Behrman's *Rain from Heaven*, which opened at the Golden Theatre on Christmas Eve, three months after *Judgment Day*. Set in the drawing room of Lady Lael Wyngate's English country manor house, Behrman's is a well-made play that could have come from the pen of Arthur Wing Pinero, Somerset Maugham, or Sidney Howard. Amid a lot of talk, infidelities, and conflicted couples is a contention between those Americans and English characters who would found a league of Anglo-American Aryan youth and those who are refugees from a Continental anti-Semitism and fascism that hovers turbidly in the play's background. Gerald Bordman notes the stage success of *Rain from Heaven*, which ran for an impressive ninety-nine performances.[6] This is not surprising, for American audiences in 1934—perhaps caught between isolationism and naïveté—were not yet ready for stronger dramatic fare about anti-Semitism and Nazis. Indeed, Behrman neatly keeps the unpleasant subject matter from the American doorstep by locating it, for no good reason, in an aristocratic British home. Resident at Lady Lael's house, moreover, is Hugo Willens, a German refugee musician who is one-eighth Jewish, has, therefore, been persecuted by the Nazis, and has spent time in a concentration camp.[7] Despite what would naturally be life-changing trauma, he appears at Lady Lael's seemingly unruffled except for a new cynicism and a determination to return to Germany to fight the only roughly defined evil there. At the conclusion of the play, as Hugo speaks of his plans to depart, he and the other characters speak of events in Germany using clichéd images and the most general of terms:

> LAEL. You are leaving to fight a mania as ravaging as a forest fire that burns down everything before it, leaving stumps and ashes where there had been strength and growth. I don't want it to consume you. . . .

HUGO. No, I'm determined at last to view the world—including myself—completely without illusion. It's a matter of life and death. I see now that goodness is not enough, that kindness is not enough, that liberalism is not enough. I'm sick of evasions. They've done us in. Civilization, charity, progress, tolerance—all the catchwords. I'm sick of them. We'll have to re-define our terms. (272)[8]

Fascism thus may seem a threat to a British society ruled by social class prejudices and to German-Jewish octoroons, but in Behrman's drama it does not (yet) pose a direct and potent threat to American democracy and rugged individualism.

Quite the contrary is the case in an important work that brings to life the horrors of fascist dictatorship and places them hypothetically, very believably, and very disconcertingly in contemporary America. In 1935, Sinclair Lewis, Nobel Prize laureate and arguably the most important American writer of his day, published his novel *It Can't Happen Here*. Set in Vermont, it describes the rise and frightening success of an American fascist coup. Within a year, Lewis, with the assistance of film writer John C. Moffitt, produced a dramatic version of his novel for the Federal Theater Project.[9] Originally, Moffitt and Lewis wrote a filmscript of *It Can't Happen Here* for MGM Studios, "who shelved [it] for fear that it might offend Hitler and Mussolini."[10] Subsequently and with great éclat, on 27 October 1936 the Federal Theatre opened its production of *It Can't Happen Here* simultaneously in eighteen cities, including New York, Boston, Miami, San Francisco, Chicago, Indianapolis, Los Angeles, and Seattle. In 1938, Lewis and Moffitt revised the script, and a new version premiered in Cohasset, Massachusetts, with Sinclair Lewis himself playing the leading role of Doremus Jessup.[11] Also among the cast was a young and as yet unknown Barry Sullivan.

Writing his novel and then his play-text in the early 1930s, Lewis found himself witnessing the unsettling rise of fascism and demagoguery both abroad and at home. In Europe, there were Hitler, Mussolini, and Franco. At home, there was the specter of Huey Long's demagogic reign in Louisiana, the openly anti-Semitic radio broadcasts from Detroit of Father Charles Coughlin, and the formation of the American Nazi Party by Gerald L. K. Smith and Governor Eugene Talmadge of Georgia. Using a rural New England setting and the joblessness of the Depression, *It Can't Happen Here* suggests the myopia of Americans who could witness the rise of Hitler and Nazism in Germany, or even of those homegrown demagogues who would create dictatorship and racism in the U.S. and say, "It can't happen here."[12]

Fostering the election of Windrip (Lewis's stand-in for Hitler or Long) as the next U.S. president, the Vermont Commissioner of the Corpos (the storm troopers of dictator Windrip), woos a young, unemployed college graduate, saying:

You see, I've been dealing with a lot of lads from good families who have been ruined by the arguing and experimenting of the last three administrations. The country's gone soft. But Windrip will discipline it, if he has the help of men like you. . . . We're recruiting more and more college men. Don't you find it good to be really *needed*, these jobless days—drafted for a man-sized job—with pay! (32)

Indeed, although the Corpos is mainly comprised of lower-class roughnecks and rednecks, the play shows Windrip's regime making clever appeals not only to unemployed college graduates but also to businessmen with labor problems and to feckless physicians with failing medical practices. Lorinda Pike, as her name suggests, is a pugnacious, feisty, unmarried newspaperwoman and the play's *raisonneuse*, who astutely remarks, "The Corpos *intend* everything. They tell the industrialists they'll stop strikes. They tell the workers, unions will be sacred. They tell the well-to-do they'll lower taxes. They tell the poor they'll have twenty-five hundred a year" (43).

In the course of *It Can't Happen Here*, Lewis and Moffitt vividly stage the fatal blackjacking of a plainspoken Vermonter who refuses to support the Corpos and Windrip's presidential campaign. The violence continues and intensifies after Windrip is elected, suspends democracy, and enforces his will through the Corpos and their weapons. Windrip himself never appears in *It Can't Happen Here*, but his disembodied, declamatory voice is heard in a bombastic radio address. More importantly, the dictator's strength is palpably and frighteningly dramatized as his Vermont commanders and troops psychologically and physically intimidate citizens in scenes meant to be indicative of similar ones being enacted in every state. Of course this brings home to the audience as well the similar scenes actually taking place in fascist Europe. The play's action spans approximately two years, during which time the United States has become a police state, the government controls all industry, concentration camps are in place, private property has been seized, and men and women are reduced to enforced labor just short of outright slavery. It is the enactment of physical violence and the scars of abuse on actors' bodies that render *It Can't Happen Here* an effective stage vehicle, one far more potent than Rice's comparatively restrained *Judgment Day*, in which the physical violence is spoken of but never shown.

At the center of *It Can't Happen Here* is newspaperman Doremus Jessup, an embattled icon of freedom of the press and American democratic principles more generally. In an effective scene, the audience sees with horror Doremus's son-in-law, a very likable but outspoken physician who opposes the quack the Corpos have installed as the new hospital director, physically roughed up and taken outside. The audience then hears the report of the gun and realizes with horror that the young husband and father has been shot to death. When the Corpos seize Doremus's newspaper and compel him to continue publishing their propaganda, Doremus joins the revolutionary American democracy underground and secretly distributes anti-Corpos leaflets. When his young grandson asks, "Why do the Corpos do things like killing Daddy?" Doremus answers, "Because they

1. *It Can't Happen Here* (1936). George Henry Trader and Tom Greenway. Courtesy of the New York Public Library.

hate free people, like your father, that want to know the truth! They hate the— oh, the free-inquiring, critical spirit" (104). And when his subversive activities on behalf of freedom and truth are uncovered, when he is beaten and remanded to a concentration camp, Doremus becomes a contemporary Nathan Hale and a martyr for American freedoms:

> I'll take my beating gladly. Maybe the other cautious citizens will hear of me now and begin to fight. It was our laziness that let the rats like you come in, but now my blood may wash you out. [*He tears loose from the* OTHER CORPO.] Go on! I am ready! (110)

By the conclusion of the play, an audience has experienced with shock the believable deaths, physical abuse, mental breakdown, and enslavement of the principal heroic characters; it now witnesses Doremus Jessup's family, the avatars of American democracy, making their refugees' escape across the border into free Canada.

It Can't Happen Here is far from a subtle play, but in its bluntness and in the power of the violence it depicts lie Sinclair Lewis's wake-up call to the United States, his cry for sympathy toward refugees streaming to American shores in the wake of Nazism, and his urgent insistence that America move from apathy to engagement.

During the years that immediately followed the productions of Rice's *Judgment*

Day and Lewis's *It Can't Happen Here,* Hitler's power and threat grew quickly and frighteningly. And that threat becomes a more immediate one for Americans, who have begun to learn from journalists and from the increasing numbers of arriving refugees telling their poignant stories about the atrocities being perpetrated in Europe. Playwrights, however, seemed to shy away from using one of the theatre's most potent weapons, the enactment of physical violence in a live setting. Frequently they seemed strangely loath to present the intimidations and persecutions inflicted by Nazis on Jews, communists, and other dissidents. But one 1930s playwright who was never afraid to bring physical violence to the theatre is Clifford Odets. His powerful *Till the Day I Die* (26 March 1935), written as a companion piece to *Waiting for Lefty* when that play went into Broadway production, is actually the only American play of the era to dramatize in any extended way the oppression and brutality then occurring in Germany.

Till the Day I Die, set in 1935 Berlin, concerns the capture and torture of a German communist, Ernst Taussig, to force him to reveal the names of his comrades. As a play about communist ideals and loyalty to the Cause versus loyalty to an individual (even one's brother) or to one's own survival, *Till the Day I Die* toes a conventional leftist party line. Despite the torture and suicide of the main character, Odets's play has none of the call to action that propels the audience of *Waiting for Lefty* to action and to call for "STRIKE." Gerald Weales calls *Till the Day I Die* "an exercise in revolutionary theory in which the individual must be willing to sacrifice himself for the group," and Gerald Rabkin writes, "the play ends, not with the conversion of the previously uncommitted, but with the affirmation by the committed that their existence is contained in the collective of which they are a part."[13]

As a play about the codes of fealty to the Communist Party, *Till the Day I Die* is uninteresting and not the stuff of memorable theatre. Where the force and power of the play lie, however, is in the presentation of Nazi callous ruthlessness and in the scenes of physical violence. Ernst Taussig, Odets's protagonist, is an erstwhile violinist and now a communist activist. When a Nazi officer in scene 2 slams the butt of his rifle down on Ernst's fingers, Odets's stage direction reads, "ERNST, *writhing with pain, puts his smashed right hand under his left armpit and almost faints*"(105).[14] And this is the first of a series of painful moments, which when acted convincingly, will make the audience cringe with horror and mental pain. The finger smashing is followed in quick order by scene 3, in which Nazi goons at intervals interrupt their pinochle game and beer drinking to kick an elderly man to the floor, spit beer at him, and beat him senseless. They do much the same to a young boy. As Ernst, here a surrogate for the audience, watches these proceedings in horror, "*Suddenly* TROOPER 2 *in a fury lets fly at* ERNST *who slowly crumples to his knees*" (111). And in the subsequent scene, Odets evinces the terror of a Jew who is trying to pass as an Aryan major in the Third Reich's military. When a captain threatens to expose the major, telling him that a Jew would never pull the trigger of a gun, the stage direction reads, "*At his close range the* MAJOR *suddenly pulls the trigger. The*

CAPTAIN *gets the whole automatic charge in the belly. Grabs himself with both hands. Slowly crumples in a soft pile*" (119). This is followed by the Major putting the muzzle of the gun in his mouth and, in a stage blackout, ending his life.

Odets may have taken some of these moments from actual accounts, and their enactment onstage is strong stuff.[15] Using vivid physicality conveyed by live actors only a few feet away from the audience, Odets, in short, makes the savage Nazi cruelty, at which other playwrights only hinted, up close, immediate, and personal. Whether Odets intended it or not, *Till the Day I Die* is ultimately far less about loyalty to the communist cause than it is about hatred of the Nazis and their tactics. By extension, it is a powerful alert to Americans to witness and be shocked by the Third Reich, its politics, and its methods of wielding power through physical assault.

Hatred of the Third Reich is likewise a major ingredient in two muddled, melodramatic plays that, not surprisingly, failed on Broadway. Oliver H. P. Garrett's *Waltz in Goose-Step* opened on 1 November 1938 at New York's Hudson Theatre, and Jacques Deval's *Lorelei* opened four weeks later on 29 November at the Longacre. Each ran for a mere seven performances. Notwithstanding their literary and dramatic flaws, *Waltz in Goose-Step* and *Lorelei* are remarkable for their comments about the plight of German Jews in the 1930s. The former is also noteworthy for its suggestion of a link between Nazism and homosexuality. *Waltz in Goose-Step*'s convoluted plot centers on the internal intrigues among ambitious, conniving, decadent Nazis and their conflicts with August, their leader (obviously an ironic portrait of Hitler). At the center of the play is Josef Straub, a young German pilot with a Jewish mother and an unknown father. The secret exploded in the course of the action is that Straub's father is none other than August, the Nazi leader himself.

The revelation of Straub's father's identity gives *Waltz in Goose-Step* occasion to characterize what was happening to the Jews in Germany under Hitler. To his mother's shock and the audience's, when Straub learns his father's identity, he does not turn against the leader but, in a dramatic turn, exclaims, "I'm glad. I'm proud I'm his son" (3.20).[16] His mother argues that men like his father have robbed Straub of his place in Germany, but Straub retorts with the German anti-Semitic clichés of the time. Their dialogue is worth quoting at length because it documents rhetorically—though not visually—the situation the playwright hopes to bring to the attention of his audience:

MRS. STRAUB. Is it your country? Or mine? Or your people's any longer?

STRAUB. If it isn't it's their own fault—the Jews' fault. They brought it on themselves. . . . Our country should create its own culture—not adopt one out of the Ghetto.

MRS. STRAUB. Why all of a sudden? Do you know the real reason? Because when conditions get bad, people have to have brains to make money. And the others can't do things as good as the Jews. So they steal everything we got—rob us. Our business. Our money. All we worked to build up they take away with guns. Still they're afraid maybe the Jews are so smart they'll get it back again. So they beat us. Drive us out of the country. Kill us. . . . I don't understand. Why they had to murder your Uncle Jacob. That I don't understand. Well and strong when they took him away. Two days later he's dead. And they wouldn't let us see the body. Then your cousin, Rebecca. Through the streets, they paraded her, with a filthy sign around her neck. Because she loved one of their boys and he loved her. Every night they're handcuffed together, dragged up on the stage, for the audience to make dirty jokes about. That I don't understand.

STRAUB. You can't blame The Leader—for everything wrong that happens.

MRS. STRAUB. Who started it—calling us dirty Jew dogs? Who got poor, stupid people that don't know any better all excited against us? Who would murder us all—half a million people—if he wasn't afraid of the rest of the world, of the boycott? So he kills another way that won't look so bad. He's starving us to death. That's what *he's* doing. We can't work. We can't make business. And so our little children starve. Your Uncle Aaron's girl, Rachel—little helpless Rachel, nothing but skin and bones—her food she has to pick out of garbage pails.

STRAUB. I know how you feel, Momma. But you can't make it all so simple. The Jews made us lose the war. They made a bad peace, that ruined and degraded the whole country, millions of people. We have to rise and fight if we're to be a world power again. But the Jews controlled everything, banks, stores, newspapers. And they were pacifists. They had to go. That's all. (3.21–22)

Although *Waltz in Goose-Step* never shows interactions between Germans and German Jews, it goes further than any other American play of the 1930s in detailing the oppression of Jews by the Third Reich.

The Jewish situation in Germany is also introduced tangentially in Deval's *Lorelei*, which features a speech in which a German Jew speaks of what is happening in his country:

I'm not speaking as Samuel Kronberg. . . . [but] For the hundred thousand of my race who have been exiled, tortured, jailed, outlawed . . . For the thousands of my race who are starved and beaten in concentration camps, like lepers and murderers. I'm speaking for the flogged and slaughtered herd of German Jews! (1.11)[17]

Both these plays fail on several counts. In addition to their hopelessly confused and confusing plots, their comments on the atrocities then taking place in Germany are not only peripheral to their melodramatic story lines but are never shown to have any clear relevance to America or Americans. Finally, since *Waltz in Goose-Step* and *Lorelei* were never published and each had only seven performances, they had no impact on either theatre audiences or readers. They are, nonetheless, of some interest for being among the only American dramatic works of the 1930s to point up in any detailed way onstage the Third Reich's anti-Semitic practices.

The matter is very different in the case of Robert Sherwood, who not only takes sides against fascists but also, more importantly, suggests that the ominous events in Europe are the product of human greed costumed as jingoism. Perhaps the anxiety about the possibility of another world war is nowhere better expressed than in Sherwood's famous Pulitzer Prize–winning drama, *Idiot's Delight*, which opened at the Shubert Theatre on 24 March 1936 with a cast that included Alfred Lunt, Lynn Fontanne, Sydney Greenstreet, and Richard Whorf. Stranded in a resort in the Italian Alps close to the Swiss and Austrian borders, with the Bavarian Alps of Germany in distant view, Sherwood's group of characters, who are Italian, Austrian, German, French, British, American, and allegedly Russian, face the onset of World War II.

As war breaks out, the microcosm of characters begins to reflect national attitudes. The German research doctor, closing in on a cure for cancer, returns to Germany not to cure disease but quite the reverse: to assist in the development of germ warfare. He accepts that the world is peopled by maniacs, exclaiming, "Why should I save people who don't want to be saved—so that they can go out and exterminate each other? Obscene maniacs. Then I'll be a maniac, too. Only I'll be more dangerous than most of them. For I know all the tricks of death! . . . We are all diseased" (161).[18] The honeymooning British couple returns to England, where the groom will join the army in solidarity with the French and against Germany and Italy. The Italian captain is resigned to war, and his words reveal simultaneously his complacency and Sherwood's deepest fears, "The map of Europe supplies us with a wide choice of opponents. I suppose, in due time, our government will announce its selection—and we shall know just whom we are to shoot at!" (13). Quillery, the angry French communist, reviles the Italians for their Fascism, predicts that the German doctor will return to the Fatherland because his cure for cancer "might benefit too many people outside of Germany—even maybe some Jews" (81), and condemns the English as hypocrites and butchers who have instigated war "because miserable little Italy dared to drag its black shirt across your trail of Empire" (82). The American takes a more detached view, asserting, "We have become a race of drug addicts—hopped up with false beliefs—false fears—false enthusiasms" (42–43).

At the dark center of *Idiot's Delight* stands Achille Weber, a manufacturer of munitions and a character perhaps inspired by Bernard Shaw's Andrew Undershaft, three decades and one world war after *Major Barbara*. Quillery and Sherwood see Weber as the embodiment of corporate greed and evil that bears much of the responsibility for the war that is about to happen. And Quillery's denunciation of Weber and what he represents captures the dark cynicism at the root of *Idiot's Delight* as it also disturbingly predicts some of the events that would soon take place in Europe:

> The great Monsieur Achille Weber, of the Comité des Forges! He can give you all the war news. Because he *made* it. You don't know who he is, eh? Or what he has been doing here in Italy? I'll tell you. He has been organizing the arms industry. Munitions. To kill French babies. And English babies. France and Italy are at war. England joins France. Germany joins Italy. And that will drag in the Soviet Union and the Japanese Empire and the United States. In every part of the world, the good desire of men for peace and decency is undermined by the dynamite of jingoism. And it needs only one spark, set off anywhere by one egomaniac, to send it all up in one final, fatal explosion. Then love becomes hatred. Courage becomes terror, hope becomes despair. But—it will all be very nice for Achille Weber. Because he is a master of the one League of Nations— The League of Schneider-Creusot, and Krupp, and Skoda, and Vickers and Dupont. The League of Death! And the workers of the world are expected to pay him for it, with their sweat, and their life's blood. (79– 80)

At the conclusion of the play, all the characters have fled the Italian Alps save Harry Van, the American performer (Alfred Lunt), and Irene (Lynn Fontanne), the pseudo-Russian with whom he had had an affair years before in Omaha. Together, and reminiscent of the characters at the conclusion of Bernard Shaw's eve-of-World War I play, *Heartbreak House,* they watch the bombs falling on Italy and ironically sing "Onward Christian Soldiers."

But at this point in his development, Sherwood is an optimist who is writing *Idiot's Delight* as a cautionary tale. In a postscript to the play, Sherwood writes that he believes "the world is populated largely by decent people, and decent people don't want war. Nor do they make war" (189). He argues instead that decent people have been deluded and "intoxicated by the synthetic spirit of patriotism, pumped into them by megalomaniac leaders," but ultimately feels that the people will come to their senses, "that a sufficient number of people are aware of the persistent validity of the Sermon on the Mount, and that they remember that, between 1914 and 1918, twelve million men died in violence to make safe for democracy the world which we see about us today" (189, 190). And if the fascist leaders of Germany, Italy, and Japan are met with "calmness, courage and ridicule," they will wilt. Sherwood's idealism is admirable, though it was soon to prove naïve. *Idiot's Delight* is meant to encourage the U.S. and its allies to resist war.

As Brenda Murphy, writing of *Idiot's Delight,* astutely puts it, "a great deal happened between 1936 and 1939."[19] Indeed by the end of the decade, the question of whether the United States should enter the fray against Hitler and Mussolini became a pressing one. Caught up in the discussion of that question were concerns about whether an American way of life needed protecting in the face of Fascism's growing strength. It is not insignificant, therefore, that the titles of plays concerning the American dilemma had a patriotic ring to them, for example, Sidney Howard's *The Ghost of Yankee Doodle*, Robert Sherwood's *Abe Lincoln in Illinois*, Philip Barry's *Liberty Jones*, George S. Kaufman and Moss Hart's *George Washington Slept Here* and *The American Way*, and Elmer Rice's *Flight to the West*. Sidney Howard's *The Ghost of Yankee Doodle* (1 November 1937) is perhaps the first important play to mark the growing debate in the United States over whether the country should remain aloof and neutral concerning the problems and political developments on the other side of the Atlantic or if the U.S. should side with the British and French and take an active stand against the German and Italian fascist regimes.

The Ghost of Yankee Doodle is a family play, and, as one character observes, "The family's a mirror. One of those old-fashioned, bull's eye, convex mirrors that reflects a whole room reduced and concentrated. You can see all civilization in the family. You can see what's wrong with the world" (26–27).[20] Clearly these blunt—maybe even heavy-handed—words are an astute description not merely of *The Ghost of Yankee Doodle* but of almost every family play ever written. Reflected in the convex mirror of Howard's family play, however, is a spectrum of views about American political neutrality vis-à-vis events in Europe. The Garrisons are an American blueblood family with liberal leanings (possibly their name is even meant as a reminder of William Lloyd Garrison) who gathers for Christmas at a time when Hitler's and Mussolini's rise to power pose a palpable threat to European democracy and political stability. Another war in Europe seems inevitable. In the years after World War I, however, the Garrisons, like so many Americans, are weary of war and wary of American involvement in a European conflict. For them, American neutrality or isolation must be maintained. One brother, Rudi Garrison, describes a political cartoon he is about to publish in the family-owned newspaper he edits. The cartoon shows Santa handing out diplomas to Americans while two teams—one of which is Germany, Italy, and Japan, and the other, France, England, and Russia—stand by. The brother explains what the diplomas say on them: "The blessings of isolation. Trade at your own risk. The usual crap. This big one's our National Honor. See? It's marked 'Keep Me Home' " (12). To the hawkish "Old Guard Republican" Senator Callory, who wishes America to enter the fray not because of political commitment but only because American merchant ships have been sunk, Rudi retorts, "Foreign trade's a fine thing, I know, and business can't do without it, but we're not taking chances on war just to earn money for you businessmen" (13). Rudi's brother, John (played in the original production by Frank Conroy), argues for neutrality on more high-minded, pragmatic grounds: "We're not just Christian pacifists, you know. Till the nations can learn how to behave themselves, though, neutrality's cheaper than any alternative. As somebody said: Life is the only wealth" (13–14). His Harvard undergraduate nephew, Roger, exemplifies the attitude of young Americans who lost fathers, family members, and friends as a result of the recent Great War, a war in which he feels the U.S. suffered heavy casualties because it foolishly meddled in a conflict that did not concern it. Speaking for himself and his Harvard class-mates, Roger smugly argues the standard position of post–World War I isola-tionism:

> And I'll tell you what we've concluded, Uncle John. This isn't like your war. . . . No martyred Belgium or *Lusitania* this time. They were great stuff! Made you want to fight! Oh, I know! What did we get out of it but Allies' debts and the soldiers' bonus! And this war's between Hitler and Karl Marx and those of us who've no use for either of 'em hope it ends with both of 'em out of business, and let's us, for God's sake, stay clear of it! . . . That's how the rest of the country feels too, I expect. (15)

To which his Uncle John chimes in, "Because our real responsibility's keeping this country out. I thank God France and England are holding their own. If they weren't it might be harder to keep out" (15).

As *The Ghost of Yankee Doodle* progresses, various domestic and love relation-ships take on symbolic value. James Clevenger, a powerful figure who owns a chain of influential newspapers given to yellow journalism, enters the play and successfully proceeds to use his newspapers to fan the flames of patriotism and war. For him, the end of American neutrality spells the end of Depression joblessness and labor unrest; a workman exclaims, "It's a great day for the whole entire American labor movement that's had its bellyful of neutrality!" (103). For the young people, war will provide their chance for heroism. By the conclusion of *The Ghost of Yankee Doodle,* some of the characters have altered their stances, but the brother who opted so confidently for neutrality comes to speak the lines that give the play its title: "Our Yankee ancestors made our kind the guardians of man's faith in himself! Not in leaders or dogmas or governments, but himself! . . . Liberalism: a goal man's never been able to attain, a hope man's never been able to abandon. . . . It isn't easy to walk the middle way" (143–144). His prior neutral stance is now an embattled one, and so, by extension, are American ideals now also embattled.

The Ghost of Yankee Doodle is a drama that waffles, and in that way it seems to touch the nature of American equivocation in 1937 about constant and om-inous news coming from Europe. Howard's play rejects those hoping to thrust America into the war, for they are motivated by crass, selfish, materialistic rea-sons or by shallow, saber-rattling jingoism. The Garrison family members, who maintain their liberalism and their desire for neutrality, are admirable, yet they come to recognize that the forces of economics and jingoism will eventually overpower them, annul their neutrality, and sweep them headlong into World War II. Howard calls *The Ghost of Yankee Doodle* a tragedy, and in a sense, it is tragic, for at its conclusion, the characters have chosen different stances toward the war, all of which are either tainted or nugatory. Favoring war to revitalize American industry or for pure heroic adventure seems no better than opposing the war on communist principles because it represents a conflict about property. The Garrison family, with their desire to protect American lives through American neutrality, are impotent idealists who stand no chance of averting the waves of war that are about to crest on American shores. Perhaps the wavering quality of *The Ghost of Yankee Doodle* made Howard the perfect choice to write the screenplay for *Gone with the Wind* soon afterward.

Howard's panorama of a family and its attitudes is meant to be his convex mirror of the times. *The Ghost of Yankee Doodle* reflects the times as well in ways unintended by the playwright, for the play never raises or considers as reasons for American entry into the war the issues of military aggression and human suffering in Europe or the Nazis' program of intimidating Jews. Other plays of the period, however, will do so.

More often than not, the plays that sought to convince audiences of the need for American involvement in Europe and in World War II made Americans aware of the dire situation in Europe and then forcefully stressed the threat of those developments to American democracy and the ideals upon which this country was founded. The individual rights guaranteed by the Constitution and more particularly by the Bill of Rights were in jeopardy from the forces of fascism and dictatorships in Germany and Italy. Not merely was it America's duty to help those peoples whose democratic rights were being trampled, but, more importantly, Americans needed to realize that if Germany and Italy gained enough power through their conquests in Europe, they would soon come across the Atlantic and rob Americans of all they held dear.

In this regard, George S. Kaufman and Moss Hart's great hit (but nowadays little remembered) play, *The American Way*, is singularly revealing. Starring Fredric March and his wife, Florence Eldridge, *The American Way* opened at the Centre Theatre in Rockefeller Center on 21 January 1939. Having already made their mark as America's leading comic playwrights, Kaufman and Hart drew large audiences to their play, which boasted an unusually large cast and many large group scenes. The play's vibrant patriotic strains were, moreover, the very thing to move a theatre filled with patrons who had come to New York to visit the 1939 World's Fair. Against a panorama of American history from the defeat of William Jennings Bryan by McKinley in 1896, through World War I, the Lindbergh flight, and the Depression, to the present (1939), *The American Way* traces the individual life of Martin Gunther from his arrival at Ellis Island in 1896, yearning for the freedoms of American democracy, through his prosperity in the fictional small city of Mapleton, Ohio, to his death defending American ideals in 1939.[21]

On the surface, *The American Way* is an unabashedly chauvinistic paean to America, the ideal of the American self-made man, the great goodness of the American way of life, and the sacrifices Americans make for their country in

2. *The American Way* (1939).
(Left to right) Norma Clerc,
Florence Eldredge, Fredric
March. Courtesy of the New
York Public Library.

times of political and economic stress. The unbridled patriotism of the play
moved even otherwise dispassionate reviewers. The two comments reprinted on
the dust jacket of the first edition of the play register the kind of emotional
reaction Kaufman and Hart were clearly hoping for.[22] Columnist Walter Winchell is quoted as saying, "*The American Way* is as exciting and as beautiful as
the American Flag. Long may it run"; and John Anderson in the *Journal-
American* is quoted as writing, "No audience that I can remember in my time
on the aisle has been so shaken with emotion as we all were at the Center
Theatre on Saturday. . . . Here was no longer a theatre but a place of pilgrimage;
no time to sit in judgment, but to stand at attention. Salute!"[23] Hart's recent
biographer, Steven Bach, comments rather more wryly that "the Center Theatre
was sodden with tears. . . . On balance, tears at *The American Way* were un-
earned. . . . They were feel-good tears at a feel-bad time."[24]

Kaufman and Hart's play, however, is more than a vehicle to wring tears and
trigger a knee-jerk patriotic response from the American public. Its linear structure describes a timeline from 1896 to the play's last scene in 1939. One might
ask, as *The American Way* moves through the first four decades of the twentieth
century, Where is the life of Martin Gunther headed? Kaufman and Hart
shrewdly chose as their setting not an urban melting pot but a small community
in the American heartland—Mapleton, Ohio—the same fictional community
Hart would use a few years later when in 1943 during the war, he wrote *Winged
Victory* for the Air Forces. They also avoided the pitfall of ghettoizing *The*

American Way into a play about anti-Semitism by creating a German (and spe-cifically non-Jewish) immigrant as their main character.

The American Way's last scenes, toward which all the previous ones have been relentlessly heading, concern Gunther's confrontation with his grandson, Karl, whose father sacrificed his life for the American way in World War I. The Gunther furniture factory and the family prosperity are lost during the Depres-sion, but the immigrant patriarch's chauvinistic love of America prevails undi-minished. Such is not the case for his disaffected and unemployed grandson, who falls easy prey to the pamphlets and rhetoric of his fascist, subversive, brown-shirted friends. The confrontation between grandfather and grandson captures the clash of values that Kaufman and Hart wish to italicize. When a local banker reveals to Gunther young Karl's attraction to fascism, a debate ensues:

> KARL. You've got no right to stop me. How do *you* know—how does *he* know—what it's like for me? For millions like me. You're living in the past—the world's moving. You don't know what's going on. We've got different problems now. And the same old system can't meet them any longer.
>
> BROCKTON. You see what's happening, Martin. No place is safe from it, even America.
>
> KARL. Go ahead—wave the flag. Let the bands play. But if you stop listening to "The Star-spangled Banner" for a minute, you can hear the whole rotten system crashing around your ears. . . . What's so wonderful about the American way of doing things, compared with any other way? Look at *you!* What have *you* got after all these years? Nothing!
>
> MARTIN. I will tell you what I have got, Karl. I have got everything that I wanted from America, and more. I came over here a poor boy, with nothing, and I got from America riches and years of happiness. All right, the riches have gone. That does not matter. But freedom there still is, and that is what *does* matter. I don't care how they are trying to change this country, or what name they call themselves. They are all the same—all these things—they are un-American. What really matters, Karl, is that you, and the young people like you, should take over this country, and keep it what it has always been.
>
> KARL. Try that speech when you're looking for a job, grandpa, and see where you get. You're sentimental about this country, but I'm not.
>
> . . .
>
> MARTIN. To live where there is freedom, Karl, that is the greatest thing in the world. Yes—yes, I *am* sentimental about this country. If America meant liberty before, think what it means now. (143–145, 146–147)

Karl is unconvinced by his grandfather, and the scene changes to a park that the audience remembers as the earlier setting, the 1908 Fourth of July *pro patria* and civic pride celebration. Now that same park becomes disconcertingly the setting for a fascist *contra patria* rally in 1939. Unsavory young men in brown shirt uniforms with military belts appear until there are about thirty of them onstage. Their leader, surrounded by his three guards, steps forward. The image is that of Hitler and Mussolini in their military uniforms, delivering their impassioned, rhetorical speeches:

> THE LEADER. [*His voice the voice of a fanatic*] You all know our mission. We must fulfill our part. Then and only then can America fulfill *her* destiny. There are forces in this country who accuse us of being un-American; in reality we are in the truest sense of the word Americans, the real patriots of this country. [*A cheer from the men*] Our program in the United States is this: We seek the spiritual regeneration of the youth of America after the model of the homeland. When we have attained this goal, we will organize the youth of this country and give them economic reinforcement and political schooling. Thus prepared, economically rejuvenated and politically active, our youth shall then be used, under our leadership, in the coming struggle for the reconstruction of America! [*Another cheer*] Let us not swerve from our high purpose; we must remake this country for Americans and Americans only. Other countries have cleaned their houses; the time is coming when we must do the same. (148–149)

In an equally impassioned speech, an aged Martin tries to break up the meeting, exclaiming:

> Read! Read the history of America! Again and again we have fought our way through. And now, just because one man—*one man*—stands over Europe and tells us that democracy is finished, that this country is no good, are you going to believe him? . . . Democracy is *not* finished; it still exists in many countries of the world, and we are not going to let it die! We are going to keep up the faith until this evil force is wiped from the face of the earth! (152)

The leader strikes Martin with his belt and, to the horror of Karl and the audience, the old man, representing American democratic values, is beaten to death.

In many ways, the Horatio Alger panorama of *The American Way* is a preparation for this moment, for Gunther's fatal beating by the fascists and for a eulogy by the local banker, in which he says, "I see in the life of Martin Gunther, and even in his death, high hope for America. It will go on, this country, so long as we keep alive the thing that Martin Gunther died for. Let us keep this land of ours, which we love so dearly, a land of hope and freedom" (155). At a time when the U.S. was beset by the psychological depression attendant on the economic one, a time, consequently, ripe for the appeals of fascism on the right and communism on the left, Kaufman and Hart clearly saw America in danger. Shrewdly using a huge cast, they created an extravaganza of emotional, sentimental patriotism that produces the flag-waving reviews of Walter Winchell and John Anderson but that also imbues its audience, the American public, with the spirit to take a stand against the forces of Hitler and Mussolini. Although *The American Way* is not urging this country to declare war, it certainly is preparing its audience for that strong possibility.[25]

Small-town America is also the backdrop of an American classic less extravagant, less patriotic than *The American Way*. Opening just eleven months prior to *The American Way*, Thornton Wilder's *Our Town* is set in a fictional New Hampshire town not so very different from the Ohio town created by Kaufman and Hart. But whereas *The American Way* is a dramatic vehicle of huge proportions, *Our Town* is based on the premise that less is more, and so it creates its effects with a nearly bare stage, pantomime, and a few simple chairs and ladders.[26] At first glance, the events leading to World War II would seem to have no bearing on Thornton Wilder's remote New England town, Grovers Corners, New Hampshire, in the years 1901, 1904, and 1913—the dates of the three acts of *Our Town*. But of course since the Stage Manager opens *Our Town* by giving the audience the names of the playwright, director, producer, and actors there is a fourth date, the present, which for the opening of *Our Town* was January 1938, when the military actions in Europe were already at play, even though U.S. entry into the war was still nearly four years away. Throughout *Our Town*, Wilder seems to have war and America's seemingly inevitable involvement in that war in mind, and he seems as well at pains to provide the audience with a useful perspective on the meaning of war, preparing it for the events he could see looming in the near future. From the outset, Wilder suggests that the chronicle of daily life, the very thing that *Our Town* records, is more important, enduring, and meaningful than either technological advances or wars. Speaking of what will be placed inside the cornerstone of the new bank in Grovers Corners, the Stage Manager says:

> So I'm going to have a copy of this play put in the cornerstone and the people a thousand years from now'll know a few simple facts about us— more than the Treaty of Versailles and the Lindbergh flight.

Obviously the Lindbergh flight, the Treaty of Versailles, and, by extension, the war which that treaty concluded are placed well in the background. Foregrounded is the record of daily life.

Prior to the Stage Manager's comment on the Treaty of Versailles, Wilder provides another revealing comment on war. Mrs. Gibbs tells her neighbor Mrs. Webb that the only traveling her husband does is his biennial pilgrimage to Civil War battlefields. Mrs. Webb responds, "Well, Mr. Webb just *admires* the way Dr. Gibbs knows everything about the Civil War. Mr. Webb's a good mind to give up Napoleon and move over to the Civil War, only Dr. Gibbs being one of the greatest experts in the country just makes him despair." Impressively, within a short forty years after the dramatic events of the American Civil War, and after the high price paid in human lives and general devastation during that war, Wilder indicates that it had already become trivialized and commodified into a hobby and a list of tourist sites. By 1901, the bloody battlefields of Gettysburg and Bull Run had been transformed into tourist attractions for Civil War hobbyists like Dr. Gibbs. Spoken in 1938, these lines about the Civil War enable the audience to realize that ultimately what will become World War II will not be the end of civilization as we know it, and that before the end of the twentieth century there will be people like Dr. Gibbs who will become World War II aficionados, spending their leisure time as antiquarians of *that* war, traveling to *its* battlegrounds. Of course Wilder's implicit prophecy has proven correct.

In the first act of *Our Town*, Wilder comments on war in another but related key with his remarks on Joe Crowell, the newspaper boy:

> Want to tell you something about that boy Joe Crowell there. Joe was awful bright—graduated from high school here, head of his class. So he got a scholarship to Massachusetts Tech. Graduated head of his class there, too. It was all wrote up in the Boston paper at the time. Goin' to be a great engineer, Joe was. But the war broke out and he died in France— All that education for nothing. (10)[27]

The passage reflects Wilder's despairing feelings about the losses caused by wars, not merely of bodies but of talented men. These are feelings that many Americans in Wilder's audience could respond to, imbued as they were with the strong current of pacifism and isolationism that affected this country in the wake of World War I and of the human toll that that war took. Yet *Our Town* is not a pacifist play. Rather it accepts wars as part of the human condition, and it conveys a strong sense that the losses of lives and objects brought about by war, though hard to bear, are not permanent: that life goes on and losses are replenished. Thus, at the beginning of act 2, Joe Crowell has already been replaced on his newspaper route by his younger brother Si, even as the loss of Joe's intellectual gifts will be replaced by those who follow. For Wilder, then, war and loss are poignant moments in mankind's script, but the script does not end there, for the life of the human race goes forward, unimpeded by individual deaths.

This is made manifest in the last act of the play, in which the Stage Manager, surveying the gravestones in the Grovers Corners cemetery, emphasizes *Our Town*'s Olympian view of war. He notices graves dating back to the American Revolution, ones sought out by those who "want to make sure they're Daughters of the American Revolution," by people who are thus little better than armchair war buffs like Doc Gibbs. And the Stage Manager goes on archly to point out to the audience:

> Over there are some Civil War veterans. Iron flags on their graves . . . New Hampshire boys . . . had a notion that the Union ought to be kept together, though they'd never seen more than fifty miles of it themselves. All they knew was the name, friends—the United States of America. The United States of America. And they went and died about it. (80–81)

He then turns to the other graves in the cemetery, graves of ordinary Grovers Corners townsfolk, whom we have seen and come to know in the course of the previous acts. Wilder thereby once more suggests to his 1938 audience that wars and war deaths, those past and those inevitably to come, are part of the eternal verity of human existence, a part of life's natural course. Whether death comes on a battlefield in France or in Gettysburg, or whether it occurs in Grovers Corners, it is just death, finally just a part of the life cycle.

Like *Our Town*, William Saroyan's *The Time of Your Life*, which won both the Pulitzer Prize and the Drama Circle Award for 1939–40, seems at first glance a play quite remote from Hitler, Nazism, and current events in Western Europe. Indeed, with the exception of Malcolm Goldstein, who sees the threat of war in *The Time of Your Life*, most critics have regarded Saroyan's play as Brooks Atkinson did in his *New York Times* opening night review, as "a prose poem in ragtime with a humorous and lovable point of view."[28]

Certainly *The Time of Your Life* seems only obliquely and vaguely about world events, but when read in the context of its time, a whole new and dazzling sense of the play emerges. Indeed, Saroyan seems to create in Nick's Pacific Street Bar a very pacific, sheltered, directionless group of diverse characters presided over by Joe, an uncommitted, benevolent, barroom Prospero. Nick's saloon, an image of American harmony within melting pot diversity, is described as "a good, low-down, honky-tonk American place that lets people alone" (67).[29] The free-flow atmosphere, however, is systematically interrupted by the several appearances of Blick, the mean-spirited and bullying policeman who threatens the denizens of the bar, intimidates and denigrates them, and is physically abusive toward them. When Blick enters, all pacific activity in Nick's Pacific Street Bar stops and dissolves into paralysis and terror. Saroyan's stage direction reads, "There is absolute silence, and a strange fearfulness and disharmony in the atmosphere now" (62), and Nick angrily confronts the bullying policeman with, "You're out to change the world from something bad to something worse. Something like yourself" (64). As the play progresses, Blick becomes increasingly identified with the image of Hitler and associated as well with a force innately hostile to the ineffable Americanness of America.

The last act of *The Time of Your Life* takes place with a map of Europe spread out on Joe's table; with Joe's companion, Tom, dashing out to buy copies of *Life*, *Liberty*, and *Time*, magazines whose names bespeak the themes of the play; and with Joe's feelings of guilt about the capitalist gains that have made him wealthy but have also immobilized him in the saloon where he sits enthroned as its benevolent ruler. Into this atmosphere enters Blick with the manner of a petty fascist tyrant manhandling a young newsboy: stripping the spiritually bruised Kitty Duval of her clothes, her dreams, and her self-respect; pummeling an African-American dishwasher; and roughing up the eccentric codger Kit Carson, the character who represents yarn-spinning pioneer America.

Blick's manner is unmistakably that of the Gestapo, and his relentlessly menacing presence finally forces Joe from his Olympian detachment and splendid isolation into a failed attempt, but an attempt nonetheless, to shoot Blick. Moments later, however, Blick is shot dead by Kit Carson, the spirit of America and of rugged pioneer individualism, and Blick's demise is, furthermore, italicized by the pinball player's tapping the pinball machine, finally hitting the jackpot, and thereby, in a *coup de théâtre*, causing the machine to send up waving, triumphant American flags. There is no formal exhortation to the audience or soapbox rhetoric in *The Time of Your Life*, but the play does conclude importantly with Joe's rousing himself from his detachment and from his barroom throne, leaving the saloon, and re-entering the outside world, presumably to become engaged or re-engaged with its problems. The play is set in October 1939, and Joe's departure from his splendid isolation clearly seems—a month after Germany's invasion of Poland—Saroyan's pointed cue for the American public to do likewise.

As world events grew increasingly grim, Saroyan's nudge to his countrymen is followed by rather more forceful pushes and shoves from other playwrights. Robert Sherwood's role in prewar "getting involved" drama is, therefore, an illuminating one. His 1936 Pulitzer Prize hit *Idiot's Delight*, though it heard the sabers of war beginning to rattle in Europe, was meant to be an antiwar play. Two years later, Sherwood changes his position, and his most famous play, *Abe Lincoln in Illinois*, is not merely a dramatized biography of young Lincoln on his way to the presidency but also a drama about a thoughtful, peace-loving man who sought to avoid the issues that were dividing the nation.[30] In Sherwood's play, Lincoln must come to recognize that, although the times will be hard ones and although a great many lives will undoubtedly be lost on both sides in a civil war, he must take a stand, even if that stand means declaring war on the South. The analogy with the decision being forced on peace-loving liberals, like Sherwood himself, in the late 1930s is pellucid.[31] But it is Sherwood's Pulitzer Prize–winning *There Shall Be No Night*, which opened on Broadway on 29 March 1940, as Hitler's aggression continued to build, that marks Sherwood's most undiluted statement and his complete conversion from the pacifism he had championed only a few years earlier.

In *There Shall Be No Night*, once again peace-loving, neutral people are driven from their high-minded disengagement and forced finally to take a spirited and moving stand against fascism. In this case it is the pacifist and politically neutral Kaarlo Valkonen, a Finnish Nobel Prize–winning physician, and his American wife who embody American well-bred disengagement from political events. The ideological distance Sherwood travels in a short time from *Idiot's Delight* to *There Shall Be No Night* is accented by the fact that the principal actors in both plays are the same: Alfred Lunt, Lynn Fontanne, Sydney Greenstreet, and Richard Whorf.

Sherwood's *There Shall Be No Night* describes the Russian invasion of Finland, an invasion the playwright sees as one orchestrated by the Nazis. It pointedly recognizes as well that if Americans wait too long, the U.S. will also be in danger of Nazi takeover. In the preface to *There Shall Be No Night*, Sherwood writes:

> Like many another who hopes he is a Liberal, I had great faith in the Soviet Union as a force for world peace. . . . But with the assault on Finland the last scales of illusion fell. I knew this was merely a part of Hitler's game of world revolution. . . . The sole purpose of [Nazi] propaganda in the United States, as it had been in France, was to spread confusion and disunion, to weaken American resistance so that we would provide an irresistible temptation to Hitler to continue his conquests westward. (xxvii–xxviii)[32]

For Sherwood, American failure to act would eventually spell the demise of democracy in general and American democracy in particular. As a result, Sherwood's characters Valkonen and his wife, Miranda (Lunt and Fontanne), are, like Prospero and *his* Miranda, ultimately compelled to forsake their idyllic remove from world events in order to play an active role in European politics.

Sherwood's hard-hitting drama introduces a German diplomat who raises the specter of the extent of the Nazi design and reveals that American neutrality is a structural part of Hitler's grand design:

> I assure you the United States is secure for the present. It may continue so for a long time, if the Americans refrain from interfering with us in Mexico and South America and Canada. And I believe they will refrain. They are now showing far greater intelligence in that respect than ever before. They are learning to mind their own shrinking business. (89)

The American newsman in the play also reflects cynically on his country by comparing the U.S. to Pontius Pilate, who, when Christ was crucified, declined to act, saying, " 'Bring me a basin of water, so that I can wash my hands of the whole matter' " (122). He remarks wryly as well that the news of a Russian invasion of Finland will have little impact on blasé American ears in comparison to the radio adventures of Renfrew of the Mounted Police, sporting events, and society page gossip.

In the figure of Kaarlo Valkonen, Sherwood presents both the coming of political consciousness to a disengaged pacifist and a model for American awakening and consequent engagement in world affairs.[33] In a stroke of playwriting

3. *There Shall Be No Night* (1940). Alfred Lunt and Edward Reguello. Courtesy of the New York Public Library.

excellence, Sherwood raises admiration for the courage of the Finns and equates Finnish and American ideals. Valkonen's coming of age takes place in an abandoned country schoolroom whose walls are hung with passages evoking democratic solidarity taken from *The Kalevala,* the Finnish national poem. Valkonen makes immediate the equation between Finland and the United States by remarking, "Every Finnish child learns about the Kalevala—just as Americans learn those words about Life, Liberty and the Pursuit of Happiness" (148). In the play's stunning climax, Dr. Valkonen rips off his Red Cross armband, which represents his well-meaning neutrality, and leaves the schoolroom to bear arms against the invaders, knowing full well that he will face almost certain death by doing so. That it behooves a neutral America to follow Valkonen's example, Sherwood makes abundantly clear.

Indeed, much of the country was still strongly antiwar, and *There Shall Be No Night* was denounced by antiwar reviewers, with performances picketed by antiwar demonstrators.[34] The play and its call for active engagement were, however, a great success among the general public, and after its New York run, it had a very successful national tour until that tour was abruptly halted after the attack on Pearl Harbor. By that time, Russia had weighed in on the side of the Allies, whereas an overrun Finland had become an Axis ally. Because of these events,

President Roosevelt himself allegedly stepped in to curtail the tour of the play. *There Shall Be No Night* gave its final performance a week after Pearl Harbor, supposedly because the story was too incendiary and conveyed the wrong messages about Finland and Russia.[35]

In *There Shall Be No Night*, the threat of Nazism to the U.S. is made manifest, though the action is played out far away from the United States, in Finland. Six months later, the Nazis come closer to American soil when, on 30 December 1940, the Playwrights' Company, which had produced *There Shall Be No Night*, opens Elmer Rice's drama *Flight to the West* at the Guild Theatre in New York. In this play, a wide-ranging group of characters is on a flight from Lisbon to New York. Among the passengers are two Nazi operatives coming to the States to bring the doctrines, dictatorship, and human cruelty of Nazism to the U.S. The entire play takes place in flight, and the Nazis on board are subdued before the plane lands, before Nazism can literally set foot in the United States. But clearly Rice warns that matters have now gone a step beyond *There Shall Be No Night*. The Nazis are already winging their way to New York.

As his *Street Scene* (1929) and *We the People* (1933) reveal, Elmer Rice was unusually adept at writing and staging panoramic plays, in which characters from different walks of life come together to convey a situation and stage-picture of mural proportions. Although not written on quite the scale of Rice's earlier plays, *Flight to the West*, produced a year before Pearl Harbor, creates for its American audience a meaningful panoramic snapshot of wartime issues. Clearly the play was designed to motivate its audience to take an active stand against Hitler and the increasingly tragic events being played out in Europe. Attending the pre-Broadway opening of *Flight to the West* in Princeton, New Jersey, Albert Einstein, himself a refugee from Hitler's Germany, remarked, "If it does not succeed, it is not the fault of the play, but of the public."[36] Einstein here registers his awareness that Americans were resistant to taking a firm stand against Hitler or entering a war that they saw (or wished to see) as a European domestic squabble in which the U.S. had no cause to meddle. *Flight to the West* is in large part directed to that recalcitrant audience by showing in strong terms that European issues and conflicts are not confined to Europe, but are in transit to American shores.

Among the passengers aboard Rice's plane is Charles Ingraham, who is the author of the pacifist tract *The Betrayal of Democracy*. Although not the principal character of *Flight to the West*, Ingraham is Rice's version of Sherwood's Karl Valkonen. Indeed, when Ingraham and an admiring passenger, Charles Nathan, discuss the failure of pacifism in the face of current events, *There Shall Be No Night* is immediately recalled (even down to a reference to Finland):

> CHARLES. But I don't exaggerate when I say that your books were a sort of Bible to my generation. We read them—especially *The Betrayal of Democracy*. You taught us how some old men in Paris made America trade away the Fourteen Points to get the League of Nations and then how

4. *Flight to the West* (1940). (Left to right) Grandon Rhodes, Harold Dyrenforth, Lily Brentano, Karl Malden, Paul Henreid, Boris Marshalov, Kevin McCarthy. Courtesy of the New York Public Library.

some old men in Washington shut us out of the League. . . . What follows is that a year ago, three months ago, in fact, I knew exactly where I stood and why on this question of war and peace. But there's been Finland and Norway and Holland. And I've seen Paris bombed and France defeated. . . .

INGRAHAM. I'm in about the same fix you're in. You see, I'm having a hell of a time right now trying to get straightened out myself.

CHARLES. You mean you've changed your point of view, too?

INGRAHAM. Well, a man doesn't readily throw overboard the convictions of a lifetime. For twenty years, I've devoted myself to decrying war and the war makers, agitating for disarmament, for a world commonwealth. But, more and more, I began discovering to my horror that my facts and arguments were being used in ways that I had certainly never intended, by the rabid isolationists. By the critics of democracy, even by the Nazi propagandists. I'd been deluding myself with the belief that I was a clear thinker with a constructive program, but now as I look at myself, all I see is another confused liberal.

CHARLES. Well, my God, I'm certainly glad I talked to you—because if you feel that way, you can imagine the state I'm in. I see all this going on around me and I get the feeling that I should be doing something about it. I've even been playing with the idea of training to be an army pilot. (21–23)[37]

In this exchange, the play urges its audience to rethink post–World War I pacifism. And, as Charles contemplates joining the Air Corps, *Flight to the West* further implies replacing current American disengagement with new and positive action.

Like Howard in *The Ghost of Yankee Doodle* and Sherwood in *Idiot's Delight*, Rice goes on to suggest the culpability of American business interests. He demonstrates that American big business has co-opted Ingraham's pacifism for its own ends, that the banner of peace and neutrality is being waved in order to obfuscate worship of the almighty dollar. Indeed, the golden calf of capitalism is partly responsible for America's turning its back on morality and the proper course of action in the face of the Third Reich's turpitude. Gage, the Texas oilman aboard Rice's plane, has a large stake in oil contracts with Germany, and representing the voice of American big business, he urges laissez-faire. He is promptly answered by Louise Frayne, the feisty reporter and Rice's spokesperson for the conscience of America and the endurance of its democratic principles:

GAGE. Mind you, he's [Hitler] done a lot of things I don't like. So has Stalin. So has Musso. . . . I don't believe he's [Hitler] got any interest in Washington . . . the Nazis have plenty to do in Europe, without bothering us—that is, providing we don't coax them into it. Matter of fact, I had that right from Hitler himself. . . . Anyhow, I don't see that sticking out our necks is going to get us anywhere. Seems to me it's much smarter to talk business with Hitler and get our share of world trade than to get ourselves blown to bits, fighting Europe's battles. . . . Well, when you come right down to it, I'd rather play ball with him, than fight him and get licked.

LOUISE. I'll be God-damned if I would! Oil contracts or no oil contracts, I'd rather die fighting for freedom than live in a Hitler-dominated world. (55)

Although Rice works on his audience through these ideological confrontations, he does so with equal—perhaps greater—effectiveness visually. The passengers flying to the United States from Europe also include an American scholar and his family. He appears with eyes bandaged, for he has lost his vision through Nazi violence. His Belgian wife is on the edge of mental breakdown, and his young daughter appears with one arm missing. They are a stirring visual reminder to the audience of what Hitler is perpetrating and provide the human example that complements and gives substance to the play's more abstract arguments about neutrality versus engagement.

The central action around *Flight to the West* is triggered by the array of characters on board the airplane circle realizing that their fellow passengers include Dr. Hermann Walther, an official at the Third Reich's embassy in Washington, and Count Vronoff, a Nazi agent and fifth columnist traveling under an assumed name en route to a teaching post at the University of California, where he will presumably engage in subversive activities. When Walther expounds his Nazi and racist ideology, it is enough to make any good American cringe: "I speak for a young, vigorous, and determined race, which clearly understands the role it is destined to play in human history and which rejects the whining beatitudes and the weak slave morality of your dying Jewish-Christian culture" (146). Louise Frayne gives voice to what Rice hopes his play will lead audience members to feel: "I wish our government would kick every German diplomatic officer and business agent out of the country," she asserts. "They're just there for one purpose—to create confusion and dissension and prepare the way for Nazi penetration. And the sooner we do something about it, the better it will be for us" (135). Clearly Walther and Vronoff are up to no good, and they are ultimately prevented from entering the United States. But the progress from *There Shall Be No Night* is perceptible. Now the Nazis are not just talking about the United States as a future target; their advance guard is already on its way. That they are stopped in *Flight to the West* is fortunate, but the script of actual events may not have such a happy and theatrical conclusion.

It is almost a lockstep progression from *There Shall Be No Night* on 29 March 1940 to *Flight to the West* on 30 December 1940 to Lillian Hellman's *Watch on the Rhine,* which opened four months later on 1 April 1941 and won the Drama Circle Award for 1940–41. Hellman takes the next step beyond Rice, by bringing Europe to America and situating the threat of Nazism directly in the drawing room of a prominent American family in no less a place than the nation's capital itself. In *Watch on the Rhine,* Sara Muller, an American, her European anti-fascist husband, Kurt, and their children have lived in hiding, in poverty, and on the run. They have now crossed the Atlantic and come to the Washington, D.C., home of Sara's socially and politically prominent mother and brother, Fanny and David Farrelly, so that Sara and the children can be safe while Kurt returns to Europe to continue the fight against Hitler. For Sara and her family, the Farrelly home where she grew up is now alien and almost incomprehensible both for its physical opulence and for its political style, which is an amalgam of naïve ignorance, studied denial, and laissez-faire avoidance. As Hellman describes it in her stage directions, the family drawing room itself seems a microcosmic physical image of America: there is taste but no commitment, "no styles, no periods" (231).[38] It is that very lack of focus and style that has, pointedly, allowed the Farrellys mindlessly to invite Teck de Brancovis, a petty European aristocrat and Nazi operative, as a long-term houseguest in the Farrelly home. The analogy between this and a neutral United States in early

5. *Watch on the Rhine* (1941).
(Left to right) Peter Fernandez,
Eric Roberts, Paul Lukas, Ann
Blyth. Courtesy of the New
York Public Library.

1941, also mindlessly doing business as usual with the Third Reich and harboring Nazi agents, becomes patently clear.

When the ardently anti-fascist Kurt and the Nazi agent de Brancovis clash within the Farrelly home, the Farrellys are forced to learn political realities and to awaken from their isolationism and political slumber. "By this time all of us must know where we are and what we have to do," says Sara, and Kurt remarks ominously of his in-laws, "Fanny and David are Americans and they do not understand our world—as yet." Furthermore, Sara bluntly tells the Farrellys' Nazi houseguest that for Americans the discovery of fascists on their home turf is like wealthy inhabitants of a mansion discovering that the vermin of the slums have found their way into their home: "We know how many there are of you. They don't yet. My mother and brother feel shocked that you are in their house. For us—we have seen you in so many houses."

When Sara's European husband, Kurt, explains his political commitment to the Farrellys, his is, ironically, the very commitment that is *supposed* to underlie American democracy. Hellman thus posits a European martyr defending American ideals, and the Americans in her play thereby seem all the more negligent and reprehensible for their neutrality and isolationism, for their abandonment of basic American values and ideals. The watch on the Rhine must, Hellman implicitly argues during the course of her play, become the watch on the Potomac. And the newly awakened Washingtonians, Fanny and David Farrelly, close the play with

FANNY. Well, here we are. We're shaken out of the magnolias, eh?
. . .

DAVID. We are going to be in for trouble. You understand that?

FANNY. I understand it very well. We will manage. I'm not put together with flour paste. And neither are you—I am happy to learn.

The *we* is not only Fanny and David, but *we* the audience. As Richard Moody eloquently states in his study of Lillian Hellman, "the terrifying face of Fascism hangs like a gargoyle over the Farrelly household. No longer can the Atlantic and Potomac shield us from the Nazi menace."[39]

Another play, which actually precedes *There Shall Be No Night*, *Flight to the West*, and *Watch on the Rhine* and which exploits Nazis in America for rather melodramatic ends, is Clare Boothe's *Margin for Error*. To most Americans, Clare Boothe Luce is remembered as a diplomat and as the wife of Henry Luce, the powerful publisher of *Time* magazine. In the American theatre, writing as Clare Boothe, she is remembered for *The Women*, the acerbic satire of women getting divorces in Reno. Forgotten is her uneven but nevertheless sometimes perspicacious and forceful *Margin for Error*, another drama of the period that weighs in about the need for Americans to involve themselves in World War II and to see that the Third Reich was already making incursions on American soil. Written after Boothe had traveled to Europe with her husband and seen firsthand the terrible events unfolding there, *Margin for Error* opened on Broadway on 3 November 1939, a mere ten weeks after the German invasion of Poland, but is consciously set, as the stage directions tell us, "prior to September, 1939" (xxii).[40]

Called on its title page "A Satirical Melodrama," *Margin for Error* is a curious olio of detective fiction, satire, and political suasion. Its single setting is the library of the German consul general in an American city. Prominent onstage are a map of Germany, a bust of Adolf Hitler, and a stand containing both Nazi and American flags. The play concerns the melodramatically evil and corrupt German consul portrayed in the original production by Otto Preminger, who also directed the play. Very consciously, Clare Boothe draws characters who are overblown, sometimes even ludicrous archetypes. She does so partly to satirize them and partly to create a wartime American morality play.[41]

At the conclusion of the first of *Margin for Error*'s two acts, and with all the characters in the room listening to one of Hitler's stentorian speeches, proclaiming "Sieg Heil"s from a radio at high volume, the consul is suddenly discovered lying dead in his chair. In classic detective fiction mode, all the characters have good reason to have murdered the consul; the second act consists of the whodunit investigation led by Officer Finkelstein, who, as a Jew, is himself not above suspicion.

The play is pure formula, and Clare Boothe knows it, but she attempts to employ that formula for higher ends. Indeed, what she is saying to the American theatre public is "I'm going to give you the politically disengaged theatre fare you so enjoy but use it to make you aware of what is going on in the world and even in your own country." Thus in the confrontation between the corrupt German consul, Baumer, and Denny, a shrewd American journalist, what might otherwise be a moment of mere comic repartee becomes an occasion for comparative ideology:

> DENNY. Baumer, we can't argue. We begin from opposite premises. You believe the citizen was born to serve the state. We believe the citizen is the state—
>
> CONSUL. Our belief has created a great Germany.
>
> DENNY. All the returns on Germany are not in yet. Don't forget. America's still the richest and freest nation.
>
> CONSUL. I hope you can defend this fat Eden.
>
> DENNY. Any time you think so, just try to come and get it!
>
> CONSUL. Then it may be too late. By that time America may have caught the disease which has weakened its sister democracies. The little disease they picked up in Munich—
>
> DENNY. Oh, we're thinking about that too, Baumer.
>
> CONSUL. Fortunately, that's all you Americans do, is think! (81)

The words of the consul are meant to raise the hackles of every audience member. Consequently, when the consul is assassinated while the radio blares forth what Boothe repeatedly calls "The Awful Voice," the audience's revulsion toward the consul, Hitler, and Nazi Germany is transferred onto the deservedly dead body onstage. In short, Boothe allows the audience to share with every character onstage the desire to see the consul dead.

A comedy of murderers ensues when it is discovered that the consul has been shot by one character, stabbed by another, but has actually died by accidentally drinking a poisoned beverage he had brewed for someone else. Thus the consul dies thrice over, comically enacting every character's and every audience member's wish fulfillment about the Nazis. More importantly, by having the consul unwittingly poison himself, Boothe prognosticates the ultimate self-destructive fate of the Third Reich.

But Boothe's satiric gaze is directed not merely at the Nazis, who are all shown finally to be boobies and cardboard villains, but also at her fellow Americans who tolerate such patent villains to reign not merely on the stage of the Plymouth Theatre but on the stage of Europe. In the preface to the published version of his wife's play, moreover, editor Henry Luce writes:

6. *Margin for Error* (1939). (Left to right) Leif Erickson, Elspeth Eric, Bramwell Fletcher, Otto Preminger (back to audience), Sam Levene, Burt Lytell, Phillip Coolidge. Courtesy of the New York Public Library.

> *Margin for Error* has, I think, an importance outside and beyond the theater. Its importance does not arise from the fact that it at last clarified a surging, turgid rush of American emotion in the World Crisis and, having given a name to action, made action possible—for it did no such thing. Its importance lies in exactly the opposite direction. For it demonstrated that Americans were afraid—afraid to think. Americans were afraid of the kind of thinking where thought is fused with emotion—the only kind of thinking that leads to conclusions and to action. (ix)

He goes on to say that the play shows that Americans "*desired* to be confused, were at great pains to confuse themselves, applauded the confusion, hoped they might painlessly confuse themselves straight through World War II, and wake up in a fine mood of clarity on some happy summer's day. . . . In short *Margin for Error* indicated that the United States of America was advancing into its own Munich—a zigzag isolationist course from which it may or may not extricate itself with honor and success" (xi). Luce's words were written in January 1940, nearly two years before America declared war, and it took the bombing of Pearl Harbor to bring America out of its political doldrums and into battle.

II

In the era before Pearl Harbor, the plays that attempted to rouse America and Americans into action display an impressively wide variety of theatrical techniques, styles, and tactics. It is almost as though the playwrights are groping for just the right dramatic formula that would propel the audience from their seats and into action. Kaufman and Hart employ extravaganza; Boothe couches her argument in the form of a consular whodunit; Sinclair Lewis conjures up an American dystopia; Sherwood writes a history play about Lincoln and in another play uses the invasion of Finland as his backdrop; Rice chooses a courtroom, Saroyan a barroom, and Hellman a drawing room; and Rice attempts as well the mode of Chaucer or Vicki Baum in which characters, each with a separate tale to relate, are brought together on a pilgrimage, in a hotel, or on a plane. Some of the approaches are more successful than others. The struggle for a dramatic form equal to the critical moment of history before Pearl Harbor is lucidly reflected in the plays of Maxwell Anderson, who makes three disparate dramatic attempts to focus the attention of the American public on events in Europe. His *Key Largo* (27 November 1939), *Journey to Jerusalem* (5 October 1940), and *Candle in the Wind* (22 October 1941) could not be more dissimilar. The first is a verse play about the aftermath of the Spanish Civil War; the second, also in verse, an anti-Nazi play in the form of a historical drama depicting Christ's youthful Passover pilgrimage in Luke 2:41–49; and the third, a romantic melodrama in prose about enduring love in the face of Nazi totalitarian oppression.

Self-consciously written in blank verse, *Key Largo* seems Maxwell Anderson's attempt to write a war play in the form of a Shakespearean tragedy. With an appropriately regal name, his tragic hero King McCloud (played in the New York production by Paul Muni), like Shakespeare's Hamlet, has a cowardly streak that led him to back down from the fight against evil in Franco's Spain and momentarily to back down again when he returns to the United States and faces a local despot. And like Hamlet, King Lear, Othello, and Timon of Athens, King McCloud plays out his tragic struggle in a setting at the geographic limit of civilization, where land and men meet the chaos of sea: the Florida Keys.

The long prologue to *Key Largo* takes place on a battlefield in northern Spain. There, fighting against Franco, McCloud's amalgam of pragmatism and cowardice in the face of what he recognizes as a losing battle is pitted against the idealism of his aptly named comrade, Victor d'Alcala (portrayed in the New York production by José Ferrer). Although Victor and his comrades are killed in the struggle against Fascist rule in Spain, they nevertheless achieve victory, if only an idealistic one. Anderson consequently reflects on mankind's never-ceasing struggle against tyranny:

> Hasn't it always looked the same, the fight
> for freedom? It's never respectable. It's led

> by unscrupulous fanatics, each one eyeing
> the other's throats. They're followed by a rabble
> that pulls down the walls and lets the roofs
> fall in on them. A lot of people die,
> good and bad, but there is more freedom later,
> for the next generation, there is. If you want a clean,
> Armageddon battle, all the beasts of hell
> against the angels of light, you won't get that,
> not in this world. (10–11)[42]

And the tyranny here is one that for the audience is embodied not only by Franco but also by Mussolini and Hitler. Indeed, McCloud despairingly exclaims:

> Was there ever a crusade
> without an ignominious end? Before
> we came to Spain we should have thought of that.
> The knights in rusty armor crippling home
> with an increment of blood and bone diseases
> from Palestine—leaving the infidels
> in charge as usual. Or the A.E.F.
> over-seas for democracy, and winning—
> along with other diseases—
> this Mussolini and Hitler. Yes, and Franco,
> very likely. (15)

Victor and his comrades, aware they will die, remain in battle but not in vain, for, as Victor says, basic to humanity is a hatred of injustice, "And that means the Hitlers / and the Mussolinis always lose in the end" (23). McCloud, by contrast, deserts the struggle, cynically remarking, "nothing / you win means freedom or equality / or justice" (22).

Beset by remorse, McCloud has sought to expiate the guilt he feels for his desertion by seeking out the families of his friends and informing them of their sons' heroic deaths. The final stop on his journey of atonement brings him to Key West and to Victor's father and sister, Allegre (played by Uta Hagen). In the Florida backwaters, McCloud and the audience learn of the local tinhorn gangster, Murillo, a miniaturized American version of Mussolini, Hitler, and Franco. Indeed, behind his back, Murillo's gang even calls him Mussolini. And when Murillo attempts to seduce Allegre and is rebuffed by her, he makes perfectly clear what he symbolizes. She scornfully tells him that she has no respect for him, to which he sneeringly replies, "You will have. It's the same with women as with nations, baby; the fellow with the most guns and the most money wins. Always. Because that's what the nations want! And what the women want!" (50). In short order, too, Murillo, like Hitler occupying Czechoslovakia and Poland, invades the d'Alcala home, using it for his mobsters and their crooked dealings.

In the face of the despotism and unalloyed evil of Murillo and, by inference, his European despotic counterparts, Anderson offers some of the long-range optimism implicit in Wilder's *Our Town*. Although McCloud once again flinches from taking a stand against despotism, d'Alcala, remembering how fish survive against all evolutionary odds, voices Maxwell Anderson's notion that the spirit of what is good in mankind will finally prevail against annihilation at the hands of a Murillo, or a Hitler and a Mussolini:

> For conditions
> among the fish were quite the opposite
> of what you'd call encouraging. They had
> big teeth and no compunction. Bigger teeth
> than Hitler or Murillo.
> Over and over again the human race
> climbs up out of the mud
>
> . . .
>
> It may be that the blight's on the race once more—
> that they're all afraid—and fight their way to the ground.
> But it won't end in the dark. Our destiny's
> the other way. There'll be a race of men
> who can face even the stars without despair,
> and think without going mad. (114)

Anderson's tragic hero, King McCloud, has his moment of Aristotelian anagnorisis at the conclusion of *Key Largo*, finding his better self and finally taking action against the tyrant. And like Hamlet, he kills and is killed by his enemy.

Unfortunately, both Maxwell Anderson's verse and tragic action fall far short of Shakespeare's. In *Key Largo* he chooses the high road of verse drama and inflated language to write a tragedy that produces neither pity nor fear. The aims of *Key Largo*, however, are quite clear: to affirm the survival of mankind, to argue that men will ultimately choose pursuing a higher good over yielding to the tyranny of despots, and to awaken a cowardly America to follow the example of King McCloud and bear arms against the sea of troubles in Europe.[43]

Anderson followed *Key Largo* with *Journey to Jerusalem*, which starred a sixteen-year-old Sidney Lumet as an adolescent Christ. In the preface to the play, Anderson reiterates the philosophy of d'Alcala:

> Before I wrote *Journey to Jerusalem* I had come to a realization, along with many others in these bitter years, that there was no answer to Hitler and the rule of force except some kind of faith, faith of men in themselves and in the race of men. A Hitler is only possible in a despairing nation,

a nation of men who have lost faith in their dignity and destiny. . . . If we are to oppose Hitler we must believe in ourselves, as individuals and as a nation. And if we are to believe in ourselves we must—and there is no way out of it—believe that there is purpose and pattern in the universe. . . . (v, vi)[44]

Also in the preface, Anderson once again reaches for Shakespearean analogue, arguing that Hitler's "philosophy is that of Iago, and his attitude toward his fellow men is likewise that of Iago toward Desdemona and Othello and Roderigo and Cassio" (v). The play itself juxtaposes faith in the Messiah to the tyranny of Herod and the Romans. Despite the clarity of Anderson's preface, however, the connections in the actual play-text between the times of Christ and those of the present are vague and shadowy at best.

Anderson is far more successful in reaching an audience when he descends from the clouds of lofty verse and the stiltedness of a New Testament costume piece. Written in prose and directed by Alfred Lunt, *Candle in the Wind* was an effective stage vehicle for Helen Hayes to do a star turn, even if the play's dramatic substance is thin and sentimental. Indeed, *Candle in the Wind* has much the feel of 1940s radio soap operas, with characters introduced for little apparent reason, motivations unclear, and a portrayal of love unsullied by reality.[45] But should *Candle in the Wind* be written off simply as weak playwriting from the author of such fine plays as *High Tor, Winterset,* and *What Price Glory?* The critics were dismissive, but Burns Mantle's passing comment is revealing: "This serious study of the curse of Hitlerism superimposed upon an American actress' romance disappointed the critics, but with the help of Helen Hayes, who played the heroine, found and interested a considerable public. After 95 performances in New York the play was taken on tour and played out the season." (5).[46] It may just be that Maxwell Anderson knew what he was about, that his aim was not to please the critics then or now, but to write the sort of play that would bring home the threat of the Nazism to audiences that wept also at romantic films, read newspaper feature stories written by "sob sisters," and tuned in to afternoon radio dramas like *Helen Trent, Our Gal Sunday, Ma Perkins, Life Can Be Beautiful,* and *Mary Noble, Backstage Wife.* Although *Candle in the Wind* may not be a literary triumph, the fact that it played as many performances as it did suggests that it served its purpose as dramatic material that would sway audiences to feel that American neutrality should be replaced with commitment and a declaration of war against the forces of European fascism.

Madeline Guest, the heroine of *Candle in the Wind,* is (like Helen Hayes herself) a famous American actress. She is temporarily living in France and disengaged from events in Europe until she falls in love with an anti-Hitler French journalist and freedom fighter.

At the outset of the play, the Germans have occupied France, but Madeline's understanding of the situation is merely the secondhand, naïve knowledge of Nazi tactics possessed by most Americans. As one of her American friends puts it, "I only know what the correspondents say in the Ritz Bar. Some maintain that conquest can't be permanent—that it's only skin deep. Others say that this is the beginning of the new ice age, and the Nazis are coming down like a snow cap over civilization. As for Americans, they were given their last warning months ago" (12).[47] When Madeleine's lover, Raoul, who has escaped from Nazi captivity, makes his initial appearance in the play, Madeline exhibits the typically American talent for avoiding unpleasant situations. She immediately suggests he escape France with her and leave the country's political troubles behind. Raoul, however, pointedly objects and, like Kurt Muller in Hellman's *Watch on the Rhine* (which had opened five months earlier), conflates his political stance with American ideals:

> I think I'd love your country, because it's yours. But it's not mine. What if America were sometime in desperate straits, and the men of America ran away? What would you think of them? . . . I am a Frenchman—and fight for France. For many years I fought with my pen against them, but not well enough. Not well enough, darling, and so now we must all fight as we can—desperately—with whatever arms there are. . . . You'd die for it too, if it came to a choice. . . . Rather than live ignobly. (24–25, 26)

When Raoul is captured and Madeline remains in France to try to free him from the local concentration camp where he is held prisoner, she and the audience are forced to see and know the Nazis face-to-face.

Anderson does not allow the gaze of the play ever to penetrate into the concentration camp. Suffering or tortured inmates are not shown, but the play creates harsh portraits of hard-bitten, doctrinaire Nazi officials and presents in strong terms the suffering of those whose loved ones have been incarcerated. The American heroine, Madeline Guest, becomes a stage representative of the U.S., and her increasing involvement in the terrible events playing themselves out in Europe at the hands of the Nazis becomes Anderson's cue for his audience. Erfurt, the Nazi official, tells her, as she enters his office at the concentration camp, "you have stepped, when you enter this room, from one world to another—from the old world to the new. You have stepped from freedom and chivalry and legend, into science, reality and control" (41). He concludes by making his "you" not just the heroine but a feminized U.S. itself, scoffing, "You are spoiled and soft, you Americans. You have never come up against sharp iron. It is your destiny to be beaten!" (46). The play thus throws down the gauntlet to all in the audience. As the curtain falls on the first act, the Nazi official tells Madeline to return to America where she belongs, and she responds with new-found resolve, "I will stay, and I will win!" (46).

As *Candle in the Wind* progresses into its second and third acts, Madeline increasingly loses her feminine and genteel qualities to emerge as a powerful and masculine opponent of those who purport to be the true men, the master race. For Germans of the Third Reich, a "female" emotion such as pity is a sign of weakness. Indeed, with twisted Nazi logic, the German commandant sees Shakespeare's Edmund in *King Lear* not as an arch-villain but as a tragically flawed hero whose weakness is his lapse of ruthlessness when he relents and says, "Some good I mean to do, despite of mine own nature," for, as the commandant explains, "Shakespeare's got the whole moral system upside down. In real life the strong and the ruthless win, and the weak suffer. And that's how it should be, or must be" (73, 74). The villainy and egotism of the Germans is, Anderson implies, beyond that of even one of Shakespeare's worst malefactors, and the Germans are, moreover, hostile and opposed to Western culture, Christian pity, and Shakespeare as the icon of all that is good in Western thought and art. At this point, audience members whose gorge did not rise at such patent Philistine dastardliness would need to be ideologically comatose. And for the literate in the audience, Anderson's call is for slow-acting Americans finally to take up the role of Edward in opposition to the more than bastard German Edmunds.

By the end of the play, Madeline, cuing her American countrymen, has gone from a beautiful and helpless American actress to a virile fighter actively engaged in the battle against a savage German world order. "They've made soldiers of us all—women and children and all," she exclaims. "They've even made one of me" (107). And the closing speeches of the play drive the point home:

> ERFURT. We take our enemies one at a time, and your country is last on the list. But your time will come.
>
> MADELINE. Yes. We shall expect you and be ready for you. In the history of the world, there have been many wars between men and beasts. And the beasts have always lost and men have won. (116)

Erfurt here delivers the message that runs through so many of the pre–Pearl Harbor plays, that when Germany has subdued Europe, the U.S., currently putting its ostrich head in the sand, will be its next easy target.[48] In response, Madeline sounds Anderson's perhaps heavy-handed call for Americans to be men, for them to stand up like St. George against the Teutonic beasts of Europe.

III

In the panorama of wartime plays before Pearl Harbor, Frederick Hazlitt Brennan's *The Wookey* is something of a curiosity. Brennan, who began as a journalist and movie critic, became a freelance Hollywood screenwriter. Opening on 10 September 1941 at the Plymouth Theatre in New York and starring Edmund Gwenn, *The Wookey* is a bittersweet comedy that celebrates British fortitude. Beginning with England's entrance into the war and subsequently set during the 1940 Blitz of London, Brennan's drama follows the travails and courage of the

Wookeys, an East End, working-class family headed by a father who operates a small boat in the London dockyards.

The Wookeys and their friends are ardently and comically lower class. These are the "small" people whose lives are dramatically affected and scarred by those who set world events in motion, and these are the people who give their lives at Dunkirk. Their home, near the targeted London docks, is repeatedly bombed by German air strikes. In one of those bombings, the innocent and lovable Mrs. Wookey meets her end. The play is a medley of character roles, from the blowzy Aunt Gen to 'Orace Wookey (played by Gwenn), the stalwart paterfamilias, and it is geared to make the American audience warm to these affable, brave little people whose lives are so badly damaged by the merciless Germans and by the limited military means of a heroic England. But even in this American play set in Britain, the American ambivalence about entering the war is given voice by Mr. Wookey, the lovable lower-class Everyman who is initially staunchly against war. It is only when the events of the war touch his immediate family that he becomes an engaged combatant.

Once Mr. Wookey's family is injured, once he sees the ravages of German warfare in Dunkirk and during the Blitz at home, his animus toward the Germans is aroused and he becomes a spokesperson for why the ordinary (American) citizen should take a stand. In their way, Mr. Wookey's unsophisticated sentiments forcefully go to the heart of the matter. He argues, "I'm a British subjeck an' I speaks me mind, war or no war. This bugger 'Itler, 'e wants ter boss the 'ole world. We should ha' kicked 's ribs in five years ago"(78).[49] In his own way, despite the crudeness of his formulation, 'Orace Wookey has an ultimately astute understanding of Hitler's appeal to the German people:

> Oh, 'Itler this and 'Itler that—you mikes me tired. 'E ain't a warrior. 'E ain't a general. 'E's a blarsted prison-keeper! 'E's what Jerry allus wanted to be. That's why Jerry follors 'im. 'E's promussed Jerry 'e'll mike a prison of the 'ole bloody world. (110)

Despite his negative views on Hitler and the Germans, however, Wookey does not easily surrender his reluctance to enter the war. In this regard he is not unlike the Americans in the audience who are watching him onstage. His down-to-earth understanding and assessment of Hitler's character and motivations, however, are certainly as eloquent in their own right as the high-toned verse of Maxwell Anderson or the more sophisticated speech of Rice's or Sherwood's or Hellman's characters.

A writer of brilliant social comedies like *Holiday, Paris Bound,* and *The Philadelphia Story* and of the remarkably fine philosophical plays *Hotel Universe* and *Here Come the Clowns,* Philip Barry seems, to his credit, to have felt it was his duty as a playwright to write about the threat to American liberties posed by Italian Fascism, Nazism, and communism. Barry's talent for writing witty repartee, however, was ill suited to serious wartime issues, and his awkward dramatic

7. *Liberty Jones* (1941). (Center) Nancy Coleman and John Beal. Courtesy of the New York Public Library.

allegory, *Liberty Jones* (5 February 1941), written partially in verse, has the subtlety of a brickbat, and it closed after twenty-one performances. Nevertheless, Barry clearly hoped to use his playwriting skills to take a stand on the American situation as the country faced the threat of European fascism. Despite the glaring failure of *Liberty Jones*, Barry's patriotic intentions demand recognition and respect. In this regard, he stands in powerful contrast to Eugene O'Neill, who had received a Nobel Prize and was considered America's top playwright, but who is the only prominent American playwright alive at the time never to write a play about the war or wartime issues.

Phillip Barry's *Liberty Jones,* directed by John Houseman, is an allegory, in which the title character is believed to be terminally ill and confined to bed at the Washington home of her uncle, Samuel Bunting. In the bedroom, she is surrounded by symbols of America: a gilt eagle, statues of angels and the Virgin, portraits of American naval officers, and a snare drum from the American Revolutionary War. She is visited by the characters Tom, Dick, and Harry, who are concerned about her and her malady, the symptoms of which are that she lacks the strength to fight off the allegorical figures called The Three Shirts, who are dressed in red, black, and brown, and who obviously represent Stalin, Mussolini, and Hitler. Very likely, Barry calls them The Three Shirts instead of giving them names to stress their inhumanity. In its flat-footed way, *Liberty Jones* points an accusing finger at a weak America using appeasement to stave off The Three Shirts by granting them space in Washington's Rock Creek Park. There The Shirts grow in size and try to seize Liberty herself, forcing Tom, Dick, and Harry (the symbols of American freedom) into combat. Tom, who marries Liberty and who has in the past appeased The Three Shirts, is compelled finally to speak sternly:

> [*Suddenly his voice changes.*] Listen, you thugs, I love this girl. Do you think I'll let you take her from me now? . . . I don't think you understand me: she is my wife, my home, my children. I love her fully, deeply, passionately. I love my obligations to her, her gifts to me. I love her a thousand times more than you love your strength, your power, your race, your pride, your conquests. (157)[50]

Tom uses his sword to pierce the shirt fronts of The Three Shirts, who deflate and lie inert like spent balloons at Liberty's feet. Having found her strength and her health, the once ailing Liberty (like America) can exclaim, "I am a girl no longer. I am a woman grown. Now I am afraid of nothing in this world or any other!" (163). In its way, the growth of Liberty from naïve girl to mature woman replicates the change experienced by Madeline Guest in *Candle in the Wind*.

Allegory is also the form used by minor playwright Ellis St. Joseph in an equally heavy-handed play, *A Passenger to Bali* (8 February 1940), in which the naïve and well-meaning Capt. English, captain of a commercial freighter, takes a passenger on board his ship. This passenger is the Rev. Mr. Walker, an allegorical figure of fascism, who pretends to be a missionary on his way to Bali to convert the natives.[51] Quickly, the true nature of the false Rev. Walker emerges, and he assumes what the stage directions tell us is "a grim Mussolini-Hitler pose" (62). Everywhere the ship tries to dock, the fascist Walker causes unrest. Captain English, perhaps like Chamberlain, comes to see Walker for what he is and despises him but finds that conciliation not only fails but also evokes the fascist Walker's scorn, as he sneers, "Give me a civilized man every time! You can bluff him, beat him, trick him, buy and sell him!" (128). Ultimately Capt. English and his crew abandon their ship, leaving it to Walker and letting him fare as he may. In other words, fascism is not killed, only ostracized. The play ends with the stage directions, "*The fog shrouds everything. The ship's bell, swinging with the rise and fall of the ocean, tolls a requiem . . . a warning*" (139), a warning meant for the American audience.

IV

The American plays written in the years before the United States commits to the war serve as a reading of the country's skittish pulse. Americans were still recovering from the losses of World War I and trying to emerge from the depths of the Depression. It seemed a time to address domestic woes rather than to attend to the ills of other countries. Indeed, during the period before Pearl Harbor, the U.S. had not yet decided whether to stick to its post–World War I isolationism and pacifism or to stick its neck out and commit to another war across the ocean. Not surprisingly, the general feeling that emerges from the wide spectrum of war-related plays during this period is one of national ambivalence. The specter of fascism growing in strength and moving ever closer to American shores is countervailed by the desire of Americans to cultivate their own gardens and leave European battles to the Europeans. Perhaps nowhere is that dilemma of neutrality versus engagement seen more strongly than in two Group Theatre plays of the 1939 season: Irwin Shaw's *The Gentle People* (5 January 1939) and Robert Ardrey's *Thunder Rock* (14 November 1939). Both plays bring the full acting and directing talent of the Group Theatre into play. The first, directed by Harold Clurman, included in its cast Sam Jaffe, Roman Bohnen, Franchot Tone, Karl Malden, Sylvia Sidney, Elia Kazan, Lee J. Cobb, and Harry Bratsburg (later to become famous under the stage name Harry Morgan). The second, directed by Kazan, again included Cobb, Bohnen, and Bratsburg, plus Myron McCormick, Luther Adler, Morris Carnovsky, Frances Farmer, and Robert Lewis. One wishes that these gifted actors had been given stronger dramatic material with which to work, but both *The Gentle People* and *Thunder Rock* are landmark plays for revealing and charting the ways American playwrights of the period sought to change American attitudes toward the war. The plays reflect, as well, how the playwrights themselves struggled with their own difficult metamorphoses from strong pacifist convictions to (often reluctant) acknowledgment that pacifism was not a viable answer to the aggression of fascist dictators. It is remarkable, too, that in these two plays staged by the Group Theatre, a theatre that was nothing if not politically committed, the question of isolation or engagement is not clearly determined. Instead, it remains unresolved.

April 1936 saw the Broadway production of Irwin Shaw's *Bury the Dead*, possibly to this day the single most celebrated antiwar play. Fewer than three years later, however, Shaw's *The Gentle People* records the playwright's changed attitude. Edmond Gagey regards the play as a call "to positive action." Shaw's biographer, Michael Shnayerson, claims that "Shaw had intended to make the point that America was a last refuge of the free in an increasingly Fascist world, and a melting pot that needed protecting." Malcolm Goldstein is probably closest to the mark when he argues that through this play Shaw sought a "united front against fascism" but nonetheless recognized that that was unlikely to happen.[52] *The Gentle People*'s subtitle is *A Brooklyn Fable*, and in his prefatory epigraph Shaw asserts, "This play is a fairy tale with a moral. In it justice triumphs and the meek prove victorious over arrogant and violent men. The author does not pretend that this is the case in real life."[53]

The two protagonists of *The Gentle People* are elderly men with symbolic names: Jonah Goodman and Philip Anagnos (i.e., one who comes to discover or know). The two sit fishing on the bow of a boat moored at a Brooklyn pier, seeking to escape from the realities and unpleasantness of their daily lives. Their anglers' idyll, their splendid isolation, is rudely disturbed by Harold Goff, a flashy, braggart, two-bit gangster, who seems to work hard at imitating George Raft. Goff tries to extort protection money from the old men, and he simultaneously arouses both the sexual and economic lust of Goodman's daughter Stella, who dreams, like the impassioned followers of Hitler and Mussolini, of escaping from the diurnal humdrum and financial constriction of her Depression-era life.

Only in one brief moment of *The Gentle People* does Shaw make a direct connection between the Brooklyn events depicted onstage and the larger world. Speaking of the increasing voracity of Goff and the racketeers whom Goff represents, Goodman says:

> I read once in a book that if a lion once tastes human blood, from then on he never is satisfied with anything else. This is pertinent to our case. ... What does history show? Look at Mussolini. They fed him Africa, now he has his teeth on Spain. They let Hitler taste Austria, he is dribbling at the lips for his other neighbors. (47)

Although *The Gentle People* is appropriately gentle in connecting Brooklyn and Europe, Shaw's play is nonetheless unmistakably about the threat and allure of fascism, and about the need for Americans to end their denial of the fascist threat and to take action. As Eberhard Brüning argues, "zugleich wird angedeutet, daß Faschisten und Gangster, ob in Europa oder Amerika, gemeinsame Züge aufweisen" [It is shown simultaneously that fascists and gangsters, whether in Europe or America, display shared characteristics].[54]

Remarkably, in less than three short years, Shaw makes a radical change from *Bury the Dead* to *The Gentle People*.[55] But *The Gentle People*'s consciously simplistic ending leaves matters unresolved. Realizing that their peaceful, recreational, and escapist fishing can no longer withstand Goff's extortionist appetite, Goodman and Anagnos lure Goff, a non-swimmer, onto their boat, take him out to sea, and push him overboard. By killing Goff, they take action, freeing the waterfront of its strong-armed, tin-pot despot. They also liberate Stella Goodman from her destructive false dreams of instant romantic adventure and capitalistic affluence. Yet the conclusion of *The Gentle People* is simply too good and too pat to be true. Shaw knows it and wants his audience to know it too, as his epigraph makes unmistakably clear. Shaw understands that even as late as 1939, America, like Goodman and Anagnos, wished to deny the realities of the world and to find escape instead in its own political anglers' idyll, an escape that his own *Bury the Dead* had helped put in place. Yet even as *The Gentle People* attempts to awaken Americans to the dangerous movements brewing in Europe, refracted throughout the play are doubts about whether this is possible or even good. Shaw finally leaves unresolved the question of whether his Brooklyn fable is merely idealistic fiction or a fable that can come true.

Perhaps the most stunningly equivocal piece of the whole pre–Pearl Harbor period is Robert Ardrey's *Thunder Rock,* the drama the Group Theatre presented eleven months after staging *The Gentle People* and, even more important, just two months after the world-shaking German invasion of Poland. In fact, not only in its subject matter but remarkably in its textual variations as well, *Thunder Rock* bespeaks the indecision about World War II that characterized late 1930s America. Ardrey's play is remarkable in another way as well. It is one of the only—perhaps *the* only—play of the period to see the conflicts and dangers across the Pacific. All the other pre–Pearl Harbor plays of note look exclusively across the Atlantic to Hitler, Mussolini, and Europe.

The setting of *Thunder Rock* is splendid isolation itself: "the lighthouse on Thunder Rock, a speck of an island in northern Lake Michigan" (vi).[56] There Charleston, the lighthouse keeper, once a newspaperman and author engaged in social issues and causes, has retreated from the world, claiming that "society itself is a lost cause" (23). Visited by his old comrade Streeter and by Flanning, the lighthouse inspector, the reclusive Charleston scoffs at their concern for the state of the world. With breathless excitement, Flanning offers a snapshot summary of issues facing America in 1939, which Charleston greets with consummate disinterest:

> FLANNING. How's everything going to come out? Hitler, Mussolini. The dictators vs. Democracy. Fascism, Communism. War vs. Peace. Look at Uncle Sam, the battleships he's building. What happens next? Refugees, what's the world going to do with all the refugees from Europe? Right here at home, business gets better and we've still got unemployment. Strikes, capital vs. labor—It's drama, my boy, sheer stark drama.
>
> . . .
>
> CHARLESTON. I'm sorry, Inspector, I respect your curiosity concerning the future, I just don't happen to share it. (12–13)

Similarly, Charleston's friend Streeter declares that he has decided to fly planes in the Sino-Japanese war to help the Chinese in their struggle against Japanese invasion and domination. "The time comes round, you've got to do something. That's all there is to it," argues Streeter. "You can't stand by and watch forever" (20). But standing by and not even watching is precisely what Charleston is resolved to do.

Turning his back on contemporary events, retreating spatially to his remote lighthouse off the Michigan Upper Peninsula, Charleston also retreats chronologically from the modern world. A ship that went down in 1849 near Thunder Rock lost all its passengers and crew, and Charleston, endowed with the dazzling mental gift of being able to conjure those drowned passengers back to life in his imagination, has moved back into time past and now lives among them. His literal jump back in time is a metaphor for America's willful desire to look backward and deny the present, even as Charleston's retreat to his lighthouse is an obvious comment on American isolation, neutrality, and disengagement in the face of events in Europe and Asia.

As Charleston's shipwreck victims come increasingly to life in his imagination, they take on a life of their own. Each of them, Charleston and the audience discover, has cynically or dejectedly given up and abandoned some social, personal, or scientific problem to which he or she saw no possible solution or resolution in 1849. With 20–20 contemporary hindsight, however, Charleston and the audience realize that solutions and resolutions were just a few years away, that the characters would have triumphed had they persevered. Learning a lesson from this, Charleston recognizes that he must depart from his lighthouse of isolation, re-enter the world, participate in world events, and take his stand, even if the forces against him seem invincible or the current world situation seems impossible to ameliorate.

But how Ardrey's third-act ending works itself out offers a stunning insight into the playwright's ambivalence and the ambivalence prevalent at the time. In the published acting version of the play, the 1849 characters disappear, and as they do so, Streeter returns by means of Charleston's mental conjuring. In actuality, he has died in China while flying his plane against the Japanese, but now he returns to the lighthouse together with his Chinese mechanic and comrade, Chang. While the imaginary Streeter is explaining to Charleston that it is the plight of the honest, simple, oppressed Chang and his fellow Chinese that led Streeter to make a commitment to enter the struggle against Japan, Charleston's radio goes on, announcing the start of World War II:

> Ladies and gentlemen, today, September First, Nineteen Thirty-Nine, may become a day in world history long remembered. Berlin: Adolph Hitler delivered a speech believed to be the keynote to the general war in Europe. Warsaw, Poland: Frontier reports say that Polish soil has been invaded by German motorized units. London: Prime Minister Chamberlain will address the House of Commons this afternoon. Invocation of the Anglo-Polish pact is expected. Ladies and gentlemen, at 8 P.M. this evening this station will present a symposium on the subject, Can America escape the impending European conflict? (81)

A reborn, recommitted Charleston tells Streeter, "There's no such thing as escape. . . . Always, from the point of view of the man who fought, his defeat seemed inevitable. . . . And yet—one after another—obstacles to civilization do get smashed. Sooner or later. Like the obstacle that darkens our day. [*A slight pause.*] We'll win, Street. It's the one inevitability. Now or later, today or in a thousand years—we'll smash this thing" (82–83). Charleston resigns from his isolated post at the Thunder Rock lighthouse, but what exactly he will do next remains unknown as he leaves the stage. In other words, if America and Charleston cannot escape from world events, what should then be their course of action?

The acting edition of the play leaves that question up in the air. Whatever Charleston's course of action, this version of *Thunder Rock* suggests that America can and must, like Charleston, abandon its isolation and become actively engaged in world events.

Thunder Rock was published again in 1950 in Robert Ardrey's anthology, *Plays of Three Decades*. The conclusion of the third act in that version is very different from the published acting version. In the 1950 script, Charleston's friend Streeter does not reappear, but as the imagined 1849 characters fade, Charleston is left alone to hear an abbreviated radio announcement of Germany's invasion of Poland, preceded by the sound of a plane that is bringing Cassidy, Charleston's replacement as keeper of the lighthouse at Thunder Rock. When the two men confront each other, Charleston is a new person ready to go out into the world, but Cassidy is a replication of Charleston's reclusive old self coming to the lighthouse in order to remove himself to the furthest extremity from world events. In the last moments of the play, Charleston makes much of his having fought in Spain, and as he departs, the audience knows he will now re-engage himself in wartime causes. Which particular causes those will be or how he will do so remain unarticulated. When Charleston leaves behind his lighthouse retreat and his isolationism, one recalls the similar concluding action when Joe finely leaves the Pacific Street Bar, his island and his isolation, in *The Time of Your Life*.

But Charleston is replaced by Cassidy, and in scripting that, Ardrey makes the audience aware that for every Charleston awakening from isolationist slumber there is a Cassidy who earnestly seeks it. The sense, then, is that Americans are likely, at least for the foreseeable future, to remain in their national stalemate, caught between the push for activism and the desire for isolation. The one glimmer of hope for activism that emerges in this ending of *Thunder Rock* lies in Charleston's prediction that the spirits of the shipwrecked dead on Thunder Rock will before long work their magic on the reclusive Cassidy.

The strong activist ending of the first version of *Thunder Rock* and the more equivocal ending of the second version suggest the uncertain state of Ardrey's own view.[57] But the story does not end there. As Malcolm Goldstein has written, in the promptbook for the Group Theatre's production of *Thunder Rock*, Charleston is given a speech that problematizes the ending of the play still further, for it argues neither for activism nor isolation but for an informed pacifism:

> America's going to war. . . . No . . . she's got a bigger job than war. Peace. Peace in the face of war, that's the job, and she can do it. . . . Don't force the world to go our way, force won't work. Show them, show them that our way is best. . . . A people at peace can put men to work at better jobs than destruction. A people at peace can have butter to eat and the luxury of justice. America's got one high obligation to preserve the last peace on earth. That's our job.[58]

Whether added by Ardrey himself or, more likely, by the Group Theatre, this speech adds still another dimension to the equivocation of *Thunder Rock*. What is important here is that the three very different final moments of *Thunder Rock*—some of them written postwar—throw into sharp relief the indecision and dialectics that characterized not only Ardrey and his play but also both the nation from 1935 to 1941 and the war-related plays produced during that period.

V

In all the prewar plays, theatre audiences sat safely in their seats watching events unfold in drawing rooms, courtrooms, airplanes, embassies, and other familiar stage spaces. It took the medium of radio drama to bring the terror of invasion and dictatorship more immediately to the attention of the public and directly into the American home. Arguably the most powerful message about the dangers of American apathy, isolationism, and pacifism came from poet and playwright Archibald MacLeish, who saw in radio and poetry a way to fashion powerful drama that could thrust an audience headlong into the situation in Europe and arouse them to prepare themselves for the worst (x).[59] Writing in his foreword to the radio play *The Fall of the City*, MacLeish asserts, "The ear accepts, accepts and believes, accepts and creates. The ear is the poet's perfect audience. And it is radio and only radio which can give him public access to this perfect friend."[60] Using the powerful radio acting and radio announcing skills of House Jamison, Orson Welles, Burgess Meredith, and Dwight Weist, MacLeish places his audience directly in a city on the verge of attack and subjugation by a dictator or military strongman.[61] Cleverly, MacLeish does not give the city a local habitation and a name, though it is clearly a city in the Western world. Drawing on the idiom of radio's on-the-scene news broadcasts, the Voice of the Studio Director (House Jamison) in "orotund and professional" tones informs the listeners of *The Fall of the City*, "This broadcast comes to you from the city" (3), and moves to the Voice of the Announcer (Orson Welles), who creates the scene in the ears and imagination of the play's listening audience:

> We are here on the central plaza.
> We are well off to the eastward edge.
> There is a kind of terrace over the crowd here.
> It is precisely four minutes to twelve.
> The crowd is enormous: there might be ten thousand:
> There might be more: the whole square is faces. (4)

As the radio play continues, the inhabitants gather in an atmosphere of increasing tension, knowing that a conqueror is allegedly on his way. In the style of Greek tragedy, which MacLeish consciously imitates, a breathless messenger arrives, warning the chorus, comprised of citizens, and the chorus leader, who is the Announcer, that the conqueror is fast approaching the city. MacLeish's generally trimeter verse line effectively italicizes at once the messenger's gasps for breath and the urgency of his message:

> There has come the conqueror!
> I am to tell you.
> I have raced over sea land:
>
>   . . .
>
> Be warned of this conqueror!
> This one is dangerous!
> Word has out-oared him.
> East over sea-cross has
> All taken—
> Every country.
> No men are free there.
> Ears overhear them.
> Their words are their murderers
> Judged before judgment
> Tried after trial
> they die as do animals:—
> Offer their throats
> As the goat to her slaughter.
> Terror has taught them this. (10–11)

The internal rhymes and alliterations work together here to conjure up, in a few lines and in general terms, what the world and Americans were in more specific terms coming to recognize as Hitler's geographic aggression and the atmosphere of surveillance, arrests, kangaroo courts, concentration camps, and mass slaughter that marked the Third Reich's regime.

Employing the rhetoric of post–World War I pacifists, the Voice of the Orator (Burgess Meredith) argues, in a verse line very different from and far more eloquent than that of the Messenger, that the way to overcome the conqueror is through peace, appeasement, and words, not armed resistance:

> What is the surest defender of liberty?
> Is it not liberty?
> A free people resists by freedom:
> Not locks! Not block houses!
>
>   . . .
>
> This conqueror unresisted
> Will conquer no longer: a posturer
> Beating his blows upon burdocks—

. . .

There *is* a weapon my friends.
Scorn conquers!

. . .

Let this conqueror come!
Show him no hindrance!
Suffer his flag and his drum!
Words . . . win! (13–14, 15, 16)

To this, a second Messenger (Dwight Weist) warns that the conqueror uses as his rationale an image of his enemy that is of his own devising, and that the multitudes are worshiping him for it:

He brings his own enemy!

He baggages with him
His closest antagonist—
His private opposer.
He's setting him up
At every road corner—

. . .

And the people are shouting
Flowers him flinging
Music him singing
And bringing him gold
And holding his heels
And feeling his thighs
Till their hearts swell
And they're telling his praises
Like lays of the heroes
And chiefs of antiquity. (19–20)

Of course the play here brings to mind Hitler and Mussolini's identification of Jews, gypsies, gays, and political dissidents as the enemies that must be annihilated while the tumultuous cheering crowds pay their wildly enthusiastic homage to *Der Führer* and *Il Duce*. Like the pacifist orator, the priests of the city encourage the populace to trust in religious faith, which they claim will save them from conquest, "Turn to your gods! / The Conqueror cannot take you!" (22). A general then in vain exhorts the cowardly citizens to resist the conqueror.

Certainly MacLeish's message to his radio audience is that pacifism, acquiescence, and denial permit the conqueror his conquests. *The Fall of the City* concludes with the disconcerting collapse of a democratic, peace-loving place, much like the U.S., and the frightening image of a Hitler ruling the world:

> The city is doomed!
>   There's no holding it!
> The age is his! It's his century!
>
>   . . .
>
> The age demands a made-up mind.
> The conqueror's mind is decided on everything.
>
> His doubt comes after the deed or never.
>
>   . . .
>
> He's one man: we are but thousands!
> Who can defend us from this one man? (29)

MacLeish's play concludes as well with the even more frightening idea that the cowardly citizens of a once democratic state can and will rationalize the need for a fascist dictator. The Voices of the Citizens exclaim, "Masterless men / Must take a master!" and "Rigor and fast / Will restore our dignity! / Chains will be liberty!" (30). As the dialogue and verse work together to place Mac-Leish's American listening audience in the middle of the conquered city and amidst its citizens, the call for an active stand against the political developments in Europe is made and viscerally felt.

Even more compelling than *The Fall of the City* is MacLeish's verse radio play of the following year, *Air Raid*, in which a town tries to proceed nonchalantly with daily life and to ignore the ever-louder motors of planes coming closer and closer. The desperate desire of the townspeople to deny the ominous planes and what they portend—"What's a war to us—there's always another. / All that noise to tell us there's a war" (20)—is counterpointed aurally by the escalating, deafening sounds of the planes' engines.[62] Once again, MacLeish denies his listeners the comfort of voyeurism, placing them directly in the action, "The town is in those mountains: you are there / You are twenty-eight miles from the eastern border: / You are up on top of a town on a kind of tenement" (7).

MacLeish proves himself a master of both radio sound and poetic sound as the tension of *Air Raid* mounts, not merely as the loud plane engines indicate that the enemy is approaching the town but also as the pulsating, frequently tetrameter rhythm of the male voices contrasts to the largely pentameter and hexameter lines of the women. A climax in which sound dominates meaning comes as Men's Voices shout:

> Air Raid!
> Air Raid!

Air Raid!
Air Raid!
The bombers!
The bombers!
The bombers!
The bombers! (22)

The women, however, scoff at this male anxiety and at the Sergeant who warns of impending disaster, for the women believe that wars are men's affairs and do not affect the daily lives of women. One woman sarcastically quips to the Sergeant:

Listen to me policeman!
Perhaps it's true they're coming in their planes:
Perhaps it isn't true. But if it is
It's not for housewives in this town they're coming.
They're after the generals: they're after the cabinet ministers. (24)

And another says:

We're women. No one's making war on women—
The nation with no land: without history:
The nation whose dates are Sunday and Monday: the nation
Bounded by bread and sleep—by giving birth. (25)

MacLeish, using the rhetoric of the Sergeant, makes abundantly clear to his American listeners, who may, like the women, believe that the war is just another run-of-the-mill war, that this war and this enemy is not like any other. This enemy, this Hitler, will not spare women and has ideological agendas that transcend the traditional, less imaginative desire for more land:

It may be thought
He makes his wars on women!
It may be thought
This enemy is not the usual enemy!
That this one is no general in a greatcoat
Conquering countries for the pride and praise:
That this one conquers other things than countries!
It may be thought that this one conquers life!
That life that won't be conquered can be killed!
That women are most life-like! That he kills them! (27)

The stage directions convey the shattering crescendo that follows at the close of the speech, "*The women's voices rise again in a great shriek of laughter. Over their laughter, clear and lifting and lovely as laughter itself rises the Singing Woman's scale. Under it, dull, heavy, flat come soft explosions"* (28).

The women are still not won over and scoff at the enemy, caricaturing him in terms that any American who had seen photos and newsreels of Hitler or Mussolini would instantly recognize. The chorus of women, one after another, still asserts with amusement, "He gets his photograph made in his belt and his buttons! /. . . . He gets his photograph made with his fist stuck out! /. . . . And his chin stuck out! /. . . . And his chest stuck out!" (28–29). The amusement, however, ceases when the planes arrive. The women shout to the pilots, "It's us do you see! / It's us don't you see us!" which is answered by *"A crazy stammering of machine gun hammers above the rising roar,"* and *"For an instant the shrieking voices of the women, the shattering noise of the guns and the huge scream of the planes are mingled, the voices are gone and the guns are gone and the scream of the planes closes to a deep sustained music note level and long as silence"* (35). The play ends with the stage direction, *"the diminishing music note again. Over it the voice of the Singing Woman rising in a slow screaming scale of the purest agony broken at last on the unbearably highest note. The diminishing drone of the planes fades into actual silence"* (36).

Through the power of the verse and through the dramatic art sound that radio enables, the American listeners are placed inside the besieged town, amid the machine gun fire and the agony of the fatally wounded women. The listeners thus feel viscerally and immediately the terror of the air raid, and they come to recognize the folly of believing that Hitler and Mussolini are just this era's generic enemies, a replay in modern dress of past enemies. *The Fall of the City* and *Air Raid* command attention and deny the audience the ability to bury their heads in the sand or to continue with equanimity the so-called splendid American isolation.

What becomes clear as one surveys the drama of the prewar period in the U.S. is the increasing anxiety among American playwrights of the 1930s and early 1940s and the increasing intensity of their dramaturgy as events in Europe became more and more profound and minatory. There is, furthermore, on the part of the American stage's gaze, a curious zooming in on and zooming out from wartime issues. And some issues are almost totally ignored. *The Ghost of Yankee Doodle* and *The American Way* look across the ocean at events in Europe from the relative safety of small-town America. *There Shall Be No Night* and *Flight to the West* pose the threat of Nazi fifth columnists coming to the United States, and *Margin for Error*, *Watch on the Rhine*, and *Liberty Jones* present subversives having already infiltrated U.S. cities. *Key Largo*, *It Can't Happen Here*, *The Time of Your Life*, and *The Gentle People* use images of localized despotism in America as analogies of the more widespread despotism in Europe.

Few plays of the period, however, actually take place in Europe. *Judgment Day* is set in a nameless East European country, *There Shall Be No Night*, in Finland, *The Wookey*, in London during the Blitz, and *Candle in The Wind*, in France under the Vichy government. Yet all these are at the periphery of the Holocaust in Europe. With the exception of the thoroughly unsuccessful and unpublished *Waltz in Goose-Step,* no plays are set in Germany, Italy, Poland, or Austria. Today one thinks of the 1935–41 period as a time when Jews were oppressed by Hitler and his followers, were forced to wear the yellow *Judenstern,* lost their jobs and had their places of business destroyed, were often separated from family and relations as they fled Nazi-occupied countries, or were herded into concentration camps. These realities were not unknown. Although great attention is paid to American democratic ideals and their possible loss should the forces of fascism invade American shores, there is a remarkable near silence in American plays about the Jews, *Kristallnacht,* and deportations to concentration camps. Gays and gypsies are never mentioned. Clearly for Broadway as well as for Washington, the sense was that Americans might go to war over the threat to democratic principles but not over the oppression of European minorities.

With a few exceptions, military headquarters and battlefields are also largely eschewed. Except for *Thunder Rock,* Japan and events in Asia likewise do not find their way into the drama. It takes American entry into the war to bring some of these issues and settings into prominence. But surely the many American dramas presented during the years immediately prior to Pearl Harbor alerted Americans to war issues and allowed them to see the oncoming storm clouds. On that fateful Sunday morning of 7 December 1941, when the Japanese attacked Pearl Harbor and 1,102 crewmen aboard the USS *Arizona* lost their lives, the United States may not have been militarily prepared. American theatre audiences, however, had been prepared for years. Politically astute playwrights, writing in the 1930s and early 1940s, had foreseen and shown the inevitability of American entry into World War II, preparing theatre-going Americans for the battles that lay ahead.

TWO

The Drama of the War Years

I

With the Japanese attack on Pearl Harbor and the subsequent American declaration of war against Japan, Germany, and Italy, American troops joined with the Allies to wage war across both the Atlantic and the Pacific. Whether the United States should go to war was no longer a matter for debate. War was now a fact and was fast becoming a fact of American daily life. The outrage of Pearl Harbor had moved the American public to favor war for the first time since World War I. Boys in military uniform were to be seen everywhere, high school and college students were enlisting or being drafted in large numbers, and a spirit of adventure and danger was in the air. Hardly an American family was without someone serving his country. The new fashion rage for male children was the sailor suit, and even women's fashions featured epaulets on the shoulders. Soon women joined the war effort not just by rolling bandages, baking fruitcakes, and writing letters from home but by joining the military themselves: through the WAACs (Women's Auxiliary Army Corps), which in July 1943 became the WACs (Women's Army Corps); the WAVES (Women Accepted for Volunteer Emergency Service); the SPARS (derived from the Coast Guard motto *Semper Paratus*); the Marine Corps Women's Reserve; and the Army Nurses. And when the men went off to war, women assumed positions on the work force in areas that had once been exclusively male vocational preserves.[1]

Ethnically homogeneous rural American towns with military training camps found themselves overflowing with young men from all over the country and with a variety of ethnic and religious backgrounds. And in their off hours, those diverse young men often explored what the town had to offer in the way of alcohol and sexual adventure. The top brass in Washington were now the military brass, and waging war became the main business of government. National chauvinism and jingoism ran high, marred only by the inevitable and dreaded lists of casualties and of men missing in action. Army helmets commemorating the dead and missing could be seen hanging on American front porches. Crepe was a frequent decoration visible on neighborhood door fronts.

It did not take long before a new wartime vision of the U.S. was projected on the American stage. Playwrights were no longer faced with trying to convince audiences that the country should enter the war. Instead they turned to the new task of helping the public to understand better the causes for which lives were being sacrificed, the dangerous nature of the enemy, the heroism of the troops at the front, the excellence of American military know-how, and the impact of the war on the lives of those at home. There were references onstage, too, to the less savory aspects of life on the home front: businessmen exploiting wartime industry to line their own pockets, women finding new men while husbands and boyfriends were overseas, and Nazi fifth columnists appearing on American soil, intent on sabotaging the war effort. Some topics, however, like the actual strategies of the war, the diplomatic challenges, or the death camps where six million Jews, gypsies, dissidents, and gays lost their lives, were rarely mentioned. Yet amid all these serious topics, Thalia's comic spirit was not quelled. The social changes brought on by the war provided rich fodder for comic writers, and theatregoers were eager to put aside the daily newspaper headlines about battles, victories, and defeats to enjoy the lighter side of life during war. In their way, the war-related farces and social comedies sometimes spoke as revealingly of wartime sensibilities and American concerns as their darker dramatic contemporaries.

Action movies came into their own during the 1940s as filmmakers increasingly realized that a great strength of cinema lies in its ability to film battle scenes. Movie cameras could range around outdoor terrain or could photograph hundreds of movie extras dressed as soldiers in battle attire and capture the dynamics of combat. Recording or simulating war was a relatively easy feat for Hollywood. All those extras could be employed for a brief time and not for every performance. The many battlefront films made during and just after World War II are eloquent evidence for the special power of war films and their ability to capture military action on the screen. However, the landscape of battle, from Shakespeare's Henry plays to the present, is where live theatre feels the pinch of its limitations. The confined indoor space of a playhouse, the awkwardness of bringing the armies or machinery of war onstage, the prohibitive cost of employing scores of actors on a daily basis, even if the stage were capable of holding them all, render battlefront drama a major challenge for live theatre. More often than not, playwrights will, therefore, eschew actual combat scenes and confine themselves instead to a small set of soldiers in one encampment, barracks, or trench. Perhaps because of such impediments, there are but few American battle plays of any note written during World War II.

Maxwell Anderson, one of America's most respected playwrights at the time of World War II, did write two battle plays—*The Eve of St. Mark* (7 October 1942) and *Storm Operation* (1 November 1944)—for theatre audiences, but both were less than successful in bringing the feel and scent of military combat to the stage. It is only after the war is over that a couple of successful battlefront plays are mounted: Harry Brown's *The Sound of Hunting* (20 November 1945) and William Wister Haines's *Command Decision* (1 October 1947). And Anderson's *The Eve of St. Mark* is not meant to be primarily about combat. Instead, this play is representative of one of American drama's burdens during the war. Its importance lies not in its theatrical excellence but in how, ten months after the U.S. declares war, it seeks to chart for the audience the meaning of the transition from peacetime to wartime. It also tries to chart what happens to soldiers, drafted for a year of service in a peacetime army, when the country suddenly goes to war and they are shipped overseas for an unexpectedly long period of service and placed in combat with a fierce enemy.

The Eve of St. Mark moves between the soldiers and the folks back home, suggesting the ways in which domestic lives are—and will continue to be— affected as families go from the hardships of the Depression to those of a country at war. To enunciate these large-scale issues, Anderson creates a rural Everyfamily living on the western edge of New York State's southern tier. Very likely Anderson was thinking of the families he knew during a boyhood spent in a host of Pennsylvania, Ohio, Iowa, and North Dakota towns.

In large part, *The Eve of St. Mark* is about Pvt. Quizz West, whom we follow from his first appearance when he comes home on furlough in April 1941, eight months before Pearl Harbor, until his death on a Pacific island a year later (five months after the U.S. enters the war). It is also very much about the typical American family and the innocent young sweetheart Quizz leaves behind. There is, moreover, a powerful sense in *The Eve of St. Mark* that Anderson is straining to create a drama of profundity about what World War II will mean to American men in uniform and to their loved ones.

The play opens with notes of change. A farmhand, whose Depression-era indigence has brought on the desertion of his wife and the placement of his children in welfare institutions, finds work with the Wests, who are shorthanded on their farm because their son, Quizz, has been drafted. Anderson never follows up the story of the farmhand, but clearly he is placed in the play to suggest that, for better or worse, the war will alleviate the unemployment that had been brought about by the Depression. At the same time, the drafting of teenagers makes their parents feel their own age and the brevity of life. As Quizz's mother, Nell, laments, "But the war does rush everything. It sort of crowds us toward the exit"(6).[2] There is a concomitant sense of urgency as Quizz must use a single day off to return home, see his parents, propose to Janet, whom he has known for too short a time, and leave again for camp so as not to be AWOL. To create a sense of wartime momentum in scene 1, Anderson pointedly makes it all happen too quickly. He contrasts this with the lack of urgency among the soldiers as they banter and throw dice in their barracks in the subsequent scene.

But even as Anderson pencils in the changes felt in America's Depression-edged rural communities like that of the Wests by a country preparing for probable war, so too does he note the transformations felt in small towns now housing military bases populated by boisterous and randy young men. With poignant ambivalence, a promiscuous young woman in the town where Quizz and his comrades are stationed laments the alterations in her community and in what were once innocent girls like herself:

> I hate the whole damn army! What did you have to come to this town for, anyway, with your whole army, spoiling everything! We didn't ask for you! We didn't want you here! We had everything nice, and we went to church on Sunday, and I could'a got married, and then you come along with your army and it's all spoiled! I want it the way it was before you came along! . . . They want to have a drink and then they want to go out and look at the stars! Astronomy! Only they never see the stars! Oh, no! And I hate you all and the whole God-damn army and I want it to be the way it was! (38)

Anderson here helps his audience to discover the new geographies of "on base" and "off base" and to understand how those geographies establish revised configurations of sexuality and alcohol consumption for both soldiers and the once sleepy small towns that the soldiers now inhabit and alter.

As American entry into the war becomes increasingly imminent, Anderson tries to chart the nervousness of the family and the way in which the premarital commitment between Quizz and Janet intensifies. Knowing that he will likely be shipped overseas for combat duty when the U.S. enters the war, Quizz, who is twenty-two, and Janet, who is a senior in high school, find themselves unexpectedly transformed from naïve youngsters to adults making life commitments. At the close of act 1, they confess to one another their sexual inexperience and consciously decide to engage in premarital sex, lest the impending war rob them of sharing that experience. It is only a *deus ex militia*, an eleventh-hour call for Quizz to return to the base, that prevents them. But this is not Anderson as an advocate of chastity but as a writer who plans to use that chastity in poetic ways during the second act. Significant, however, is the way in which *The Eve of St. Mark* recognizes how the war catapults young people prematurely and headlong into adulthood.

As a work of theatre, *The Eve of St. Mark* wanders with uncertainty among characters who lack color and depth. In the middle of the second act, however, when America is in the war and the soldiers find themselves in April 1942 on a lonely Philippine island, beset with malaria and fighting a losing battle against the Japanese, the play comes together to make its point. Although canon and artillery fire punctuate the play's final scenes, neither the Japanese nor actual combat is shown. Instead, the focus is on the brave company of soldiers who are ill and stranded but attempt to hold their position against the Japanese who outnumber them, are better equipped, and have blown up the American medical supplies containing the much-needed quinine for those men suffering from malaria. The soldiers are faced with evacuating or going to their deaths to ensure the safety of the other American troops in the region. Above all, Anderson, early in the war, uses theatre to provide civilians dramatic access to the hardships of battle, to men sacrificing their young lives and futures, facing death for their country. One soldier astutely points out, "There are tens of millions back home who have hardly been touched at all, tens of millions who have risked almost nothing" (85). Some of those tens of millions are the members of Anderson's audience, but they will now know and presumably honor the sacrifice of GIs such as those depicted in the play.

Jumping off from Keats's "The Eve of St. Mark" and the idea that one day separated chaste lovers can communicate, Anderson creates what would later be called "magical realism" so that Quizz can speak to his mother and to Janet, asking their advice about whether to stay or leave the embattled island. This allows Anderson to provide a set of answers that captures the kinds of attitudes felt by Americans as they learned more about the war or experienced directly its armed conflicts. Quizz's mother speaks the understandable words of parents, for whom the safety of their young is uppermost, "Oh, my son, does it matter about giving up one place to the enemy? It won't matter as much as your lives. It's better to live. If you live now you can fight them again. And we'll see you. We'll see you here again" (89). When the play's magical realism enables Quizz to communicate with his Janet, he breaks into Andersonian verse, enunciating for the women in the audience the thoughts Anderson believes are in the hearts of America's best fighting men:

> Sweet, we had no home. No place and no time,
> and it seems to me I'm only a ghost forever
> if I should die and you've never been mine in the night,
> as if I'd never lived, and left no record—
> no son and no name—and another must take my love,
> my lost uncompleted love.
>
>   . . .
>
>   So if I die now
> I give you to another.

And his decision to remain on the island becomes an amalgam of honoring his country and honoring his loved ones:

It is something in myself I don't understand
that seems to require it of me. It seems to be
the best of me—the same inner self that turned
to love you and no one else, that says
give more than is asked of you, be such a man
as she you love could honor at a secret altar
knowing all you've thought and done. (90–92)

The stilted poetry is better expressed by another soldier, a descendant of Patrick Henry, who questions the sacrifice the men will make by remaining on the island but then concludes that he is like his ancestor "who preferred death rather than slavery. . . . And you know, I want to sink those God-damn Jap boats; I want to sink all of them" (98).

Exactly how Japan might enslave America is not articulated in any detail but left as a general threat. *The Eve of St. Mark* likewise never makes very specific for what principles and issues, other than some generalized sense of honor and love of country, the men are sacrificing themselves. "We're fighting for our lives and fighting to keep men free" is as close as the play seems to come to endowing World War II with a purpose. A disembodied radio voice broadcasting to the families at home tells them:

"Have you noticed that our soldiers almost never talk about the war, almost never discuss our reasons for fighting? I've noticed it. And have you wondered why? I think I know. This is the first war in history where there's no possible argument about who's right and who's wrong. We're fighting for our lives and fighting to keep men free. You can't argue about that. You don't need any oratory to convince people, nor songs to keep up their spirits in such a war. And so it's a war without oratory and without songs— because we know very well what we're doing." (107)

The lack of specific charges against the enemy here is significant, for it is indicative of many wartime plays to follow which pit the West against the Japanese. The cruelties enacted on European populations after German invasion provided American playwrights with material for demonizing the Third Reich. The hatred of the Japanese always seems rather more generalized and unfocused.

Two years after *The Eve of St. Mark*, with the war in full swing, Maxwell Anderson wrote a second war play, *Storm Operation*. This time he set his action across the Atlantic, with American troops invading North Africa and preparing themselves for combat against the Germans in the area around Maknassy, Tunisia. In the prologue to the play, Peter, the main character, picks up where the soldiers on the Philippine island in *The Eve of St. Mark* left off, but the level of patriotic rhetoric has been ratcheted up a notch:

I didn't want to be a soldier. Nobody did, only we knew the job had to
be done, and we had to do it. And the only way to fight a war is to make
the other fellow so Goddam sorry he picked on us that he'll never want
to do it again. And the only kind of soldier to be is the best there is.
That's why we went through all that infiltration hell. We've got to be so
good they'll never want to see us again. (7–8)[3]

The image is one of American soldiers putting the neighborhood bullies in their
place so that they will not attempt intimidation ever again. There is no sense
here that those bullies have an ideological agenda or that the Allies have a
counteragenda, other than making the bullies sorry they picked a fight. In short,
here and elsewhere in his play, Anderson's attention is on the hardships and
exploits of the Allied troops who are engaged in doing their arduous job, working to defeat the enemy. There is little articulation of the causes of that enmity.

What Anderson does articulate in *Storm Operation* is the growth of his characters under fire and some of the realities of interpersonal relationships among
military personnel during war. He gives his audience, as he does in *The Eve of
St. Mark,* the romantic heroism of soldiers laying down their lives for their
country's cause, but in *Storm Operation,* he gives them as well a rather more
down-to-earth insight into the modes of behavior and thinking that war engenders in those on active duty overseas. Of special interest is Anderson's rendering
of what World War II meant for the women who served alongside the men.
Although the codes of good taste and what was discussable onstage in the 1940s
prevent Anderson from going into detail, he nevertheless does not disguise the
fact that romantic and sexual affairs between enlisted women and men were
common, frequently transitory, and might well involve a man with a wife back
home.[4]

Storm Operation presents on the one hand a classic love triangle in which Sgt.
Peter Moldau, an American, and Capt. Sutton, a British (and married) officer,
compete for the affections of Lt. Thomasina "Tommy" Grey, an Australian army
nurse. On the other hand, it offers a frank insight into the limitations placed
on commitments during war and how, more importantly, these limitations re-
define the roles and positions of women. For women especially, the play makes
clear, the constraints of war paradoxically offer a new freedom and selfhood.
The precariousness of war, moreover, justifies *carpe diem* relationships for members of both sexes. Given the limited possibilities in 1944 for speaking openly
about sexual matters in the theatre, the dialogue between Peter and Tommy,
who have had a past affair at another location but did not consummate it with
a marriage, is remarkably straightforward:

PETER. I did love you. But if you're in a war you're married to the war.
You can't promise anything, not if you're honest. Because you never know
where you're going to be, or how long you'll be gone, or whether you'll
come back, and you haven't got a thing in the world except what's in your

pack and what you get at the end of the month. You don't belong to yourself and you don't know about tomorrow. That goes for men and for women too.

TOMMY. I know. There are a lot of girls who get to be—part of the army. A man dies—and they go with another. And then he's killed. And there's another. And pretty soon they don't expect anybody to come back and it doesn't matter so much who it is. (47)

Later, as Peter and Sutton quarrel over Tommy like dogs over a bone, Anderson scripts a stunningly feminist speech:

TOMMY. I believe I heard you say that Peter took your girl. . . . Well, he didn't. Nobody takes me from anybody. If I leave one man and take up with another, it's my own doing. I do as I please. That's one thing a girl gets out of this war. She's not property any more. She's a person in her own right—as good as a man—and as much her own as a man. You two quarrel over anything you like, but don't think for a minute you're quarreling over me. The only tag I wear is the dog-tag around my neck. (72–73)

These assertions are impressively ahead of their time.

To this feminist moment, however, Anderson implicitly contrasts the situation of a technical sergeant, Simeon, who has paid eight hundred francs to a local trader for a woman who will be his slave in all matters, including sexual. In this case, the woman is seen, through the double lenses of gynophobia and xenophobia, as no better than a stray animal. Simeon is reminded that in the past he has brought back to camp a lost baby camel and three baby chimpanzees, and "Now you pick up a dirty female Moslem wearing a yakmish and with no education which she can use standing up" (24). The native slave woman, Mabroukha, does prove to be a valuable Sacajawea for the soldiers as they deal with the local inhabitants and the unfamiliar North African terrain. Her inclusion in *Storm Operation* troubles in useful ways Tommy's bold feminism, for while Mabroukha registers the ambivalence about gender and race among both the troops and Anderson's audience, she also embodies precisely the gendered commodity Tommy so vehemently refuses to become.

Although *Storm Operation* is often flat-footedly preachy, it is Anderson's admirable if imperfect attempt to do two things at once: first, to render the feel and smells of battle and battlefront decisions to the civilian audience sitting in the comfort of New York's Belasco Theatre thousands of miles from the North African battle lines; and second, to remind that audience of what Anderson thinks the war is about. To write *Storm Operation* and get a firsthand feel of the war, Anderson flew to North Africa to spend time among the troops stationed at the front.[5] Anderson's characters assert that what happens in war cannot be described or conveyed. It can only be truly understood by those who have experienced it:

> Oh, hell, in this war anything can happen. And nearly everything does.
> When this war is over and we get home and they begin to ask us what
> was it like we're going to open our traps to say something and then we're
> going to realize nobody at home will ever know—and we can't tell 'em—
> and we're going to shut our traps and keep 'em shut. Because it's impos-
> sible. . . . No, this mucking war is out of this mucking world and out of
> range of the English language. I defy anybody to tell anybody what Africa
> is like. You can't even describe the stink of it, let alone how it feels to be
> here and what it does to you. (88)

Using the art of theatre, *Storm Operation* is an attempt to allow the audience
vicariously to experience the North African campaign in a way that narrative or
written record would be incapable of doing. And part of what the audience
experiences is that very poverty of language that prevents the soldiers from articulating their experiences and feelings in a limpid way to others and even to
themselves.

Storm Operation conveys, too, the ways in which combat creates a unique
environment with discrete ethics of its own. The play, for example, allows the
audience to witness the Americans in the desert trying to ambush German units.
When a soldier steps on a mine, he screams in pain and thereby gives away the
American position. The dialogue that follows is obviously meant to give the
audience vicarious, near "firsthand" experience of wartime's unique situational
ethics:

> PETER. He was all blown apart and screaming so loud you could hear him
> all up and down the valley. That's what brought the snipers down on us.
>
> SIMEON. I don't know what you could have done about that.
>
> PETER. I could have shot him and kept him quiet. That's what the Captain
> said I should have done. And he's right. . . .
>
> CHUCK. You just can't do things like that.
>
> PETER. In a war you do. You have to. It was one dying man's life against
> a dozen healthy men. That's the logic of war and that's one of the things
> we have to learn. (84–85)

"The logic of war" as it is conceived in *Storm Operation* is also made manifest
in the self-sacrifice of soldiers for their comrades, in the situational sexual mores,
and in the special relationship of those in command to those who must follow
them. The play's several situations, comic and serious, depict the camaraderie
and rivalry among the men, the relationships between the Americans and the

Arabs with whom they must deal, the dangers the men face as they square off against the Germans, and the travails of the wounded and dying. These all are meant to convey to an audience at home the ineffable feel and smell of the war being waged by their loved ones overseas. *Storm Operation* is moderately successful in that effort.

Anderson is rather less successful in educating his audience about the specific American goals of the war. The play's central character, 1st Sgt. Peter Moldau, tells his men, "But all I want really is for you and me and the rest of us to get together and kick the Germans out of there" (109). As Anderson's mouthpiece, he preaches:

> A lot of men die around you—and you don't think about it—you put it out of your mind and go ahead—just being a soldier—and then suddenly it all catches up with you. And you hate the war and all it does to you— and you know you have to go on with it, but you've got to know something's coming after it—you've got to know this isn't all there is . . . I'll go ahead and learn to be ruthless and learn to be hard, and learn to be a better soldier, but I can't do it unless there's something beyond, unless there's something to come back to. . . . But you aren't living. You're just taking orders and eating rations and killing—and you're nothing—nothing—unless you've got a line out to that blessed place back there where there are homes and children and peace. Or a line to the future—or a hope of somebody that loves you and doesn't let go. (111–112)

We are left with generalities. The meaning of the war seems reduced to a platitude about making the world a better place in general and making the future for Americans in particular brighter. In what specific ways the world can be a better place or human life improved is left unarticulated. The Germans need to be "kicked out of" wherever they are, but why that is important or what sort of life or government the Germans espouse is not told. Nor is there a sense of the territorial or philosophical issues at stake in World War II. It is not that Anderson did not know these things or that his thinking is shallow. Rather it seems that he wants his audience to feel almost viscerally that the sacrifices made by fighting men during World War II are not for discrete political issues but for a larger, inspired vision of a brighter future for Americans and for mankind.

The weakness of *Storm Operation* is that the action of the play does little to validate its noble spoken sentiments. A more impressive battlefront play, though not one that was successful on Broadway, is Allan R. Kenward's *Proof through the Night,* or (as it was later called) *Cry Havoc.* Opening on Christmas day, 1942, at the Morosco Theatre as *Proof through the Night,* Kenward's play closed a week later on 2 January 1943. Burns Mantle records that in Los Angeles it had a rather more successful run under the title *Cry Havoc,* and under that title was subsequently published and made into a successful Hollywood motion picture.[6]

Although short-lived onstage, *Cry Havoc*, with its all-female cast, is in various ways a revealing and sometimes extraordinary play. It is set in the shelter used by a group of gallant female nurses and hospital volunteers caring for the wounded and constantly under artillery fire during the devastating siege of the Bataan Peninsula early in 1942. As is typical of the military plays of the period, *Cry Havoc* brings to the stage women from various walks of life and various parts of the United States. There are also two volunteer sisters from England. Although WACs are present in *Storm Operation*, *Cry Havoc* is the single war front play to spotlight the heroism of women under fire. To be sure, the play's rather thin plot seems a mere excuse for Kenward to make theatre audiences aware of the heroism of the women who were serving and laying down their lives in the thick of battle alongside American GIs.

By focusing on the nurses and staff volunteers, *Cry Havoc* movingly and successfully renders onstage the terrible pressure of nursing the severely wounded while under fire from the ever-nearing Japanese. Yet *Cry Havoc* does this without ever showing the wounded to the audience, concentrating instead on its group of women at the point of physical and psychological breakdown. The tone of the play is set almost as soon as the curtain rises, when Doc, the head nurse, tells the new recruits—and by extension the audience—what will soon take place:

> More often than not, the work that you will be called upon to do is distasteful, and you might think it out of your province, but it must be done—the enemy will attempt to dislodge our position as soon as they can bring up their big guns. Anytime now a hell worse than you ever imagined will break loose. (13)[7]

And that hell does break loose as the play progresses.

The background sounds of armed conflict resound and intensify in the course of *Cry Havoc*. As they do, the women show the increasing signs of fatigue and frayed nerves after days of caring for the wounded. Such is war, the play asserts. And when one of the British sisters is missing and believed dead, Doc, the voice of wise experience, explains both what war is like and the importance of the female presence in wartime:

> I understand better than you'll ever know. I don't have to think back very far to remember seeing those same planes bombing a town in China. I was helpless to do a thing but watch that death pouring out of the sky. I found myself flat on the ground, pounding it with my fist and bawling like a baby—we can't help that, but we can rise above it. . . . There never has been anything pretty about war. . . . Men have always destroyed and women have always come along behind and tried to put back the pieces. (29–30)

In speeches like this and in its projection of the women who have made a sacrifice and will, before the play is over, heroically give up their lives to the Japanese, *Cry Havoc* attempts to use drama to bring home to American audiences the reality of the war in general and Bataan in particular, even as it tries to evoke the special role that women volunteers have made and continue to make as the war continues.

There are two plot lines in *Cry Havoc* that deserve attention. The first is that the women know that the Japanese are making increasingly accurate strikes at their base because there is an unknown traitor in their midst. As one reads through the American plays of the war years, that theme of a traitor in our midst recurs frequently. The idea of a fifth column at work in America and among American troops, subverting American liberties and seeking to deliver the country into the hands of the enemy, seems to reflect a national paranoia not unusual during war. One can understand, too, how that fear continued during the Cold War and how fascist fifth columnists were replaced during the subsequent Cold War by Reds, pinkos, and Fellow Travelers. Revealing, too, in *Cry Havoc* is that, although the play takes place in the Pacific, the traitor at work in the midst of the women is not a Japanese but a German operative. Here, as elsewhere, it seems that although the Japanese as a people are demonized, their motivations are not well enough understood to have them traduced onstage. Consequently, in the middle of the Pacific, it is the flaxen-haired Connie who proves to be not a Japanese but a German operative, trained, as she importantly reveals, in a German bund in America (98). And her scorn, which seems geographically out of place in Bataan, is the typical German "master race" scorn for Americans that surfaces in play after play:

> CONNIE. What an inferior bunch of cattle you really are with your moving picture idea of heroics and stiff upper lip—right now while your musical comedy army is being pushed around—while all of your little toys are being taken from you—you bask in the conceit that everything must have a happy ending—How?—Did you ever stop to think how?
>
> GRACE. What do you think's going on back in the States right now, dearie?
>
> CONNIE. [*Viciously*] Strikes—big shots keeping the tools of war from being made because of money or politics—Labor union racketeers kidding the dumb laborers that now is the time to get even with those big shots—and so, more strikes. An inferior race that needs the regimentation of the German master race, and hasn't long to wait. (102–103)

Kenward nicely has Connie not merely pluck the chords that will evoke American patriotic pride but put her finger as well on the worst American fears about the ways in which the legacy of the 1930s Depression era could undermine the 1940s American war effort. The reply given to Connie is a rousing endorsement of American ideals and a tribute to America's fighting women:

Funny thing about your kind—you've never really understood our kind—and there's not much to understand when you boil it down. Take what's left of us here—we're a pretty average bunch—we're not heroes—we're not even soldiers—we're just a bunch of scared girls who hate war and death almost as much as we hate what your superior race has to offer—"Superior race"—that's a beautiful way to describe a people who twist their men into cold machines and turn their women into breeding animals. . . . No—you keep your way, we'll take ours, but this time we'll make you understand us so completely that you'll never forget, because this time—we understand you. (103)

Clearly, Kenward is not retorting to Connie but attempting to use his play to educate his audience and focus them on what he sees as the main issues of the war.

Although *Cry Havoc* is significant for its portrayal of women at war, it is also a rather groundbreaking play in another respect. One of the women is Stephany Polden, always referred to as Steve. She has been a machine operator in a cannery in the Pacific Northwest and is, as the stage directions explain, "a large, raw-boned, muscular gal who carries herself like a man" (8). In the Broadway production, this role was played by, of all people, a twenty-one-year-old Carol Channing! Although the word *lesbian* is never used, *Cry Havoc* is ahead of its time in its sensitive portrayal of Steve, who does not at first recognize her own sexual orientation.[8] When Steve attempts to calm down Grace, one of the other women, an agitated Grace flings her away, exclaiming, "take your paws off me. Always wantin' to put your arms around people—callin' 'em 'Honey' and strokin' their hair—why don't you go out there and fight with the rest of the men—you—you Freak!" (55). With that, Steve's self-realization is born, and she asks Grace, "Do they really call me a—a—" (58). She then seeks guidance from Smitty, one of the older, seasoned nurses:

> STEVE. Is there anything wrong with me, Smitty? Am I different from them, Smitty? Tell me honest, Smitty, I gotta find out. I'm so confused.
>
> SMITTY. If there was anything wrong with you—anything to be ashamed of, you'd know it. You'd know it here, Steve—[*Touches her heart.*]—long before anybody else.
>
> STEVE. But I don't, Smitty. I've never even thought—
>
> SMITTY. [*Interrupting.*] And you mustn't. Right now you're confused—hurt—Cancers grow from that kind of hurt, Steve—It's a word that's hit you below the belt—shake it off while it's still a word, Steve, because accepting it makes it real and gives it a chance to grow. (64–65)

That is as far as Kenward takes the lesbianism question, for Steve is soon shot dead by Connie, the Nazi infiltrator. But even that far is very far for 1942. What

Kenward here daringly raises is the issue of same-sex attraction among women in the World War II armed forces, an issue that was largely closeted until recently.[9]

When *Cry Havoc* appeared as a film in 1943, it was made into a vehicle for Hollywood stars Margaret Sullavan, Joan Blondell, Ann Sothern, Fay Bainter, and Ella Raines. Not surprisingly, the lesbianism was completely excised from the filmscript. But Kenward's playscript, though not a stage success, deserves serious and close attention for its realistic portrayal of battle conditions on Bataan, its unique limelighting of women on the battlefront, and its daring presentation of lesbianism among the female troops.

Cry Havoc opened and closed on Broadway in a matter of days. A slightly more successful battlefront play appeared a month later, on 3 February. Janet and Philip Stevenson's *Counterattack* (based on a Russian play by Ilya Vershinin and Mikhail Ruderman) opened at the Windsor Theatre and ran for just over two months, closing on 17 April.[10] By all rights, *Counterattack* should have been a greater success, for several theatre talents were involved in the production. Staged by Margaret Webster, *Counterattack*'s cast included Morris Carnovsky, Sam Wanamaker, Richard Basehart, and Karl Malden. As with *Cry Havoc*, whose setting is limited to the nurses' quarters in Bataan, *Counterattack* adjusts its battlefront situation to the limitations of the stage by situating the play in a cellar on the Eastern Front in 1943. Two Russian soldiers (Carnovsky and Wanamaker) are put in charge of seven captured German soldiers and one German nurse. When the shelling above ground seals off the cellar, the play becomes a battle of wits for the two Russians to stay in control of the Germans.

Despite their "master race" boasts, the Germans prove mean-spirited, ultimately turning upon themselves in a high-pressure situation. When one of the Germans breaks down under pressure, he indicts the whole Nazi enterprise, exclaiming, "You don't know! You'll never know how foul it is. All of them—double-crossing everybody—even themselves—so nobody knows who's who or what's what. For ten years, life's been like that! A stinking sewer full of toads—spitting poison on each other! Shoot them all, Russian. They're not men any more. They're monsters!" (3–4). The power of the Russians, by contrast, lies in the loyalty they have to one another, a loyalty instilled through a society built on collectives. As was the case in *Cry Havoc*, the presentation of actual warfare seems too great an undertaking for the stage, and there are only the sounds of tanks and shells. Moreover, extolling the communist system and having a Russian soldier named for Karl Marx seems an anachronistic throwback to the leftist theatre of the previous decade and, despite the Russians having become Allies, somewhat out of place amid the American pro-democracy patriotic spirit that held sway during the war years.

Counterattack has little to say and surely had little appeal for an American audience, whose concerns about the war were likely focused on American troops and American problems. Nonetheless, it ran for eighty-five performances. It is worthwhile to see *Counterattack* in the context of another drama produced two months earlier that is also about the German attack on Russia, and also reminiscent of the 1930s agitprop style employed by Clifford Odets in *Waiting for Lefty*. Opening on 29 November 1942 at the New School for Social Research and produced by Erwin Piscator, Dan James's *Winter Soldiers* was awarded the Sidney Howard Memorial Award by the Playwrights Company. The play's huge cast prevented the Playwrights Company from producing it on Broadway. Instead they seem to have passed it into the hands of Piscator, the famous European émigré playwright-director. *Winter Soldiers* is not exactly a battlefront play, but one that focuses on the arrogance and shortsightedness of the German military leadership, which moves troops from as far away as Yugoslavia to the Russian front and to a position twenty miles outside Moscow in order to take the Russian capital. Juxtaposed to the arrogance and brutality of the German command is the courage and determination of the ordinary citizens, the little people of Yugoslavia, Czechoslovakia, Poland, and Russia. They thwart the intended progress of the troop trains from Yugoslavia by delaying and even blowing up some of the trains. As a result, the Russians have sufficient time to arm, successfully defend Moscow, and gain an underdog's victory over the Germans. The play consists of separate scenes of counter-Nazi courage and resistance in each Eastern European location along the way. Each group is projected as a brave and tiny David pitted against the German Goliath. That strength of the individual resisters which wins the day is the theme of *Winter Soldiers*. A Yugoslavian professor, broadcasting the message of resistance over the radio waves toward the beginning of the play, explains:

> This is Freedom Station—Yugoslavia—I am speaking now to you, my fellow countrymen of Austria.
>
> Tonight—as on so many other nights, the news is black.
>
> But days and nights have been black before. This monster Hitler's nothing new. We've known him by a hundred names: Persian King and Greek tyrant; Feudal Lord and Emperor of the French; Russian Czar and Oriental despot. They all made edicts: "It is forbidden." "Verboten." "Defendu." "History ends with me." And where are they now? Buried in the trash of history for all their swords and guns and lies.
>
> The Nazis tell us it is hopeless to resist. They tell you: "We have the railroads and the highways, the communication lines. We have the factories and the armies and the police. We have a state machine that will last forever. We're steel. You're human. You bleed and die. But we go on forever!"
>
> They lie! I tell you they lie! Machines rust and rot, but Man is indestructible! It is the people who go on—not the machines! (1.3.26–27)[11]

Rhetorically and dramatically powerful, *Winter Soldiers*, according to Burns Mantle, "caused more stir than had any other production in the history of that experimental theatre." Not surprisingly, Mantle selected it as one of the ten outstanding plays of the season, reproducing an abridged version of its text in his annual volume.[12] Probably its off-Broadway location and its large but unknown cast kept *Winter Soldiers* from being the hit it deserved to be. In this sense, it was not unique.

The war years did produce some plays that concern the role of soldiers abroad though not engaged in combat. The best of these is the dramatic version of John Hersey's best-selling novel *A Bell for Adano*, published in 1944. The stage version of *A Bell for Adano* was written by playwright and screenwriter Paul Osborn (*The Vinegar Tree, On Borrowed Time, Mornings at Seven, The Innocent Voyage, Point of No Return, The World of Suzie Wong*). Shortly after the publication of the novel, it was produced by Leland Hayward and presented at the Cort Theatre in New York on 6 December 1944. By that time, the war was winding down, and the play's New York audience was treated to a vision of future peacetime rebuilding in Europe and the re-establishment of prewar relationships with wartime foes, in this case the citizens of Italy.

Like Hersey's novel, Osborn's play centers on the figure of Major Victor Joppolo, played onstage by Fredric March. The aptly forenamed Victor Joppolo is put in charge of the de-Mussolinification of the small, conquered fishing town of Adano. The play not merely looks ahead to the task the U.S. knew it would have to undertake after the war but prepares the American audience for the importance of a postwar commitment in Europe. As Joppolo enters the posh Italian marble Adano city hall, only recently a fascist headquarters, he remarks, "Less than an hour ago, I landed here and walked through the streets to this building. I saw the filth of the town—the poverty in which these people have been living. I am told some have had no food for three days" (17).[13] Joppolo's mission is to restore the town to its pre-fascist equilibrium; the play's mission is to suggest that Americans not think of themselves as undilutedly virtuous Samaritans, capable of no indiscretions, as they rescue and re-educate an erstwhile enemy. That point is nicely made when Joppolo tells the Adano citizens, "I assure you that the Americans want to bring only good to this town. But, as in every nation, there are some bad men in America. It is possible that some Americans who come here will do bad things. If they do, I can tell you that most of the Americans will be just as ashamed of those things as you are annoyed by them" (18).

Hersey's novel is essentially a string of mostly comic and genial episodes. The same is true of Osborn's play. But underlying these episodes in the play is the strong message present in so many wartime American dramas: that the principles of democracy are the basis for the best kind of government, that they are just and worth fighting for. Joppolo's Italian villagers, as well as the theatre audience, are shown the difference between dictatorship and democracy, between a government ruled by corrupt officials versus one based on the equality of free men. And for their part, Osborn's American theatre audience is also reminded of the reason American involvement in World War II is so important. This is captured in one of Joppolo's several speeches to the people of Adano whom he has selected to help him get the town back on its feet:

> Something has just occurred that makes me feel that you do not all understand exactly what we are trying to do here. It's important that we understand each other. This has to do with what we think—how we feel. Adano has been a Fascist town, but as I told you when we appointed you to your positions it is no longer being run that way. It is now being run as a Democracy. I am afraid some of you are forgetting that or perhaps you do not know exactly what a democracy is. I will tell you. [*He starts to tell them, leaning forward, but finds it difficult.*] One of the main things about a Democracy is that the men of the Government are no longer the masters of the people. They are the servants of the people, elected by the people, paid by the people with their taxes. Therefore, you are now the servants of the people of Adano. I too am their servant. When I go to buy bread, I'll take my place at the end of the line and wait my turn. Now, if I find any of you are not willing to act in this way, I shall remove you from office. Just remember that you are now the servants—not the rulers—of the people of Adano. (29)

The overwhelming sense not merely in this speech but in the play as a whole is that Allied victory is imminent and that the task ahead is not the defeat of Mussolini and Hitler but the replacement of Fascism with American-style democracy.

The play preaches as well the importance of Americans' not being rude conquerors and vandals but models of civility. When an intoxicated group of American soldiers takes over an Italian house and destroys the precious antiques during their drunken spree, Joppolo reprimands them in severest terms, but he goes on to create the play's message of what American behavior should be during the inevitable postwar rebuilding process:

> We got a tough job ahead of us. . . . In our Army we've got damn near every race in Europe:—no other country in the world has so many men who speak the language of the countries we've got to invade, whose parents have come from there. And that's our chance, because until there's something stable in Europe, our armies will have to stay here. . . . And just as good as we can make things over here, that's just how good they'll be at home. What you guys do today may have a whole lot to do with what your kids, and their kids, will be doing for years to come. For God's sake, let's grab this chance to bring some sort of sense and decency and hope into the world again. It all depends just how good we can be. (95)

The image here is a curiously double one. More war and further invasion still lie ahead. At the same time, there is a clear recognition that once the war has been won by the Allies there will be, for both a ravaged Europe and the United States, a difficult period during which international friendships, as well as the destroyed towns and cities of Europe, will have to be caringly rebuilt. *A Bell for Adano* is a play about soldiers, and it is the American soldiers who are winning the war in the present and who are meant to win the peace in the future. But it is even more than that. No one has spoken more warmly and eloquently of this play than John Mason Brown, who wrote:

> To most men national governments are faraway forces, as abstract and distant in small communities as local governments are real and near. . . . This is where Joppolo comes into the picture, and where the abstraction known as "government" ceases even now to exist. . . . In a village such as Adano and by the very nature of his task, Joppolo is bound to be more than an American. Whether he knows it or likes it, he is America. He is "Little America" incarnate, which is one way of saying he is really the big and abiding America. (284)[14]

In terms of shaping American attitudes toward the soon-to-be-defeated enemy, *A Bell for Adano* is, both as novel and as play, a work of landmark significance.

A month after *A Bell for Adano* opened, it was followed by John Patrick's heartwarming, sentimental, and enormously successful *The Hasty Heart*, which opened at the Hudson Theatre on 3 January 1945 and ran for 207 performances. Here again, the cast is one of soldiers, but this time the focus is on those recuperating in a military hospital "somewhere to the rear of the Assam-Burma front" (3).[15] Although *The Hasty Heart* is only superficially about the war and more largely a sentimental story about the humanizing of a dour, reclusive, and socially offensive Scot, the play, in ways rather different from *A Bell for Adano*, does look ahead to the postwar future. The men in the hospital recover not merely from their war wounds but from the hardness and selfishness the war has instilled. In a sense, Patrick's play seems meant to nurse its American audience back to a gentle and kindly prewar sensibility.

II

As Robert Sherwood had so masterfully done in *Abe Lincoln in Illinois*, two wartime playwrights produced enormously successful historical plays, in which the issues of World War II are projected through a prior and analogous time in American history. Sidney Kingsley's *The Patriots*, which won the 1942–43 Drama Critics' Circle Award, was presented by the Playwrights Company and opened at the National Theatre in New York on 29 January 1943. Florence Ryerson and Colin Clements's *Harriet* opened in New York at Henry Miller's Theatre on 3 March 1943. Both are historical dramas that, despite their respective American federal period and Civil War settings, are thoroughly about World War II. Both plays once again sound the notes of the dominant leitmotif running through the drama of wartime America: the belief in the superiority of American democracy and its values, and the importance of defending the rights granted by the Constitution against the tyrants who would replace a democratic government by and for the people with a fascist dictatorship.

The version of *The Patriots* published in the 1995 collection of Sidney Kingsley's *Five Prizewinning Plays* edited by Nena Couch contains an illuminating preface by Kingsley that does not appear in the original 1943 edition of the play.[16] In that preface (with no date given but written in later years) Kingsley lucidly spells out the connection between his play, set in the period following the American revolution, and the events of World War II:

> If there was a play that was written out of the questions raised by the fearful epoch of World War II through which we were passing, it was *The Patriots*. Hitler was rising, threatening the concept of democracy and so, on the other hand was Stalin. There were some who felt that the coming struggle for world domination was between fascism and communism, and democracy was pushed aside as a vital world force. . . . I set out to write a play about democracy. I intended it to be a contemporary play; but in the searching for first principles, I found that a study of the American Revolution provided me with a more specific answer to the questions raised by the terror that was in the air. (169)

The Patriots centers on the figure of Thomas Jefferson and more particularly on his fight for a democratic form of government in opposition to the monarchist views of Alexander Hamilton. The prologue to the play, depicting a Jefferson returning to the United States after years of service in France, not only sets the stage for the events to follow but, as Jefferson daydreams about his role in the Continental Congress drafting the Declaration of Independence, Jefferson's words are obviously as much about the motivations for America's entry into World War II as they are about the sentiments that led to the War of Independence:

> There is not a man in the whole empire who wished conciliation more than I. But, by the God that made me, I would have sooner ceased to exist than yield my freedom. And in this, I know I speak for America. I am sorry to find a bloody campaign is decided on. But, since it is forced on us, we must drub the enemy and drub him soundly. We must teach the sceptered tyrant we are not brutes to kiss the hand that scourges us. But this is not enough. We are now deciding everlastingly our future and the future of our innocent posterity. . . . Now is the time to buttress the liberty we're fighting for. . . . *Now*, while men are bleeding and dying. (182–183; 15)

It is hardly surprising to learn that *The Patriots* was written while Kingsley was serving in the armed forces.[17]

While ostensibly dramatizing the fight for American democracy's survival in the last decades of the eighteenth century, *The Patriots* is simultaneously a powerful reflection of the country's 1940s wartime determination. And Kingsley's play works in both directions. That is, its depiction of the Jeffersonian struggle to place the country on a firm democratic foundation is enhanced and made meaningful by the World War II fascist threat to what, a century and half later, the U.S. had come to cherish as its democratic way of life. At the same time, however, *The Patriots* rededicates its 1943 audiences to the Allied cause by reminding them of the Jeffersonian principles which, Kingsley suggests, forged the working and successful political philosophy that has served as the guiding spirit of this country.[18] Nor is the audience reminded only of Jefferson but of Tom Paine, when in 1943 the actor portraying Washington laments to Jefferson about the situation in 1793. Washington's comments are, furthermore, blatantly laced with a pejorative reminder of Neville Chamberlain's famous 1938 declaration about achieving "peace in our time":

> Peace in our life? . . . Paine wrote it. Was it in *The Crisis*? "These are the times that try men's souls. The summer soldier and the sunshine patriot will, in this crisis shrink . . ." . . . I read Paine's essay. You know, it lent me new strength. I had it read to my men through trumpets. Nailed it on trees for them to read. It helped them. Gave them sore-needed courage. Do you remember the passage on the Tory innkeeper who was opposed to the war because—[*He finds the phrase he's been searching for*]—that's it— "He wanted peace in his lifetime"? And Paine looked down at the innkeeper's children crawling on the floor and thought, "Were this Tory a man, he would say: If there must be conflict with tyranny, let it come in my time. Let there be peace and freedom in my children's time." (222; 133)

Kingsley here uses *The Patriots* to renew the power of Paine's message. And he does so in the minds of his wartime audience at the National Theatre and at every theatre where *The Patriots* would subsequently be performed. In Jefferson's ringing words to Alexander Hamilton that message is unmistakable: "Our people who fought the revolution from a pure love of liberty, who made every sacrifice, and met every danger, did not expend their blood and substance to change this master for that. *His voice grows strong.* But to take their freedom in their own hands, so that never again would the corrupt will of one man oppress them. You'll not make these people hold their breath at the caprice, or submit to the rods and hatchet, of a dictator" (236; 176). One can well imagine a 1943 audience bursting into spontaneous applause at the conclusion of this speech.

Another very popular and significant play, nowadays curiously overlooked by both theatre historians and those concerned with women playwrights, provided American women a role model and reference point. In the middle of the war (March 1943) Florence Ryerson's play *Harriet*, written with the assistance of her husband, Colin Clements, opened in New York. Dedicated to Eleanor Roosevelt and directed by Elia Kazan, *Harriet* was a dramatic vehicle and something of a costume piece for America's leading lady of the theatre, Helen Hayes. The play presents the travails and literary success of Harriet Beecher Stowe and of her famous novel *Uncle Tom's Cabin* during the Civil War period.

Robert Sherwood had already drawn the analogy between the American Civil War and World War II in his 1938 stage success *Abe Lincoln in Illinois*. Whereas Sherwood suggested the need for male commitment to American ideals, Florence Ryerson effectively renews those ideals for women living through a period of violence and warfare. At one point and in ways similar to Kingsley's evocation of Paine's words in *The Patriots*, Ryerson in *Harriet* has Harriet Beecher Stowe read lines from *Uncle Tom's Cabin* lines that inspired Americans in the nineteenth century and are meant by the playwright to do so again in the new wartime context of 1943:

> "Their night was now far spent, and the morning star of Liberty rose fair before them. Liberty!—electric word! What is it? Is there anything more in it than a name,—a rhetorical flourish? Why, men and women of America, does your heart's blood thrill at that word, for which your fathers bled, and your braver mothers were willing that their noblest and best should die?" (193)[19]

Soon after these lines, Stowe's oldest son, who has joined the Union army, lies in an army hospital seriously, perhaps fatally, ill. At a time when no one foresaw the war's end, Helen Hayes as Harriet sounded words meant to give voice and comfort to American women whose sons were likewise lying near death in military hospitals, "I speak as though there is no sorrow like my sorrow, yet I know that this heartbreak is everywhere. There is scarcely a house in the land without its dead" (196).

Ryerson's Harriet justifies the meaning of the war and its carnage when her daughter, Georgie, whose fiancé has gone off to war, echoes what were surely the sentiments of many women in 1943 as she exclaims toward the conclusion of the play, "Why should we care if some men, somewhere, want to keep slaves? What difference can it make to us? I say, let them keep their slaves so long as it ends this ghastly war. Let them do what they like, and give us a chance for happiness!" (205). But Florence Ryerson addresses these questions by concluding *Harriet* with an enormous salvo of uplifting patriotic commitment. Harriet Beecher Stowe returns from meeting President Lincoln, and we know immediately that her words are not about Lincoln and the Civil War but about Roosevelt and World War II:

> One hour with our President has lifted my spirits and endowed me with new strength. He made me see that this war, which seems so final to us now, is but one small pattern in a vast tapestry of struggle. Since the dawn

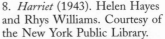

8. *Harriet* (1943). Helen Hayes and Rhys Williams. Courtesy of the New York Public Library.

of history there have always been tyrants, great and small, who seized upon and enslaved their fellow men. But, equally always, there have been noble souls who bravely and gladly gave up their lives for the eternal right of man to liberty. The hope of today lies in this: That we, as a people, are no longer willing to accept these tyrants, and the world they make, without question. We are learning that a world which holds happiness for some but misery for others cannot endure. (211)

The curtain comes down on the play with a resonant offstage voice singing the words of "The Battle Hymn of the Republic." Ryerson's message is directed to all Americans in her wartime audience, but especially to the female members of that audience.

Not surprisingly, *Harriet* enjoyed a measure of Broadway success and ran for 114 performances. Even after the war it continued to be staged, often in schools (including my own high school), well into the late 1950s, for Ryerson provided just the perfect mixture of dramatized historical biography and the sort of uplifting patriotic message that an audience needed and wanted to hear during the worst year of the war.

The Patriots and *Harriet* employ specific historical moments from the American past to illuminate the contemporary war issues. In Thornton Wilder's *The Skin of Our Teeth*, history is seen in another light, as the playwright ambitiously and often brilliantly uses the entire sweep of human history to place World War

II into a larger context. In many ways, *The Skin of Our Teeth* iterates the theme of human endurance that colored Wilder's prewar *Our Town*. Although Wilder began writing *The Skin of Our Teeth* before Pearl Harbor, he did not complete it until a few weeks after that memorable day.[20] After its pre-Broadway opening at the Schubert Theatre in New Haven (15 October 1942), *The Skin of Our Teeth* made its New York premiere at the Plymouth Theatre on 18 November 1942. The playwright was absent at the opening because he was by then actively involved in the war and stationed overseas as an army intelligence officer. Fifteen years later, in the preface to *Three Plays*, he wrote, "[*The Skin of Our Teeth*] was written on the eve of our entrance into the war and under strong emotion and I think it mostly comes alive under conditions of crisis."[21] It is important, consequently, to consider *The Skin of Our Teeth* not merely (as it is usually seen) as a play about man's ability to retrieve his situation from destruction at the last moment and to begin again, but also as a consideration of the nature of mankind written within the context of the world's most wide-scale, international, and savage war to date, a war in which the playwright himself was actively engaged.

When *Our Town* ran on Broadway, it had been frequently compared with Kaufman and Hart's *The American Way*, which opened eleven months later and which also centered on a typical American family in small-town America. The Kaufman and Hart play had starred Fredric March and his wife, Florence Eldridge. Now, three years later, this onstage and offstage duo, who had made their mark in *The American Way*, were engaged to play the lead characters, Mr. and Mrs. Antrobus, in *The Skin of Our Teeth*, the new play by the author of *Our Town*. Like *The American Way*, *The Skin of Our Teeth* is about the classic American family well known to theatre and radio audiences. But like *Our Town*, it is also about the family of man and the human situation from the beginning of time to the present. Although it can be seen as an extension of the ideas explored in *Our Town*, *The Skin of Our Teeth*, with its pairing of March and Eldridge, also brought to Wilder's new play reminiscences of *The American Way* and of that play's upbeat portrait of American values in the face of rising fascism. When Jed Harris, who had directed *Our Town*, turned down the chance to direct *The Skin of Our Teeth*, Wilder had the good fortune to secure the services of a then young actor-director, Elia Kazan, who was recommended by Wilder's disciple Robert Ardrey and whose sole prior Broadway directing credits were Ardrey's *Casey Jones* (1938) and *Thunder Rock* (1939). Kazan's acting apprenticeship with the politically committed Group Theatre and his experience directing the fanciful *Thunder Rock* (produced by the Group Theatre) may have been the fortuitous combination that unwittingly gave him the appropriate qualifications for directing *The Skin of Our Teeth*.[22]

Starting with Adam and Eve, the repeated survival of mankind by the skin of its teeth is Wilder's large theme, and in the play's successive three acts the Antrobus family, who live in Excelsior, New Jersey, survive first the great ice age glacier, then a version of the biblical deluge, and finally a war of great scope and devastation. At the close of each of the first two acts, the end of the world is imminent, but the beginning of each subsequent act gives proof that the dread event did not take place. In the first act, Wilder nicely uses the fact that, historically, the great glacier did actually stop just shy of New Jersey. Likewise and analogously, in the world as it is represented onstage, the scenery is continually collapsing or disappearing, and the actors miss their lines or become ill. Yet the play itself manages by the skin of its teeth just barely to proceed from act to act, from its beginning to its non-conclusion, as the audience is sent home but told, "This is where you came in. We have to go on for ages and ages yet. You go home. The end of the play isn't written yet" (142).[23] In its way, *The Skin of Our Teeth* is a forerunner of Samuel Beckett's *Waiting for Godot*, in which characters also complain that they do not wish to go on, but do. And like Beckett's drama or Vladimir's song about the dog who came into the kitchen and stole a crust of bread, *The Skin of Our Teeth* perpetually keeps ending and starting over again.

Importantly, in the third act of *The Skin of Our Teeth*, the play's pattern changes: the end of the world is not about to happen but, rather, has just been averted. Calamity is not imminent but has just passed. As in *Our Town*, the miracle of life is that it continues on. Sabina, the Antrobus's maid (famously acted by Tallulah Bankhead), exclaims to the audience, "The whole world's at sixes and sevens, and why the house hasn't fallen down about our ears long ago is a miracle to me"; she follows this by unwittingly quoting from The Book of Common Prayer, "In the midst of life we are in the midst of death, a truer word was never said" (4). For a country embroiled in the global turmoil of World War II, the whole world was indeed at sixes and sevens. Wilder's flying scenery may well have been inspired by the antics of Ole Olsen and Chic Johnson's 1938 slapstick musical comedy *Hellzapoppin'*, which was still running in 1942. But surely in 1942, the collapsing walls and scenery would also bring to mind for those attending a performance of *The Skin of Our Teeth* the destroyed buildings and scenery of wartime Europe, captured so vividly in movie house newsreels and newspaper photographs.[24]

Likewise, refugees fleeing the glacier appear at the Antrobus house. In 1942, the very word *refugees* was highly charged, with hordes of refugees fleeing the Holocaust arriving on American shores. Among the refugees seeking shelter in Excelsior, New Jersey, are Homer, who recites in Greek the opening lines of *The Iliad*, Moses, who recites in Hebrew the opening lines of Genesis (40–41), and a physician. And Miss Somerset, the character who plays the role of the actress playing the role of Sabina, breaks through the fictions of the play and turns to the audience, saying, "Oh I see what this part of the play means now! This means refugees. Oh, I don't like it. I don't like it" (34). Mr. and Mrs. Antrobus react to the immigrants respectively with 1940s American attitudes of welcome and xenophobia:

MRS. ANTROBUS. George, these tramps say that you asked them to come to the house. What does this mean?

ANTROBUS. Just . . . uh . . . These are a few friends, Maggie, I met on the road. But nice, real useful people . . .

MRS. ANTROBUS. Now, don't ask them in!
    George Antrobus, not another soul comes in here over my dead body.

ANTROBUS. Maggie, there's a doctor there. Never hurts to have a good doctor in the house. (36)

Here as elsewhere in *The Skin of Our Teeth*, Wilder brings the entire history of the world into an engaging discourse with the history of World War II to date and with wartime America in 1942.

In act 3 of *The Skin of Our Teeth*, Wilder pointedly cites the eternal source of evil in the world, the evil that Americans were fighting in World War II, and locates it in the character of Henry, the Antrobus son who, we are told early in the play, was once called Cain. Portrayed in the original production by Montgomery Clift, Henry is Wilder's representation of envy, racial prejudice, and greed: the elements eternally present in every human and the source of mankind's ills. As Sabina aptly says, "I don't know how to say it, but the enemy is *Henry;* Henry *is* the enemy. Everybody knows that" (119).

In act 1, Henry is first identified with the envious Cain and the murder of Abel. In act 2, as the embodiment of white racism, Henry, with no cause other than the pleasure of offering violence and with slingshot poised for release, menaces a Negro chair-pusher on Atlantic City's boardwalk (67). In act 3, Henry's seething discontent, arising from a sense of oppression and envy, is figured as a version of the disruptive fascist malady Americans were seeking to extirpate by entering into a war against Hitler, Mussolini, and Hirohito.

Talking in his sleep, Henry sounds like Hitler talking to the Germans about the Jews, "Fellows . . . what have they done for us? . . . Blocked our way at every step. Kept everything in their own hands. And you've stood it. When are you going to wake up" (126). And Henry, as Wilder explains in the stage directions, "*is played, not as a misunderstood or misguided young man, but as a representation of strong unreconciled evil*" (127). As father and son square off, their speeches resonate with the ideological oppositions that set Allies against Axis, even as Wilder looks ahead to a peacetime when the victors will attempt to reconcile with Nazis and fascists, bringing them back into the fold of humanity:

ANTROBUS. You're the last person I wanted to see. . . . I wish I were back at war still, because it's easier to fight you than to live with you. War's a pleasure—do you hear me?—War's a pleasure compared to what faces us now: trying to build up a peacetime with you in the middle of it.

HENRY. I'm not going to be a part of any peacetime of yours. . . .

ANTROBUS. Henry, let's try again.

HENRY. Try what? Living *here?*—Speaking polite downtown to all the old men like you? Standing like a sheep at the street corner until the red light turns green? Being a good boy and a good sheep, like all the stinking ideas you get out of your books? Oh no, I'll make a world, and I'll show you.

ANTROBUS. How can you make a world for people to live in, unless you've first put order in yourself? Mark my words: I shall continue fighting you until my last breath as long as you mix up your idea of liberty with your idea of hogging everything for yourself. (128–129)

Greed, anti-intellectualism, jealousy, and Oedipal anger are the dominant elements in the venomous brew of evil that seems to course through Henry's veins. By extension, those same elements seem, in 1942, to characterize the forces against which the Allies were fighting.

Wilder's audiences, seeing *The Skin of Our Teeth* while World War II was at its height and two and a half years before it was to be over, were given, in the third act, a foretaste of the peacetime that was to come in 1945 as Sabina opens the act, shouting, "Mrs. Antrobus! Gladys! Where are you? The war's over. The war's over! You can come out. The peace treaty's been signed!" (104). As *Our Town* had assured an audience prior to American entry into World War II that individual lives are lost in war but that life continues and wars fade into history, *The Skin of Our Teeth* assures an American audience, now actively embroiled in the war, that mankind will endure and survive this war, even as it has every other war and every other cataclysm.

By envisioning the peacetime beyond current events, Wilder's play asserts itself as a comedy in the way Shakespeare's *The Winter's Tale* and *The Tempest* are comedies, projecting the world as it can be after tragedy. Mr. Antrobus reveals to his wife and to Wilder's audience, "But during the war,—in the middle of all that blood and dirt and hot and cold—every day and night, I'd have moments, Maggie, when I *saw* the things that we could do when it was over. When you're at war you think about a better life; when you're at peace you think about a more comfortable one. . . . All I ask is the chance to build new worlds and God has always given us that. . . . Maggie, you and I will remember in peacetime all the resolves that were so clear to us in the days of war" (135, 140). Thus well before World War II has ended, Wilder writes *The Skin of Our Teeth* to prophesy that the forces of good will prevail and that a brave new postwar world should be informed by lessons learned during war and tragedy. At the same time, Wilder makes clear that the forces of ill will and evil, the Henrys and the Calibans, never die and are with us, creating havoc from generation to generation.

III

In their individual ways, Kingsley, Ryerson, and Wilder provided the kinds of messages the American wartime audience needed and wanted to hear. Such a

9. *Sons & Soldiers* (1943). (Left to right) Leonard Sues, Karl Malden, Gregory Peck, Geraldine Fitzgerald. Courtesy of the New York Public Library. Used by permission.

time is the wrong moment for indictment of a country, its leaders, and its past decisions. Yet this is what Irwin Shaw and Lillian Hellman imprudently did in writing their respective plays, *Sons and Solders,* which opened at the Morosco Theatre on 4 May 1943, and *The Searching Wind,* which opened nearly a year later at the Fulton Theatre on 12 April 1944. Once again, as he had in *The Gentle People,* Irwin Shaw shows in *Sons and Soldiers* his change of attitude from the strongly pacifist position he propounded in his 1936 masterpiece *Bury the Dead. Sons and Soldiers* brings together several theatre talents. It was the last play to be directed by Max Reinhardt before his death, and it gave a young, handsome, and then unknown actor, Gregory Peck, a leading role that would catapult him to Hollywood stardom. Supporting Peck were Geraldine Fitzgerald, Stella Adler, and Karl Malden (who had previously been cast as the policeman in Shaw's *The Gentle People*). *Sons and Soldiers* closed after only twenty-two performances, and both Malden and Shaw's biographer, Michael Shnayerson, place the blame for the play's failure on the overbearing sets designed by Norman Bel Geddes.[25]

Far more than excessive set design causes the weakness of Shaw's drama. It stems as well from the playwriting itself. The play begins in 1915, when Rebecca Tadlock (Geraldine Fitzgerald) is told that her life is in peril if she gives birth and that she should have an abortion. *Sons and Soldiers* then flashes forward as Rebecca contemplates the life- and career-to-be of Andrew (Gregory Peck), the son she is carrying. For most of its three acts, the play has little clear focus except to depict Andrew as an unfocused, discontented, and rather feckless young man, overprotected by his mother. His father recedes into the background, his brother Ernest dies fighting the fascists in Spain, and on the day before Pearl Harbor Andrew prepares to go off to war, but not before finally marrying the neighborhood girl who has pursued him since childhood. The climactic speech comes toward the conclusion of the play, but it is a speech poorly prepared for by preceding action and is given by Andrew's father, who suddenly emerges from the shadowy periphery of the drama to indict himself and, by extension, the United States for sitting idly by during the years between the wars and allowing the world to get out of hand:

> I was born the same day as Adolf Hitler. He could do something to *kill* my sons. I should've been doing something to *save* them. I'm guilty, guilty. I'm ashamed to stand in the same room with you, you ought to slam the door on me. . . . I'm an old man and one son's dead and another's going to war, and all I did was pay rent and taxes. . . . The war was being fought for twenty-five years. And I didn't know it. . . . I waited for my sons to grow up and fight in it for me. I should've been out screaming on street corners. I should've grabbed people by their lapels in trains, in libraries and restaurants and yelled at them. . . . "Love, understand, put down your guns, forget your profits, remember God. . . ." I should have walked on foot through Germany and France and England and Russia. I should've preached on the dusty roads and used a rifle when necessary. I stayed in this one town and paid the grocer. Versailles, Warsaw, Ethiopia. Manchuria. Madrid, Munich. . . . Battlefields, battlefields, and I thought there was one war and it was over. I'm guilty, I'm guilty, slam the door on me. . . . (148–149)[26]

This somewhat inchoate recrimination returns the play to 1915 and Rebecca's decision to give birth to her sons regardless of the dangers to her health and of what she has envisioned about the future of her children. Perhaps even more than Shaw's weak plot, his sour picture of the American head-in-the-sand attitude during the years between the wars was doubtless one a wartime audience did not wish to see.

Lillian Hellman's *The Searching Wind* as a drama is a far more finely crafted and incisive play than Shaw's *Sons and Soldiers,* but for understandable reasons it is also Hellman's least acclaimed, least appreciated work. Whereas *Sons and Soldiers* flashes forward from 1915 to 1941, *The Searching Wind* is set in the wartime present, and its scenes move back and forth between the present of spring 1944 and the past years of 1922, 1923, and 1938. Hellman creates a triangular love relationship among American diplomat Alexander Hazen, his wife, Emily (portrayed by Cornelia Otis Skinner), and his sometime lover Cassie Bowman. Ordinarily this would be the stuff of a 1930s Broadway success by Somerset Maugham, Sidney Howard, or S. N. Behrman. But Hellman con-

10. *The Searching Wind* (1944). (Left to right) Dudley Digges, Mercedes Gilbert, Montgomery Clift, Cornelia Otis Skinner. Courtesy of the New York Public Library.

sciously takes the well-made and well-worn Broadway paradigm of a man caught between two attractive women and plays it off against a backdrop of critical wartime world events, so that the love affairs become trivialized and blameworthy in the context of Mussolini's entry into Rome and the growing menace of Nazism. The urbane repartee of the main characters sounds effete, self-indulgent, and culpable when it is juxtaposed to the speech of a Nazi official who triumphantly explains Hitler's insistence on annexing the Sudetenland and the probable future aggression of Germany toward Russia.

The indictment of an older generation who did next to nothing to stem fascism but indulged themselves instead in their own marital and extramarital affairs is passionately made by the Hazens' son, Sam, played by Montgomery Clift, who has served in the army, been wounded, and is about to suffer the amputation of his leg because of the war that his self-absorbed, weak-willed, feckless parents essentially allowed to happen. While Sam and his battalion are in the trenches of Italy among dying American soldiers, one of Sam's buddies hands him a society pages clipping reporting the Hazens' attendance at a social occasion with several international luminaries. He sardonically comments, "Glad to be sitting in mud here, Sam, if it helps to make a carefree world for your folks." Sam then learns that the people at the party his parents have attended are decadent Europeans ready to do business with the Nazis and sell out their countrymen. His friend warns, "Sam, . . . if you come from that you better get away from it fast, because they helped to get us where we are" (95).[27] Filled with disgust at his parents' behavior, Sam accuses them, "I am ashamed of both of you, and that's the truth. I don't want to be ashamed that way again" (96). His anger is Hellman's anger at her country and at the U.S.'s failure to take a stand at a time when the thrust of fascism could still have been stemmed or quelled. Though Hellman's point may be well taken, at the height of a hard-fought war she could hardly hope to win applause for a work that is so sharply accusatory, that blames her country for letting the war come about.

Recriminations for the U.S.'s failure or reluctance to enter the war abounded in plays mounted during the years immediately prior to Pearl Harbor. As the cases of *The Searching Wind* and *Sons and Soldiers* sharply demonstrate, criticism acceptable before war seems unacceptable during the years of active military engagement. Quite the contrary is the case for another theme—traitors in our midst—that begins in the years before the war but is intensified during the war. Nationally, outside the theatre, President Roosevelt begins in 1938 and 1939 to step up the FBI investigation of fascists, communists, and subversives. In the theatre, Nazi and fascist operatives in the United States had already made their unwholesome appearance, particularly in Elmer Rice's *Flight to the West*, Lillian Hellman's *Watch on the Rhine*, Clare Boothe's *Margin for Error*, and Philip Barry's *Liberty Jones*. Once America declared war, enemy activity on the American home front becomes a frequent feature of government-sponsored plays and is the central issue in an important wartime drama, James Gow and Arnaud d'Usseau's *Tomorrow the World*.

Even before *Tomorrow the World*, the transition from prewar to wartime concern about enemy operatives is registered in a minor play, *Letters to Lucerne*, written jointly by Austrian-born Fritz Rotter and American-born Allen Vincent. *Letters to Lucerne* was written before Pearl Harbor but opened at the Cort Theatre two weeks afterward (23 December 1941), ran for only twenty-one performances, yet was nonetheless featured in the *Best Plays of 1941–42* Burns Mantle volume.[28] It is set at an international girls school in Lucerne and begins on 31 August 1939, a day before the German invasion of Poland, and concludes several days thereafter. During that critical time, the girls, who are American, British, French, German, and Polish nationals but are at school in neutral Switzerland, begin to take sides and mirror the attitudes of their respective countries.

Of particular interest in *Letters to Lucerne* is the way Erna, the once-beloved German student at the school, is immediately seen by her classmates and erstwhile friends as a traitor in their midst. They believe their assumptions are rendered credible when they open Erna's letter from home, read of her mother's esteem for Germany, and learn that Erna's brother, Hans, in love with Olga, their Polish classmate, has been killed during the bombing of Warsaw and been awarded the Nazi Iron Cross for his heroism during the invasion. Using the metaphor of an American-run girls school in Switzerland, the authors of *Letters to Lucerne* attempt to capture in miniature the way in which the invasion of Poland infects a once-neutral world and a once-neutral America with the belief that every person of German origin is a subversive working for the enemy. Set at the moment that touches off World War II and produced at the moment two years later when America declares war, *Letters to Lucerne* warns against such snap judgments. The high point of the play comes when it is learned in a second letter smuggled to Lucerne that the prior patriotic letter from Erna's parents was written to foil the Nazi censors and that Hans purposely crashed his plane to avoid bombing Olga's city and "because it was the only thing he could do—the only way he could protest and deny the terror that has swept over our country" (104).[29] At this early moment in the war for the U.S., the American audience is encouraged to assume the best about people and to refrain from the racial profiling of Germans. As the war intensifies, however, and as American paranoia about enemy operatives increases, the attitudes toward Germans and German Americans harden, as they do in *Tomorrow the World*.

James Gow and Arnaud d'Usseau's *Tomorrow the World* is a remarkable dramatic artifact, one that nicely registers a range of American issues and anxieties at the height of the war. It premiered in New York at the Ethel Barrymore Theatre on 14 April 1943, featured Ralph Bellamy and Shirley Booth in leading roles, and ran for a record five hundred performances. As John Anderson wrote in his opening night review of the play, "It is more than an engrossing play; it is a plain warning, forceful, dramatic and challenging."[30] The title of the play of course refers to Hitler's 1932 assertion, "Today Germany, tomorrow the world," and its simple plot concerns the rescue from Germany and arrival in a Midwestern university town of twelve-year-old German boy, Emil Bruckner, who has been thoroughly indoctrinated with Nazi ideology before leaving Europe. He is the nephew of widower, professor, and scientist Michael Frame, who is engaged in research to help the American war effort, and of Frame's unmarried sister, Jessie. Opposers of Hitler and fascism, both Emil's parents have been condemned and exterminated by the Nazis. His mother was the sister of Michael and Jessie, and his father, a German freedom fighter and Nobel Prize winner, had been Michael's closest friend and mentor. After his parents' deaths, the orphaned Emil has been brainwashed by the Nazis and consequently has come to the Frame home programmed to serve the ideals of *Der Führer* in the American heartland.

In several ways, Gow and d'Usseau's drama seems a barometer reading of American home front attitudes toward the war, and as such, *Tomorrow the World* is an unusually illuminating work. At the center of the play is Emil Bruckner, the young German boy whose characterization touches wellsprings of classic American angst. Prewar plays like Clare Boothe's *Margin for Error*, Elmer Rice's *Flight to the West*, and Lillian Hellman's *Watch on the Rhine* project the fear of enemy operatives and fifth columnists at work undermining the democratic fabric of American society, a fear that lasts well beyond World War II, when it

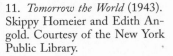

11. *Tomorrow the World* (1943). Skippy Homeier and Edith Angold. Courtesy of the New York Public Library.

becomes transformed into the rage for extirpating American Reds and pinkos during the Cold War.

Remembering that *Tomorrow the World* opened on April 1943, at the height of the war, a time when Hitler and his cohorts were thoroughly demonized in the mind of the American public, one can well imagine the gripping effect on the audience of Emil's appearance onstage in his Nazi uniform. The figure of a youthful, blond boy who comes down the stairs into the living room of a typical mid-American home giving a Nazi salute dramatically and instantly delivers the image of an enemy lodged dangerously in the bosom of the nation. The moment is captured in the photo reprinted on the play-text's dust cover, and the stage directions read:

> For a moment the stage is empty. Then EMIL appears on the stairs, wearing the uniform of the Nazi Jungvolk—the tan shirt with red arm band and its swastika insignia, the black shorts which leave the knees bare, the tan stockings and the high black shoes. A sheathed dagger is thrust through his belt. He comes down the stairs, stops in the hall, glances toward the dining room, then comes deliberately into the living room. He surveys the living room professionally, as if establishing the precise strength of the enemy. . . . Then his eye is caught by the desk. Obviously it is the desk that holds all the secrets.(48–49)[31]

The threat that Emil embodies is not just manifested in his enemy uniform or in his visible and dangerous weapon. More alarming is his ransacking Professor Frame's desk and attempting to discover the secrets hidden therein. The image initiated here is soon greatly heightened when Emil goes beyond the living room desk drawer and attempts to steal classified materials from his uncle's wartime science lab, hoping to pass them on to Nazi agents. Gow and d'Usseau seem here to be tapping into the historically recurrent American paranoia about subversives in our midst, a paranoia that would carry over in a new key to the next decade and lead, for example, to the arrest and indictment of Alger Hiss for allegedly acting as a subversive and passing government documents to the communists.

The brainwashing of Emil by the Nazi propaganda forces is made especially poignant and ethically reprehensible because he is a minor. The Nazis, the play suggests, systematically indoctrinate their youth with hate and cloud their minds with misinformation long before they are able to make independent adult determinations. And the indoctrination of Emil, as it appears in *Tomorrow the World*, is redolent with the German ethnically pure "master race" ideology, reviling the United States for its ethnic diversity.[32] Emil, as megaphone for the tenets of Nazism, exclaims:

> I am a German, and I shall always be a German. America is a cesspool. To be an American is to be a member of a mongrel race. The American blood stream is a mixture of the scum of the earth. The only pure-blooded American is the Sioux Indian. (56)

In part, Emil also echoes Hitler's remarks blaming Germany's troubles, defeat in World War I, and subsequent inflation on foreigners and alleged enemies of the state such as Emil's father. Parroting what has been drummed into him in Germany, Emil accuses his father and asserts:

> In 1918 Karl Bruckner betrayed Germany on the home front. He fomented revolution. If it had not been for him and the Jewish Bolsheviks, Germany would have won the war. He was one of those who made Germany weak. He was responsible for the inflation and the Communists. . . . We Germans were soft. We forgot our great destiny. Then *Der Führer* came. He gave us back our courage. With *Der Führer* to show the way, it is our position to conquer the world. (60–61)

This also reminds the play's audience of the Third Reich's aim of world domination and heightens the play's castigation of the Germans for poisoning the minds of innocent children like Emil.

In its presentation of Emil and the Nazi ideology he spouts, *Tomorrow the World* takes a strong and hostile stand toward the values and tactics of the Third

Reich. At the same time, however, it also registers a strong strain of liberalism that urges the audience to see and judge others as individuals rather than to make assumptions on the basis of nationality or ethnicity. In this way, *Tomorrow the World* astutely captures the conflicted feelings of the wartime American public which saw Germans as the demonized enemy but also knew that in many instances Germans were their ancestors and that Germany, in the past, had been a center of learning and culture. Even Emil's genial scientist uncle, Professor Frame, learned his science and was trained in Germany. In their drama, then, Gow and d'Usseau seem eager to make clear that, although some German Americans are Hitler sympathizers, not every American with a German accent is a Nazi. This is borne out when Emil, assuming that Frieda, the Frames' German-born housekeeper, must be loyal to Hitler, attempts to enlist her aid for the Nazi cause. She is appalled and tells Emil's uncle explosively:

> He's a devil, Professor! A devil, like they make them in Germany these days! He thinks he's a spy for Hitler. He wanted to open your telegram! . . . [*Turning on* EMIL *bitterly*] You! It is you fellows who make every one hate Germans! You wear your swastikas. You march! You kill! And all the Germans get blamed—people like *me* get blamed! (52–53)

At the same time, however, Fred Miller, the German-American janitor who cleans Professor Frame's laboratory where classified, war-related research is carried on, is shown to be a member of the *Bund* and a small-time Nazi fellow traveler.

Other conflicting American attitudes are evoked by Gow and d'Usseau in their portraits of Emil's maiden aunt, Jessie, and Michael Frame's fiancée, Leona Richards. The unmarried Jessie is a representation of American conservative social and political behavior. For her, what she deems "socially respectable" behavior is everything. She has little use for Karl Bruckner, her dead brother-in-law and Emil's father, because his persecution by the Nazis left him and her sister penniless. She also sees Karl as German and, consequently, an enemy, regardless of his political commitments:

> JESSIE. If it hadn't been for him, Mary would have been alive today. Well, maybe it's a good thing that she didn't live. Look what happened to him. Practically a criminal, and then he died in prison.
>
> MICHAEL. For God's sake, Jessie! He died in a concentration camp.
>
> JESSIE. Well, he must have done *something*.
>
> MICHAEL. He did plenty. Can't you understand! Karl was fighting then the very thing we're fighting now! He was on our side!
>
> JESSIE. He was a German, wasn't he? (12–13)

When her nephew, Emil, appears in his Nazi uniform, she exclaims with vehemence, "We're at war, aren't we? He's the enemy. He's a German, just as I knew he would be. They're all the same. Lying, arrogant, deceitful—goose-stepping. If it was up to me, I'd exterminate the entire German race!" (54). The satire directed against Jessie clearly makes her as racist and reprehensible as the Nazis she reviles. Her desire to "exterminate the entire German race" is no better than Hitler's "final solution" for the Jews.

Yet, Gow and d'Usseau complicate the figure of Jessie by having her succumb to the blandishments of Emil, who senses that she is a lonely woman about to lose her place in her widower brother's household, since he is about to remarry. From being his antagonist, Jessie becomes Emil's protector. He locates her vulnerability, tells her what she longs to hear, and massages her discontent over her brother's imminent marriage to Leona. When Emil nearly kills his cousin Pat, Michael and Jessie have an illuminating confrontation:

> MICHAEL. He was sent home from school yesterday for fighting, and lo and behold, you were treating him like a new-found friend. Why was it? Tell me, Jessie. Was it because he hated Lee? And you resented her too? Suppose you tell me, Jessie. Let's get this out in the open.
>
> JESSIE. It's true, Michael. . . . I let the child deceive me.
>
> MICHAEL. He found the weak spot in all of us.
>
> JESSIE. It was worse than that. I let him talk against Leona. I let him brag that he would make it impossible for you to get married. Then, when he almost killed Pat, it was as if I had been in league with a murderer. (140–141)

Jessie's behavior, which has gone from antipathy to sympathy, enables the audience to understand the appeal of fascism not merely for disgruntled Americans but also for those countries whose troubles made the siren song of Nazism appealing and led them to align themselves with the Axis. Yet her realization that she has served as an accomplice in evil prevents the audience from entirely forgiving her actions even though they understand their cause.

Most revealing in *Tomorrow the World* is Gow and d'Usseau's presentation of Leona Richards, who is soon to marry Professor Frame. She is Emil's teacher at school and is Jewish. In the second act of the play, we learn that Emil has chalked obscenities, presumably anti-Semitic obscenities, on the sidewalk. When Leona confronts the boy about this, he vehemently cries out at her, "It's a lie! A Jewish lie! . . . A Jewish lie from a Jewish whore!" (102). The familiar anti-Semitic Nazi rhetoric overcomes her, and she delivers a hard slap to Emil. It is a stage moment at which one can well imagine applause from the audience as Leona enacts their desire. When Frame comes to the boy's defense, arguing that Emil is just a child with a problem and Leona has surely handled problem children before, Leona replies in one of the play's central moments:

But Emil isn't just a case of maladjustment. He's *perfectly* adjusted—but to a Nazi society! He's been taught contempt for people who don't use force. He's been taught that Americans are soft. And sure enough, we've been soft with him. He's found that he can push us around. And he'll go on pushing us around until we give him the one answer he understands—a licking . . . it's long overdue, Mike. A licking. Not in anger, not in haste. But a deliberate, carefully planned licking. (106–107)

Clearly this serves as more than a justification for Leona's striking Emil. It pointedly explains, justifies, and supports America's involvement in the war.

In a way remarkable for 1943, when American engagement in the war was intense and when the revelation of Jewish extermination in the death camps was making its first horrific impact on the public consciousness, Gow and d'Usseau suddenly modify their passionately anti-German stance and look ahead to post-war compassion for those in Germany simply caught up in the times. When Emil nearly kills Mike's daughter, Mike and Leona exchange roles. Mike is now ready to turn Emil over to the police and send him to a correctional facility. And it is Leona who preaches another way. It is she, the Jew and victim of anti-Semitism, who astoundingly, two years before V-E Day, preaches understanding and prognosticates what was to become in postwar Germany the process of de-Nazification:

> LEONA. Yesterday I made a bad mistake. . . . Today you're trying to do the same thing. . . . I don't know any more than you how to handle this boy. But I know we've got to try. We can't turn our backs. We can't put him behind bars, nor simply wipe him out. You can call it pride if you want, but I won't admit failure like that, and I won't let you. . . . And it's not just our problem. There are twelve million other children just like him in Germany. They can't all be put behind bars. They can't all be exterminated.
>
> MICHAEL. Of course not. But what we decide for Emil Bruckner has nothing to do with post-war Germany. You're talking way up in the clouds.
>
> LEONA. But don't you see, Mike. If you and I can't turn one little boy into a human being—then God help the world when this war is won, and we have to deal with twelve million of them! (160–161)

Tomorrow the World thus creates a scenario that allows the audience first to vent their anger at the Germans but then to move beyond that anger and desire for revenge to envision a future characterized by humane reformation. This follows the underlying theme that replaces the idea of enemies in need of extermination with one of humans who err and can be re-educated. It is of a piece, too, with the idea that among the Germans and German Americans there are Nazis and Nazi sympathizers, but there are also decent Germans like Karl Bruckner and

Frieda who uphold democracy and in no way deserve to be counted among the numbers of the enemy.

I V

That Emil in *Tomorrow the World* is especially hateful toward the Jewish Leona brings home one of the major aspects of Nazism. Nowadays, when we reflect on World War II, we often think first of the unspeakable horrors of the Holocaust; of the extermination of six million Jews; and of names like Dachau, Buchenwald, Theresienstadt, Belsen, Sobibor, and Auschwitz. We remember the indelible images of people in striped rags liberated by Allied troops from the Nazi death camps, looking more like mobile skeletons than human beings and framed by terrifyingly ironic signs that say "*Arbeit macht frei.*" And we remember the dramatic piles of shoes and of human hair, the devastating relics of those millions killed in Nazi concentration camps. But during much of the war, Americans remained largely ignorant of what was actually transpiring in the concentration camps that dotted Nazi-controlled Europe.[33] To be sure, as early as 1934 there is a mention of concentration camps in S. N. Behrman's *Rain from Heaven*, but there is a sense that such camps were merely internment camps for political dissidents. A year later, when fascist concentration camps appear in Sinclair Lewis's nightmare fantasy *It Can't Happen Here*, those camps are once again holding areas for those deemed enemies of fascist dictatorship. In 1941, Maxwell Anderson in *Candle in the Wind* places a Frenchman, working with the French underground against the German occupation forces, in a concentration camp. But other than the commandant's office, *Candle in the Wind* offers no glimpse of the camp nor any sense of what it is like.

Although refugees coming to American shores doubtless brought tales of concentration camps, tales that many likely thought exaggerated or apocryphal, actual documentation that the concentration camps were death camps was not released until well into the war. Indeed it was not until the brief report published 29 June 1942 in the *New York Times* (via the *London Daily Telegraph*) that Americans and the rest of the Allied world read, "Germans have massacred more than 1,000,000 Jews since the war began in carrying out Adolph Hitler's proclaimed policy of exterminating the people, spokesmen for the World Jewish Congress charged today."[34] Buried as it was on page 7 and couched in the terms of possibility rather than certainty, this article, though of historical importance, had little impact on the American consciousness. It took another four months before the information became more real with the revelation in the *Times* that the June report was essentially correct:

> Declaring that the Nazi program to reduce the number of Jews in Poland by 50 per cent this year was a "first step" toward complete annihilation, the report said: "The most ruthless methods are being applied. The victims are either dragged out of their homes or simply seized in the streets. . . .

Dr. Stephen Wise . . . learned through sources confirmed by the State Department that about half the estimated 4,000,000 Jews in Nazi-occupied Europe had been slain in an "extermination campaign."[35]

Even then the story was relegated to page 10. The horrific truth that began to leak out with greater intensity in subsequent months did much to reconceptualize a war which until then had been largely seen as a struggle between (an American-style) democracy and fascist dictatorship, yet the horrifying dimensions of what we now have come to know as the Holocaust did not fully come to light until after V-E Day when the camps were liberated.[36] Then Americans saw photos and film footage of the camps themselves, with their crematoria and gas showers; piles of human hair and shoes and body parts; and the look of the skeletal survivors with their horrific recollections and unspeakable wounds, psychological and physical. The indelible photographic images of the camps and the tales told by survivors (with numbers often tattooed on their arms) which have come so powerfully to mark our consciousness and our conception of World War II largely emerged toward the conclusion of the war and were not, therefore, a central part of public imagination while the war was being fought. Indeed, it was not until the summer of 1942 and the *New York Times* reports that American stage dramas registered the issues of the Holocaust. Thus, the subject of Leona's Jewishness in *Tomorrow the World* was a highly charged one, coming as it did ten months after the *New York Times* reports. It came as well just one month after Ben Hecht's impassioned dramatic performance piece about the plight of Jewry during the war: *We Will Never Die.*

In response to the loss of millions of Jewish lives to the Nazis and their allies, Ben Hecht (together with Peter Bergson, alias Hillel Kook, who had rescued many European Jews and brought them to Palestine) produced an unconventional play and a highly emotional, rhetorically powerful, dramatic propaganda piece, *We Will Never Die*, about the importance of Jews in world culture, the genocide in Europe, and the need for Jewish national as well as just religious and ethnic identity. On 9 March 1943, Hecht's *We Will Never Die*, which featured Paul Muni and Edward G. Robinson in the leading roles, opened to huge crowds at Madison Square Garden. It was produced by Billy Rose, directed by Moss Hart, and featured music by German refugee Kurt Weill. It was eventually to play in six cities and to well over 100,000 people. Hecht's piece is simple and direct, and aimed, just as agitprop plays of the 1930s were, at the emotions of its audience in order to raise their consciousness.[37] That *We Will Never Die* prompted Governor Thomas E. Dewey of New York to declare a day of mourning for the Jews who had been killed by the Nazis suggests that Hecht's piece fulfilled its mission.

In part, *We Will Never Die* seems to assume a Jewish audience or one familiar with the sounds and symbols of the faith. The background set for the piece is a large projection of the Ten Commandments, which are illuminated, darkened, or beclouded in response to the dramatic material presented, and the dialogue is preceded by the always electrifying blast of the shofar, the ram's horn that is blown on the Jewish New Year and on Yom Kippur, the Day of Atonement, the most solemn day in the Jewish calendar. Indeed, the script makes clear that it is the Yom Kippur shofar sound, a sound which at once aurally italicizes the knowledge of mortality and which is also employed to conclude the Yom Kippur service and, metaphorically, to herald what is hoped will be a good year.

A central part of every Yom Kippur service is Yiskor, an extended memorial service that keeps alive the memory of family members, friends, and martyrs who have died. *We Will Never Die*, without mentioning the Yiskor service, nonetheless picks up that idea as the play begins and as a rabbi intones to the audience:

> We are here to say our prayers for the two million who have been killed in Europe, because they bear the name of your first children—the Jews.
>
> Before our eyes has appeared the strange and awesome picture of a folk being put to death, of a great and ancient people in whose veins has lingered the for so long earliest words and image of God, dying like a single child on a single bayonet. . . .
>
> We are here to honor them and to proclaim the victory of their dying. . . .
>
> Though they still fill the dark land of Europe with the smoke of their massacre, they shall never die.
>
> For they are part of something greater, higher and stronger than the dreams of their executioners. . . .
>
> We are here to strengthen our hearts, to take into our veins the pride and courage of the millions of innocent people who have fallen and are still to fall before the German massacre. (1,2)[38]

The service in the play begins with "Shema Israel, the prayer that holds the last words of the millions who have died in the massacres by the Germans" (3). The indentations and separation of lines in the typescript text, moreover, indicate *We Will Never Die*'s rhetorical strategy and strength. The "Shema Israel" prayer is delivered by twenty-one rabbis who come on to the stage while the prayer's responses are sounded by an offstage choir. A narrator then remembers the history of Judaism from Abraham the first Jew to the present, but soon focuses poignantly on the contemporary plight of European Jews:

> Today in the dark lands of Europe the Germans are seeking to destroy the creed written by Abraham and that now belongs to the whole world.
>
> Statisticians have estimated that it costs $50,000 for the Germans to kill a single allied soldier. This is an expensive gesture.
>
> The killing of a Jew is less expensive. It costs nothing.
>
> The Jew is without weapons, without a flag. He is the step son in the

house. The laws of nations do not include his safety, his honor or his inheritance. (5)

In addition to the arousal of audience response to the slaughter of Jews by the Nazis, one can see here the seeds of Hecht's subsequent postwar piece, *A Flag Is Born,* which would urge the establishment of Israel as the Jewish homeland and state.

The narrator of *We Will Never Die* proceeds to give a litany of great Jewish patriarchs—including Abraham, Moses, David, and Bar Cochba—that segues into an even more impressive litany of significant Jewish contributors in more recent times to science, invention, music, art, literature, and statesmanship. This section of the piece concludes with the homely but heart-wrenching last dispatch from Corregidor by Jewish, Brooklyn-born Irving Strobing, and it ushers in a dramatic account of how Jewish soldiers are serving during World War II under a multitude of national flags belonging to the armies of the Allied countries in Europe and in North and South America, and how these Jewish servicemen are serving and laying down their lives in the name of a free world and in a multitude of critical and bloody battles. Again the Jewish homeland issues of *A Flag Is Born* are foreshadowed:

> FIRST SOLDIER: There is only one flag missing over the head of the Jew—his own.
>
> SECOND SOLIDER: There is only one wail heard from the Jews of the free world—the wail at the Wall of Jerusalem—the wail for the right to fight. Here two hundred thousand Jews, sturdy pioneers of the new land of Palestine are crying out for a place on the battle front.
>
> Over two million brothers in Europe have died as Jews. Let us fight as Jews to avenge them. We will fight well. (22)

As rhetorically effective as *We Will Never Die* is, however, it is nonetheless fueled almost solely by the rhetoric of words, of dramatic narrative. There is no staged dramatic action or conflict but rather the voiced invocation of the helplessness of Jews who are merely sojourners in other nations and who are now the objects of Nazi tyranny.

It is hard to give a name to *We Will Never Die.* Certainly it is not a play or even an agitprop play, for it lacks both conventional plot and action. To call it a pageant would be a misnomer, for a pageant suggests a focus on visual display. In some ways, *We Will Never Die* is a narrative pageant not unlike wartime radio plays but with seen actors and an impressive set. Probably because the atrocities of the death camps had not yet been seen and the brutalities against Jews related only secondhand, *We Will Never Die* speaks of rather than stages those atrocities and brutalities.

The final section of the piece prophesies U.N. deliberations when the war is over with a long conference table flanked by the flags of all nations (except that of the Jews). "Three Germans, two in frock coats and one in uniform, with the swastika on their sleeves, enter and sit down with their backs to the audience—facing the Tablets" (22–23), and the narrator declaims:

> Of the six million Jews in German held lands the Germans have said none shall remain. The four million left to kill are being killed—according to plan. When the time comes to make the peace these will have been done to death.
>
> And these millions who were hanged, burned and shot will have died without the dream of abasements to be avenged or homelands to be restored. For when the Jews die in massacre they look toward no tomorrow to bring their children happiness and their enemies disaster. For no homeland is ever theirs no matter how long they live in it, how well they serve it or how many of its songs they learn to sing.
>
> When the plans for the new world are being thrashed out at the peace table when the guilts are fixed and the color and shape of the future determined, there will be nothing for the Jews of Europe to say to the delegates but the sad, faint phrase—"Remember Us." (24–25)

This is followed by a long and descriptive list of Nazi violence acted out against Jews, each concluding with "Remember us," as, for example, "In Riga a thousand of us arrived on a transport from Germany as conscripted laborers. We had been traveling in sealed compartments for many days without food. The Germans in Riga unlocked our compartments and looked us over. They decided we were too weak to be of any use in the factories. They put us into sealed wagons and drove us into the fields and dynamited us. Remember us who were the workingmen" (27).

We Will Never Die concludes poignantly with a now ironic remembrance of the dead:

> Let their dying be not without meaning. Let the manner of their dying be one of the measures of the German soul. Let their myriad corpses piled in the streets, fields and rivers of Europe be as the hound of Heaven on the heels of evil men. . . .
>
> The Jews have a prayer for their dead. It is the prayer called the Kaddish, the prayer that begins Yis-ga-dall v-yis-ka-dash. It is the prayer spoken by the hearts heavy with grief for the dead. But it does not speak of grief. It is the greatest poem of the Jewish soul. For in grief, however great, it affirms the glory of life, and blesses God. Let us sing this prayer for the voiceless and the Jewish dead of Europe. (30)

This statement is ironic because the date of the piece is 1943. The devastation of war and its toll in human lives were far from over, and the next two years of the war would witness the deaths of still millions more Jews at the merciless hands of the Nazis.

Even with the revelations that the concentration camps were actually death camps carrying out mass genocide, it took some time before the drama seemed able to address that horror in any very direct way. Perhaps the most moving wartime play touching on the subject of the camps (though not depicting them) is Edward Chodorov's *Common Ground,* which opened 25 May 1945, less than two weeks after V-E Day. Alas, as the excellence of *Common Ground, Decision,* and *Those Endearing Young Charms* now attests, Edward Chodorov is a playwright of considerable talent who never got his due. Perhaps consciously invoking the situation and structure of Robert Sherwood's prewar *Idiot's Delight,* Chodorov presents in *Common Ground* a disparate group of American performers who, during the war, have been on tour entertaining American troops. Their plane has been shot down, and they find themselves in an Italian castle, where they have been captured and are being held prisoners by the Italians and the Nazis.

Their captors know who these entertainers are and scoff at their P.O.W. status. The oldest and most accomplished among them is the Jewish-American comedian Buzz Bernard, who is told that he will be shipped to a Nazi death camp for Jews. The others—Kate and Nick, who are respectively Irish-American and Italian-American; Alan Spencer, alias Alan Steiner, of German descent; and Genevieve "Geegee" Gilman, an American ingenue hoping to achieve stardom— are offered the chance to survive if they will entertain the Italian and German military and serve to direct propaganda to the American troops, persuading them of the falseness of the American cause. The German commander, Hofer, instructs them of their task:

> You will dance. We will make a grand tour, mm? We play in Italy, Austria, Budapest, Berlin perhaps—I give you a private railroad car. You will be quite happy. And they will be quite happy in America to hear what you do—mm? So. First we go to Naples—Rome—Florence—[*To Nick*] Where you will speak to your people and you will tell them how all Italians in America pray for the success of the Fascist armies. How all Americans, but some Jews and financiers, do not wish to fight—we will tell you what to say. [*Looks at Alan*] And in German-speaking places—in Austria and so forth—you, Steiner, will tell how you waited for the chance to come back to your own people. And so forth. And after you are finished, Berlin will decide what to do with you—both. The girl [Geegee] will be sent back to America. The Irishwoman [Kate] to her own country. The Jew, of course, will go to a concentration camp in Germany immediately, today. We don't need him! (45–46)[39]

If the Americans do not accept the traitorous script they are offered, they will be shot. The lose-lose situation is worthy of the best dramatic dilemmas concocted by those seventeenth-century playwriting talents Beaumont and Fletcher.

The group of entertainers is confronted, furthermore, by an American now working for the enemy. Ted Williamson, an erstwhile American actor who, disgruntled with his lot in the U.S., has become an ardent fascist sympathizer, now seeks to win over the captured Americans to his point of view. What Chodorov accomplishes here is a powerful twist on d'Usseau and Gow's Emil, the teenage subversive Nazi brainwashed by the Germans who invades an American household. Here Williamson, a turncoat American actor living in Europe, seeks to convince the captured performers of the rightness of the fascist racist cause compared with what he believes is the innate weakness of American multi-ethnic society. Giving voice to that strain of American fascist sympathy current in America before the war, during the war, and even nowadays in the Ku Klux Klan and neo-Nazi organizations, he says sardonically:

> You're a real American. And Albert Steiner here—he's a real American. And this Irish biddy. And a Jew comic. [*Burlesque melodrama*] And I'm a traitor? Don't you people ever learn anything? Is it going to take another war to make you realize how right Adolph is? What difference does it make who wins? As soon as the fighting stops—then watch. This war is a pity. Adolph made a mistake. He began in the wrong alley. Europe is full of little countries where the people all look alike, and they're proud of it. America is the place! We're just lousy with all kinds of animals that look different, smell different—and hate each other at the bottom. There's no real common ground—and after a hundred and fifty years of kidding, they're getting less and less polite about it. Why don't you face that? I did. That's why I'm here—You're fighting "Fascism," aren't you? I'm going to show you the stack of magazines and newspapers we get every week— all printed in America—and all yelling for Fascism! . . . Christ—if Adolph had started the ball rolling in *America*—and concentrated on *that*—only that—I'd be sitting in 21 right now—and not a sheeny in the joint—and there wouldn't have *been* any war. Because the rest of the world would have just tumbled into line. (31)

Williamson articulates the repeated claim that American multi-ethnicity provides no common ground of national unity and fosters instead a country comprised of mongrels. Obviously, the title of Chodorov's drama makes clear that the playwright questions and condemns the racist premise promulgated by Williamson and by those who think as he does.

Buzz Bernard, the American-Jewish comedian, is not given the choice offered to the other captives. His fate is to be sent to a German concentration camp. *Common Ground* is, thus, an important breakthrough in providing American theatre audiences with an image of concentration camps as death camps. To be sure, Chodorov does not present a camp onstage, but Buzz Bernard offers a graphic description of the camps and of his coming to terms with the Jewishness he formerly denied. Bernard's comments are compelling and Chodorov's audience, Jewish or not, would surely have been moved:

> It came to me in Algiers—when I was having lunch with that fellow, the English correspondent who saw the death camp in Poland—where the Germans took the shoes off the children, and stacked them up neatly, according to size, before they—One camp, he said—a million and half people—I could see he was still shaking, and I asked him, "Do you understand it?" He said, I beg your pardon?" I said, "Do you understand it— underneath—what is it?" He said, "The Nazis, Mr. Bernard—" and so on, with the Nazis—Nonsense! Nazis. Yes. But not just the Nazis—not just the "Germans"—that's nonsense. But something gave them permission. . . . I would like to die like a man—and like a good Jew—Which is funny—because even a year ago I would never have said "Jew." I never in my life thought much about it. I knew that's what I was—and I knew there was something not exactly kosher about being a Jew—but it didn't bother me. . . . I'm trying to remember what I thought I was—when I was a boy. And all I can think of is that I thought I was an American. (67–68)

Chodorov evokes in graphic terms the horror of the death camps, but he also points an accusing finger at a world, including America, that is an accessory to the crime of genocide by tacitly condoning racism and racial profiling, and by pointing a finger as well at those, like Bernard, whose desire to assimilate has led them to deny their ethnicity. *Common Ground* is strong stuff and delivers some hard punches.

The moving conclusion of the play is not an eleventh hour rescue but a poignant realization on the part of all the captured entertainers—even those whose first reaction was to cooperate with the Italians and Germans in order to save their skins—that they do share a common ground as Americans and that they cannot capitulate to fascism. As Alan says, "So that's it. So we all found out we're Americans. . . . Marvelous, isn't it? . . . You can't die any better than *that,* can you? Did Nathan Hale do it any better? Or Joan of Arc? What the Hell—You know *all* the people I've seen die have been pretty damn good at it—I wonder why? . . . We routed the enemy!" And Nick replies triumphantly, "Yeah! The Americans won!" (78–80).

A raised American consciousness about the persecution of Jews in Europe and about prejudice toward Jews at home probably played some role in giving attention to another facet of American prejudice: the plight of the Negro. During World War II, as in prior wars, African-American soldiers served valiantly, but they served in all-black, segregated units. A war allegedly waged against Nazi racist theories naturally threw America's own assumptions of white racial superiority into ironic relief. Thus, several wartime and immediately postwar plays raised the uncomfortable issues of American racism and segregation. These plays, written by white playwrights, provided a prelude for Lorraine Hansberry's *A Raisin in the Sun* as well as for other plays of the late 1950s and 1960s by gifted, militant, revolutionary African-American playwrights such as Douglas Turner Ward, LeRoi Jones (Imamu Baraka), Ed Bullins, Lonne Elder, Alice Childress, Charles Fuller, Kingsley B. Bass, Jr., Ossie Davis, and Ben Caldwell.

In 1927, Dorothy Heyward had been the co-author, with her husband DuBose Heyward, of *Porgy and Bess.* Fifteen years later, as World War II was being fought, she co-authored with Howard Rigsby another hard-hitting play about African Americans, *South Pacific,* which opened at the Cort Theatre on 29 December 1943 and marked the first professional theatre appearance of Ruby Dee. Perhaps because of its subject matter and perhaps because it is excessively melodramatic, *South Pacific* ran for only five performances. It is, nevertheless, worthy of some attention because it is a drama ahead of its time. When the curtain rises, Heyward and Rigsby present two American seaman, Dunlap and Sam Johnson, one white and one black, whose respective ships have been destroyed by Japanese fire in the Pacific, and who have been washed ashore on a Pacific island held by the Japanese. Under Japanese thrall are not only the native dark-skinned islanders but also Dr. John, a black physician from Papua New Guinea, and Ruth, a black missionary and nurse. When the two marooned soldiers meet Dr. John and Ruth, they learn that the dark-skinned Sam will likely be able to pass as a native and go unnoticed by the Japanese, but if discovered, the white Dunlap will be killed.

To Sam, the situation is liberating because for once the white man is in the minority, an endangered species among the island's populace of color. Embittered by a lifetime of smarting under racist prejudice in America, Sam believes he has serendipitously fallen into a nonwhite racial paradise, and he rejects any notion of his working with Dunlap or with Dr. John and Ruth against the Japanese who occupy and now rule the island:

> DUNLAP. Japs don't bother you?
>
> SAM. They never did anything to me.
>
> DUNLAP. Just blasted a ship out from under you!
>
> SAM. That's war.
>
> DUNLAP. Maybe you'd like to see them win this war!
>
> SAM. I don't give a damn who wins it. Just don't try to drag me into it. That's all I say. Don't try to tell me I got to fight for something I never had—and never going to get.
>
> DUNLAP. You're getting it. You're getting everything—slowly. But if they win you never will! . . .

SAM. You want us to go out and kill and maybe get killed. . . . Then why don't you give us something to fight for? Why don't you give us the same reasons you got? . . .

DUNLAP. This isn't a color war! It's a war of one kind of men against another kind. Understand that?

SAM. I heard your line of talk too much before—and I heard it fancier than you'll ever say it.

DUNLAP. Listen Johnson, any place else, I wouldn't have anything to do with you. Not because the color of your skin makes any difference, but because I just don't like the color of your guts! (1–12–14)[40]

South Pacific suggests that Sam's anger is understandable though out of place in wartime. The play goes on to prophesy that during the postwar period full civil rights and equality for African Americans will be slowly granted.

After some time elapses and U.S. ships approach the island, Sam continues in his refusal to help, this time specifying the reasons for his anger toward white Americans and thereby implicitly citing for the audience the injustices that must be remedied:

SAM. I told you where I stood.

DUNLAP. You stood against *intolerance*. If the Japs and Nazis control the world,—

SAM. I heard all that.

DUNLAP. You're lining yourself up on the side of intolerance.

SAM. I'm not lining up on any side. I'm keeping out of it.

DUNLAP. By not fighting against them you're fighting for the Japs. . . .

SAM. Yeah? I suppose my country needs me.

DUNLAP. You're right.

SAM. Well, they should've needed me younger—when they didn't have any job for me, or any vote, or any room for me 'cept in a tenement. (2.2.41–42)

By falling in love with Ruth, who is innocently devoid of any race prejudice, Sam does come to see that he must fight against the Japanese, who symbolize racial intolerance, but he does not do so until after the black Dr. John, the white Dunlap, and a beloved native boy have been killed. Although *South Pacific* closed five days after it opened, it is nonetheless an important indicator of how the issues of World War II helped set in motion the civil rights agitation that began to heat up after the war was over.

A connection between the war and the home front is more strongly and far more excellently made in Edward Chodorov's *Decision*, a drama that opened on 2 February 1944 at the Belasco Theatre, where it ran for 161 performances and was selected as one of the Burns Mantle best plays of 1943–44.[41] Reviewing the production for the *New York Times*, Lewis Nichols commented, "Edward Chodorov has written a sincere study of the fight against Fascism in this country, and his players act it to the hilt. Between them they take it out of the category of pamphlet and make it a real evening of theatre." And the review in the *New York Journal-American* mentioned that Chodorov "had them on their feet and cheering."[42] Nevertheless, *Decision* is an unrecognized work and one that deserves a great deal more attention than it has hitherto received.

The setting of *Decision* is a generic American city (but clearly neither a Southern city nor New York). Two plots importantly intertwine in the home of Mr. Riggs, the local school principal. First, his son, Tommy, has just returned from active duty in Europe, where he has served his country patriotically on the battlefield fighting fascism and fascists. Tommy has been wounded in the line of duty and consequently been returned to the U.S. for continuing but noncombat duty stateside. But while Tommy has been fighting overseas, important industrial changes have taken place at home. The stepped-up need for armaments and troop supplies coupled with a diminished wartime domestic work force have led the U.S. government to pass legislation opening factory and munitions plant doors—including those of the local Anderson Company plant—to a new class of workers: American blacks. Strongly opposed to this new social and financial empowerment of African Americans are powerful local reactionary forces which do not wish to see social changes in America. The villain of *Decision*, the racist Senator Dufresne, never appears, but his tools, the town newspaper editor and his paid goons, do. Part of Chodorov's point here is that the true powers behind American fascism and racism work in safety behind the scenes. They are strongly felt but never seen.

At the Anderson plant, there has been racial violence resulting in some fatalities, but those riots, it becomes clear, have been fomented by the operatives of the racist senator, who wishes to lay blame for the deaths on allegedly violent blacks, thereby abrogating racial integration among the munitions plant workers. Keeping the color bar in place, Chodorov suggests, is far more important to the champions of racial segregation than either Allied victory in World War II or properly arming American servicemen. Riggs, the school principal and respected community member, has accepted the role of mediator and defender of the black workers. This leads to a direct confrontation with Masters, the newspaper editor and mouthpiece for Senator Dufresne. Chodorov uses the heated exchange between Riggs and Masters to lay bare the play's issues in the most limpid of terms:

12. *Decision* (1944). Gwen Anderson and Laurence Hugo. Courtesy of the New York Public Library. Used by permission.

MASTERS. I was born here, in a white native Protestant community—I'm going to get rid of this army of niggers and trash that Anderson has presented us—along with the rape and disease which he and Washington gave us for nothing.

RIGGS. Have you tried to correct these conditions—?

MASTERS. Correct? I'm no "idealistic reformer," man! You high-flying Hottentot missionaries want to "Win the war and reform the world!" Bunk! We won't *win* any war if we keep giving in to these damn socialist slogans—or what we do won't be *worth* winning!

RIGGS. I disagree with you completely, Masters. I believe that we will win *only* if we extend democracy to its fullest everywhere—and now—so that all men understand exactly why we fight. Especially our own millions of colored citizens.

. . .

MASTERS. Going to free the nigger all over again? Well, he's not going to be free—not to stand up and work as an equal with decent white men—

and certainly not to draw the same pay—not permanently—not around here—not while I'm around!

. . .

RIGGS. Would you have Mr. Anderson refuse to obey the decisions of the government in time of war—?

MASTERS. Yes! When they're decisions made by a bunch of communistic New Dealers and labor racketeers! Kowtowing to Washington bureaucrats doesn't spell patriotism to me! (35–36)[43]

The issues here are powerful and powerfully presented, especially for 1944, nearly two decades before the civil rights movement would reach its full momentum.

Tommy, Riggs's son, just returned with wounds from the battlefields of Italy, is used in *Decision* to represent the war raging across the Atlantic, while his father is waging an analogous war at home. As Virgie, the Riggs family's former black maid who now works at the plant, says to Tommy, "Your father don't wear no uniform maybe—but he been fightin' just the same—and with *no* gun" (58). And as Riggs himself, who is after all an educator, says somewhat didactically to both his son and the audience:

I respect the fundamental law of our country—justice and equality for all—and I believe you were fighting to preserve it. I think you will understand, son, when I saw it violated, every day, here before my eyes—I couldn't resist doing my share in the battle against Dufresne and those who plan a Fascist-minded future for us. . . . I believe we are living, now, in the midst of a very real civil war—a war that must be decided before you come home for good—or you will come home to the ashes of the cause for which you fought. (63, 64)

Decision does not, however, end with the triumph of Riggs and of enlightened community members. The forces of bigotry, the tools of the racist senator, find the father of a female student and get him to level false charges of child molestation against the principal. Riggs is swiftly taken into custody and mysteriously found dead in his holding cell the following morning. He has seemingly used his suspenders to hang himself, but it is obvious to all that he has been murdered.

With the assassination of Riggs between acts 2 and 3, the emphasis in the final act shifts so that Tommy, who in anger and disgust is ready to leave his hometown forever, must (along with the Chodorov's audience) be convinced to remain and fight in a war at home that is, finally, no different from the one he had been fighting in Europe. He must be led to see that the workers, fighting bigotry and racism in his hometown, who rally to his support after his father's wrongful death, are like the soldiers who fought at his side in the World War

II battles against fascism in Europe. When Tommy's idealistic fiancée rallies him to the cause, she is obviously speaking not merely to him but to Chodorov's wartime theatre audience:

> You know better than any of *us* what it means to fight side by side with people who depend on you—for their lives. And that's what's happening here—but you won't see it. In back of you and me and Mr. Anderson— are all those people—who are just *like* an army!—But with eighty different generals shouting at them—trying to make them go this way—or that— and what your father did was give them a feeling of *unity*, because they trusted him—and now all that might be wasted—because you won't help. (79)

The political directive of *Decision* is obvious. The end of the play is not a happy ending but a rally to arms. A negative review of *Decision* denounced the play-wright: "Mr. Chodorov hasn't learned the most elementary principle of dramatic construction, which is that you cannot have a good man evilly put upon without making his persecutors pay for the crime."[44] While most students of the theatre would disagree with the reviewer's essential principle for creating dramatic art, the open-ended conclusion of the play, which tosses the issues into the audience's lap, may have left playgoers uncomfortable. Indeed, if we judge *Decision* by its immediate impact, we realize that in 1944 the message delivered by *Decision* fell if not on deaf ears then on ears of American audience members not yet ready to act upon what they had heard. It may well be, however, that works such as these began the process of undermining the racist monolith that informed the thinking and assumptions of a great many Americans.

V

Notwithstanding the tragic events and the serious stage dramas of World War II, the spirit of comedy did not abandon the prosceniums of Broadway. Indeed the progeny of Mars and Thalia were many and robust. And as children of the same parents, they share among themselves some clear family resemblances. Existing alongside the offspring Mars fathered with Melpomene, the brood of wartime comic dramas more frequently exhibits the common gene of farce. An easy and not incorrect conclusion seems to be that lighthearted, war-related comic plays provided audiences, in the midst of wartime crisis, a much-needed antidote to their serious cares. The comedies, moreover, addressed with mirth and ebullience some of the major and often troubling dislocations of prewar peacetime life Americans were experiencing during the war. In the years after the U.S. declared war on the Axis powers, Americans were confronted every day on the radio and in the newspapers with terrifying reports of new battles and casualties. Every day they received news of family members and friends killed, injured, or missing in battle. There were air raids and food rationing, husbands and sons away at war, and wives and daughters finding new roles in the labor force or serving as wartime volunteers. Added to the traditional sight of men on the streets dressed for work in hats, jackets, and ties was the new and increasingly familiar sight of men in uniform.

The influx of soldiers from all over the U.S. to army camps located across the country changed the economics of towns adjacent to military bases. But more important, the soldiers far away from home, facing a war of unknown duration, in need of relief from the duress of life in boot camp, and contemplating battles on foreign shores from which they might never return, brought to many once placid American towns new waves of drunkenness and sexual desire. Suddenly young women in small towns discovered handsome, clean-looking young men dressed in attractive uniforms to replace the enlisted and drafted hometown boys. The war also brought with it the need for many married women to return to parental homes for moral, economic, or child care support while their husbands were overseas. Housing and hotel accommodations near army bases (and in Washington) were in short supply, and people sometimes found themselves sharing rooms and housing with strangers. These serious matters are also well-suited backdrops for comedy, and the playwrights of the day were quick to recognize the potential of the war's social dislocations as fodder for stage comedy. Often the comedies written during the war years are little more than the classic situations of farce but peppered with men in uniform and the unusual circumstances that occur during wartime.

Within ten months of American entry into the war, Josephine Bentham and Herschel Williams staged their very successful wartime comedy, *Janie* (10 September 1942), which ran for 642 performances at Henry Miller's Theatre.[45] Bentham and Williams's comedy of teenage misadventures was surely inspired by the impressive success of the then-popular radio series *A Date with Judy* and by the enormous popularity of Sally Benson's collections of her *New Yorker* stories, *Junior Miss* (1941) and *Meet Me in St. Louis* (1942). The latter was, of course, made by Vincente Minnelli into the now legendary 1944 Judy Garland film. The former was transformed by Joseph Fields and Jerome Chodorov into a hit play (18 November 1941) to which, despite its own success, *Janie* was often invidiously compared. Indeed, John Anderson's opening night review of *Janie* waggishly quipped that it was "Junior Missed."[46] Set in Hortonville, "a small city in the United States," *Janie* centers on the risible misadventures of Janie Colburn and her high school girlfriends when their lives and romantic fantasies are impacted by the presence of young recruits at the army base located at the edge of Hortonville.[47]

The actual plot of *Janie* is trivial, but in the figure of Janie's father, the editor of the local newspaper, Bentham and Williams help bring to light some significant wartime issues. One of these is that, with American industries newly focused on producing goods for the war, equipment for civilian uses came to be in short supply. Consequently, Mr. Colburn has been to Washington to plead with the Priorities Board for a new printing press for his newspaper. His reasoning throws into relief a range of disparate issues:

> As I told 'em in Washington, the *Hortonville Times* is a paper that's indispensable now. We've not only got this Army Camp right on top of us, we have those new war plants, and all these people needing their morale kept up. (12)

Of these, the wartime scarcity of an item such as a printing press is foremost, but Colburn's comment italicizes as well the increased reliance during the period on the news media as a source of daily information for charting the progress of the war and for keeping up the good spirits of the civilian populace. The authors do not seem entirely to sympathize with Colburn, for they put in opposition Colburn's partner, John Van Brunt, who has written an editorial that argues the opposite view and asks for "the need for a little co-operation with the government. . . . I felt we ought to get along with the tools we had" (13–14).

Colburn's reference to the appearance of a military base and a war plant in Hortonville evokes the sense of a new 1940s American labor geography that reshaped the social landscape of many small- and mid-sized American towns through the influx of military personnel and through the new presence of industrial workers producing goods for use by the armed forces. Moreover, Colburn's comments indicate that there the landscape has also changed in Washington, the hub of American domestic wartime operations. He complains that he has been a victim of the accommodations shortages that were to beleaguer visitors to the American capital during the war years: "And where d'you suppose I slept that night? In that damned town! Sitting up in a chair in the lobby of the Mayflower Hotel" (13). In Hortonville as well, the housing shortage has left its mark. Colburn learns that his partner, John Van Brunt, has been evicted from his bachelor lodgings: "Those officers at the camp took over the Hortonville Hotel. John had to give up his old rooms there" (14).

Janie, written only months after American entry into the war, is impressively early in picking up the scent of two wartime domestic issues. One is male uneasiness about women's emergence from their housewifely duties to take an active (even if still circumscribed) role in the war effort. Mrs. Colburn serves on local committees to foster relations with the army base and with the local Fighter Command, whose job it is to spot potential enemy aircraft. Her husband, concerned that his daughter, Janie, has been written up in a magazine for organizing a teenage necking party, chides his wife, "It's all your fault Lucille. If you'd spend more time on your children and less on these war thingamajigs! In the last war it was the men who left their homes" (15–16). But one can see that what is a risible comment in 1942 will resurface two years later in Rose Franken's *Soldier's Wife* as a very real anxiety about the effect of altered gender roles for women brought about by the war. One can sense, too, that the enterprising younger female generation embodied by Janie will not grow up to be like the two mother figures in the play, the one a subservient wife and the other an erstwhile Southern belle and overbearing mother (a forerunner of Tennessee Williams's Amanda Wingfield).

The other social issue to surface and be anticipated in *Janie* is that, during an era when many women married soon after graduating from high school, the teenage girls in the play begin to replace traditional prospective spouses, the hometown boys, with the boys stationed at the army base who come from all corners of the United States. The implications for families remaining geographically close to one another and for future American demography are clear. *Janie* also challenges the restrictive social stance of an older generation opposed to a party Janie throws for the soldiers. The play recognizes that the boys at boot camp will soon be men at war, some of them never to return from battlefronts. Janie's reply to her parents' consternation about the party invokes a compelling combination of incipient feminism and poignant recognition of World War II realities:

> COLBURN. Now, have you anything to say for your self? . . .
>
> JANIE. Oh, yes, Father. I've got my own point of view about this.
>
> MRS. COLBURN. Be respectful, Janie.
>
> COLBURN. I never heard anything so outrageous in my life. You can't have a point of view. What is it? . . . You had two hundred soldiers careering around in here.
>
> JANIE. But where those soldiers are going, they won't be careering around, Father. And my point of view is—maybe some place where they're going, they're going to look back and say, "That was kind of a swell party we had that night in Hortonville." (111)

In short, beneath a conventional *Junior Miss–* and *A Date with Judy–*style comedy, one can recognize the beginnings of the social fissures World War II was to bring.

Three weeks after the opening of *Janie,* the team of Howard Lindsay and Russel Crouse, who had written the 1939 runaway success stage adaptation of Clarence Daly's *Life with Father* and produced the 1941 hit *Arsenic and Old Lace,* opened its comedy *Strip for Action* (30 September 1942), starring Keenan Wynn and comedian Joey Faye at New York's National Theatre. Like several other comedies produced during the war years and allegedly about soldiers, *Strip for Action* ultimately has very little to do with the military or the war. The comedy is set inside the Bijou Theatre in Maryland, and its zany, metatheatrical plot concerns Nutsy (Keenan Wynn), a drafted burlesque comedian who manages to engage some civilian friends employed in burlesque and to co-opt the army in order to stage a strip show for the entertainment of the troops. Although occasionally offering a satiric look at the satyric proclivities of men in the military, *Strip for Action* is largely an excuse for putting strippers and comedians on the Broadway stage, perhaps in defiance, as Gerald Bordman suggests, of Mayor LaGuardia's prohibition of burlesque in New York City.[48] Indeed, the idea of subverting and of co-opting authority is part of the fun of *Strip for Action*, for Nutsy manages to get approval for his show from one of the high-ranking officials of the War Department. And the stiff, censorious general in charge of the military camp becomes a comedy "straight man" in spite of himself when he precedes the raising of the burlesque show curtain with instructions, delivered deadpan, to his soldier audience:

> As you were! Men of the 202nd Field Artillery, you've come here tonight to see a show—a burlesque show. It has been arranged for you by the War Department. These are my orders: During the show I want no whistling, no stamping, nor rude remarks made to the actors, no throwing of any articles on the stage. You're going to see a lot of girls in the show—and you're going to see a lot of them. Now I know you haven't seen many girls lately—but when the show is over, you will leave the theatre by the front door. And I don't want any of you around the stage door. Don't try that because you won't get away with it. I'll be there myself. (189)[49]

Enhanced by the acknowledged wartime removal of men from the usual society of women, *Strip for Action* seems little more than the age-old conflict between authority and saturnalia, with an onstage audience of men on active duty dressed in their uniforms and well-endowed women "stripping for action."

The Doughgirls, written by Joseph Fields and directed by George S. Kaufman, which opened at the Lyceum Theatre (30 December 1942) three months after *Strip for Action*, can also be seen as a piece of lightweight comic relief for an American audience feeling the stresses of combat and casualties during the year that followed Pearl Harbor. A madcap comedy in the style of Kaufman and Hart, *The Doughgirls* seems to have been just what audiences wanted; consequently, it ran for a record 671 consecutive performances, not closing until 29 July 1944. As in *Janie*, *Strip for Action*, and many other military-inflected comedies of the period, *The Doughgirls* has nothing to do with the geopolitical, ideological, and combat issues of the war. It does, however, point out a range of domestic issues stemming from the changes the war brought to American social life.

The hotel room shortage in Washington, already noted in *Janie*, provides the backdrop for *The Doughgirls*. The improbable comedy centers around three couples who find themselves unexpectedly sharing a single hotel suite in a Washington hotel. By sheerest comic coincidence, the three women who end up in the same hotel room with their "spouses" turn out to be old friends, and it is soon revealed that none of them is legally married to the man who has brought her to the hotel.[50] Edna is with Julian, who has been separated from his wife for several years but is not yet divorced. He is in Washington because he and a Soviet chemist have found a way of producing artificial rubber for the army. Vivian is with Colonel Harry Halstead, who is reluctant to get married because of the uncertainty that the war has brought to American life. And Nan is with a military pilot, Tom Dillon, but, since Nan's divorce has not been finalized, she and Tom are not yet married. To this farcical mix is added Sylvia, Julian's mercenary wife; Brigadier General Slade, who has an eye for pretty women and who hires Vivian to take dictation; and Natalia Chodorov (played by Arlene Francis in a much-acclaimed performance), a gun-toting Soviet army sergeant and a comical take-off on Garbo's Ninotchka.[51]

What is impressive about *The Doughgirls* is its implicit but rather clear acknowledgment of the early stages of the American sexual revolution and the way it is given momentum by the war. In an earlier period, the play's three leading female characters would have been frowned upon and stigmatized as fallen women, but in Fields's comedy the pre- and extramarital relations are quite acceptable, even to the point of characters' playing fast and loose with military regulations.[52] Nan, for example, explains her relationship with Tom:

This fella, he's an aviator—well we fell in love, ya might say, on the spot. But I didn't have my divorce yet from the fella to who I was married to— well, this here flyer got stationed at Bolling Field and I went to live with him as man and wife— . . . Well, it seems he signed some papers for the Army, accepting money for a wife, which was me—but which I wasn't at the time. And I ain't yet. (36)[53]

In its own way, *The Doughgirls*, amid farcical situations that pile up exponentially, daringly takes for granted the sexual arrangements fostered by the war.

Another madcap Broadway meringue, which opened at the Longacre Theatre on 5 May 1943 and ran for over a year (497 performances), is Phoebe and Henry Ephron's *Three's a Family*. The Ephrons in later years were to write *Take Her, She's Mine* (1961) and numerous film scripts. In *Three's a Family*, they reiterated the comic device of *The Doughgirls* and, invoking the wartime premise of a housing shortage, engineered a farce in which too many people reside in a small New York apartment.[54] As an extension of the housing problem, one moment in *Three's a Family* provides a nice insight into the 1940s baby boom. When Sam Whitaker, the father of the family in the Ephrons' comedy, is questioned about the wisdom of his son Archie's impending fatherhood, given the uncertainty of the war years, Sam replies:

There are mighty few things in the world today that makes as much sense as that. And Archie's not the only one. There are thousands like him. They're twice as much in love with their wives as they would usually be, because they have half as much time. They're trying to jam a whole lifetime of love into a couple of months. When you get a situation like that, you're bound to get a lot of babies. . . . A baby gives them a stake in the future—Gives them something to fight for, and something to come back to. So what you think is a lot of half-baked, foolish kid stuff makes as much sense as the *United States Constitution and the Twenty-One Amendments.* (55)[55]

The rest of the comedy is pure froth and wartime comic relief.

A far more compelling and insightful comedy, though one that ran for only fifty-three performances, is Edward Chodorov's *Those Endearing Young Charms,* which starred a dashing Zachary Scott and opened at the Booth Theatre on 16 June 1943. In *Those Endearing Young Charms,* Chodorov writes a 1940s comedy of manners with the Restoration *beau monde* replaced by an American world at war and with Etherege's Dorimant and Harriet or Congreve's Mirabel and Millamant reconfigured as a rakish Lieutenant Hank Trosper and a witty Helen Brandt. Typical of comedy of manners, the intelligent repartee exchanged by Hank and Helen marks them, we realize, as destined for one another. We recognize, too, the play's two other characters, Jerry and Mrs. Brandt, as, respectively, modern versions of the dull, unsuccessful suitor and the older generation "blocking" character.

Those Endearing Young Charms is noteworthy for the way it emphasizes and dramatizes two important wartime social issues. First, there is the frank presentation of Hank Trosper, who is a navigator on a bomb squad about to be sent to the Pacific and, as he sees it, probable death. The audience is made simultaneously to understand Hank's calculated randiness and yet to reject it. Cold-bloodedly and cynically, he wants to grab his sexual pleasure with Helen because a few days hence he will be in combat with a good chance that his plane will be shot down and that he will die in action over the Pacific. He explains his sexual pragmatism to his friend Jerry, whose position in the army is not likely to bring him into combat or face-to-face with death:

> Do you know what the life strength of a bomb crew is? . . . What are you kicking about? Drill? Canned milk? You've got a ninety percent chance of mustering out. You're right about Helen—she's something to remember. The expectancy of a bomb crew is figured in minutes. You're wasting your time appealing to my heart. I left it on the statistical chart in the War Office.[56]

He adds dispassionately that if he has to, he will even marry Helen if that is the only way he can bed her before he departs the following day for combat, "She isn't going to chase me out over the Pacific, is she? I didn't invent this, kid—it happens every day. If I die like a hero—the government will send her my medal—and a pension. If I pull through—[*Picks up the money*] They say this is great stuff for heart trouble" (63). Hank's unabashed *carpe diem* attitude surely represents an aspect of sexual mores during the war. As one looks back on 1943 wartime morality, Edward Chodorov's presentation of it in *Those Endearing Young Charms* is illuminating, even though it very likely hurt the play's popularity with Broadway audiences who wanted to see servicemen as Galahads imbued with romantic love and not driven by lust and pragmatism.

Even more significant and stunning is Chodorov's presentation of women. By comparing a mother who made marital and sexual decisions during World War I to a daughter who is a making them during World War II, Chodorov deftly points out the changes in female gender roles and values from one generation to the next. In 1918, Mrs. Brandt opted for a circumspect and a conservative view of marriage that led to a not unhappy but pedestrian domestic relationship. In 1943, that is not the right choice for her daughter, Helen:

> MRS. BRANDT. Jerry's father wanted to marry me—before he left—Yes, he did—He was a soldier—he wanted very *much* to marry me. And at the time—so did I. But there was something else to consider—something much more *important* than the way we felt—
>
> HELEN. What?
>
> MRS. BRANDT. The chance that he might never come back. . . .
>
> HELEN. Were you ever sorry, Mother, even for a minute—that you *didn't* marry him—and wait? Truthfully—truthfully—?
>
> MRS. BRANDT. How can you ask such a question? Of course I wasn't sorry. It was a very lovely, very sweet thing—but if it couldn't be—it couldn't be. I met your father. We were engaged a year before we were married. And we never had an unhappy day. . . . Some of the girls I knew *did* marry soldiers who had to leave right away—and who didn't come back—or who came back cripples—or even worse—
>
> HELEN. But a lot did—most of them *did* come back all right, didn't they? And then both people had the wonderful feeling of having done their jobs—and it was over—and they'd earned each other. Mother, I don't mean you were wrong in Nineteen Eighteen. I adored Daddy and I wouldn't have had you marry any other man. But you can't "play safe" or *plan* like that today. There isn't any such thing. It's all so different now. (52–53)

Chodorov makes clear that the conflation of the women's movement and wartime exigencies serves to create new women like Helen, independent in income and thought, who expect equality in marital and sexual relationships:

> HELEN. Mother, you were happy with Dad—if you mean you never had a quarrel. . . . But, darling—you know he never really treated you as an equal? You were almost like—a kind of housekeeper— . . . Oh, I know he loved you, and you meant a lot more than that to him—but, Mother, you

couldn't tell by looking at you both. *Really* you couldn't. I never heard you talk about anything but the shop—and the shop—and bills and money—and, if you didn't you went for days without hardly one word to each other. Dad talked his head off—but not to you. I remember wondering when we had company, why the men left the women—right away—and got together in one corner, as though they thought you weren't fit to talk about anything . . . (54)

Indeed, what draws Helen to Hank is that he treats her as an equal, argues with her, and even comes to accept her opinions.

Helen shocks her mother—and in all likelihood Chodorov's 1943 audience—when Mrs. Brandt asks her, "Did he [Hank] admit why he wanted you to go to his hotel room?" and Helen replies, "He didn't have to. And he didn't try to give me a fake reason for it, either. And I like him for that" (55). Moreover, she poignantly provides the wartime context for her position:

Two girls on my floor whose husbands have been killed—and another whose brother is in the Merchant Marine, and she hasn't heard from him in a year? And that girl, Edith, I brought up here last week—whose father is a doctor in the Navy—and she doesn't know what's become of him—and there are lots of people whose men are all over the world—All they do is live from day to day—Do you think it would make any difference to them whether I or *anyone* slept with a man? (77)

Despite their banter and hard-bitten pragmatism, despite the fact that love-making precedes declarations of love, Hank and Helen are meant for each other, do fall in love, and do make commitments. As Hank leaves for the air war in the Pacific, he concludes, "Say, I might not be such a screwed up pretzel as you think. I know what I'm fighting for—you don't have to sell me. Aren't you beautiful and nice? Well, if I'm fighting for you, I'm fighting for what's beautiful and nice" (91).[57] Its conventional ending aside, what is remarkable and important in *Those Endearing Young Charms* is the remarkable frankness with which it depicts the *carpe diem* sexual realities that flourished during World War II.

Half a year later, a smash hit comedy, *The Voice of the Turtle*, came along and picked up some of the issues raised in *Those Endearing Young Charms*, but softened those issues in such a way that it enjoyed unprecedented success with Broadway audiences. Written by John Van Druten and starring Margaret Sullavan and Elliott Nugent, *The Voice of the Turtle* opened on 8 December 1943 at the Morosco Theatre, eventually moved to the Martin Beck Theatre and then to the Hudson Theatre, and closed on 3 January 1948, more than four years later and well after the war was over.[58] Although it raised some eyebrows about premarital sexual relations, it allayed its audience's objections through its romantic charm. As Wilella Waldorf, the reviewer for the *New York Post*, aptly wrote of Van Druten, "An old farceur, he has a fine sense of timing and a feeling for good taste that shall quite disarm any squeamish member of the audience who may be inclined to feel a trifle shocked by the frankly sexy theme of the play."[59]

An important difference between Chodorov's and Van Druten's plays is that the somewhat strident and off-putting sexual self-assertion of Chodorov's heroine is replaced in *The Voice of the Turtle* with an ingenuous, questioning, and guilt-edged dialogue spoken by Van Druten's heroine, Sally (Margaret Sullavan), in response to her louche, sexually liberated, worldly-wise friend, Olive:

> SALLY. Well, it's not going to happen again. Sex, I mean. Not for a long, long time. Not till I'm thirty. It should never have started in the first place. . . . If I'd stayed home in Joplin, none of this would have happened.
>
> OLIVE. Don't they . . . in Joplin?
>
> SALLY. Olive, tell me something. Something I want to know. . . . Well, *do* ordinary girls? I was raised to think they didn't. Didn't even want to. And what I want to know is—don't they? They don't in movies. Oh, I know that's censorship . . . but . . . the people who go and *see* the movies . . . are they like that too? Or else don't they notice that it's all false? . . . Even in Shakespeare, his heroines don't. Ever. Juliet carries on like crazy about not. I don't know whether what Mother and Father taught me was right, or true, or anything. Were you raised like that? (18–19)[60]

Similarly, Van Druten replaces Chodorov's cad, Hank, who had been played by the dangerous-looking Zachary Scott, with a well-educated Princeton graduate bruised and made mildly cynical by a past love affair gone wrong, Sgt. Bill Page, portrayed by a wholesome and innocent-looking Elliott Nugent. When the play was made into a 1947 film, Ronald Reagan assumed the role of Bill Page. The review of a 2001 New York revival of *Voice of the Turtle* again suggests how Van Druten shrewdly softens the portrait of Bill Page: "Nick Toren, a slim young actor with a fine, resonant speaking voice and a rich-kid-brought-to-earth aspect that suits the circumstances of his character, is terrifically appealing in his balancing of the eager hedonism of a young soldier and the courtliness of a gentleman that he may not have known he possessed."[61]

Shrewdly, too, Van Druten allows Sally and Bill to fall truly in love and to spend one night in the same apartment but in separate rooms before allowing them, at the conclusion of the second of the comedy's three acts, to have sex and sleep together in the same room. Indeed, whereas in *Those Endearing Young Charms* Helen stridently casts off her mother's World War I–era morality and values, in *The Voice of the Turtle*, at the conclusion of the first act and a day before the couple finally fall into each other's arms and into bed, there is some dialogue between Sally and Bill that recognizes in an affable way that new times have produced new rules:

BILL. I was just remembering a novel I once read about life in 1910 . . . where the heroine was compromised because she was seen coming out of a man's apartment after dark.

SALLY. I guess things *have* changed. . . . although I don't know that my mother would . . . *quite* understand this. It's silly because it couldn't be more sensible. But there are a lot of people who still wouldn't believe in it. (59–60)

Likewise Bill begins the second act by having made his bed, percolating coffee, and squeezing orange juice for Sally. When Sally comments, "it's not a man's thing to do," Bill pointedly retorts, "You'd be surprised what a lot of men are doing nowadays" (66). In short, *The Voice of the Turtle* is and continues to be a successful romantic comedy that earns its success in part by positing, in an unthreatening and amiable way, the beginnings of a new American sexual morality enabled by the exigencies of wartime.

As both *Those Endearing Young Charms* and *The Voice of the Turtle* suggest, for a young serviceman with a weekend pass, there could be little time for the amenities given to romance and courtship. The marital or sexual point had to be reached quickly. A year after *The Voice of the Turtle,* such telescoping of romantic time is the yeast for the musical confection concocted by Betty Comden, Adolph Green, Leonard Bernstein, and Jerome Robbins, *On the Town,* which opened at the Adelphi Theatre on 28 December 1944 and packed the house for 436 performances.[62] And two weeks prior to *On the Town,* it was likewise a main ingredient in Norman Krasna's comedy success *Dear Ruth* (13 December 1944 at Henry Miller's Theatre). Chodorov's *Decision* daringly raises and explores a new wartime sexual morality, Van Druten's *The Voice of the Turtle* seeks to makes it acceptable, but *On the Town* and *Dear Ruth* duck the question of coitus. Reverting to traditional comic courtship, they are warm, "feel good" works that allow the audience to be entertained and to leave the theatre with their conventional moral attitudes still intact.

The American comedies produced during the years between Pearl Harbor and V-J Day point out changes in both sexual geography and time on the American home front. Servicemen frequently left behind their moral constraints when they left behind their hometowns to be trained at camps adjacent to small towns or at bases in harbor cities. Soldiers and sailors on leave or on weekend passes could also be seen everywhere in large (especially coastal) American cities, hoping to find romance, sex, or both. As becomes clear, furthermore, in plays like *Those Endearing Young Charms, The Voice of the Turtle, Dear Ruth,* and *On the Town,* the periods from wooing to wedding or from courtship to congress had to be fast-forwarded to fit the time frames of weekend passes and shore leaves. Furthermore, not unrelated to the changes the plays reflect concerning the sexual geography and sexual mores are the changes in the American vocational geography and the new possibilities and power afforded women. Premarital and casual sex had always been there and was startling only because it was coming out from under wraps. The idea of women taking over traditionally male vocations was a far more threatening matter. Perhaps that is why in Ruth Gordon's comedy *Over 21*, a female invading a traditional male vocational domain at the play's conclusion becomes as incongruous as a pickle slice placed atop a cream pie.

On 4 January 1944, *Over 21*, a comedy written by and starring Ruth Gordon and staged by George S. Kaufman, opened at the Music Box Theatre. Filled with then fresh and effective comic confusions, which nowadays have become situation-comedy clichés, *Over 21* charmed Broadway audiences.[63] The situation comedy is, moreover, much enhanced by physical comedy. The setting is a bungalow for officer candidates on the periphery of Tetley Field in Miami during the summer of 1943. The poorly equipped bungalow contains fixtures in odd locations, an idiosyncratic refrigerator, and doors and windows with lives of their own. The stamp of Kaufman is also visible, for *Over 21* has much of the feel of Kaufman and Hart's madcap comedies.

Underneath the high jinx of *Over 21*, there are two points of note. The plot of the comedy deals with the decision of forty-year-old Max Wharton, a prominent and influential New York newspaper editor, to enter officer candidate school.[64] His wife, Polly, a celebrated novelist and screenwriter, has chosen to accompany him to his basic training in south Florida during the summer and before air conditioning. Why does this affluent couple, he at forty and she in her late thirties, leave their comfortable existence and residences in New York, Hollywood, and the Hamptons to enter basic training in South Florida and move into a bare-bones bungalow? Max feels strongly that he must make a substantive commitment to the war effort beyond writing editorials for his paper. As his wife explains, "Because if we lose there won't be any paper. That's Max's main reason for being in the Army" (31).[65] Since Max is "over 21," he has an especially difficult time competing with the younger men who are better equipped than he to handle all the technical training. When Polly articulates this, it is Ruth Gordon's indirect way of making the public aware of how technically well-trained American military officers are:

> This'll give you an idea of what Max has to go through. . . . "The resultant of two vectors is defined as the single vector which will produce the same effect upon a body as is produced by the joint action of the two vectors." . . . And this is simply *nothing*. That's only one tiny unimportant little thing he has to learn. He has to learn everything in this whole book. And I don't know how many more. (30)

But the patriotic dedication to the war effort by this glamorous, "over 21" couple is the lesser of the two noteworthy elements of *Over 21*.

The more important aspect of *Over 21* is what it adds to the data the wartime plays of the 1940s—and perhaps especially the comedies—provide about the reconceptualizations of women's roles during the war years. In a sudden and unforeseen twist at the play's conclusion, the dilemma of what will happen to Max's editorial position on the newspaper after he successfully completes his training and receives his commission is stunningly resolved in the dialogue between Polly and Max's editor, Robert Gow:

> POLLY. Robert, you don't have to sell the paper. You've got help like you never dreamed of. . . . How'd you like help that's hotter than a pistol? The biggest ball of fire since Haley's [*sic*] comet?
>
> GOW. I'd like it. Who?
>
> POLLY. Me. Ever heard of her?
>
> GOW. You! Yuh, but, Polly, what makes you think you can do it? You never did anything like it before!
>
> . . .
>
> POLLY. Women never ran railroads or built airplanes or were welders before. . . . Look at the kids flying bombers and fortresses! Yesterday, they were cutting rugs at college! Men who never left their home towns before, today they're scrambling up those hills to Rome! . . . This is a world of changes. The waltz is on the wane, kiddo. You better oil up your joints or you'll turn quaint.
>
> . . .
>
> GOW. But the newspaper business, Polly—there's a lot to know.
>
> POLLY. Lamby, it's a luxury of the past to be doing something that's your business to do. So, once more into the breach, dear friends, and mama'll handle the home front! (65)

In this dialogue, so much out of keeping with the rest of the play's nonsense, there is a clear and concise evocation of several changes effected by the war. College boys became men and juvenile pastimes were put aside for the serious business of the war. Men were suddenly removed from regional American geographies and traditional vocations to find themselves on other continents and trained for new wartime jobs. And for women, the war brought radical occupational changes and new responsibilities. Polly herself will presumably move from genteel lady novelist to hard-bitten New York newspaper editor. As she so colorfully puts it, "mama'll handle the home front."

By far the most impressive and revealing wartime comedy was written by a particularly ingenious and, in her own way, daring writer, Rose Franken, a playwright who, perhaps because of her judiciousness, has been largely and lamentably overlooked by feminist scholars.[66] Rose Franken created what might be the

13. *Soldier's Wife* (1944). Frieda Inescort and Martha Scott. Courtesy of the New York Public Library.

single most important women's play of the war, *Soldier's Wife*, which opened in New York on 4 October 1944. While World War II was still raging, Franken foresees that the war will soon end and prognosticates ensuing postwar marital and gender problems.

Soldier's Wife centers on Kate Rogers, whose husband, John, went off to serve in the Pacific, leaving her behind as a male-dependent, pregnant woman. During John's absence, however, Kate has given birth to their son and begun to raise him. She has learned to do the things on which she had been used to depending on her husband: repaint furniture, correct the wiring in a lamp, and fix a temperamental radio. Left on her own, she has become able not only successfully but adroitly to manage her domestic and economic affairs.

When a wounded John is discharged from the army and returns to his now considerably less helpless wife, he experiences difficulty and male anxiety as he tries to get his new bearings, and asserts, "You're the sort of woman who ought to stay off a step-ladder and keep away from machinery even when you're not pregnant" (25).[67] Wisely, Kate recognizes that the war and the disparate experiences of men and women in that war have moved husbands and wives in new and unexpected directions. Their lives and gender roles will never be quite the same again, as she tells Florence, her widowed sister:

They're all going to come home with that look of having been through things we didn't know anything about. How are we ever going to make it up to them? He came in here as if he didn't belong, as if he weren't sure. . . . And then I started to show off about that damn fool lamp. It was the worst thing I could have done—it gave him the feeling I didn't need him any more, I could get along without him.

To this, her sister sagely replies, "But the war hasn't changed either of you, it's given you significance" (27). And John eventually realizes how the war has radically changed who women are:

JOHN. Both you and Florence have let me rant on about what happened to me—and neither of you said a word about what happened over here. Just a couple of strong women.

KATE. [*As a simple statement of fact*] Women have to be strong these days.

JOHN. And it scares the bejesus out of a man. We're coming home to women who've gone through their own kind of hell and who can take it the same as we have. Suppose I don't go back to fight. What do you need me for? The war's made a man of you—

KATE. [*Battling his hysteria*] John, it's sick for you to talk like that. I didn't want to learn to do without you, I *had* to!

JOHN. [*After a brief struggle with himself*] You're right, Kate. And the learning of it has been your quiet bloodshed. (44–45)

Still, when Kate is offered the chance to write a daily newspaper column, John feels the threat and sting of castration:

Last week we were just an ordinary married couple. Now Kate's got an earning capacity that makes mine look sick.—We're not the only ones it's happening to, though. There's a chap down at the lab who's got a punctured ear-drum and his wife is a Captain in the Marines.—A little farfetched, but the same principle. (119)

The resolution of *Soldier's Wife* is a problematic one. Franken essentially snatches power from men only finally to restore it to them. Nevertheless, for the men and for the audiences, there is a new recognition that male power is no longer absolute. Kate declines the daily column, announces she is pregnant again, and proposes that she and John buy a Newfoundland dog, leave New York, and move to the suburbs.[68] Contemporary feminists would doubtless disapprove, but in 1944, Franken wisely knew how to make her point effectively without offending either her audiences or her Broadway producers. Obviously what Rose Franken is rather shrewdly doing in her popular comedy is something very important: using comedy to educate audience members of both genders, but especially women, about what the end of the war, already imminent when *Soldier's Wife* opened, will mean for the readjustment of gender roles and the consequent revision of domestic partnerships.

VI

It is illuminating to see Franken's essentially comic material cast in a far more emotional way in 1943, a year earlier, by a promising and still relatively unknown young playwright just beginning to make his mark: Arthur Miller. On 31 December 1943, Miller's one-act play, *That They May Win*, opened at the Victory Committee of Welfare Center in Brooklyn. An agitprop play in the style of Clifford Odets's *Waiting for Lefty*, Miller's *That They May Win* presents Danny, a wounded husband who has fought in Italy, where he has killed twenty-eight enemy soldiers and received a medal for heroism, who returns home to his wife and new baby to discover that they are living in dire poverty because the army allotment is not enough to meet the cost of living.

The response to the family economic dilemma by Delia, the wife, reveals an amalgam of motives. Like Franken's Kate, Delia is a product of wartime feminism, but a feminism unwilling to threaten a husband's masculinity, and to this are added elements of both patriotism and sheer economic necessity:

> You don't understand, Danny, I *want* to work. . . . I do. Even if we didn't need the money. [DANNY *looks at her anew*.] I want to . . . I want to help out. I thought of it ever since you wrote how hard the boys were fighting, and everything about how they were trying so hard. I'd like to help out. I'm not kidding. . . . So I was thinking . . . you're not really cured yet. And maybe if you stayed home and looked after the baby, just till you could take a full-time job . . . well, I'd work. We could live on forty-two a week. We could just about make it nice. (54–55)[69]

Miller astutely tackles the intersection of gender politics, patriotism, and indigence by having Danny, in what seems like a face-saving move for his endangered masculinity, accept his wife's desire to work, saying, "I think maybe you ought to have a job. I just didn't want you working because you had to. I mean it's different this way" (55).

Suddenly and with a strategy worthy of his playwriting role model, Clifford Odets, Miller transforms his one-acter both dramatically and ideologically. As Delia and Danny face the dilemma of child care should they both wish to work, and Danny begins to raise his voice to his wife in anger and frustration, a Distressed Man from the audience shouts up to scold him for his tone. At that point, actors who have been planted in the audience wrest the play from the actors onstage to propel both the dramatic action and the point of view in a new direction. Danny and Delia have been blaming themselves for their indigence and experiencing the friction caused by the difficulties of becoming a two-income family in the face of wartime rising prices and price gouging by rapacious merchants. The men in the audience, however, radicalize the situation as, with voices that echo those in *Waiting for Lefty*, they angrily seek to transfer from Delia and Danny to the government the burden for the unjust economic hard times faced by the very families that have made sacrifices for their country:

> Listen! Don't it stand to reason in a democracy? The big guys have organizations to lobby for laws *they* want in Washington. What about the people waking up and doing the same thing? . . . We the people gotta go into politics. Politics is just another way of saying how much rent you'll pay; and how much bread, chopped meat and milk your food dollar will buy, and what you'll have to pay for Junior's new shoes! You have to go to those Senators and Congressmen you elected and say, "Listen here, Mister! We're your boss, and you have to work for us! Get us more funds for the OPA so there'll be money enough to see that price control is really enforced!" (58)

Remarkably, Miller places the power for social reform into the hands of the new breed of American women that the realities of World War II have produced. The play envisions a home front army of women who will be trained to be volunteers helping the OPA with price enforcement. To this idea, the audience member called Distressed Man quips, "the women I meet are all too dumb; most of them can't even spell July." But he is given Miller's stinging retort by the audience member character called Man Who Knows:

> They aren't dumb, my friend; look what they learned to do in this war. They learned how to weld, how to run a drill press, how to build a P-47, how to hold a home together while their husbands are away fighting to win the war, how to vote. And they're learning that women can fight in this war too, right here on the home front. Their army is the Consumers' Council and their machine guns are market baskets, and someday, when Johnny comes marching home, they'll be able to say to him, "Okay, soldier, I was a soldier too!" (58–59)

In this little-known one-act play, which is written during the depths of the war and which precedes *All My Sons* by four years, Arthur Miller impressively captures an important aspect of wartime economic and price issues. More important, whereas *Over 21* lightly touches on changing occupational and gender roles for women, and whereas *Soldier's Wife* discreetly brings to audience attention the new possibilities for women but quells their threat by having Kate return happily to domesticity, Arthur Miller's *That They May Win* unabashedly and directly celebrates revised female occupations, attitudes, and gender roles. Miller elevates women from the helpless "girl I left behind me" to an army of truculent women warriors, pugnaciously and ably waging fierce war on the domestic battlefront of economics and price ceilings. In short, the pronoun in the title of *That They May Win* is purposely ambiguous, referring not merely to the men at war but also to women and their ability to play an active role in both winning the war and winning equality with men. *That They May Win*, like *Soldier's Wife*, also suggests that after the war, things will be different from what they were for American women and in American families.

Postwar changes are projected as well in two impressive, revealing plays that opened just weeks after V-E Day. One, *The Wind Is Ninety*, looks back at the war and registers the pain of American families who lost husbands, fathers, and sons during the war. The other, *Foxhole in the Parlor*, looks ahead to the problems of servicemen returning from the war. And yet they both register new but similar end-of-the-war messages.

Opening on 21 June 1945, just six weeks after V-E Day, and closing, after 108 performances, on 22 September 1945, a month after V-J Day, *The Wind Is Ninety* is a healing play that puts American wartime casualties into a useful perspective for those who have suffered personal losses and for the American public more generally. Some of the play's power may derive from the fact that the playwright, Captain Ralph Nelson, was not only an actor and writer but also a U.S. Air Forces serviceman who had, consequently, known wartime grief first-hand from both the military and civilian standpoints.[70] *The Wind Is Ninety* is told from both of those perspectives. Starring Wendell Corey (in his first Broadway role), Kirk Douglas, Frances Reid (who had played Martha Jefferson in Kingsley's *The Patriots*), and the juvenile brother and sister actors Dickie and Joyce Van Patten, *The Wind Is Ninety* bears some resemblance to Anderson's *The Eve of St. Mark* in its supernatural or magical realism style. The spirit of the dead Captain Don Ritchie (Wendell Corey), an air force pilot who has been killed in action, returns to his family to observe them and help them cope with the news of his death. He is accompanied on his journey back to his family by the ghost of the Unknown Soldier of World War I (Kirk Douglas). Nelson creates for the audience an effective binocular perspective as it sees the impact of Ritchie's death on the posthumous Ritchie himself as well as on his parents, young son and daughter, and wife. One wonders how much the playwright, who is listed on the play's title page as Captain Ralph Nelson, vicariously projects himself into the role of Captain Don Ritchie.

Much of *The Wind Is Ninety*'s strength derives from having Ritchie, unseen by his family, onstage watching his family as they think of him, read his letters, receive the government telegram informing them of his death, and then react to that news. As he watches his family and as he is mentored by the Unknown Soldier, Ritchie hopes not just to help them bear his death but also to remain alive to them, guiding them into the future as they carry him in their hearts. The dialogue signals to the audience that the family onstage is Everyfamily, and that all Americans should be guided in the future by the cherished memories of those who gave their lives in the war:

CAPTAIN. They're just people, I suppose, like any others. But that's *my* father and that's *my* mother. That's *my* wife and those are *my* kids. Can you remember that feeling, Soldier? That's why I had to see them now. To help them, if I can, over the shock of learning I'm dead. It will hurt them. I don't want that pain over me. I thought—maybe, being here—I could help them some how. . . . Is there any way I can talk to them? Any way I can reach them?

SOLDIER. It's up to them.

CAPTAIN. If they only knew I was all right. That I'm not leaving them for good.

SOLDIER. You're alive still, if they'll keep you alive in their hearts. (31)[71]

The play poses the problem, however, of what Americans should keep in their hearts. Is it only to be the memories of the dead man when he was alive? More pointedly, the play asks the question, "Why did so many Don Ritchies have to die?"

With the war all but over, *The Wind Is Ninety* seems consciously to eschew the usual argument of men giving their lives in a just cause: to preserve American freedoms from the tyranny of fascism. Instead, the play very consciously focuses away from wartime ideology and moves toward a peacetime lamentation for what seems to be the innate pugnacity of mankind. Doc, Don Ritchie's father, reacts cynically and bitterly to the news of his son's death, saying to his now-widowed daughter-in-law:

Doc. I suppose we had it coming to us. From the moment of birth we lead a life of violence. The infant leaves the peace of the maternal womb. Strange hands grab it up and slap it to give it life. From that moment until the instant of death life is violent. I brought my son up decently, and he was a good son. Yet before he died, he killed too. I never taught him that. They gave him a medal for shooting down some men before they had a chance to kill him. And now, someone will get a medal for killing him! . . . We honor these men for the ribbons on their chests and the blood on their hands.

JEAN. Father Ritchie—remember why he fought—

Doc. For the things he believed? So did the men he killed. I honor my son, Jean. I honor your husband, your children's father, my wife's child. But the civilization that made the man—*No!* Is this the best we can do with five thousand years? (52–53)

Ritchie and the Unknown Soldier, in another key, ask much the same question but begin to give the audience an answer:

SOLDIER. How did you live your last two years? Why did you? Why did you die? Don't you want them to know?

DON. Do you know why?

SOLDIER. Eleven million men are fighting because they suffer one disease. Eleven million homesick men. But I don't know *why* they die. I don't know why you died—or I. I can't answer the mothers who ask on what altar their sons were sacrificed.

DON. Then why am I here?

SOLDIER. You are the one to answer that, Don. You and a million serial numbers on white crosses. A legion of dog tags clanking against the breasts of a million families. We're going to be a national conscience, Don. Disturbing, haunting, shaming what happened. Spitting on the way we died our only lives. A national—*no*—a world conscience. (76–77)

Ritchie, the dead son, husband, and father, does finally find his way into the hearts and future of his family. He will not be forgotten but will forever be close to them, imbuing their lives with his spirit and values. For the playwright, however, clearly the lives and deaths of Don, the Unknown Soldier, and all those whose lives were claimed in World War II are to be an abiding presence among all men and women, inspiring them to avoid all war in the future and thereby to end the waste of human lives that wars bring about. It is impressive that *The Wind Is Ninety* ends not on a note of triumph but with an appeal to the conscience of mankind to create lasting world peace in the future.

The day before *The Wind Is Ninety* opened, Elsa Shelley's *Foxhole in the Parlor* closed after forty-five performances. Opening at the Booth Theatre on 23 May 1945, two weeks after V-E Day, Shelley's drama already touches on postwar issues and even makes timely reference to the conferences that led to the establishment of the United Nations: Yalta (February 1945) and San Francisco (a month before *Foxhole in the Parlor* opened).[72] Returning home and the legacy of the war are the subjects of the play.

After his roles as the sensitive or disillusioned young man in Robert Sherwood's *There Shall Be No Night*, Thornton Wilder's *The Skin of Our Teeth*, and Lillian Hellman's *The Searching Wind*, Montgomery Clift was surely the perfect actor to star in *Foxhole in the Parlor* as Dennis Patterson, a soldier who has carried the dead and wounded from the battlefields of the war and emerged from a foxhole uninjured when his two close friends, standing next to him, had their heads blown off by enemy artillery. As a result of his traumatic experiences, Dennis returns home shell-shocked. His horrific experiences on the battlefield led him, as they had many soldiers during the war, to army hospitals for the mentally wounded. Now having been released from the army hospital and returned to his Greenwich Village apartment, Dennis remains emotionally high-strung: his hands tremble and he is despondently cynical and despairing about any hope for lasting world peace.

In the course of the play, Shelley combines two not unrelated issues: first, that men are returning from the war not only physically wounded but also mentally scarred; and second, that the servicemen returning from the war front have a special need to believe that their sacrifices were not made in vain. Shelley understands, too, that although families were prepared for soldiers to return with limbs amputated and in wheelchairs, they tended to be unprepared for the equally debilitating and challenging mental injuries. Nor were they fully aware that most such mental injuries could be successfully treated and healed, even as physical injures are. In *Foxhole in the Parlor*, Shelley implies, furthermore, that it will be the women's task to exorcize their men's wartime demons and nurse them back to mental health.

Shelley's drama compels her end-of-the-war audience to spend time with the psychologically bruised and understandably high-strung Dennis; with Ann and Tom, his sympathetic and artistic neighbors; and with Kate, Dennis's irritatingly unsympathetic sister, who can only label him insane and make plans to commit him to an asylum. Ann visits the army mental hospital, speaks to Dennis's doctor, and reports what she has heard. Through Ann's account, Shelley allows her civilian audience a vicarious glimpse into the ordeals that soldiers faced during the war, whereby the audience is able to move a step closer in understanding the terrible origins of the mental injuries experienced by returning servicemen:

> Oh, Tom, what I saw in that hospital I shall never forget! . . . They have thousands of soldiers there, young lads most of them . . . emotionally confused . . . upset by the terrors of battle.—Oh, poor Dennis . . . what he must have gone through! (29)

> When the shooting started Dennis was sent up as a litter-bearer. . . . The litter-carriers are right in the thick of combat. Carrying the wounded off *during* the battle. And the dead, too. . . . It seems Dennis was under constant exposure to artillery and air bombardment for eleven days . . . then was knocked out by this shell blast, and was taken to a field hospital, unconscious. When he awoke he was upset and tense . . . "his sleep disturbed with battle-dreams." . . . when he was well enough he was returned to duty. But shortly after that he was captured. "Was in a German prison camp for six weeks." . . . He escaped from the camp! . . . "After bayoneting all the German prison guards." . . . He and his buddy . . . a fellow by the name of Henry . . . made their way back to the lines together and rejoined their unit . . . Well—some months later Henry was killed in combat and died in Dennis' arms. Dennis wanted to carry him from the field, but was forbidden, because there were so many *wounded* men. He was ordered to leave his dead buddy lying there on the battlefield . . . So Dennis became

"agitated, and screamed. . . . ran about bewildered and exposing himself to the fire." (33–35)

Performed as it was between V-E and V-J Days, *Foxhole in the Parlor* alerted Americans to the reality that many soldiers would not be coming home in triumph simply to resume the lives they had led before the war and as though nothing had happened to them.

But *Foxhole in the Parlor* prepares its audience as well for the reality that soldiers would also come home imbued with idealism and with a need to see a world that had learned its lessons from the war. Shelley's drama is thus not merely about shell shock but also about the desire for world peace and for World War II to have had meaning. The published version of *Foxhole in the Parlor* appeared after the play had been performed and after V-J Day, so that the published play-text concludes with the triumphant announcement of the Japanese surrender. But even in the June before V-J Day, Shelley foresaw the end of the war and the consequent beginning of domestic problems as well as peacetime initiatives. Dennis struggles not merely with his psychological wounds but even more significantly with his driving desire to explain the need for world peace. He remembers his deceased comrade Henry, who was Jewish and who linked the idea of peace with the Passover ritual:

> That last night . . . Henry and I were in a foxhole together, waiting. We were to attack at dawn. Henry was Jewish and that night it was the first night of Passover.—So as we waited there in the foxhole, Henry told me the meaning of the Passover. And he told me that HOPE is the meaning of the Passover—hope of salvation. At one point of the feast, a vacant chair is placed at the table; a cup is filled with wine and placed in front of the vacant chair; they open the door and the prophet Elijah is invited to enter. Everyone watches the wine in the glass. If it is diminished, Elijah has been there and salvation is at hand . . . And Henry said when he was a little boy, he was always so sure that there was less wine in the glass; but salvation never came . . . And I thought to myself, when Henry had told me this, that *now* salvation MUST come! . . . This is my message . . . At the Peace Conference, you are to place a vacant chair . . . you are to open the door . . . you are to invite God Almighty to enter and preside! And you are to make a COVENANT with God about keeping the peace! . . . You have before you the holiest assignment ever given to man. The destiny of mankind. (54)

For Shelley, this is as much her message as the acceptance of postwar trauma and neuroses. Americans of the present, Shelley implies, will need to understand the scars of the immediate past while working to ensure that the past never happens again. Or, as Dennis himself exclaims, "We soldiers were promised that we were going to war to END WAR. We want that promise kept. . . . The peacemakers! They can lay the foundations for a permanent peace or they can fire the first shot of the Third World War" (73).

The final lines of *Foxhole in the Parlor* provide an apt conclusion, as well, to the abiding concerns of American wartime plays even as they simultaneously open a gateway to the new concerns that would inform many postwar plays. From the attack on Pearl Harbor to the conclusion of the war in Europe and the Pacific, however, the commercial plays on the American stage sought to keep American spirits high while training the thoughts of the audience on the dangers of the totalitarian fascist governments to which the U.S. stood in firm opposition. Plays such as *Tomorrow the World, Winter Soldiers, The Common Ground,* and *We Will Never Die* kept the evil of the enemy fresh in mind. The sacrifices and achievements of fighting men and women in the cause of their country and of democracy are the stuff of *The Eve of St. Mark, Cry Havoc,* and *A Bell for Adano.* The events of the war were put into historical perspective in *The Skin of Our Teeth, The Patriots,* and *Harriet.* The several fine comedies produced during the war provided not merely comic relief for dire newspaper headlines and tragic events but also suggested, in their way, what comedy always suggests: that the human spirit is irrepressible and that the *élan vital* cannot be conquered by tyrants and hard times. As the war drew to a close and Allied victory was clearly on the horizon, playwrights began to look to life after the war. For better and for worse, things would not easily return to what they had been in the 1930s. Men returning to civilian life and the work force and men returning physically and mentally scarred by the war would require special attention. Having done men's work during the war, women would not so easily slide back into homebound domesticity. And what of this country's race problems and lingering anti-Semitism? Most important, however, is the question *Foxhole in the Parlor* raises: How will society prevent World War III?

The commercial theatre was not the only theatre to address the issues of the war. A more complete picture of the relationship between drama and war emerges as we add the perspectives of government-sponsored theatre and radio plays to the wartime plays of Broadway. What emerges, too, is how significant a role theatre played in shaping the American consciousness during the war years.

THREE

The Dramatic Art of Uncle Sam: The Government, the Drama, and the War

I

On 14 June 1943, the reigning glitterati of the day—Eleanor Roosevelt, Mayor LaGuardia, the Duke and Duchess of Windsor—were at the 46th Street Theatre in New York to witness the Broadway production of five one-act plays written and acted by enlisted men. The performance, called *The Army Play by Play*, was the remarkable product of the U.S. Army and the genius of famed producer John Golden. In his introduction to the published version of the plays, Golden explains how, working with the Army Special Service Staff, he created the John Golden–Second Service Command One-Act Prize Play Contest, which garnered 115 original play scripts from American soldiers at army camps around the nation (x–xii).[1] A selection committee that included Elmer Rice and Russel Crouse chose the five best scripts. Golden asserted that staging the plays "became my patriotic duty" (xii–xiii). The five scripts chosen were mounted and presented on Broadway to raise funds for the Soldiers and Sailors Club. The opening performance earned $100,000, and the plays were subsequently staged for President Roosevelt at Hyde Park. They then opened officially on 2 August 1943 at the Martin Beck Theatre in New York, where they ran for forty performances and later were produced at theatres and army bases around the country.

One wonders what sort of instructions Crouse, Rice, and the others on the selection panel might have been given about the criteria for choosing scripts. One wonders, too, about the 110 scripts not chosen. Their whereabouts are, alas, not known, and it would be illuminating to know the issues they raised. But the five surviving and published scripts that comprise *The Army Play by Play*

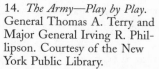

14. *The Army—Play by Play.*
General Thomas A. Terry and
Major General Irving R. Phil-
lipson. Courtesy of the New
York Public Library.

were written and performed, for the most part, by first-time playwrights and by
inexperienced nonprofessional actors, all drawn from the military. The five one-
acters that comprise *The Army Play by Play* thus provide a unique glimpse into
wartime military life and the war effort as it is seen and dramatized by servicemen. In part, Golden's enthusiastic and somewhat magniloquent praise is apt.
He writes:

> The plays that you are about to read are, in a sense, folk-plays, for they
> express, with disarming simplicity, the sentiments, the expressions spoken,
> listened to and lived through by our boys in the service—gleaned from
> their experiences as characters participating in the greatest drama the world
> has ever known. And so it is that these "little plays," born of this great
> Drama, tell the story, not of death, but of living calmly, alongside of death,
> and laughing at it. (xiii)

What is impressive about the five plays is the topics they cover and those they
do not. Did the selection committee favor particular issues? Is there a reason
the atrocities being committed in Europe and Asia are barely mentioned or that
the cultural diversity among the troops is a topic that arises often? We are not
likely to know the answers to these questions. It is, however, important to recognize that what we do have in *The Army Play by Play* is a government initiative
to use drama in shaping both civilian and troop attitudes toward World War II

and American involvement in that war. It is important, as well, to value *The Army Play by Play* as five dramatic artifacts that register in fairly undiluted ways the feelings, issues, and points of view of talented enlisted men who were encouraged by the military to express themselves through playwriting and whose plays were subsequently performed by ordinary soldiers rather than professional actors. Filled as they are with the personal and patriotic feelings of actual American servicemen, the plays were surely highly effective vehicles for boosting the morale of both military and civilian audiences. The scripts and the performances had the powerful cachet of presenting truth seemingly unvarnished by the gloss of pre-established agendas or prior professional training on the part of either playwrights or performers.

Of the five plays contained in *The Army Play by Play*, three center on barracks life. *Where E'er We Go* by Pfc. John B. O'Dea of Fort Lewis, Washington, is a lighthearted portrayal of restless soldiers cooped up at dull, rain-soaked Fort Lewis outside Seattle, waiting for furloughs and expecting to see battle action.[2] *Button Your Lip*, subtitled *A Farce in One Act*, by Cpl. Irving Gaynor Neiman stationed at Chanute Field, Illinois, is a comedy of mishaps and misadventures stemming from misplaced military records and the appearance of 1940s film star Dorothy Lamour in a USO entertainment being performed at the army camp. A third play, *Mail Call*, written by Aviation Cadet Ralph Nelson stationed at Americus, Georgia, is a more serious play located abroad *"somewhere in the Theatre of Operations"* (101) and centered around the kinds of mail GIs received while fighting for their country and more specifically around the decision of whether to open a package of food from home addressed to a deceased comrade and then whether to devour its contents.[3]

What is common to these plays and to others in *The Army Play by Play* production (as well as to the many plays and films of the period set in army barracks) is the portrayal of a military unit as an American microcosm, an American cross-cultural snapshot. Of course it is important to interject here that, during World War II, African Americans were segregated into their own units, and thus the supposed American cross-section is not a racial one. It is always purely white, devoid not only of African Americans but also of Asian Americans, Hispanics, and other persons of color. In *Mail Call*, for example, Johnson is from Oklahoma, Luckadoo, from Tennessee, and Spider, from Alabama; Abe Meitelbaum is *"a wiry little New York Jew"* and the son of a Jewish tailor, and Minnick is said to be *"representing New Jersey"* but with a girlfriend in Montana. The family of the deceased McKinley is sketched in as a generic American family, straight from a Norman Rockwell scene on the cover of *The Saturday Evening Post*. Here, as in so many wartime plays, is the strong message that this is a war that bonds all Americans from all walks of life to face a common enemy, one that threatens American democracy and the American way of life. The enemy poses a major threat, as well, to a national unity that is, paradoxically and ineffably, engendered by the country's ethnic and regional diversity. In many ways, then, dramas such as the ones in *The Army Play by Play* scripted an

American cross-cultural comradeship and worked to dismantle the regionalism and ethnic (though not racial) divisions that were a legacy of the Civil War and that continued to be a force in pre–World War II America. The cultural diversity valorized in these plays, moreover, set the stage as well for the breaking of barriers—including those of color—that took place in the postwar period and continues to this day.

In the two pure comedies contained in *The Army Play by Play*—*Where E'er We Go* and *Button Your Lip*—issues of importance leech into the humor of the scripts. The attitude toward women, for example, is revealing. During the war years, Broadway offered a plethora of comedies like *Dear Ruth, Janie,* and the Leonard Bernstein musical *On the Town*, depicting the ultimately chaste, moral love affairs and flirtations between military men and the sweet girls they pursue. In *Where E'er We Go,* however, the talk by the soldiers suggests, rather more realistically, a less-than-chaste attitude. "The way I figure it," one of the soldiers argues, "a dame's a dame. Just because she's a guy's wife, what the hell? At least then you *know* she ain't a virgin" (10). The casual attitude toward sex here and the impressively irate physical response to this from a married soldier make clear the abiding World War II issue of changing sexual mores and the recognition that wives and girlfriends were not always faithful during the long periods when their men were overseas or at military installations far from home. A related change of the social landscape is expressed when the furloughs are canceled and the men cannot make a trip to see their friends, girlfriends, wives, and families back home. One of them then comments: "Maybe you wouldn't have had as good a time as you think. Things are a lot different at home now. All your pals are in the Army or Navy—there wouldn't be any guys around—even the girls are working or in the WAAC's" (29). Underlying the comedy of *Where E'er We Go,* moreover, is the sensitive presentation of the anxiety soldiers in training experience as they wonder to which theatre of the war they will likely be shipped. Perhaps it was this combination of anxiety and comedy that led to *Where E'er We Go*'s also being selected for inclusion in *The Best One-Act Plays of 1943*.[4]

Button Your Lip is pure farce. It focuses on the similarity between officers and draftees as it pokes gentle fun at the ways in which officers can make mistakes. In *Button Your Lip,* the men cannot be shipped out without their records, which have been misplaced or lost. The Lieutenant and the Sergeant farcically keep cutting off Joe the draftee who is desperately but unsuccessfully trying to give them important information. Obtuse despite his Yale education, the Lieutenant, the highest-ranking officer, is made the butt of gentle comedy. Never allowing Joe to relay his information, the Lieutenant exits, saying that the soldiers will have to be processed all over again if the records are not found. Ultimately one learns that the records have been misplaced not by Joe the draftee but through the absentmindedness of a still higher-ranking officer, the Captain. The implicit message here is that the young recruits with limited formal education are frequently more worldly-wise than their older, more educated, and sometimes socially advantaged officers. There is no hostility here, but rather the various military ranks are reduced to a comical lowest common denominator.

Although it is Joe the draftee who is the comical center of *Button Your Lip*, another common soldier closes the farce:

> *Final piece of business. At last entrance of* CORPORAL, BRAD *steps out of shower room, sans bathrobe, but with a towel tied around his middle. We see that what he has been hiding under the robe is an elaborate "God Bless America" tattooed across his chest.* (97)

Thus, whereas a play such as *Where E'er We Go* stresses the unitedness of the United States, *Button Your Lip* implicitly shows a unity of American troops that transcends social class and the divisions of military rank by bringing together all the men under the banner—or in this case tattoo—of "God Bless America."

Closing of ranks and unity is played out in a more serious and moving key in *Mail Call*, in which the men, once again representing an American regional and cultural cross-section, write a heartwarming letter to the family of their dead comrade, even though they know he was overcome with fear and was killed running from the battle scene. The letter they write is technically true:

> "The enemy attempted a bridgehead on our beaches. The assault was heavy, and we fell back to our secondary defenses. It was touch and go, but when the time came, your son was the first on his feet, the first to run, without waiting for orders. It was his initial run that unified the rest of us.
>
> "A shell got him, but I was with him the moment he died." (133)

Replete with double meaning, the letter underscores for the audience the theme of troop unity that the armed forces and the plays selected for *The Army Play by Play* is clearly trying to promulgate. Indeed, what emerges rather pellucidly from these plays is the American government's eagerness, through the vehicle of drama, to provide models of national unity for both military and civilian audiences. For the Germans, by contrast, a major issue was precisely ethnic homogeneity and superiority. The United States covers a large geography containing an ethnically heterogeneous population, and in the 1940s it was still feeling the residual effects of the regional separations italicized only eighty years before by the American Civil War. The government, then, has an understandable interest in sponsoring drama which depicted men rising above regional, ethnic, and religious difference to unite in support of their country and its wartime agendas.

The obverse of this unity is felt in *The Army Play by Play* through the introduction of the theme of treachery and betrayal. Despite its overall farcical tone, *Button Your Lip* raises the question of treachery when Joe is mistakenly blamed for the disappearance of military records and is suspected of being a spy or saboteur. The important theme of treachery or subversion is palpably stressed in the works chosen for presentation and publication by the committee appointed by the U.S. Army to select the best plays in the Army playwriting contest. In *Pack Up Your Troubles* by Pfc. Alfred D. Geto of the 1204 SCSU HQ, 2nd Service Command, the serious and the comic awkwardly intersect. Two nervous army privates, Benson and Clark, perhaps modeled on the comedy team of Abbott and Costello, sneak out of their barracks before dawn to use a telephone booth that is off limits between taps and reveille. Their aim is to call a hospital on Long Island and learn the condition of Benson's wife, who is giving birth to their first child. The dialogue is one of comical camaraderie between the two men as they envision what might befall them by way of court martial and punishment if they are spotted. In the risible scene during which the two affably bungling soldiers try to place their long-distance call, they learn from the pay phone operator that they are just shy of the change needed for their call to go through. Suddenly juxtaposed to this phone booth comedy is the serious public address system announcement, "Attention! All posts! Be on the lookout for two saboteurs who have been traced to this Camp. If they are in fear of being apprehended they will probably make for the nearest telephone to try and get a message through!" (155). A nervous Clark abandons his friend Benson, whose conversation with the long-distance operator becomes one of farcical confusion:

> Operator! For God's sake I'm calling Major Mabel at the Dripwell Hospital, in Laussy, Long Island–I mean–Mrs. Hospital at the Maternity Colonel! No, I haven't got the fifteen cents! You owe me four nickels already! What? My name and address? What for? No, no, no! I don't want you to mail me the nickels, I want—Operator—you don't know what it means to be a father before reveille—(156)

As he hangs up the phone in frustration and presumably amid audience mirth, sounds are heard and Benson hides under a nearby desk, where he hears the conversation of Corporals Morelski and Jones, two Nazis posing as American servicemen.

To the comic, life-affirming, and family-affirming scene of a soldier attempting to call and inquire about the birth of his child, the playwright clumsily but nonetheless pointedly juxtaposes a life-destroying plot of sabotage and the projected mass killing of American troops. This evokes the fear of traitors in our midst, a theme that not only marks some of the plays in *The Army Play by Play* but is likewise found in many American plays written for the professional theatre during World War II. The frequent celebration of a united, patriotic front composed of ethnically and geographically diverse soldier-citizens and the threat of divisiveness and disaster at the hands of fascist operatives are clearly two sides of the same coin.

In Geto's *Pack Up Your Troubles*, the Nazi operatives passing as American army corporals, Morelski and Jones, embody the worst American fears of Nazis invading the U.S., taking American lives, and destroying the democratic way of life Americans treasure. Once again the theme of traitors in our midst is sounded. Morelski and Jones's plan is to cause mass destruction by blowing up a troop train:

> CPL. JONES. When that troop train blows up it will be the biggest military disaster on the Home Front in the nation's history!
>
> CPL. MORELSKI. The train is moving out on Track 12. That's not even a quarter of a mile away!
>
> CPL. JONES. As soon as the train passes switch 44—Boom!—and the Berlin School of Sabotage honors two more of its graduates!
>
> CPL. MORELSKI. I have to laugh, too, to think how we got into the Army!
>
> CPL. JONES. Only The Gestapo could think of something so clever like breaking into the draft board and putting cards from the dead file into the live one and then intercepting the mail! . . . And to think you get stuck with a name like Morelski!
>
> CPL. MORELSKI. Some Polish dog! But what about *you!* Jones! American hick!
>
> CPL. JONES. It will feel good, Mein Herr, to be Steuhmer and Waldhardt again! (156–157)

Later they project giving the army rookies "a Nazi education" so that, consequently, the "Fifth Columns in America will rise up!" (160). The operatives are of course apprehended before the troop train is destroyed, but one can feel in the text the concern of the army playwright about the possibility of enemy infiltration in the American armed forces. One can understand as well that the Special Service Branch of the U.S. Army chose *Pack Up Your Troubles* as one of the five plays to be presented nationwide at army installations and at civilian playhouses, for it was meant to put both soldiers and civilians on the qui vive about possible saboteurs and enemies of America in their midst.

The fear of subversion and the paranoia generated by that fear blend in striking ways with the theme of cross-ethnic and cultural camaraderie in what is by far the most effective play in *The Army Play By Play* collection: *First Cousins* by Cpl. Kurt S. Kasznar of 1204 SCSU HQ and Service Command.[5] It is dedicated *"to the thousands of foreign-born American soldiers"* (31). The play takes place in the hull of a German submarine, where four captured Allied soldiers are being held. Once again, as in *Where E'er We Go* and *Mail Call*, the soldiers represent differing backgrounds, as is made clear by their self-introductions during the prologue to the play. Mack Thompson tells the audience that he is an army sergeant from Long Branch, New Jersey, whose mother is a cook for a rich

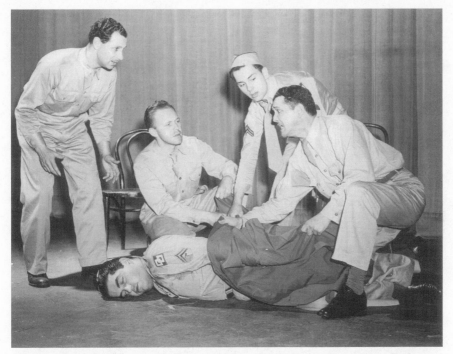

15. *The Army—Play by Play*. (Left to right) Cpl. David Reiser, Pvt. Melvin Parks, Cpl. Ralph Geisler, Sgt. Barry Thomson, Cpl. Kurt Kazner (horizontal). Courtesy of the New York Public Library.

family. He asserts in his opening speech, "I am glad to fight for my country" (33). Sam Cohan is a private from the Jewish section of Brooklyn and the son of a printer. He, too, asserts, "I am proud to fight for my country" (34). Clide Humphrey is British and with the Royal Navy. His entire family was killed during the Blitz. He ends his self-introduction with "I'll kill anyone that won't help me destroy the Jerries" (34). Finally, Private Karl Schramm says he was born in Chicago but is the son and grandson of German immigrants. Educated in New York, he was sent to Germany to attend university in Heidelberg and afterward worked there for I. G. Farben. When the war started, he explains, "Mama got excited and upset and must have made some silly remarks. Father had a hard time proving to the FBI that he was not pro-Hitler. I am an American and proud to fight for freedom and independence" (34–35). Their solidarity, however, is challenged by the extremity of their situation, and then challenged further when it becomes known that the commander of the submarine, Baron von Schramm (played by the playwright himself), is Karl Schramm's first cousin.

The confrontation of the two cousins enables Kurt Kasznar in *First Cousins* to demonize the Germans even more intensely than they are in Geto's *Pack Up Your Troubles*:

This miraculous coincidence pleases me greatly. It will save me much explanation and prove to you how ridiculous your efforts are in opposing the Reich. You people of America are not a nation—You're just a polyglot mixture of races, bloods, ideas, opinions and lower classes. How dare you aspire to equal the master race. Like my cousin here; every one of you that has lived under the weak influence of your hypocritical democratic regime.... But the moment when each one of the Germans, Italians, Spaniards, Austrians and our gallant yellow Aryan allies, the Japanese feels the call of his true country—your flimsy would-be nation topples like a house of cards. (47–48)

The aspersion cast here on the "polyglot" nature of American society touches on the very aspect of America that this play and the others chosen for inclusion in *The Army Play by Play* seek to extol. Indeed, the U.S. Army office sponsoring the Army playwriting competition and selecting the winning plays seemed especially bent on stressing the American championship of diversity as a radical contrast to the racial purity espoused by the Nazi regime.

A central issue of *First Cousins* is once more the fear of the traitor. Under the circumstances, Sam, Mack, and Clide begin to assume that Karl, who speaks German, French, and even Yiddish, must be a Nazi operative in an American uniform. Not knowing that Karl means to deceive his Nazi cousin, Karl's comrades and the audience believe their worst fears have been realized when Karl asserts:

First you must know that I have been working in America for the Reich since 1939. Enlisting in the Army was a chance. My work was made much easier after the Signal Corps taught me a few of their tricks. I have been fortunate enough to be responsible for the sinking of several transports off the Atlantic Coast. You guys are like a bunch of women. (54)

Later, in a surprise move, Karl stuns his German cousin by hitting him on the head with a pistol, assumes his cousin's voice, orders the submarine to surface, saves the day for the Allied soldiers, and proves his loyalty to the United States. In the play's final moment, Karl is asked what will happen when the submarine surfaces. He replies, "We'll raise a white flag and float right into Liberty's arms." *First Cousins* then concludes with Mack exclaiming, "ttnshun . . . Karl Schramm . . . American," as all the men salute and the curtain falls (60). In a neat and dramatically effective way, Kasznar's short piece seems to capture many of the themes in *The Army Play by Play* collection as a whole, themes that the Army wished to promulgate. *First Cousins*, like the other four plays, stresses national solidarity built upon a foundation of American ethnic diversity, a fear of subversion, a demonization of the Germans, American patriotic pride, and a powerful sense that an America imbued with moral rectitude will prevail over the forces of prejudice and dictatorship.

I I

While the Army's playwriting competition was going on and drawing its material from the pens of ordinary servicemen, the Army Air Forces committed themselves to a much larger, splashier theatrical project, one that pulled out all the stops in its attempt to use the stage for conveying an image of life in the Air Forces and the commitment of those who serve in that branch of the military to the American public. Early in 1943, General H[enry]. H[arley]. "Hap" Arnold, the Chief of the Army Air Forces (1941–46), summoned the popular playwright Moss Hart to Washington. Hart had by then made his reputation as the co-author, with George S. Kaufman, of three zany American comedies that had become—and are still—classics of the American theatre: *Once in a Lifetime* (1930), *You Can't Take It with You* (1936), and *The Man Who Came to Dinner* (1939). He had also written with Kaufman *The American Way* (1939), the serious, patriotic runaway hit play dramatizing the history of a German immigrant from his arrival at Ellis Island in 1896 to his life in Mapleton, Ohio, the loss of his son in World War I, and his own final moments protesting against fascist elements in his community.

It seems likely that *The American Way* inspired General Arnold to tap Hart for the job of writing what was to be an enormously ambitious, government-sponsored, patriotic, and theatrical undertaking: *Winged Victory: The Army Air Forces Play* (1943).[6] What the Army wanted was a play, ready for production in fall 1943, which would extol and promote the Army Air Forces, and which would raise money that would go into the coffers of the Army Emergency Relief Fund. To this end, the manpower of the army was put at Hart's disposal. All he had to do was come up with a winning, patriotic play about the Air Forces. Burns Mantle and Steven Bach both relate how Hart traveled on a research trip to scores of Air Forces training camps so as to learn firsthand what life in the Air Corps was like. It then took Hart three weeks to write *Winged Victory* and seventeen days to stage it (32–33).[7] Or as one writer put it, "From blue-print to happy landing on Broadway, *Winged Victory* was produced in the manner of a new super-bomber."[8]

In order to create another powerful, moving, patriotic play, Hart returned in *Winged Victory* to his fictional town of Mapleton, Ohio, where he had set *The American Way* and which by then was almost as well known to the theatregoing public as Grovers Corners, New Hampshire. This time his play was about the young men who eagerly join the Air Forces; their loyal families, spouses, and girlfriends; and the pleasures and pains of serving one's country in a time of need. *Winged Victory* calls for a very few female parts, but there are scores of male parts and an oversized orchestra and chorus, all filled by men in uniform. Indeed, over three hundred military personnel onstage and an oversized military band in the orchestra pit surely created in the audience a sense of national strength, patriotism, and the will to victory.[9] Several of the actors were already well-known stars, then serving under the Stars and Stripes, others were on the brink of making their mark as celebrities, and still others, who were drafted for the production but would not go on to postwar careers in the entertainment industry, would remember *Winged Victory* as their one glorious wartime moment in front of the footlights. When *Winged Victory* opened at New York's 44th Street Theatre on 20 November 1943, among the large cast of *Winged Victory* could be found, sometimes playing minor roles, such names as Sgt. Kevin Mc-Carthy, Pvt. Barry Nelson, Pfc. Edmond O'Brien, Pfc. Edward ("Ed") Mc-Mahon, Sgt. George Reeves (in the 1950s to become television's first Superman), Sgt. Ray Middleton, Pvt. Karl Malden, S/Sgt. Peter Lind Hayes, Pvt. Alfred Cocozza (alias Mario Lanza), Pvt. Lee J. Cobb, Pvt. Red Buttons, Pfc. Martin Ritt, Pvt. Alan Baxter, Pvt. Walter Reed, Pvt. Whitner "Whit" Bissell, Cpl. Gary Merrill, Olive Deering, Pvt. Alfred Ryder, Elisabeth Fraser and Pvt. Don Taylor.[10] The music was arranged and, in part, composed by Sgt. David Rose (later to become Judy Garland's first husband and to write "Holiday for Strings"). One of the assistant stage managers was Cpl. Emery Battis. Even before it arrived in New York, *Winged Victory* was a smashing success during its pre-Broadway run in Boston, and Burns Mantle recalls the long lines that formed at the box office when *Winged Victory* came to New York.[11]

At its center, *Winged Victory* focuses on three friends from Mapleton—Allan Ross, Frankie Davis, and Pinky Scariano—who want to become Air Forces pilots. Fanning out from that center are the men they meet as they train, their officers, and the panorama of American soldiers who fill the stage singing Army songs and providing the impressive human backdrop for the central action of the drama concerning the boys from Mapleton and their Air Forces comrades. Indeed, Hart creates a kind of double drama. The one is a human interest drama concerning the individual lives of Allan Ross and a few other Air Forces men. The other is less a drama than a platform for showing the Air Forces as devoted to the highest principles of American idealism and as a meaningful indicator of the strength of an American military that accepts no less than the best when it places men into strategic positions such as pilots and gunners.

The story of the American boys from around the U.S. who gladly serve, endure hardships, and sometimes die for their country is something an American audience would have seen before scores of times either onstage or at the movies. At the heart of *Winged Victory*, however, are its messages (sometimes prolix and grandiloquent) about the importance and excellence of the Air Forces. Clearly, Moss Hart's play is meant to encourage young men to volunteer for the Air Forces by making acceptance into that branch of the service appear to be the highest honor one could achieve. *Winged Victory* is meant, at the same time, to give the American public the highest confidence in the Air Forces and in the men who fly the planes. Typical is the long and baldly propagandistic speech given by Captain Parker when the new recruits are about to be given the ex-aminations that will help determine their eventual classifications:

The principle of classification, I believe, can best be explained by making the statement as follows: the United States Army Air Crew is the finest trained Air Crew in the world today. One of the contributing factors to the magnificent record these men are making is the fact that Air Crew demands and gets the very best from every member. Men, in terms of classification, that means this: We can only afford to take the cream of the crop. Air Crew demands and gets the very best. Not the second best; not the third best. It must have the best. (40)[12]

The repetition here of superlatives and of stating those superlatives as unquestionable facts is what, at its heart, *Winged Victory* is about. The essence of this speech is repeated in another key before a scheduled examination when an officer tells the recruits, and by extension the audience, "No elaborate statistical study is needed to prove that the man who becomes nervous and tense in critical situations—the man who gets rattled under fire—is not the man for Air-Crew training. We must stop him *here*" (43). At the classification ceremonies after basic training, the point is once more hammered home by Captain Parker:

Gentlemen, the training you are starting from now on is going to be the toughest, roughest, fastest course you have ever taken. Those of you who have no desire to fly should get out right now, because you are going to have to take a good deal of punishment, and it's only that real desire to fly which will see you through. You are going into the most thrilling, most adventurous and, yes, the most dangerous branch of the service. You will have to have nerve and guts—that determination to fly and a determination to undergo the stiffest, toughest training there is. You men are being trained for combat flying. If there are some here who have the idea you are going to get this training, wear a pair of silver wings and have the girls sigh as you walk down the street, you are in the wrong place. You men will be trained for one thing and one thing only—to fight. . . . Whatever you're classified as, be the *best!* When you walk out of that door this morning, make up your mind you are going to be the best. Fellows, you've *got* to be! (75–76)

As the scene draws to a close and one by one the men step up to receive their classification, the hearts of the audience cannot help but swell with patriotic pride over these men, these remarkable specimens of American military manhood, and over the excellence of the American armed forces.

The graduation exercises from flight school carry the patriotic agenda of *Winged Victory* several steps further. The stage is set with a flag and a bunting-draped graduation platform supporting a full military band playing a march (probably Sousa's *Stars and Stripes Forever* or Meacham's *American Patrol*). With the opening speech of the chaplain, Hart pulls out all the stops as he asserts the

16. *Winged Victory* (1943). Don Taylor as Danny (Pinky) Scariano, Edmund O'Brien as Irving Miller, and Karl Malden as Adams. Courtesy of the New York Public Library.

congruence between military victory and God's will, and he has the chaplain glibly echo the words and rhythms of Lincoln's *Gettysburg Address:*

> Dear Lord, before you stand the pilots of America. Aid them to preserve belief in You as the firm, stable, immutable Source of their rights and liberties. Grant them victory, O God, for they are freedom-loving men. In granting them victory, You fulfill their resolve that liberty, true and universal, shall not perish from this earth. Dear Lord, for these things do our Airmen sacrifice, for these ideals do they wage war, for these they will achieve victory. (124–125)

The speech then deftly opens out to embrace the theatre audience as the chaplain concludes, "May the efforts of these men, and all the other men of our Armed Forces, keep the homes of our nation secure unto the day when Thy peace shall reign over all the earth" (125).

During the course of the play the young men make sacrifices: one of them is not selected to be a pilot, one of them must return for duty instead of going on a honeymoon, and one of them is killed. Their wives and sweethearts are role models of American wartime womanhood as they bravely await the departure of their men for the front and as they bond in support of their men and with each other. The message of proper behavior conveyed to the women in the audience of *Winged Victory* is pellucid:

> HELEN. All the things this war is about—I know them—but they're names—they're just names. Roosevelt—Churchill—London, Washington, Berlin, Moscow, Tokyo—they're something I read in the newspaper. They're not real to me. Bobby's smile and his voice, and the way he looks when he's asleep—that's real—that's my whole life—and he's over there across the bay and soon he'll be gone—and there'll be nothing-nothing. As if he'd never been. . . .
>
> DOROTHY. We're not alone. Somehow—I don't know why that helps—and it will you too, Helen, after a while. In this hotel, in every hotel in town, I guess, in a room just like this, there are women like us—waiting—feeling the way we feel—thinking the same things tonight. (174–175)

The men bond as well and even more strongly, for they bond not merely with one another but with the American ideals and with the hoped-for future of the country.

Toward the close of the play, Hart has his main character, Allan Ross from Mapleton, Ohio, and his friend Irving Miller from Brooklyn explain in unvarnished terms a visionary idealism that allows Hart to make *Winged Victory* far more than a public relations play for the Air Force. The remarkable amalgam of sentimentality and patriotic vitality in Allan and Irving's dialogue would surely imbue all but the most flinty audience member with tear-stained pride and love for the U.S., its men in uniform, and its overall mission for world peace and global prosperity:

> ALLAN. If only people learn something out of this. . . .
>
> IRVING. You know what I've been thinking, Al? Don't laugh at me now—I'm no philosopher. But I got to thinking there's a meaning to all this. When the war is over everybody is going to have the biggest chance in history. . . . To make the whole world over. Why not? Is it too much to ask after what we're doing?
>
> ALLAN. No—no, it isn't Irv. I'm a different guy from the kid who sat in that back yard and waited for a letter a year ago. It's more than just growing up. I'm different inside. . . . I've got a different idea of the world than I had a year ago. There's no boundaries in the sky. I wonder if they realize that back home.
>
> IRVING. Maybe. Maybe not. But there's something different on the way. We got to believe that or I can't keep fighting. And I'm glad I'm young

and alive and I'm gonna be part of it. . . . I don't know nothing from big words like International Law and Tariff Controls, but I do know that too many nice people in this world are ignorant and hungry. They're not just names to me now—they're people. And guys like us know how small the world really is.

ALLAN. That's it, Irv! That's it exactly. The world's got to be ready again for pioneers. Not just discovering new lands and oceans, but to make the ones we know about *work!* You're right—this is the biggest goddam chance in history. Because if it doesn't add up to that—Frankie died for nothing. (191–193)

In a sense, Moss Hart, writing in 1943 during what was arguably the worst year of World War II, enunciated not merely America's sense of the war's meaning but the sense of a global mission that later dominated the American national sense of self during the second half of the twentieth century. Here was a case in which drama and the tools of drama shaped American thought in significant ways. It is no surprise, then, that Gerald Bordman reports, "The play ran for six months, then toured widely, earning millions of dollars for the Army Emergency Relief Fund."[13] It is easy now, decades later, to fault *Winged Victory*, as Steven Bach does, for its sentimentality and unabashed patriotism.[14] But the U.S. was two years into the war. Families were in mourning for sons dead or missing, men were returning from the battlefields wounded and maimed, and there seemed to be no end in sight. What could be more appropriate or welcome than to mount, on a large stage and with scores of actors and musicians, the undiluted, unabashed, uplifting patriotism of *Winged Victory*, which foregrounded the physical and moral strength of American troops, suggested in its very title that victory was imminent, and encouraged a war-weary populace to rededicate itself to the struggle? Karl Malden, who was one of those scores of actors, recalls in his memoir, "Civilians thrilled to the sight of three hundred young men in uniform."[15] *Winged Victory* may not be the most sophisticated of dramas, but were it judged solely in terms of its national impact and popularity, it would, like Hart and Kaufman's earlier *The American Way*, surely be considered a strong contender for "the great American play."

III

The government directed *The Army Play by Play* and *Winged Victory* toward both military and civilian audiences. The shows were produced in New York and traveled elsewhere with a cast of professional and nonprofessional actors. The War Department and other government branches, however, also provided dramatic entertainment, but aimed exclusively at American troops and not at civilian theatre audiences. These entertainments were to be staged at army camps not by a designated, well-rehearsed cast, but by servicemen themselves for their own local diversion and amusement. The government merely provided the scripts and in some cases instructions for production and advertisement. Beginning in 1942, soon after the bombing of Pearl Harbor and American entry into World War II and continuing during the course of the war, the U. S. military issued a series of *Soldier Shows,* which were largely scripts and ideas for troops to entertain themselves with skits, quiz shows, blackouts, reviews, and games.[16]

Two of these volumes were USO camp shows titled *"At Ease."* The first of these was a collection of comedy sketches and blackouts, *"For use,"* as the title page reads, *"exclusively in* MILITARY AND NAVAL ESTABLISHMENTS *By personnel of the* ARMED FORCES OF THE UNITED STATES." The open-ended exclusive copyright for these volumes was not to expire until "six months after the cessation of hostilities," whenever that might be. The USO (United Service Organization), founded in 1941 by President Roosevelt, not only brought professional entertainers to American troops stationed at home and abroad but provided material, such as that in the *"At Ease"* volumes, for performance by the troops themselves for their own entertainment. A commentator in *Theatre Arts* astutely wrote:

> To soldiers, a show written by their buddies takes on a much deeper meaning than the artistic or entertainment value of the show itself. It is their show, written for them, produced for them and applauded by them. It's a wonderful feeling to sing a song that your pal in the next barracks has written especially for you and your buddies. It's a personal thing, not something that's come to you third hand. It's a personal thing because the chances are that it concerns a subject which only soldiers know about. In other words, it "belongs," whereas similar material from the "outside" is, at best, a good imitation.[17]

The government in issuing dramatic material to the troops obviously also understood the truth of this statement.

The first USO volume is titled *Comedy Sketches* and is largely comprised of blackouts and reprints of comic sketches from 1930s radio shows like *Baby Snooks* and from the comedy sketches on Morey Amsterdam's radio broadcasts.[18] What seems important is that almost no sketch bears on the war or wartime issues. Rather, they lead the soldier-actors and their audiences back to a peacetime world when laughing at the follies and errors of others either provided a sense that all was well or offered healthy comic relief from the often grim realities of a country in the midst of the Depression. Most of the sketches are innocuous, though one does wonder about the inclusion of George S. Kaufman's well-known one-acter, *If Men Played Cards as Women Do,* and five other imitations of the Kaufman model written by comedian Morey Amsterdam, *If Men Acted in Barbershops as Women Do in Beauty Parlors, If Men Attended Fashion Shows as Women Do, If Men Gave Showers for Grooms as Women Do for Brides, If Men Went Apartment Hunting as Women Do,* and *If Men Went Christmas*

Shopping as Women Do. In all these, men satirize women by taking a traditionally gender-coded, masculine situation and comically italicizing gender difference by using risible feminized language. Thus in that very male preserve, the barber-shop, we have the following feminized dialogue among the men:

WILLSON. [*Sits up beaming*] Hello, men. My, but you two look stunning!

MORGAN. How can you say that? You know my hair is a sight. [*Takes off his hat to prove his point*] But yours! Stafford and I were just saying how—er—unusual you look in your new windblown.

WILLSON. [*Flashing a big smile*] It is striking, isn't it? But I'm letting it grow out. [*Runs a hand through it*] I'm sure I'll look better with it "page-boy."

TAYLOR. Don't you dare touch it. [*Combs it again*] Your hair looks just darling as it is. . . . Now, how about your eye-brows? Think they need a little arching? (94–95)

The opening stage directions for *If Men Attended Fashion Shows as Women Do* give an indication of how these sketches were intended to be played. They read, "*All characters play the sketch in a normal, manly manner. The humor results from the fact that men are speaking words and thinking along the lines of women and not from burlesquing their actions or voice inflections*" (98). Still, in light of Allan Bérubé's research and of the anecdote Arthur Laurents relates in his autobiography concerning the all-male production of Clare Boothe's *The Women* at Fort Aberdeen, Maryland, one can but speculate about what gay subtexts and revelations may have emerged when these USO-promulgated *If Men . . .* sketches were produced.[19]

It is, however, the second of the two USO volumes that is especially startling to the contemporary reader. Titled *Minstrel Shows*, it contains two full scripts for minstrel entertainment.[20] The tacit assumption for the volume is that the USO entertainment is meant only for the white soldiers in the then segregated U.S. military. This minstrel show volume includes not only script material but instructions on how to create blackface makeup using a burnt cork and how to apply it (10–11). It includes as well the descriptions of the four comedians or "end men" who are to play the black roles. They are called Ephus, Asbestos, Chinchilla, and Macbeth. The descriptions of the four men represent very unsettling racist portraits. That of Ephus, for example, reads as follows:

End Man #1, whom we have called "Ephus," is the small, meek, nervous type. His nervousness manifests itself in many ways, such as: occasional stuttering and stammering; quivering of the lower lip; rolling of eye-balls;

trembling of body; and difficulty in having his vocal chords function when he is especially frightened. (9)

The other descriptions are likewise inflected with the markings of racial inferiority. Explicitly used as reference points for those staging these USO minstrel "entertainments" for white troops are the mannerisms and language employed by characters in the then very popular *Amos and Andy* radio show.

The minstrel scripts themselves are, as one might expect, a mixture of song, dance, and comedy. Their intended racist humor derives largely from the speech patterns of apparently not very bright black men using the poor grammar of stage black English while enacting the kind of comedy based on the presumed naïveté and inferior intelligence of dark-skinned subalterns. These minstrel shows affirm, as well, a white America's prejudiced, false assumptions about black lifestyles. In one monologue, for example, a black-faced minstrel telephones heaven to speak with Uncle Tom. The conversation closes on the following note:

> Well, it must be awful nice up there, just sitting around all day, listening to those comics like me and eating fried poultry—[*Listens*] Huh? [*Registers surprise*] You don't eat poultry?? [*He is horrified*] You're not allowed to eat chicken up there? [*Almost pleading*] Not even one little innocent drumstick? [*A look of bewilderment covers his face for an instant*] Uncle Tom, are you *sure* you're in Heaven??? *CHORD BY ORCHESTRA.* (50)

In another comic routine, a black soldier explains why he has just spent time in the guardhouse, "We wuz in a mock battle and the enemy was coming toward us and our captain yells at us, 'Shoot at will!' And I don't know which one *was* 'Will', so I shot our top sergeant!" (77). When the mirth subsides, the white soldiers who have laughed at this routine have had reinforced through comedy the reasons that the very thought of having black soldiers in their unit would be not just ludicrous but dangerous. The texts of these army minstrel shows are not hard to deconstruct, and their implicit message is that blacks are subaltern and stupid, and that it is good for the safety of all that they are remanded to segregated units.

What is so impressive here is that in 1942, the two volumes of USO materials foster both racial and sexual stereotypes. And, ironically, they are distributed to the very troops engaged in a war against ideologies of racial supremacy. Indeed, the official, government-sanctioned use of minstrel material serves not merely to valorize and enshrine racist archetypes but implicitly to endorse a belief in both the inferiority of African Americans and the need for keeping them segregated. Segregation and notions of racial inferiority were not dismantled in the armed forces until after the war. It was not until 28 July 1948, when President

Truman issued Executive Order 9981, that racial segregation was at last brought to an end in the American military.

I V

More impressive than the USO volumes, however, for both their length and their pointed material, are the government-issued scripts for three War Department original musicals designed for production by the troops themselves at army camps around the nation: *About Face! Hi, Yank,* and *P.F.C. Mary Brown.*[21] The music (and possibly some of the lyrics) for all three of these now little-known musicals were written by the then not yet famous Pvt. Frank Loesser, who was, of course, to achieve renown after the war for *Guys and Dolls, The Most Happy Fella, Where's Charley?* and *How to Succeed in Business.* It is indeed surprising that *Hi, Yank, About Face!* and *P.F.C. Mary Brown* are essentially missing from the annals of American musical comedy. Even Susan Loesser fails to mention them in her biography of her father.[22]

Irving Berlin's entertaining World War II revue *This Is the Army,* a revision of the one he wrote during World War I, is well known, especially in its 1943 film version, but the three still virtually unknown Frank Loesser shows for the armed forces have more than mere entertainment value. The Soldier Show "Blueprint Special" of *About Face!* is the product of a constellation of remarkably talented individuals. Graced by a comical cover drawing from the pen of the then already well-known cartoonist Al Hirschfeld, *About Face!* contains music and lyrics by Frank Loesser assisted by Pvt. Hy Zaret, T/Sgt. Peter Lind Hayes, Pvt. Jerry Livingston, and Lou Singer. Many of the sketches are by the gifted comedy writer Pvt. Arnold Auerbach. The talent collected for this show is truly impressive. Hayes (1915–98), who had also appeared in *Winged Victory,* was an actor, comedian, and singer who would star in several Hollywood films and become a television celebrity (often appearing with his wife, Mary Healy) in the 1950s and 1960s. Jerry Livingston (1909–87) is one of the great twentieth-century American popular songwriters. His "Mairzy Doats" (1943), written approximately the same time as *About Face!* was a runaway smash hit, as was his "Fuzzy Wuzzy." He went on after the war to write the musical score for Walt Disney's *Cinderella,* the theme music for the television series *77 Sunset Strip,* and the popular song "The Twelfth of Never" (1956). In the decades after the war, Hy Zaret and Lou Singer frequently teamed up as lyricist and composer respectively. Together in the late 1950s and early 1960s, they composed a series of recordings called *Ballads for the Age of Science,* which were sung by Tom Glazer, Dorothy Collins, and Marais and Miranda. They wrote the score, as well, in 1947 for *Patrick Henry and the Frigate's Keel: A Musical Legend by Howard Fast* (Decca no. DA-522) and the popular song "Young and Warm and Wonderful" (1958). Zaret is best known as the lyricist for the often-recorded song "Unchained Melody." Arnold Auerbach (1912–98), who wrote many of the sketches in *About Face!* had already written some of the script for the George

17. *About Face!* Cover illustration by Al Hirschfeld. Courtesy of Indiana University Libraries. © Al Hirschfeld. Art reproduced by special arrangement with Hirschfeld's exclusive representative, The Margo Feiden Galleries Ltd., New York. www.alhirschfeld.com

Gershwin film musical *Lady Be Good* (1941). In the course of his career, Auerbach wrote comedy sketches for Milton Berle, Fred Allen, and Al Jolson; with Arnold Howitt he wrote the script for the Harold Rome musical *Call Me Mister* (1946), and together with Howitt and Moss Hart he produced sketches for the musical revue *Inside USA* (1948). He was also a writer for the *Sgt. Bilko* television comedy series, and in 1955 he was one of a group of writers who garnered an Emmy for the comedy series *You'll Never Get Rich*.

Together, these talented men were largely responsible for the series of sketches that make up *About Face!* The sketches spoof army life and include very funny scenes about an army psychological examination (22–24) and a lecture for soldiers on sex (27–28). The high point of *About Face!* is the satiric scene in which a soldier receives his notice from the Civilian Selective Service, which threatens to draft him back into civilian life. In a comic reversal of those who challenged their draft notices for the military, the soldier here protests his civilian draft notice, and as a result is given some tests. First he is shown "a loud checkered suit on a hanger" and asked to identify it. Studying the suit, he pleads, "Gee, it looks familiar, I could swear I seen it before" (35). Shown "a tray with dishes and a large folded napkin," he again says he remembers them vaguely from his past but cannot identify them. When "A GIRL IN SARONG ENTERS . . . JOE LOOKS AT HER. HE IS PUZZLED. HE WALKS AROUND HER, LOOKS HER UP AND DOWN, TOUCHES HER CHEEK, THEN HER SHOULDER, THEN HE LOOKS

HOPELESSLY AT THE MAJOR." This scene ends with his saying to the major, "But Major! I've been in the Army for two years. [POINTS AT THE GIRL] What is it?" to which, before the blackout and curtain, the major replies, "How the heck do I know? I've been in for twenty!!" (35–36). Once more the government and the writers created a theatrical venue that allowed the enlisted men, both in the cast and in the audience, to release their tensions by having a laugh at the army and its bureaucracy, and it took their minds off the bloodshed that spanned two oceans. As part of the aim of pointing out the comical side of military life, Loesser and his associates wrote for the show "Gee But It's Great to Be in the Army," a humorous song that was to gain national hit status (14–15).

For *Hi, Yank,* Frank Loesser was joined by the talented Lt. Alex North, who after the war became one of Hollywood's most distinguished and sought-after composers, arranging the music for such films as *A Streetcar Named Desire, Viva Zapata! Spartacus, The Agony and the Ecstasy, Cleopatra, Shoes of the Fisherman, 2001: A Space Odyssey, The Rose Tattoo, Who's Afraid of Virginia Woolf?* and *Prizzi's Honor.*[23] The choreography for *Hi, Yank* was provided by none other than Pvt. José Limon, whose reputation as a dancer had already been established and who was, of course, to become after the war one of the truly great choreographers in American dance history. Once more Arnold Auerbach was the primary writer of *Hi, Yank*'s sketches as he has been for *About Face!*

Although *Hi, Yank* has no real plot, it centers around the figure of the Sad Sack, who first appeared in the Army magazine *Yank* and who was drawn by cartoonist George Baker. For decades after the war, Baker's *Sad Sack* was a regularly syndicated newspaper cartoon. For the script of *Hi, Yank,* Baker provided a comical cover with his well-known character and Sad Sack's equally well-known abusive sergeant. Baker's wonderful cartoons also grace the pages of the published play-text. The *Hi, Yank* volume contains not only the script but also Loesser and North's full musical score, Limon's precise choreography directions, designs, and instructions for set construction, costumes, lighting, and even an audience evaluation form.

Loesser and North's lively score heightens the comedy of the individual scenes, most of which consist of a genial satire directed at army life, especially as it is experienced by buck private Sad Sack. Surely the satire was a salubrious tonic to the soldiers who performed it and those who saw it performed. The comically harsh treatment that Sad Sack receives or the many military gaffes *Hi, Yank* depicts would undoubtedly have touched chords of familiarity for the soldiers in the audience. The servicemen could see that their boot camp experiences were not unique and that those experiences could be the object of both satire and laughter. One can imagine the sympathetic soldier audience reactions to the following exchange:

MIKE [THE SERGEANT]. You're not even smart enough to make permanent KP.

18. *Yank! The Army Show.*
Cover illustration by George
Baker. Courtesy of Indiana
University Libraries.

SACK. I am, too. Yesterday on KP I gave the cook a swell recipe. It's about me—Wanna hear it?

MIKE. No. But it's a long war. Go ahead.

SACK. You take one rookie, already green. Stir from bed at an early hour. Soak in shower daily. Mix with others of his kind. Toughen with PT and grate on sergeant's nerves. Season with rain, wind, sun and snow. Sweeten from time to time with chocolate bars. Let smoke occasionally. Bake in 110 degrees summer, freeze below zero in winter. Dress in khaki. Serves 130 million people. (6)

And there is a marvelously funny short scene that takes a comic poke at the multitude of military acronyms and abbreviations then in use (25–26). Loesser and North provide, as well, a delightful song, "Classification Blues," satirizing the Army's ineptness at translating soldiers' prewar experiences into appropriate wartime positions:

> I used to play the horses at Jamaica
> I made a million bucks before I quit
> So naturally the Cavalry is exactly where they put me

Where they put me!
Shovelin' it—

I got the Classification Blues
The Classification Blues
If they ever classified me right, that would be news
The somebody else's occupation
Living a life of aggravation
Oh what a lousy Classification Blues. . . .

I used to be the city health inspector
I knew the cure for every rare disease
So naturally the Medics is exactly where they put me
Where they put me!
Bend over please—(24)

The idea here is the same as the one that informs *About Face!:* an army that could laugh at its own foibles was an army a soldier could trust.

Amid the satire, Loesser and North provided two notable sentimental ballads that reminded the servicemen in the audience of the civilian life they had left and to which they would return when the war was over. *Hi, Yank* created an allegiance to the Army, and at the same time, the musical inspired allegiance to American domestic values. In the sentimental song "My Gal and I," a soldier sings about his sweetheart:

Once I used to worry about her
Every time we parted for a while
Now I'm never really without her
Flying with a proud and happy smile
To think that
My gal and I were once together
Yet she's beside me when the engines roar
And though we're apart I can't help feeling
She's closer than ever before. (17)

And *Hi, Yank's* feature number—requiring the most detailed set construction—is the heartwarmingly sentimental song "Little Red Rooftops," about a soldier's American postcard hometown (28).

The government's several intentions emerge in the last scenes of the show. Scene 13, the penultimate scene, depicts Sad Sack's comical revenge on his two mean-spirited sergeants. It is set, significantly, ten years in the future and after V-Day, and Sad Sack is now a multimillionaire. There are several embedded but very clear messages in *Hi, Yank:* that American victory is imminent; that the American rags-to-riches myth (embodied in Sad Sack's humble beginnings and failures but eventual social and financial success) is valid; and that in Sad Sack's postwar affluence lies the certainty that American prosperity will continue and prevail. Furthermore, as the curtain comes down on *Hi, Yank*'s final scene, the earnest and rousing song about the importance of serving one's country, "The Most Important Job I Ever Had," modulates into the reprise of "Little Red Rooftops." At that moment, the script once again emphasizes the wartime government's dedication to preserving the traditional American hometown and to the notion that when the war is over, America will return to a pastoral peacetime. Even the stage directions spell this out, instructing the producers of *Hi, Yank:*

> This is the finale of the show—the number that will set the mood for the audience as they leave. For that reason it must be spirited and rousing. It should not be allowed to drop or peter out. It must grow solidly to a solid finish. Be sure the musical number is well rehearsed and the lyrics clearly sung. Be sure this number provides a "lift" and sends your audience out feeling they've seen a good show. (43)

In the hands of talented composers such as Frank Loesser and Alex North and with the choreographic brilliance of José Limon, *Hi, Yank,* with its gentle satire, patriotic wartime spirit, and affirmation of home and family, was an important government dramatic undertaking.

Soon after *Hi, Yank,* Pvt. Frank Loesser teamed up with Capt. Ruby Jane Douglass, Pvt. Hy Zaret, and Arthur Altman to write *P.F.C. Mary Brown: A WAC Musical Review.*[24] In addition to its entertainment value, *P.F.C. Mary Brown* is an important work because it is one of the very few wartime stage works to focus on American women in the military.[25] Once again, the volume for the revue included not merely the play-text but a full musical score, lighting designs, set designs, a sample program, and Mary Schenck's imaginative costume designs.[26] In part, *P.F.C. Mary Brown* seems inspired by the catchy "First Class Private Mary Brown" song that was featured in *About Face!* and which reappears in *P.F.C. Mary Brown.* Moreover, one of the comic scenes in *P.F.C. Mary Brown* about issuing regulation WAC uniforms was likewise lifted from *Hi, Yank.* Although its disparate scenes are loosely connected, *P.F.C. Mary Brown* seems less a revue and boasts far more plotline than the other two musicals, and it nicely shows some of the concerns that brought women into the military, even as it provides a modest window into their life in the WACs. The subject was a timely one, since the WACs was a new organization formed in 1943 to replace the WAACs (Women's Auxiliary Army Corps).

Pallas Athena, the Greek goddess whose statues often depict her wearing a military helmet, had been used as the image on the WAC lapel pin. And in *P.F.C. Mary Brown,* the writers, a bit weak on their Greek mythology, begin their show with Pallas Athena leaving Mount Olympus and walking out on

Jupiter, who is incorrectly portrayed as her philandering and otherwise preoccupied husband, to join the WACs, where she encounters a number of comical
boot camp experiences.

In its comical way, the script may suggest why, like Athena, other married
women signed up to join the WACs:

> PALLAS. For year now I've been getting mighty sick of sitting around here
> on my pedestal while you go gallivanting around the Heavens.
>
> JUPE. You know perfectly well that an executive has to make a lot of
> business trips.
>
> PALLAS. [SCORNFULLY] Business trips! Every time you come back, your
> breath reeks of nectar! And what about that long golden hair I found on
> your toga last Saturday night?
> ... The trouble is, I need a change, and I'm going to get one. ... I'm
> going down to Earth and join the WAC's. (34)

Pallas's speech seems here to register a general female wartime discontent with
being homebound, whereas executive roles and travel freedom were granted exclusively to men. The military offered American men a newfound liberation,
and *P.F.C. Mary Brown* suggests that women also wished for a liberation of their
own. Pallas's cry of "I need a change" was surely one felt by many other women
in the early 1940s.

Scene 3 provides further insight into the motivations of those who joined the
WACs. The women sing a rousing song:

> In twenty-five words or less
> Why did you join the WAC
> In twenty-five words or less
> Tell me why you joined—(7)

The stanzas of the song are interspersed with disparate individual cases that
include the boredom of working at a secretarial job and then coming home and
being asked by parents to do dishes; the fact that the virile men are all in the
armed forces, leaving behind for dating only weaklings who tend to be looking
for a woman's material worth rather than her love; and, more positively, a hope
that being in the WACs can turn a girl into a modern, capable, self-assured
woman. But then the scene ends with all the women singing about the underlying and unifying reason they all joined up:

> In twenty-five words or less
> Here is the reason that we joined

For the Red, White, and Blue
To make this world a better place for you
For the Red, White and Blue
To make this world a better place for you. (9–10)

Illuminating here is the way World War II inadvertently created a nexus between a rather undifferentiated malaise with women's traditional gender roles and a woman's patriotic duty. The WACs offered women a new agency: they had the opportunity to serve their country, even as they were enabled to serve their own needs for liberation.

In the course of *P.F.C. Mary Brown*, women assume roles of control—impressive for the 1940s—whereby they can even pursue men rather than be pursued by them. In one number, they trade the traditional lady's Easter bonnet for a WAC cap. And in the musical's most satiric and remarkable scene, gender roles are comically and pointedly reversed when Henry, the civilian husband, comes to see his wife, Sue, on visiting day at the boot camp:

> HENRY. Just because I'm 4F doesn't mean I don't know something about the Army. [LOOKS AT HER SLEEVE] Still a private, I see. . . . It's awfully funny that Jean Bailey went in three months after you—and she's a corporal now. . . . Did you get the cookies I sent you? [SHE NODS] And the woolies? [SHE NODS] And did you write and thank Aunt Mathilda for that hand-crocheted ashtray? . . . Of course, it was no bargain moving back with mother. But I've met some nice fellows at the bandage-rolling class.
>
> SUE. Swell. [A LOOK AT HER WATCH] Well, I've got to run. [STANDS]
>
> HENRY. . . . Gee whiz, honey, you don't realize what it is to be an Army husband. Here I sit up all night on a crowded train, wait hours for a dirty hotel room, and now, when I do get to see you, you treat me like a camp follower! (27)

This scene is the converse of the *If Men Played Cards as Women Do* genre, and in its deceivingly simple reversal lies a new respect for—and affirmation of— women's capabilities as enlisted persons. Since *P.F.C. Mary Brown* was written for a military audience, it offers a lesson to both soldiers and WACs about the feelings of marginalization experienced by married civilian women whose husbands are in the service, and about how estranged and even alienated those in the service can come to feel toward the activities of their civilian wives. Indeed, the scene draws the line in the sand between those in the military and those at home, and then problematizes that division with preconceptions and misconceptions about gender roles.

The plot of *P.F.C. Mary Brown*, furthermore, has Jupiter reform and, following his wife's lead, join the Army. His superior masculine cynicism about Pallas and the role of the WACs takes a 180-degree turn, serving as the writers' cue to the male members of the audience. As Jupiter goes off to war, he sings:

First Class Private Mary Brown
She wore that uniform like a million dollar gown
Let the big guns roar, let me win this war
Cause I want to hurry right back, on the double, to
First Class Private Mary Brown
My wonderful WAC. (37)

The clever and sometimes sharply satiric olio of matters in the government-sponsored *P.F.C. Mary Brown* is one largely composed of patriotism, new attitudes toward women in general, and new respect more specifically for women in the military. As *P.F.C. Mary Brown* ends with the singing of "To see the dawn of peace tomorrow / We face the long night of war / As in freedom's name we serve the colors / The Women's Army Corps" (38), the audience—male and female—finds itself having begun the show with patronizing smiles at the girls in uniform but leaving the theatre with strong feelings of patriotism and respect for the American women in uniform serving the cause of their country.[27] Since *Pfc. Mary Brown* was directed by the government to servicemen and -women, it affirmed for the former the place of women in the military and valorized for the latter their commitment to their country's wartime cause.

V

That the U. S. Army should underwrite entertaining plays aimed at both the general public and at GIs and designed to inspire patriotism and positive images of armed forces is not surprising. Nor is the endorsement and sponsorship of dramatic vehicles and musicals for the entertainment of the troops. It is impressive, however, that the Army also used live theatre in a more consciously focused way, sponsoring drama designed not for entertainment but for didactic purposes. The Military Training Division of the Second Service Command at Governors Island in New York prepared dramatic training scripts that were released in mimeographed typescript form and presumably employed around the country. These scripts were used to train military personnel and educate them about preparedness, vigilance, and proper behavior. No authors are cited for these plays, and one wonders who wrote them, for several show effective dramatic techniques despite their heavy didacticism. What these scripts reflect, moreover, is an impressive trust by the U.S. military in the power of dramatic art, which can be effectively employed to shape the attitudes and behavior of both officers and enlisted men.

One such particularly poignant script is *Death without Battle*, which was used to warn of the need to use the Army-issued anti-malaria cream and mosquito netting.[28] In that play, soldiers have either skipped a training lecture on malaria entirely or have attended and now scoff at the mosquito cream they have been issued. By acknowledging the skepticism of its military audience and their resistance to training sessions in general, the script nicely uses its dramatic and didactic techniques to convert those watching from skeptics to believers. Under the guidance of Dave, who is distressed by the flippancy of his pals, there are flashbacks to Battista Grassi, the nineteenth-century Italian physician who did the pioneering work on malaria and the Anopheles mosquito. With his friends still resistant, Dave ends the play with a powerful parting shot, a letter telling him that his brother and several others became ill and died of malaria:

> WHAT DO WE HEAR BUT THAT THE REASON THERE WAS NO RELIEF FOR US WAS THAT AT LEAST HALF THE MEN THAT WERE TO RELIEVE US HAD COME DOWN WITH MALARIA, TOO. AND ON ACCOUNT OF WHAT DO YOU THINK??? ON ACCOUNT OF THE FACT THAT THEY WOULDN'T USE THAT MOSQUITO CREAM OR THOSE NETS. (11)

Drama and acting are used in *Death without Battle* to render the pathos of Dave's letter and the fortitude of Grassi meaningful to an initially skeptical or hostile audience. The play not only casts the heedless characters in the role of villains but, more important, can move an audience of recruits to take seriously their mosquito netting and antibacterial salve. Clearly the Army recognized that the magic of theatre can be more effective than lectures in a classroom setting.

Other plays in this didactic genre include *Stripes,* which is directed to military officers and meant to remind them of their responsibility as caregivers to the men who serve under them, and *The Eternal Weapon,* which unsubtly drives home the point that soldiers must recognize and value the importance of training, regardless of how much it may sometimes appear to seem like purposeless drudgery.[29] In the latter play, a soldier goes back in time and discovers the issues of preparedness and training in past wars. He then is projected into the future to discover his own death and those of seventeen others, stemming from his cavalier attitude toward training and his consequent lack of preparedness in battle. A Pfc. gives a didactic eulogy:

> No, these men here will not speak. How can they, when in the heat of battle his chance came to do the things he should have learned—when upon HIS knowledge of the arts of war his company in that vital moment fully depended—and he failed. He failed and dragged them with him. Seventeen men—seventeen good soldiers—seventeen futures now lie soundless—and in seventeen parts of America, seventeen families hang the death crepe over their hearts forever. . . . here lies the untrained soldier and around him lies his murderous work. (4.2)

Like many of the other training plays, *The Eternal Weapon* depicts soldiers questioning their chores and training and, consequently, slacking off on their responsibilities or cutting corners. This is then followed by a projection into a future in which the dire consequences of such behavior are made manifest.

Another forceful and moving example of these training dramas is *Ghost Column*, which is set on a Pacific island.[30] A battle that should have been an easy American win has, with many casualties, been lost to the Japanese. Why has this tragedy occurred? A court-martial inquest built around flashbacks provides the threefold explanation. First, lazy and flippant soldiers have allowed nails to be squandered and timber to be wasted, scoffing when they were instructed to save nails and wood from packing crates:

> Save nails! Save food! Save time! Save! Americans just ain't savers! Never were! . . . You think all this idea of saving means anything? It's just another form of discipline, that's all it is! All our lives we've been able to get anything we could pay for. And now all of a sudden, we gotta be tightwads! Do you guys really think there ain't enough to go around? Why, America is the richest country in the world! (10)

When the battle against the Japanese commences, a bridge must be constructed quickly for the American troops. But the bridge collapses for want of sufficient lumber and nails. Second, an unwell soldier refuses to see army doctors, denying his illness and insisting that it will pass. In the moments before the important battle, he has convulsions, pulls his trigger, and thereby exposes the American troops prematurely to the enemy. Finally, soldiers ignore the "Eat Fish A Valuable Food" signs. Avoiding and wasting the nutritionally sound meals served at the mess hall, they opt to sustain themselves instead on candy, gum, doughnuts, and colas from the PX. Consequently, for lack of vegetables and a balanced diet, one soldier falls asleep and fails to give warning during the battle and another contributes to the bloody American defeat at the hands of the Japanese because he cannot see well enough in the dark. The Inspector at the inquest concludes *Ghost Column* with the script's didactic message, one inflected with moving sentimentality:

> Because Corwin did not properly guard his health, because Bellows was a soldier whose extravagance was eventually to blow taps for some American boy; because Harlow and Sweeney wasted the food for which millions are starving—and through all this waste a massacre resulted— . . . And what was the one simple lesson they failed to learn? Saving. They did not know how to conserve their equipment, their health, their manpower—When they made the final desperate voyage into battle, the engagement and the lives of their comrades depended on one vital factor—Saving. . . . What those telegrams [to the families of the soldiers who died] should read is, "A certain soldier by the name of Corwin, or Bellows, or Harlow,

regrets to inform you that because he did not learn how to save—to conserve—because he did not heed the vital training lessons in America; he murdered your son—coldly—unmercifully—even before the Japs could get him—(33)

Ghost Column's loudly sounded themes of squandering and waste versus prudent conservation and of maintaining sound health practices are among those vigorously pushed by the government, not merely in this government-issued play and others, but also in government publications, advertising, and domestic propaganda.

One training play, *This Is Your Enemy,* stands out, for it reveals the hand of a rather skilled anonymous propagandist playwright.[31] It opens with force and panache as the stage directions tell us, "THEATRE IS COMPLETELY BLACKED OUT. THE SOUND OF MARCHING FEET SLOWLY INCREASING IS HEARD OVER THE LOUDSPEAKER" (1). This is followed by the command "halt" in German, and then a spotlight suddenly shines upon a pedestal marked with a swastika and upon which stands a young Nazi boy in uniform. In strongest terms he touts the strength of the Third Reich and the weakness of America and American democracy. His speech, replete with exclamation points, is clearly meant to set the audience's teeth on edge:

> The Third Reich—does that mean anything to you idiots?? We have conquered half the world and enslaved its populations! We have torn up your books, your religion, your culture and your ideology! Everything that your American democracy represents we are destroying, and next we will destroy YOU! . . . You driveling fools do not know the importance of perfect discipline in maintaining a fine machine of war. You call yourselves an Army! You *are* an Army! An Army of mongrels! A mixture of black, white, Protestant, Catholic and Jew! An Army that has risen from the cesspools of the world! . . . Since I was old enough to walk, I have held a gun ready to destroy your putrid democracy! There are millions like me, and you idiotic Americans have the audacity to think you are a match for our superior force! (1)

This is then followed by actual film footage showing Nazi soldiers on parade, close-ups of their enthralled faces as they listen to the impassioned shouted speeches of Hitler, and scenes of the destruction of homes and churches, the capture of Allied equipment, images of women's dead bodies, the theft of clothing from the corpses, and corpses sprayed with gasoline and set afire. These film clips are accompanied by continued inflammatory narration by the Nazi youth.

The playwright follows this potent preface with realistic scenes of discontented soldiers who yearn for action on the battlefront and find demeaning the seemingly unsoldierly tasks they have been assigned. They grumble and feel themselves mere shipping clerks in uniform because they are stationed stateside, far from the glories of combat, carrying out such mindless tasks as shipping paper dolls and pinwheels to the troops. The playwright renders the American soldiers with a remarkable feel for the language, slanguage, and speech rhythms as the dispirited men shirk their responsibilities, goldbrick, and malinger. The scenes of GI discontent are sneeringly punctuated by the Nazi boy's cynical, scornful, and triumphant remarks:

> Yah! You will never see combat! You are stationed in America doing work no different from civilians! You are not in the Army! You are underpaid civilians doing the work of a civilian without the freedom of a civilian! Isn't that the way you see it? Good! That is the way the Fuehrer wants you to see it, too! . . . Do you not watch the clock to be ready to leave your work exactly at quitting time? . . . Why should you drill? Why should you go on long marches-? Why should you take refresher courses in marksmanship and gas drill-? . . . What can you lose if the requisition is late? . . . No one depends on those silly requisitions you fill out. No one but the Fuehrer! Delay! He pleads with you! He knows what you are too stupid to see. He knows the combat forces completely depend on you Service Force soldiers to supply them with trained men and the necessary materiel. (13)

In the course of the play, this is countered by patriotic and didactic speeches in which the goldbricking soldiers are reviled, the importance of the service division is extolled, and the idea that this is a war to preserve American democracy is underscored (21–22, 28–29). The play ends, however, with a return to the Nazi boy, who tells the audience, "What you have just seen is, of course, your own propaganda," reminding them that America is a country of loafers, that "your lazy spirit is part of your American tradition . . . [and that] your nature is to delay!—to complain about everything that will speed your victory!" (30). *This Is Your Enemy* is indeed unabashed propaganda, propaganda leveled at servicemen and almost sure to instill pride—as well as a sense of responsibility and urgency—in working for the military at domestic supply posts instead of on the battlefield. The inflammatory figure of the Nazi youth and the anonymous playwright's firm grip on the dramatic medium ensure a powerful awareness on the part of the play's military audience that the war against the Third Reich is being fought at home as well as in Europe. The soldiers, for whose benefit *This Is Your Enemy* was produced, might well come away from the performances with a strong hatred for a demonized enemy and with powerful verbal and visual images that would remain with them long after their training period had ended. *This Is Your Enemy* and the other training plays are the government's attempt, through the means of theatre, to administer strong and memorable lessons to the troops, lessons in which stage pictures bring to vibrant life what might otherwise be the deadly prose of training manuals.

VI

The U.S. Army was by no means the only branch of the government that recognized in drama a powerful weapon for shaping the attitudes of Americans about the war and wartime issues. What might at first seem a most unlikely government sponsor of theatre also used drama to promulgate its wartime agendas. The staff of the Treasury Department during the war years commissioned and created dozens of plays for elementary schoolchildren, junior high school and high school students, and adults. The ultimate aim of all the Treasury Department plays was to promote the sale of War Stamps and War Bonds and to curtail American monetary squandering.

One must remember that during the Depression of the 1930s, many had lost their savings, financial instruments had failed, and financial institutions had gone bust. With this still very fresh in the minds and consciousness of Americans in the 1940s, asking citizens to invest in War Bonds was often a hard sell. The war, moreover, brought with it jobs and new prosperity, and, after a decade of Depression austerity, many Americans were in search of immediate consumer gratification and loath to defer that gratification by allocating part of their earnings for the purchase of War Bonds. At the same time, the war years brought the rationing of staple foods and the scarcity of material goods. Consequently, there were those ready to dedicate their discretionary money not to buying War Bonds but to hoarding clothes, meats, soap, razor blades, and other consumer goods or to obtaining scarce goods on the black market. Others felt that, with the entrance of the U.S. into World War II, the Allies would prevail and conquer quickly and handily, and that the war would soon be over. Why, then, should they stint on luxury items, save scrap metal, or buy War Bonds? The Treasury Department was worried that such attitudes posed a serious threat of inflation if Americans were willing to pay higher and higher prices for foods and other material goods that they suspected might become rationed or unavailable altogether. The great fear was that, at a time when the U.S. was vulnerable as it fought a bloody war on two separate foreign fronts, it might be further endangered if it had to fight runaway inflation on the domestic front as well. Thus, in response to the monetary needs of a nation at war and to the fear of a new inflationary post-Depression economic instability, the Treasury Department propagandized the responsibility of every American to save money, curb inflation, and share in the war effort by investing in U.S. War Bonds and War Stamps. And one of the principal instruments of that propaganda effort was drama.

Looking at these Treasury Department plays, it is revealing to see how particular groups are targeted, and in each case what propaganda strategies are employed and which issues are stressed. Cleverly, the Treasury Department targets American schools by creating a Schools-at-War program, complete with pamphlets, classroom activities, and drama programs for American youngsters from kindergarten through high school. The authors of the plays surely knew that the messages of wartime thrift and bond purchase would become a daily issue for the students as they read the play, rehearsed their parts over the course of some weeks, and then performed the material. They knew, too, that the audience for the plays would be not only the other students and teachers in the school but also a far more important target: the parents who heard their children rehearsing each day and who formed the adult and money-possessing mainstay audience for the children's plays.

Indicative of the War Stamp and War Bond drama authored for primary school pupils is *Squanderbug's Mother Goose*, which features Everyboy and Everygirl figures, Phil and Lis, who are led by a kindly neighbor, Miss Moppity, through the world peopled by modernized, wartime Mother Goose nursery rhyme characters. Here they encounter the villain of the piece, Squanderbug, who has grown fat on the money people squander when they could be investing it in War Bonds and War Stamps. He is, in short, the allegorical embodiment of a spendthrift, inflation-prone America.[32] Indeed, Squanderbug becomes a recurrent character in other Treasury plays meant for production at the grade-school level. In *Squanderbug's Mother Goose*, Lis and Phil begin by encountering Old Mother Hubbard, and one quickly sees where the play is headed:

> Miss M. Old Mother Hubbard
> Went to the cupboard
> For an Album of which she was fond.
> And when she got there
> She said,
>
> Old M. H. I declare! I've got enough Stamps for a Bond! (5)

When Lis and Phil ask about her dog, Old Mother Hubbard tells them he's in the Army, where he has enlisted in "Dogs for Defense. He's being trained for guard duty" (5). And when Lis asks, "But after all these years of getting him a bone, aren't you . . . well, sort of lonesome for him?" Mother Hubbard says she does not miss her dog ever since she's had her job, and Miss Moppity explains, "They don't know about your working on the swing shift in the airplane factory, I guess" (5–6).

Likewise, similar surprises occur when the children and Miss Moppity encounter Old King Cole, and the classic nursery rhyme is given a new wartime twist:

> Miss M. Old King Cole was a merry old soul,
> And a merry old soul was he,
>
> Lis. He called for his pipe, and he called . . .
>
> Miss M. [*Correcting her*]
> He called for his *purse*

And his money-roll,
And he called for his daughters three
And he gave his daughters
Some dollars and quarters,
And all his daughters cried:

DAUGHTERS. We'll rush right down
For some Stamps in town.
Hi, ho! How happy are we.

. . .

OLD K.C. Always glad to see young people getting in there, putting their shoulders to the wheel. Why, I'd rather see four-and-twenty Savings Stamps in my daughters' Books than four-and-twenty blackbirds baked in a pie . . . *any* day. (6–7)

When Phil inquires about King Cole's fiddlers three, he learns that one is in the Air Corps, one is in the Marines, and the third is in the Army, with King Cole commenting, "I couldn't let them go on amusing me when there was a *war* to be won" (7).

The propaganda of a play such as *Squanderbug's Mother Goose* continues to be transparent when Squanderbug is rejected, and when as Lis and Phil take their leave of Jack and Jill, those nursery rhyme characters bid them farewell with, "See you at the victory parade. Cheerio!" (12). At the conclusion of the play, Lis and Phil recapitulate the lessons of the didactic drama for their audience of schoolchildren and parents:

LIS. You know, Phil, I feel all different about everything now.

PHIL. Me, too. As long as the war lasts I won't care a peanut about driving out to the lake for a picnic.

LIS. . . . Let's start planning a Victory Garden, Phil . . . right away. . . . I haven't felt so good in a long while, or had so much fun. . . . Why, I bet I could even write an up-to-date nursery rhyme. . . .
Sing a song of sixpence . . .
A pocket full of rhymes . . .
We used to waste our money,

PHIL. Our quarters and our dimes.

LIS. But *now* . . .

BOTH. We'll both buy War Stamps,
AND KEEP UP WITH THE TIMES. [THE CURTAIN FALLS] (13)

Victory, savings, and the purchase of a financial instrument, War Stamps, unite in an amalgam of patriotism and economic good sense.

In a slightly different key, Sally Miller Brash's *The Magic Bond* creates a children's allegory in which a sad and troubled princess is saved by a palace page who lifts her spirits and makes her smile by fetching her a War Bond from across the seas in America. In the concluding words of the play, the lucky young page, now betrothed to the princess, exults:

> My Princess has her Bond safe in her hand,
> And I've had a chance to visit a glorious land
> A land with people determined to fight
> To keep love and liberty and all that is right,
> Let us all honor these Americans so true,
> Long wave their Flag . . . the Red, White and Blue! (7)[33]

The rescued princess is obviously a grim Europe rescued by an America devoted to liberty and freedom and willing to place its economic power in War Bonds which will at once ensure the rescue of Europeans and support American patriotism.

In one elementary school–level play by Mildred Hank and Noel McQueen, *We Will Do Our Share*, coins and a character called Bank-Roll, who are lying around the house, combine to help children buy War Stamps.[34] But in their far more sophisticated *Citizens of Tomorrow*, likely aimed at actors and audiences in the higher elementary-school grades, Hank and McQueen begin to spell out not merely the propaganda for buying War Bonds but appropriate wartime gender roles.[35] *Citizens of Tomorrow* is about five boys who, realizing that "V" is the Roman numeral for five, form a V for Victory club in the empty garage of a father who has sold the family automobile in order to buy War Bonds. With the help of older brother Bill, home on furlough, the boys organize their own form of wartime combat as Bill tells them, "collecting junk and paper and stuff to make the guns and supplies is fighting, too" (74). The boys reluctantly allow girls to join their club, after the girls complain of their exclusion and then offer to fulfill their gender roles, "We want to join The Victory Club . . . and [you] won't let us. Why, girls can do a lot—sew and knit and work for The Red Cross—and we can buy as many War Stamps as they [boys] can" (75).

In its final scene, *Citizens of Tomorrow* veers away from buying War Stamps and Bonds to touch on a rather different matter: the need for secrecy. The children ask Bill where he will be sent after his furlough, and he reminds them of the motto Loose Lips Sink Ships, urging them to adopt it as their club slogan (75). The playlet closes with Bill's instructing the elementary schoolchildren, "Now I've got to get to—wherever I'm going. I'll be working there, and you— well, you keep on working here. Not giving away secret information or spreading rumors. Salvaging essential material for war use, buying War Stamps every week. And doing all the other things necessary for Victory. A real Victory Club. . . .

You're—well, you're the citizens of tomorrow, you know; and I've just got a hunch that you're going to make this a stronger, more beautiful America than it's ever been before" (76). Of course once again the unambiguous message is directed to the adult audience of civilians, who are meant to cheer both their children's performance and the messages of the play.

Elementary schoolchildren were only one target of the Treasury Department's propaganda plays. The tone of these government-sponsored plays becomes more imperative and the messages more direct when the works are directed toward high school students, who would soon be eligible for enlistment and the draft, and who would begin their adult lives upon high school graduation. One can quickly see the change of tone by recognizing how Sally Miller Brash moves from the fairy-tale mode of her elementary school play *The Magic Bond* to her high school musical, *Star for a Day*.[36] In the latter, high school students await a movie star who is to make her appearance in order to help sell War Bonds and War Stamps. A whole show about the war effort on the home front is created in honor of the star's arrival. The high school girls prepare to sing a special number to the tune of "Sleepy Time Gal":

> We're wide-awake gals,
> And when this World War is thru'
> We stay-awake gals will all be singing to you.
> We hope Hitler will hang
> And all the rest of his gang,
> That's why we're stay-at-home, work-at-home, knit-at-home,
> Wide-awake gals!

To the sentiments embodied in the song, the girls' teacher, Miss Bennett, exclaims, "That's an excellent spirit. . . . You are truly ALL-AMERICAN girls!" (7). Notwithstanding the female authorship of the play or the appeal of the WACs during the war, in *Star for a Day* a woman's place was seen to be clearly in the home.

When the much-expected film star must cancel her engagement, the students take over so the show can go on. And one remembers that these same students are also on the brink of taking over leading roles in the adult community. In a sense, all the high school students are understudies for the adult roles they will soon enact. At the conclusion of *Star for a Day*, bonds have been sold and the entire school sings, to the Gilbert and Sullivan tune from *The Mikado* "Here's a How-de-do" (and without any sense of irony that *The Mikado* is set in Japan):

> Hitler is a fiend,
> He is mighty mean,
> Hirohito is a-flying,
> Mussolini is a spying,
> Let's BREAK up this scene!

Some triumvirate,
Some triumvirate!
Here's what we will do.
Here's what we will do,
Organize a special army,
Of our entire student body,
To protect our rights,
We'll show Hitler sights,
We're the kind who fight!
With our soldiers, and our sailors,
We'll defend our liberty,
And the Axis better run,
If the light of day they want to see,
For they can't win the war,
And we will give them more!
We've a lot to do today,
We must save the U.S.A.
Stamps and Bonds will lead the way,
Our land is here to stay!
Here's what we can do!
Here's what we can do!

For we're making history,
With a glorious victory,
Here's to OUR LAND,
It will ALWAYS STAND!
[CURTAIN] (13)

In a remarkably upbeat way, the demonization of the enemy leaders, the defense of American democracy, the complementary relationship of a professional and a citizen army, and the purchase of War Bonds and Stamps coalesce into patriotic fervor literally voiced by an entire high school population, directing the wartime message toward their parents and their schoolmates.

Far more serious in tone are two other rather moving Treasury Department plays for high school students, Walter Hackett's *For the Duration* and Howard Tooley and Carolyn Wood's *A Letter from Bob*.[37] Both plays (as the department's plays for adults also do) raise the conflict between, on the one hand, materialism and economic self-indulgence, and on the other hand, abjuring personal desires and gain in order to support the war effort. *For the Duration* uses as its main character sixteen-year-old Tom Hill, who is eager to spend his savings on skis and skiing lessons when his family takes its planned vacation in the mountains. By contrast, Tom's friends are investing their savings in War Bonds, and Ronald Batty, an English boy dating Tom's sister, is putting aside $18.75 of his weekly $20 allowance in order to buy War Bonds and thereby give both thanks and support to the country offering him sanctuary while his father serves in the RAF. Likewise, Curt Hansen, the Norwegian newspaper boy, now also sells War Savings Stamps to the customers on his route. Tom's father, who works in the shipyard, returns home to announce that their vacation is canceled because he is working on Sundays from now on to build Liberty ships:

> These Liberty boats we are building are well named, for they carry to our allies and to our own boys much needed supplies . . . food, guns, oil, ammunition, machinery, tanks and dozens of other vital, life-giving necessities. These boats are the connecting link between us and liberty. . . . To build a four hundred and forty-one foot Liberty ship it costs approximately one million eight hundred thousand dollars. Twenty-two hundred and fifty tons of steel plating go into it; and it takes twenty-seven thousand rivets to hold such a boat together. . . . It costs ten cents to drive a rivet into a ship. That means that each time such a rivet is driven, Uncle Sam has to sell a ten-cent War Stamp to cover the cost. You figure that an average riveter can drive one a minute and that there are twenty-seven thousand rivets in a Liberty ship, and you'll get an idea of what goes into the making of a ship. . . . to build ships you need money and manpower. A great many Americans can supply the money to buy Bonds. Men like myself can supply the manpower. And men like myself can also buy Bonds. (10)

The family then takes its vacation money and Tom takes his earnings and applies them to War Bonds.

Perhaps the most dramatically effective and hard-hitting of all the plays produced by the Treasury Department is Tooley and Wood's *A Letter from Bob*. In this play it is Mother who is the only sensible one in the family, and it is she who writes regularly to her son Bob stationed in the Pacific, where he flies a B-24 bomber. Bob's younger brother, Dan, the narrator of the play, looks back into his recent past and recognizes that he has been a foolish high school student bent on spending money frivolously. His sister, Jean, is angry with her boyfriend, who purchases War Stamps instead of spending his money to take her to the school dance. Dad is annoyed because he has been repeatedly asked—or as he sees it, badgered—to enroll his employees in the Payroll War Bond Plan.

Everything within this selfish, solipsistic family changes when a letter from their son Bob arrives. Bob's letter lucidly spells out the agenda of the play and of the Treasury Department:

> Seems like the whole family, except maybe mother, isn't even trying to do what they can to help me and my buddies out. I wonder if it's worth it all. Yes, I really do, even if I hate to say it. I thought Americans were proud of their common sense. What are you doing . . . playing games? This is a war! You say you're sacrificing. Sacrifice . . . don't give me that! Is it a sacrifice to defend yourself and your home and all the people you

love when they're all just about to be taken from you? . . . *It isn't sacrifice
. . . it's just common sense.*

. . . Do you realize when you're so indifferent to this whole thing that you
won't even sink a few bucks into Bonds and Stamps that you're playing
with human lives? They tell me the sale of War Bonds is $200,000,000 a
month below what the government expects and *needs*.

. . . Sure, you say, we get supplies here. But we see those planes come in
and we say, "Good, that's swell. But think what we could do with twice
that many . . . three times that many." Just ask a sailor who's had a ship
blown out from under him, because they didn't have a convoy. He'll tell
you how a ship could have been saved. Ask a man who's been adrift on a
little rubber raft, how the lives of all his shipmates could have been saved.
He'll tell you . . . by having enough protection to make it safe for them to
man that ship!! . . .

I don't know what you're doing over there. You must think this war is
the latest in outdoor sports. But let me tell you . . . this is no game! When
the fellow you ate dinner with last night doesn't show up for breakfast
after a raid . . . you don't have much patience with someone at home who
couldn't give up a movie, or a new coat, or part of *their* salary. . . . I don't
say this because we aren't willing to do our job . . . I'm telling you this
because you aren't willing to do yours. (9–10)

The letter is at once scolding and heartrending. Powerful and effective here is
the image of young soldiers and sailors dying valiantly for their country when
they might have been spared if only the folks at home sacrificed some of their
vanities. Audience members were surely meant to be so moved by the mingled
patriotism and sentimentality of this poignant speech that they would rush out
and buy War Bonds and Stamps. And cuing the audience, the erstwhile selfish
brother, Dan, and sister, Jean, change their ways and plan to invest in bonds
and stamps.

A Letter from Bob astutely recognizes that not everyone in the audience will
be affected by sentimentality. Some, still feeling the very recent economic hard
times of the Depression, would have fears about investing in bonds. Hoping to
address those fears, the playwrights present a skeptical Dad unconvinced by the
arguments of his son's letter. He remains recalcitrant, arguing that he feels War
Bonds are a risky investment. The counterarguments Dad is given are not those
of Bob's emotional letter, but dispassionate ones that stress the financial good
sense of purchasing bonds:

DAD. This is just as good a time as any for me to tell you just exactly
why I'm not buying Bonds. In the first place, Dan, I don't think they're
safe.

JEAN. Not safe? Why my economics teacher said that was all hokum. She
said, after all, if your Bonds aren't good after the war neither will your

money be. They both come from the government, and if one goes, so does the other.

DAD. Well, maybe that's true, but there are plenty of other good reasons. I'm putting about twice as much into the government the way it is for taxes.

MOTHER. But, Robert, we're getting twice as much protection.

DAD. I'm not complaining, Margaret, I'm merely saying that I simply don't have as much money.

MOTHER. I wonder how these men in defense plants scrape up enough money to save ten or twenty per cent of it—or even more. (19)

Dad cannot resist. He decides to buy bonds and thus the entire family is re-formed and placed on the straight and narrow path of what seems to be at once personal and national salvation. Obviously *A Letter from Bob* is here also plugging the institution payroll savings plans at the workplace. At the play's conclusion, the family receives another letter from Bob in which he writes:

Forget all about Pearl Harbor and Donkeywork. Yes, I did say *forget* about them. Just remember the guys who are fighting for you. One way you're sure of getting a message to all of us is to buy War Stamps and Bonds. That message will come to us in the form of bullets. Don't worry, Uncle Sam will see that we get them; and we'll take care of passing them on to the proper parties. (22)

Shrewdly and manipulatively, the play thus impels the audience to turn away from the past and past defeats in order to focus on future victory and glory because they have purchased War Bonds. It likewise suggests that morally correct economic behavior will be immediately converted into weapons capable of sub-duing the forces of evil.

A Letter from Bob is clearly directed to a teenage as well as to an adult, wage-earning population. It is unabashedly didactic from beginning to end, but the sentimentality of Bob's letter, the reasoned replies to Dad's skepticism, and the familiarity for an audience of each family member's selfish desires combine to make *A Letter from Bob* an effective propagandistic drama. It is hardly surprising, therefore, that it was also published in one of the Treasury Department's play collections specifically directed to an adult audience and meant for production at community centers and churches.[38]

Perhaps *A Letter from Bob* suggested to playwright Bernard J. Reins an effec-tive dramatic technique, for the same anthology contains two other powerful and moving plays by him: *Message from Bataan* and *Letter to Private Smith*. Both of these rise above the level of the usual Treasury Department play and both employ as their central dramatic device the letter home from a serviceman.[39]

Message from Bataan is an impressive and unusual piece, especially for a Treasury Department promotional play. Almost every government-sponsored play has an aura of triumph, celebrating what it sees as American values, American heroism, American moral right, and imminent American military victory. These plays usually have a domestic setting, often somewhere in mid-America. *Message from Bataan* approaches matters from a very different standpoint, using as its setting Bataan, the war front itself, the scene of a major loss of American lives and one of the war's most significant and bloody defeats for this country. Bernard Reins focuses his drama on the heroism of Bill, his military Everyman character, whose bravery among the starving, dying men on Bataan is poignantly conveyed. During his final day on Bataan, Bill writes a last letter to his younger brother, Johnny, back home and entrusts it to a friend who is leaving the area. The letter reads:

> All I want to say to you is, we're doing our best, here on Bataan. But the odds are terrific . . . and we can't expect help from the States in time to save our position. We can't expect help because our country was not well enough prepared, and has to fight across the Atlantic as well as the Pacific, and hasn't yet turned out enough weapons and trained men to break through the Japanese forces. [*Pause*] Which means there's a big job for you back home to do . . . a job for every one of you, man and woman, boy and girl. For our workers there's the job of turning out the finest planes, tanks, guns . . . turning out more of them, turning them out faster, better. For our farmers there's the job of raising more food. For everybody, and especially for fellows and girls too young to fight or do heavy work, there's the job of collecting all the scrap metal that's lying around, all the old rubber, and rags, and tin, and turning it in to be made into weapons. . . . but whatever else you do, you can buy War Savings Stamps and Bonds, and keep on buying, and buying, and buying . . . and so lend your country the money it needs to pay for so many planes and ships and tanks and guns that we soldiers and sailors and flyers will never again be caught short by our enemies. (51–52)

The didacticism is obvious, but the Bataan setting and the feelings that the recent defeat on Bataan roused in the American public give *Message from Bataan* just the fillip it needs to render dramatic what might otherwise be doggedly didactic.

The importance of plays to the War Bond effort is most clearly spelled out in the Treasury Department's 1943 publication *War Bond Plays and Other Dramatic Material for Use in Connection with War Finance Promotion*.[40] The introduction informs the reader, "Since the inception of the War Finance program, cities, towns, and villages throughout America have used plays, skits, and musicals to spread the War Finance message, to sell bonds directly to the public, and to lend entertainment and excitement to War Bond rallies, club meetings, and radio broadcasts." It goes on to assert that in the sale of War Bonds, "the play's the thing," and that "Because War Bond plays and skits have been eminently successful, the Women's Section of the War Finance Division offers this collection of plays to committees interested in using plays for War Bond promotion" (1). The reader is then given tips for producing and publicizing the plays contained in the volume.

The plays are short, usually eight to thirty minutes in length, and hit hard at the need for proper economic behavior and the purchase of War Bonds during wartime. The authors of the plays are again not known playwrights, with one exception. The keynote piece in the collection is a hard-hitting short play by the established Broadway playwright Bella Spewack, who, together with her husband, Sam, had written *The Solitaire Man* (1926), *The War Song* (1928), *The Ambulance Chaser* (1931), *Boy Meets Girl* (1935), and *Clear All Wires* (1932).[41] The duo was later to achieve celebrity by writing the book for Cole Porter's *Kiss Me, Kate* (1948).[42]

Bella Spewack's script for the Treasury Department volume is *Invitation to Inflation,* which presents the chastising and education of Carol Larrabee, a frivolous, capricious, married woman who, when she keeps an appointment to meet a friend, totes a load of parcels containing patently nonessential luxury items and black market purchases. When her friend Bess tells Carol that Carol's husband is angry about her extravagances, that her marriage is in jeopardy, and that her husband would like her to spend her money on bonds, Carol exclaims:

> You mean War Bonds? I bought a War Bond. I can't buy one a month, the way Jim wants me to—and run a house too! Do you know what beef costs? I paid a dollar a pound at—well, Jim doesn't know I spent that much—I had to tell him it was ceiling price and show him the the [*sic*] receipt and my stamp book—before he'd even eat it! But he certainly enjoyed every mouthful! Buying War Bonds is all right—but how are you going to buy them with things so high—not just beef you know! (6)

Bess then gives Carol an elementary lesson on how inflation works and how she and others like her are contributing to it, and words are not minced:

> CAROL. [*plaintively*] Why, Bess, I thought we were going to have a pleasant little chat—You make me positively uncomfortable. I feel as if I were Benedict Arnold, or—
>
> BESS. I hope so, Carol. You're just as unpatriotic as the spy who delivers us to the enemy on the eve of a battle! . . . Look, Carol, when you bought that beef in the black market—you paid a very high price. You and thousands like you force the price of food up—that inevitably forces wages up—and so the dance of inflation begins. Goods become scarce—prices get higher—until they get to the point where no wages can keep up with them. Business goes bankrupt. Factories close down. . . . We're engaged in

a war. And war means people are working on materials for the prosecution of that war. Those people are not making consumer goods. They won't until the war is won. But in the meanwhile, those goods get scarcer—and because of you, Carol—more and more expensive and harder to buy. (6)

At the end of the short script, after Bess has delivered her little economics lesson and accused Carol of treason, Carol is persuaded to return the purchases in her parcels and use the money to buy a $25 War Bond.

Spewack, like other Treasury playwrights, has seemingly learned her technique from the agitprop plays of the 1930s. *Invitation to Inflation* has something of Clifford Odets's tone in *Waiting for Lefty*'s "Young Actor" episode. Indeed, the entire collection of scripts reflects the ways in which the often politically critical and leftist agitprop playwrights of the 1930s provided the models for successful, politically conservative, *pro patria* "warprop" plays of the 1940s.

The plays that follow Spewack's are all (with one exception) by women writers, either presumably in the employ of the Treasury Department or winners of a college playwriting contest sponsored by the War Bond wing of the department. In the first of June Bingham's two contributions to the volume, *Trial by Fury* (15–19), the allegorical Squanderbug, who is a staple in several plays for children, here makes an appearance in a play for adults. Squanderbug's mission is to convince women to be vain and spend their salaries on foolish trifles instead of buying War Bonds. In the prologue, we learn that the Squanderbug is in direct contact with Hitler and is one of his operatives in the U.S. In Bingham's other play, *Cry Uncle* (20–24), a "15-minute play [which] was written expressly for women's colleges" (20), the economic didacticism of Spewack's *Invitation to Inflation* is reiterated when college co-ed Mary explains to a frivolous classmate the realities of wartime economics and the need for investing in War Bonds. She explains that the funds from bonds are needed "to foot the bill for all the Flying Fortresses and little things like that" (21) and to curb inflation. Furthermore, "the Government wants you to invest in bonds, so you'll have money to spend *after* the war. That's when there'll be beautiful new cars and heavenly clothes—and then you'll be doing the patriotic thing by spending. Because the money you spend will help get our businesses back on a peacetime basis and reemploy soldiers" (22). Like many other Treasury plays, the argument to a populace emerging from the deprivations of the 1930s is to delay gratification just a little longer, until the war is won. Then spending and vanity will not merely be allowed but will boost the postwar economy, provide jobs for ex-GIs, and be part of a patriotic gesture to put peacetime America back on track.

Several of the plays in the volume are versions for more mature audiences of Hackett's high school play *For the Duration*. In these, the right-thinking members of the family must convince other family members to desist from a prodigality that is both self-indulgent and inflationary. Into this paradigm fall three plays by Betty Bridgman, *Mother Buys a Bond* (33–38), *Father Wins the Peace* (39–43), and *Bargains in Bonds* (44–48). The first, the introduction claims, is a

"20-minute play [that] was the first War Bond play to be written and produced" (33). In this work, Father and Grandma try to instill thrift, wartime austerity, and War Bond investment in a frivolous teenage daughter and in an even more empty-headed, shopping spree–prone mother. The father, using the Joseph in Egypt philosophy of storing up the harvest of the good years to stem the deprivations of the lean ones, attempts to talk economic good sense to his wife, who is spending the family funds on luxuries and consumer goods, "Alice, people are buying things they don't need. Now when so many people are earning good money, it's time to save up for the years when there won't be so much work and such high wages. That's why I'm trying to put away as much money as possible in War Bonds" (35). He then uses the argument of helping the country through War Bonds because "The Government is fighting this war for us" (35). When his wife demurs that "we can still lose this war!" Father replies, "We can't lose, Alice, if we all work together. But even if we should lose the war we'd lose our money no matter where it was, in bonds or in banks or sewed up in a mattress. Because money represents the Government's promise to pay, just as much as bonds do" (35).

Although Grandma understands the situation, the play characterizes the other women, the mother and daughter, as incapable of understanding larger ideas. Indeed, it is curious that in this play, written by a female playwright, it is the women who seem to be the enemy because of their shortsightedness and inability to comprehend the workings of economics, so easily understood by men. It is only in the face of an immediate and personal situation, when son Bob announces that he has joined the Navy, that mother and sister reform and decide to invest in bonds. Bob makes a patriotic speech:

> All the news was about the fighting and I had no part in it. I knew I belonged out there on one of those big boats, watching for enemy planes, or learning how to aim the big guns, or—or just polishing brass and scrubbing decks. Mother, I don't care what I do or where they send me. I'm going to be fighting for my country and that's the biggest and best thing I can do with my life. If that isn't worth while, then all I've been taught in school and in church and all I've learned from you and Dad was a lot of fairy tales. (37)

Mother Buys a Bond is thus constructed with gender typing in mind, so that Father's reasoned economic principles are likely to influence the males in the audience and son Bob's emotional speech is meant to have its impact on the women, who presumably act on feeling rather than reason.

Lest Betty Bridgman be accused of sexism, however, one must point out that in her next play, *Father Wins the Peace*, it is Father who must be brought into line and learn the economic good sense of investing in the Payroll War Bond Plan. When Father shows post-Depression anxiety, exclaiming, "Who's going to stop 'em from canceling out my bonds or just refusing to pay them 10 years from now?" he is told by female family members, "Your Government is the soundest, most democratic government in the world. Maybe there *is* a lot wrong with it. But in 150 years it has never failed to pay the smallest obligation" (41). *Bargains in Bonds* replays the message but in a context aimed at a farm audience. And the same family paradigm is employed in Isobel Evensen's short piece *The New Recruit* (52–55).

Following Bella Spewack's lead are two plays by Alice B. Donovan, *Day's Work for America* (59–62) and *And We Talk about Sacrifice* (63–66). In the first, another idle, consumerist woman is satirized and brought around to seeing the value of investing money in government securities instead of fripperies. *And We Talk about Sacrifice* is aimed at women, implying that the best way to a man's wallet is through his wife. It is prefaced with the comment, "The play has particular timeliness if used in conjunction with efforts to increase the regular investments of professional men and private business men. Its use before women's club members, many of whom are the wives of these men, will 'soften up' the resistance that such regular investment might meet at home" (63). With a female audience in mind, *And We Talk about Sacrifice* plays on maternal instincts. The foolish, self-indulgent Mrs. Belmont airs her views about the unimportance of War Bonds while in a physician's waiting room. She is made to see the error of her ways by Mrs. Ciskovitz, an immigrant woman also waiting to see the physician. Mrs. Ciskovitz loves and supports America because she has lost her home in Poland, her husband has been killed in the siege of Warsaw, her baby has been killed in a bombing, and her young son has been taken to a concentration camp by the Nazis. She herself has escaped to America with nothing but the clothes on her back and has been succored by this country. Her combination of suffering motherhood and American patriotism is echoed in a different key by another woman in the waiting room who has heard nothing in four weeks from her son stationed in the Pacific. A once vain but now reformed Mrs. Belmont closes the play:

> MRS. BELMONT. Thank you so much for telling us what you did, showing us what it means to lose a war, and how important it is to win it. I shall never forget what you said.
>
> MRS. CISKOVITZ. That is thanks enough—that you do not forget. The United States must remain the great free country that it is, only so is there hope for the conquered people, hope for the world. For that, no sacrifice is too great. How fortunate you are to be able to give for victory!
>
> . . .
>
> MRS. BELMONT. No sacrifice is too great. . . . I'd like to see anyone tell me they can't afford to buy more War Bonds. (66)

Alice Donovan and the Treasury Department seem to have, perhaps naïvely, believed that the testimony of the two mothers and that of the reformed Mrs.

Belmont would so affect a female audience that they in turn would convince their spouses to support the American cause through War Bonds.

A somewhat similar play aimed directly at men, and the only piece in the collection written by a man, is Phillips Brooks Keller's *Now Is the Time* (30–32). As the preface to the play tells us, "This 10-minute play was one of the five winners in a college play-writing contest sponsored by the National War Savings Staff in the Spring of 1943" (30). In it, two reporters interview John Polifka, an immigrant from Poland who has become a millionaire and who is investing his money in War Bonds. His reasons are both economic and patriotic. First, he argues, "Speaking cold-bloodedly, I can't afford *not* to buy War Bonds. At present interest rates they're just about the best and safest investment that I could make in times like these" (31). He sees as well that War Bonds will help the U.S. and the Allies invade Europe and restore his native Poland: "The quicker this country and her fighting allies are able to invade continental Europe, the sooner will my kinsmen and my countrymen be free to recover the heritage of living without fear and, as Mr. Roosevelt has said, living without want" (32). Looking at *And We Talk about Sacrifice* and *Now Is the Time* side by side, one can see the disparate and gendered ways in which the Treasury Department sought to pitch similar material to female and male audiences.

The *Letter from Bob* and *Message from Bataan* paradigm is used once more and flavored with a soupçon of the supernatural in Ensign Elsie Mary White's *One Bullet* (56–60). The stage directions instruct prospective producers, "The plot is concerned with a farmer-father who feels that he is doing his share by raising food for the war, and sees no reason to buy War Bonds. Meanwhile his soldier-son dies for want of ammunition in the Southwest Pacific. The play can be made more timely by changing the war area mentioned to coincide with war action going on when the play is given, Southwest Pacific can become Europe; Japs—Nazis" (56). The ghost of the dead soldier-son reappears and, in a poignant, melodramatic moment, haunts the niggardly father with a reenactment of the son's dying moments:

> JIM. [*As if giving up the struggle*] I—I've no bullets left—[*turning to his father*] Dad—Dad—why won't you help me? I can't—[*sound of a loud gun report. Then Jim sinks to the floor holding his middle. He is in great pain and can hardly talk but he manages to gasp out*] Dad—I needed you and you didn't help—One bullet would have sa—[*His father kneels down beside him. His words die away and as he makes a last effort to rise he pulls a chair over. At this moment the fire goes out leaving the entire stage in darkness.*] (58)

With a shrewdly passive-aggressive tactic, the play directs guilt feelings squarely toward those in the audience who have not invested generously in War Bonds.

Certainly the most unusual and imaginative of all the Treasury Department plays is another of the five winners of the college playwriting contest sponsored by the National War Savings Staff in the spring of 1943, Mary Moore's brief

American Curiosities (49–51). This rather strange piece set in a dystopian future seeks to fan the flames of America's worst wartime paranoid fantasies. *American Curiosities* is set in an imagined postwar period in which the U.S. is ruled by the conquering Germans and Japanese. The principal characters, an archaeology professor and his wife, did not, along with many other overly self-assured Americans, heed the call to buy War Bonds. Now they are fugitives, on the run from the Germans, dressed in animal skins and hiding out for the past ten years in caves somewhere in deepest Michigan. They are chided by their loyal American sister-in-law, Hattie, now also a fugitive and dressed like a huntress. Hattie scolds the professor and his wife because they refused to buy War Bonds, support their country, or believe "that the Japanese and the Germans could make a battlefield of this country for 10 years so that the only Americans left would be living in the hills like savages. You never believe that anything can happen to upset your own peace and comfort" (50). At the end of the play, Hattie leaves behind her still vain brother and sister-in-law, who are then discovered by the Germans and shot and killed onstage. The fantasy of *American Curiosities,* which looks back to Huxley's *Brave New World* and ahead to Orwell's *1984,* realizes the deep-seated fears of Americans, pressuring them to purchase War Bond and thereby avert the future outlined in the play.

The Treasury Department plays are far from being either masterpieces of drama or models of subtlety, but they do represent significant artifacts of American wartime culture, revealing as they do the ways in which a nonmilitary wing of the government sought to employ drama as a means of suasion and propaganda. The plays reveal the issues the Treasury Department sought to stress and the different rhetorics it employed to aim its messages at elementary, secondary, and college students and at the American adult public. They reveal, too, the distinctions the Treasury Department made between male and female audience members and the distinct approaches it felt would be successful with each gender. More generally, adapting the agitprop techniques of the Group Theatre and other 1930s companies, the Treasury Department produced highly effective "warprop" plays which successfully demonized wasters and extolled War Bond and War Stamp buyers; warned post-Depression Americans of potential inflation; and sought to mobilize American civilians, from kindergartners to adults, to put their trust and savings into War Bonds.

VII

The extent to which the World War II American government used the stage to foster various agendas, to shape the minds and attitudes of the American civilian and military public concerning the war, is both large and impressive. Looking back at the wide array of government-issued and government-sponsored theatrical material, it becomes remarkably clear how great was the confidence of U.S. officials that theatre and performance could help Americans win the war. In addition to the government stage material discussed here, there was also government drama conveyed through radio. Americans across the country listened to the scripts presented on radio series such as *The Treasury Star Parade, The Freedom Company Presents,* and *This Is War.*[43] Clearly the dramatic techniques employed by the *pro patria* government-sponsored dramatists of the 1940s were learned from the largely agitprop, anti-establishment playwrights of the previous decade. Writing of American theatre during the Depression era, Morgan Y. Himelstein titles his study *Drama Was a Weapon.*[44] In the hands of the U.S. government, drama was also a weapon during the wartime years of the 1940s.

FOUR

Airing the War: World War II Radio Plays

During World War II, there was hardly a household in American not equipped with one or more radios. Radio, even more than newspapers, kept Americans in close contact with both current events and with the issues over which the war was being fought. As Archibald MacLeish proved so clearly in his powerful *Fall of the City* and *Air Raid*, radio offered a vehicle for drama and for dramatizing the war and war issues in a way that could effectively reach every American home that owned a radio. Radio dramatist Arch Oboler went to the heart of the matter when he asserted, "The writer for radio who has something to say and says it well can have, in a single hour, a larger audience than Shakespeare had in a lifetime."[1] After Pearl Harbor, American playwrights combined forces with the War Department, war support groups, Hollywood and Broadway actors, and the major broadcasting systems to produce numerous radio plays. These were usually fifteen or thirty minutes in length, enjoyed the cachet of featuring famous actors, and held the great advantage over stage drama of being able to use sound effects in such a way that audiences could feel themselves transported into the midst of battle, inside planes, and within the minds of the characters. In most cases, too, the wartime radio dramas were morality plays for the American public, meant to influence their thoughts and opinions and to help them better to define their commitment to the war effort. The shortness of the airtime for the radio plays forced the playwrights to make quick hits with strong and frequently unsubtle dramatic punches as they scripted Americans to feel that the men who died or were wounded in battle were serving in a just cause, and that a victory for America would be a victory all free men and for the principles of democracy.

In July 1943, no less a figure than Thomas Mann provided the introduction to Arch Oboler and Stephen Longstreet's collection of radio plays that were presented by the Hollywood Writers' Mobilization and were dedicated to the war effort. The published plays had been part of the Free World Theatre radio series that had been presented on the Blue Network.[2] Thomas Mann wrote of these radio plays:

> What they offer is propaganda in the best and purest sense of the word. Propaganda—not for war. It is thoroughly un-American to glorify war, as has been done in certain countries, and to blame the outbreak of the war on the Pope, the Jews, capital, Communism, Messrs. Churchill and Roosevelt, and I don't know what else. To repeat: this is not propaganda for war. At most it is propaganda for a war to which we were not in the least inclined but which was forced upon us in order to prevent evil from gaining sole mastery on earth, and which we must wage to the end for the sake of mankind's honor and for the preservation of our own free human lives. . . . One can propagate good as well as evil. . . . Now then the great advantage of this book is that the propaganda which it offers cannot and will not be so described [as evil] by anyone in a hostile sense. Its propaganda is so free of partisanship, offense and challenge, it is so natural and pro-human that hardly anyone will be tempted to utter the disapproving cry: "Propaganda!" It is good propaganda insofar as it is effective, absorbing and entertaining. And it is good propaganda insofar as it awakes our hearts which are so much inclined to drowse in indifference, and summon them to hate evil and to believe in a better world as the fruit of victory. (x-xi)[3]

Mann correctly acknowledges the patently propagandistic intent of the radio plays, even as he seeks to defuse the pejorative sense that the word *propaganda* usually carries.

American radio plays about war issues were indeed propaganda, but they were, as Mann so eloquently puts it, propagandistic in the service of humanity, freedom, victory, and a better world after the war. In their fifteen- or thirty-minute formats, they often quickly go to the heart of their issues and give a sense of being morality plays for modern men and women not watching a procession of pageant wagons but tuned to the airwaves.

There were many radio plays that brought the war and its issues directly to the listeners in ways that stage plays or newspaper reports could not. Although a comprehensive examination of the use of radio plays during World War II would require a separate and extensive study, it would, nevertheless, be an injustice to overlook the importance of that hybrid of Broadway and Hollywood.[4] What follows, therefore, will not be a complete or exhaustive study, but rather a presentation of some of the landmarks of American World War II radio dramas and the impact they likely made.

Almost as soon as U.S. troops were sent into wartime action, the powerful domestic weapon of radio plays was likewise put into action. Shortly after Pearl Harbor, powerful radio scripts reached audiences around the country, binding the nation through simultaneous radio broadcasts aired from one end of the land to the other. The first of a number of wartime broadcast drama series, launched just weeks after Pearl Harbor, was *This Is War!* a thirteen-part radio series coordinated by Norman Corwin and "produced," as the acknowledgments prefacing the published volume state, "with the cooperation of the U.S. government" (3).[5]

The *This Is War!* series began its weekly airing on Saturday, 14 February 1942. The plays in the series are blatant patriotic propaganda pieces that are frequently immensely powerful and compelling.[6] The audience consists of home front radio listeners in every city and town across the nation. Symbolic of a country uniting to fight the enemy, the series was, impressively, carried at the same moment on all four major radio networks of the day—the Blue Network, the Columbia Broadcasting System, the Mutual Broadcasting System, and the National Broadcasting Company. It aired, furthermore, at a strategic time, immediately after the news at 7:30 P.M. on Saturday night. The plays were carried on every major station around the country, so that anyone in America listening to prime-time radio on a Saturday night could scarcely avoid *This Is War!* In New York, the plays were broadcast on nine different stations across the radio dial: WEAF (NBC Red Network), WJZ (NBC Blue Network), WOR (Mutual Broadcasting), WABC (Columbia Broadcasting), WNYC (New York City Municipal Broadcasting), WINS (a Hearst station), WEVD (Eugene V. Debs Memorial Fund), WCNW (Arthur Faske), and WQXR (the *New York Times* station). In San Francisco, they were heard simultaneously on four stations. Across the U.S., 700 of the nation's 924 stations aired *This Is War!* and it was beamed overseas as well.[7] In short, it would have been hard indeed to move across the radio dial and to hear anything else.

And what one heard were plays written by writers like Maxwell Anderson, Philip Wylie, Stephen Vincent Benét, and, very often, the master of radio scripts, Norman Corwin. Furthermore, performing in the plays were major stage and screen actors, among them Robert Montgomery, Paul Muni, Fredric March, Bette Davis, Douglas Fairbanks Jr., Mercedes McCambridge, Tyrone Power, Joan Blondell, Claude Rains, Helen Hayes, John Garfield, Elisabeth Bergner, John Carradine, Jimmy Stewart, Clifton Fadiman, James Cagney, Madeleine Carroll, and Raymond Massey. The profusion of *This Is War!* broadcasts at prime time across the dial, in combination with the name recognition of distinguished writers and actors, not only suggested that the plays were of signal importance but ensured that nearly all of radio-listening America, literally millions of people across the economic and social spectrum, would tune in to these plays. The significance of these radio plays and their role in the war effort, therefore, cannot be either overlooked or minimized.

In the time just prior to American entry into the war, the hard-hitting individual radio dramas of Archibald MacLeish, *Air Raid* and *The Fall of the City*, were not isolated masterpieces. There were other radio plays alerting Americans to the situation in Europe, most notably an important series launched in 1941 to promote a heightened sense of the fundamental freedoms Americans hold dear, remind citizens of the patriotic high points in American history, and prepare radio listeners for the fight the playwrights knew full well lay ahead. Author and journalist James Boyd was largely responsible for forming the Free Company, a group of writers who, with the blessing of the Columbia Broadcasting System, banded together to create radio scripts about being American.[8] Boyd's introduction to the published collection of Free Company plays concludes, "And we see as the hope of the world, our people's capacity to guard what freedom we have and, in the face of all threats from without and within, to expand it with confidence and honest pride into something, never perfect we know, but always closer to the dream" (ix).[9]

The Free Company aired ten plays on the Columbia Broadcasting System from 23 February to 4 May 1941.[10] The playwrights were a veritable who's who of American drama of the time: William Saroyan, Marc Connelly, Robert Sherwood, Stephen Vincent Benét, Orson Welles, Paul Green, Archibald MacLeish, Maxwell Anderson, and (posthumously) Sherwood Anderson. In New York, *The Free Company* came on at 2 P.M. on Sundays. This was not prime time, but it may have been chosen as a time when American families were tuned to their radios just before or after their Sunday dinner. Coming as they did when American engagement in the conflict occurring in Europe seemed increasingly inevitable and imminent, the plays aired by the Free Company form a curious intervention during a critical moment in American life. One can speculate, too, that, more pointedly, the Free Company plays were meant to influence public opinion about the national debate taking place at that time about extending the Selective Service Act, which passed in the House of Representatives in September 1941 by a one-vote margin. Many of the Free Company programs are still hair-raising to read and were surely far more so to hear in 1941. They bristle with the tension and electricity of the times. It is not so much that the individual plays, despite their famous authors, are in themselves remarkable or small masterpieces but rather that the broadcasts scintillate, like the restiveness of an ionized atmosphere and the gusts of foreboding winds just before a major lightning storm strikes. And a few months later, with the attack on Pearl Harbor, strike it did.

For the most part, the Free Company radio dramas may be characterized as contemporary morality plays about the freedoms guaranteed to Americans by the Bill of Rights. But their often acknowledged, sometimes implicit context is the abrogation of those very freedoms in fascist Europe. As actor Burgess Meredith, the emcee for the series, stated on the air in his introduction to the series as a whole on the occasion of the first play, William Saroyan's *The People with Light Coming out of Them*, "Some of these plays have for their dramatic themes particular sections of the Bill of Rights, the right of free speech, etc. Others, like today's drama, will be more general in scope."[11] The aims of the Free Company and the nature of the involvement on the part of actors and writers are further lucidly articulated by James Boyd, one of the founders of the Free Company and the director of the broadcasts, in his introduction to the fifth play in the series, Stephen Vincent Benét's *Freedom's a Hard-Bought Thing*:

> "The Free Company" is a group of writers, actors and radio workers who have come together voluntarily to express their belief in this country. They are unpaid, unsponsored and uncontrolled; just a group of Americans saying what they think about this country and about freedom; trying to say it by means of plays as the Bible parables and Aesop's fables tell us other truths by means of stories. These plays have been written by many leading writers of America, and are being acted by important actors of stage and screen, all volunteers. (117)

There is even here a suggestion that the celebrated writers and performers banding together as volunteers in the cause of freedom are a prefiguration of Americans who will soon also be asked to volunteer in the service of their country.

Saroyan's *The People with Light Coming out of Them* opened the series on 23 February 1941. It is a tribute to American diversity, taking what purports to be a generic street block in an American town and celebrating the energy and warmth of the people who live there. The play begins with a brief dialogue between Meredith and Saroyan as the actor asks the author to write a radio play for the series:

> MEREDITH. About why you like America
>
> SAROYAN. *Why?* [*Laughing*] You might as well ask me why I like to breathe. What do you *really* want?
>
> MEREDITH. Well, Bill, tell us something about why you think this country is worth living and fighting for. Give us your reasons in a little play. You *have* reasons?
>
> SAROYAN. *Millions* of 'em. As many reasons as there are places and people. Take California, for instance. Or Texas, or New York. Take San Francisco, or Peoria. Take *any* place. [*Like a railroad conductor*] Rockville Center, Freeport, Merrick, Belmore, Wantagh, Seaford, Massapequa, Amityville, Lindenhurst, and *Babylon!* (2–3)[12]

The request, in 1941, to have Saroyan demonstrate that America is worth fighting for is an ominous one. The dark clouds of war were clearly on the horizon. Saroyan's reply, both in his statement and in the play that follows, is one that proudly centers on the happy unity of American diversity, a theme that will recur often during the war as American troops are fighting an enemy that champions racial purity and belittles the United States precisely for its mongrel ethnic hybridity.

Like all the plays the Free Company presented, *The People with Light Coming out of Them* had the attraction of featuring name actors. In this case, they were John Garfield, Edmund Gwenn, and Tim Holt, among others. It is also true that a radio broadcast like this one might well be preceded or followed by news headlines, and these created a special context for each play that neither the producers nor the authors could have foreseen. The news broadcasts surrounding Saroyan's script, for example, would have echoed what appeared in that day's (23 February 1941) *New York Times* banner headline: "NAZI STAFF OFFICERS MOVE INTO SOFIA AS BULGARIAN STUDENTS PROTEST ENTRY; BRITISH MINING MID-MEDITERRANEAN." The following week's script, Marc Connelly's *The Mole on Lincoln's Cheek*, a powerful play about freedom of speech and censorship, would have aired in the context of the day's *Times* headline: "NAZI TROOPS OCCUPY SOFIA AND KEY BASES AS BULGARIA ENTERS ALLIANCE WITH AXIS; BRITISH HINT BOMBING; U.S. TO FREEZE FUNDS." The unique dramatic potential of the radio play rests not merely on the ability to replace physical action with sound but on the time of day when it is presented and on its possible serendipitous timeliness. In the theatre, the audience tends to leave the outside world behind. When the doors close, the curtain rises and the actors appear. For two or three hours, one enters the world of the playwright, a world that may by extension have some relevance to the world outside the playhouse but that is nonetheless a separate geography. Radio moves the listener from program to program—from newscast to drama to music—with little more than the seconds it takes for commercial breaks. Radio dramas frequently run a mere thirty minutes or less and are played in the home living room. They do not, consequently, have the sense of special occasion inspired by a trip to a theatre or the wearing of fancy clothes. For radio dramas, then, the context of the outside world, of current events, is either not forgotten or at least never very far away.

Some of the plays presented by the Free Company raise important issues for Americans, and the force of the playwriting is enhanced by the talented and famous actors who acted in them. Connelly's *The Mole on Lincoln's Cheek* tackles the issue of school textbook censoring. The actors include Melvyn Douglas, Claire Trevor, Margaret Hamilton, and Charles Bickford. Quite eloquently, the play implicitly rejects inculcating students with jingoistic propaganda and champions instead the cause of teaching "true" history. A teacher called on the carpet by the local school board tells his accusers and, by extension, the radio audience around the country:

> The chief purpose of history is not to glorify the past but to insure the future. And our children have the right to be given history truthfully so they can use its lessons to solve the problems every human being faces today. The only way to make a child a real patriot is to give him history,

and not an arrangement of eulogies and flowery obituaries under the *guise* of history. (48–49)[13]

And in case the audience has not gotten the point, Burgess Meredith, at the play's conclusion, makes it absolutely clear:

> Our freedom, then, has meaning . . . that here, in our land, the truth may be taught, always. Academic freedom is the first liberty to die when dictators rule, for dictators know the power of education. Let us, like Mr. Roberts in the play, keep our eyes open for truth. Let us resist any attempt to suppress truth or distort it. (52)

The play is more than a refresher course on academic freedom, for one can feel clearly the line being drawn between "us" and "them." And the "them" are obviously the followers of Hitler and Mussolini, whom Americans will inevitably have to confront.

Similarly, the third play in the Freedom Company series, Robert Sherwood's *An American Crusader,* which featured Franchot Tone, dramatized the admirable fortitude of Elijah Lovejoy, the editor of a St. Louis newspaper who used the press to express his anti-slavery views and was murdered for doing so. At the end of the play, Burgess Meredith reminds the radio audience that upon hearing of Lovejoy's death, John Quincy Adams spoke to Congress, saying, "Elijah Lovejoy is the first American martyr to the freedom of the press and the freedom of the slave" (84). Then Meredith draws the lesson for modern times:

> Today the freedom Lovejoy fought for—freedom of the press—is increasingly denied as the enemies of all human liberty march to victory after victory. Under the threat of a world half slave, half free, let us renew again the pledge of Lincoln. Let us once more highly resolve that government of the people, by the people, and for the people shall not perish from the earth. (85)[14]

That day, too, the "enemies of all human liberty" were marching to another victory in Europe even as the United States was drawing ever nearer to a declaration of war. The large headline that spread across the entire front page of the *New York Times* on 9 March 1941, the day of the broadcast of Sherwood's drama, read: "SENATE PASSES AID-TO-BRITAIN BILL 60 TO 31; FINAL HOUSE ACTION EXPECTED IN WEEK; YUGOSLAVIA REACHES COMPROMISE WITH HITLER." Even as the U.S. began to dress for battle, the Free Company programs armed American listeners with renewed pride in the freedoms for which they would soon have to fight and prepared them for the combat that lay in their immediate future.

One of the best plays in the Free Company series concerned freedom of assembly. It is *His Honor, the Mayor* and was written by that theatrical polymath

Orson Welles. The actors for this piece are Welles himself, Ray Collins, Agnes Moorehead, Everett Sloane, Paul Stewart, and Erskine Sanford. Ever the businessman, Welles reminds the audience that these actors can be seen in his film *Citizen Kane* and in the Mercury Theatre production of *Native Son*, currently running on Broadway. But despite the self-advertisement, *His Honor, the Mayor* is a forceful drama about the American right of even the most loathsome group to assemble. The mayor of a town exclaims to those who would wish to suppress the meeting of the White Crusaders, a racist and anti-Semitic group, "But don't start forbidden' anybody the right to assemble. Democracy's a rare and precious thing and once you start that—you've finished democracy! Democracy guarantees freedom of assembly unconditionally to the worst lice that want it" (172–173).[15]

In light of the race questions that began to arise during the war and became more vocal at the war's end, it seems important that two of the ten plays of the Free Company broadcasts center on racial freedoms and the treatment of American blacks: Benét's *Freedom's a Hard-Bought Thing* and Paul Green's *A Start in Life*, the latter starring Canada Lee. It is noteworthy, too, that as the Free Company's ten-program series drew to its end, the plays became less about American freedoms and more about Nazi repression and cruelty. The final two plays in the series seemed geared to make Americans hate the Third Reich, its ideology, and its methods of repression and butchery. The first of these is Maxwell Anderson's unusually hard-hitting play *The Miracle on the Danube*. The second is *Above Suspicion*, a radio play Sherwood Anderson was working on at the time of his death and completed by members of the Free Company.

The Miracle on the Danube starred Paul Muni and concerns a German army captain who wants to carry out the savage orders of his commanders but who is prevented from doing so by a spirit that seems a mixture of Christ and the captain's inner self. What is impressive in the play is not its story line but the recounting of the atrocities the captain is required to commit. These include leading a firing squad; throwing bodies into unmarked graves; liquidating undesirables; sending prisoners in sealed boxcars to their death; and exterminating the intelligentsia and artists. In this drama, Maxwell Anderson and the Free Company prepare the audience to hate a demonized enemy, one with whom the U.S. was drawing ever closer to combat. *The Miracle on the Danube* may well have had a special impact on its audience, for on that very day, 20 April 1942, the Nazis invaded the birthplace of democracy. The *New York Times* front page headline read: "GERMAN TROOPS ENTERING ATHENS; DEFENDERS FIGHT HARD TO LAST; SENATE POLL ON CONVOYS [to Great Britain] IS CLOSE."

Featuring in its leading roles Mr. Yankee Doodle Dandy himself, George M. Cohan (in probably his last performance), and Paul Henried, Sherwood Anderson's *Above Suspicion* foreshadows Gow and d'Usseau's wartime play *Tomorrow the World*, for it concerns Fritz, a frightened German teenager who has been worked over by the Nazis and has now arrived at the home of his uncle and aunt in the U.S. In the course of the play, the audience feels the paranoia of the teenager, a paranoia that stems from institutionalized intimidation of citizens in the Third Reich. There are spies and tape recorders everywhere. No one can be trusted. The police are the instruments of brutality. Any opinion that is critical of the government will lead to the disappearance and death that Fritz reveals has befallen his parents. For an American radio public sitting amid family in the comfort of their homes and tuning in on a Sunday afternoon, the image of contemporary Germany presented in *Above Suspicion* is the nightmarish antithesis of their experience at the moment. Precisely to such an audience, the thought that surveillance and repression could happen in America is frightening to contemplate and its possibility is worth going to war in order to prevent. The ten plays produced by the Free Company in the spring of 1941 are a prelude to what was to happen in radio drama after 7 December that same year.

Certainly the single most important name in radio drama during the prewar and war years is that of Norman Corwin. There are few radio playwrights who could come close to Corwin's truly amazing talent for touching the hearts and minds of listeners with his straightforward, staccato scripts that mastered the thirty-minute form, italicized narrative with just the right music and sound effects, and often delivered a drama that was a dazzling amalgam of theatre, poetry, and oratory. It is not surprising, then, that in the fall of 1941, when American engagement in the war seemed imminent, Corwin would be engaged by his friend Archibald MacLeish, who was then part of the U.S. Office of Facts and Figures as well as librarian of Congress, to prepare a radio script for 15 December, the sesquicentennial of the Bill of Rights.

The Roosevelt administration recognized not merely Corwin's talents but recognized, too, radio as a medium for reaching the American public and shaping its views both about American values and the stance of the Roosevelt administration toward the war. When Corwin was given the assignment to write a play about the Bill of Rights, a panoply of renowned figures in the entertainment industry were put at his disposal: Jimmy Stewart, Lionel Barrymore, Edward G. Robinson, Marjorie Main, Walter Brennan, Orson Welles, Rudy Vallee, Walter Huston, Edward Arnold, and Bob Burns. The music for the performance would be played by the New York Philharmonic Orchestra under the baton of Leopold Stokowski. Corwin got off to a rocky start writing the play he was to call *We Hold These Truths,* but the attack on Pearl Harbor, eight days before the play was to air, galvanized him to finish and polish what was to become one of the high points not only in his career but in the entire history of radio.[16]

Washington saw to it that all the major radio stations across the country carried *We Hold These Truths* at prime time (10 P.M. EST) on the night of Monday, 15 December. With the country now at war, it was a combination of shrewdness and serendipity that Jimmy Stewart, who was then a U.S. Army Air Corps corporal, had been chosen weeks before to serve as the program's narrator. *We Hold These Truths,* moreover, concluded with a speech by FDR himself. Did Roosevelt become part of Corwin's program, or did Corwin's play serve as a dazzling prelude to the president's speech? Something of both is probably true. Whatever the case, purportedly sixty million Americans (or about 46 percent of the total population) heard the program that night![17] Very likely this was, at that time, the single largest audience on record not merely for any radio play ever performed, but also for any play in the history of the theatre!

With tactical shrewdness, Corwin's radio play is neatly framed by an introduction beforehand and President Roosevelt's address to the nation afterward. Introducing the evening's program to the radio audience, actor Lionel Barrymore speaks of current events and mentions that from where he speaks in California, he looks out at an ocean no longer pacific. He goes on to name the actors in the program that will follow and to make special mention of the fact that Jimmy Stewart is on loan from the Army Air Corps. He alerts the audience, too, that the president will speak at the close of the program. In other words, the Corwin drama that follows, which is about the making of the Bill of Rights and not about the war, is nonetheless pointedly politicized, since it is preceded by Barrymore's comments that place Corwin's play in a wartime context and then followed by President Roosevelt's speech, which picks up on the occasion of the Bill of Rights's sesquicentennial but uses it to indict Hitler not merely as America's enemy but the implacable enemy of the beloved freedoms guaranteed by the Bill of Rights.

The script itself of *We Hold These Truths* presents a rather straightforward historical drama about the fears and skepticism of Americans after the ratification of the Constitution, and how those fears led to the creation of the Bill of Rights. Each of the ten amendments that constitute the Bill is briefly discussed. Lending weight to the performance are the familiar voices and cadences not only of Jimmy Stewart but also of the other celebrated actors in the cast. As the Bill of Rights is ratified toward the conclusion of Corwin's script, the stage directions read, "*Music: Sneak in the song 'Jefferson and Liberty,'*" upon which a citizen (Jimmy Stewart) intones, "proud men, unsuspicious, trusting men, their fighting over and their living just begun, their building and their working and their singing just now getting started." At this point a singer—none other than the one of most celebrated crooners of the day, Rudy Vallee—bursts into song:

> Here strangers from a thousand shores,
>   Compelled by tyranny to roam,
> Shall find, amid abundant stores,
>   A nobler and a happier home.
>
> Rejoice, Columbia's sons, rejoice!
>   To tyrants never bend the knee
> But join with heavy heart and sound and voice
>   For Jefferson and Liberty. (78–79)[18]

Except for a single use of the word *Gestapo,* Corwin's play makes no mention of the current world situation, Hitler, Pearl Harbor, or the American declaration of war just a few days prior. It is instead a moving tribute to the document that serves as the cornerstone of American freedom. The rhetorical force and the heart-swelling music of the program, moreover, must have filled the millions of listeners from one coast to the other with the fortitude to face what everyone surely knew lay ahead.

Corwin's drama is, finally, the centerpiece of a larger whole, a radio event that also includes Barrymore's introduction and a live presidential address. Touching the citizenry of a nation, *We Hold These Truths* concludes (with the patriotic strains of the New York Philharmonic in the background) by having Corporal Jimmy Stewart, his voice cracking with emotion, ask, "Is not our Bill of Rights more cherished now than ever? The blood more zealous to preserve it whole? Americans shall answer. For they alone know the answer. The people of America from east, from west, from north, from south."[19] It was a spark of brilliant inspiration to use Stewart, who had become famous only two years before precisely for playing the average patriotic citizen moved to fervor in the Frank Capra film *Mr. Smith Goes to Washington* (1939). And with Stewart's emotional lines, the dialogue ends, the music ceases, and Stewart, becoming Corporal Stewart, announces the arrival of his commander-in-chief: "Ladies and gentlemen, the President of the people of the United States" (86–87). At that point, President Roosevelt begins his address to the American public, articulating what Corwin's play had discreetly refrained from uttering: the freedoms guaranteed by the Bill of Rights are what the U.S. is protecting against the vile tyranny of a Hitler, who would abrogate and annihilate those freedoms here as he has already done in Europe.

Although Roosevelt, in conference during *We Hold These Truths*, did not actually hear the broadcast but came in just as he was introduced, his speech writers surely were not ignorant of what the general (though likely not specific) contents of Corwin's play would be. Thus Roosevelt begins where the play leaves off, even picking up the thread from the Jefferson song. At the same time, however, he points his finger unequivocally to Japan, Italy, and most of all Germany as the dire foes of all that the Bill of Rights represents:

> Indeed the entire program and goal of these political and moral tigers was nothing more than the overthrow, throughout the earth, of the great revolution of human liberty of which our American Bill of rights is the mother charter.
>
> The truths which were self-evident to Jefferson—which have been self-evident in the six generations of Americans who followed him—were to these men hateful. The rights to life, liberty and the pursuit of happiness which seemed to the founders of the Republic, and which seem to us, inalienable, were, to Hitler and his fellows, empty words which they proposed to cancel forever.

FDR then rousingly calls the nation to arms in defense of those very freedoms whose 150th anniversary is being celebrated, those very freedoms that Corwin's script has just movingly dramatized, "We covenant with each other before all the world that, having taken up arms in the defense of liberty, we will not lay them down, before liberty is once again secure in the world we live in. For that security we pray; for that security we act—now and evermore."[20] Roosevelt's speech was then capped by Leopold Stokowski and the New York Philharmonic's playing of the national anthem.

The unprecedented éclat of *We Hold These Truths*—likely the greatest moment in radio since the Orson Welles's *War of the Worlds* scare—made Washington alive to radio drama as a powerful resource for the war effort. Consequently, within ten weeks of *We Hold These Truths*, and relying on the momentum from that broadcast, the *This Is War!* series was launched on every major radio station in the land. The government also realized the brilliance and mastery of Norman Corwin and again tapped him to direct the thirteen-part series.[21] Who was actually behind *This Is War!* is not entirely clear, but the acknowledgment page in the published version of the plays states that they "were produced in cooperation with the U.S. Government, the collaborative efforts of the four radio networks" (vii). The *New York Times* reported that "the companies [networks] will have the cooperation of the Office of Facts and Figures which will work with the production staff in obtaining and correlating information."[22] Reading between the not-so-subtle lines, one can see that Washington put pressure on the networks to repeat what they had done for *We Hold These Truths*. This time, the series was aired not at the congenial 2 P.M. Sunday family time used for *The Free Company* but at quintessential prime time in America: in New York and the Eastern time zone at 7:30 P.M. on Saturday immediately following the seven o'clock news. It came on at 6:30 in the Central time zone, and was rebroadcast that night for the West Coast at 9:45 Pacific time. Once again major Broadway and Hollywood stars offered their services gratis. And the series was hosted this time not by army corporal Jimmy Stewart but by Navy Lieutenant Robert Montgomery.

With *This Is War!* radio became not just a communications medium but an acknowledged wartime weapon. The *We Hold These Truths* broadcast had concluded with President Roosevelt's address to the nation. The first program in the *This Is War!* series almost begins where *We Hold These Truths* leaves off by having the Roosevelt administration's court poet and intellectual, Archibald MacLeish, read a letter from President Roosevelt thanking the networks for facilitating the "series of broadcasts devoted to the telling of facts to the people of the United States and those throughout the whole world—wherever people are allowed to listen to free words—to hear the truth" (4). The broadcasts would, in short, be carried not only by American radio stations but by radio towers beamed at Europe. MacLeish goes on to assert, "Our enemies in this war have made one use of radio, The United Peoples are making another, and a very different use—a use which will meet the Axis strategy of lies with the United People's strategy of truth," and adds that *This Is War!* is meant to convey "*a fuller comprehension of the nature of the War in which we are engaged*" (4–5).

The first play in the series, which also gave the series its name, aired on 14 February 1942. Realizing that this is Valentine's Day, Corwin shrewdly seizes on that fact to give his program a special frisson and uses the occasion to underscore the program's seriousness, bringing his audience up short in the midst of the holiday's gaiety and romance. "What we say tonight," the narrator declares, "has to do with blood and with bone and with anger, and also with a big job in the making. Laughter can wait. Soft music can have the evening off. No one is invited to sit down and take it easy. Later, later. There's a war on" (5). The program that follows announces that it wishes Americans to know who the enemy is. Corwin then robustly demonizes the Axis powers in general and the Germans, Japanese, and Italians one by one, leaving no doubt that they are the mortal foe worthy of American hostility and heroism. They are the modern embodiment of the antichrist and the very apotheosis of evil. Their villainy should be a rallying point for American justice and bravery. Writing with his signature rhetorical panache, Corwin characterizes the enemy:

> The enemy is Murder International. Murder Unlimited; quick murder on the spot or slow murder in the concentration camp, murder for listening to the shortwave radio, for marrying a Pole, for Propagation of the Faith, for speaking one's mind, for trading with a non-Aryan, for being an invalid too long. The enemy is the assassin with the swagger and the smoking gun; the stumblebum set up in business by the patron state. (11–12)

To his angry depiction he adds quotations from *Il Duce* and the harsh, alien sounds of German and Japanese.

Having built up an increasingly alarming and black portrait of the Axis, Corwin's play swings round and packs its punch at the American listening audience. With a jab at Chamberlain and by a proud rhetorical echo of the national anthem, he exhorts Americans to take this new war seriously, to commit themselves to this Armageddon, to do their part:

> We see the clear way now: not *peace* at any price but Victory at any price. Not the soft appeasing answer and the turning of the other cheek, but cannon speaking for us, and the loud persuasion of the bursting bomb.
>
> A big job in the making. A big job for Americans, a job to do with fighting. In the air and on the land and in the water. Allied fighting men are en route to a greater rendezvous tonight than any you or I shall keep before the morning.
>
> This is war. It won't be won by thoughtful editorials or by a voice like this or words like these. It won't be won by sitting home and letting others do the work. It won't be won by figuring that we can never lose because

we've never lost. It may be that America has never lost a war; but neither, for *that* matter has *Japan*.

This is war, and war is sweat and grime and mud and overtime and never-mind-the profits. This is war and has to do with blood and bone and anger, and a big job done by many. (17)

Corwin unleashes his stunning display of verbal pyrotechnics to stir the nationalism and wartime energy of Americans, many of them post–World War I isolationists.

Corwin's *This Is War!* play, which leads off the *This Is War!* series, maintains the heart-stirring zeal of *We Hold These Truths*. Not all the subsequent plays follow suit. Among the strong plays in the series, however, are three about the armed forces: Maxwell Anderson's *Your Navy* (aired 28 February 1942), starring Fredric March and Lieutenant Douglas Fairbanks Jr.; Stephen Vincent Benét's *Your Army* (7 March 1942), starring Tyrone Power; and Ranald MacDougall's *Your Air Forces* (4 April 1942), starring Lieutenant James Stewart (who had been selected to receive a commission in the weeks after *We Hold These Truths*). Surprisingly and happily, Anderson, whose stage works tend to be a tad highbrow and are sometimes written in stilted verse, seems to have an instinctive feel for the radio medium. In *Your Navy,* he literally uses all the bells and whistles at his disposal to allow the radio audience, through realistic sound effects, to feel that they are actually on a ship and in the midst of warfare. Indeed, Anderson's radio play (and other plays like it) reveals one of the great advantages of radio theatre over stage theatre: combat, explosions, disasters, and ocean-going vessels can be effectively and realistically conveyed through the use of simple sound effects. *Your Navy,* consequently, enables listeners easily and viscerally to enter the world and atmosphere of a navy vessel torpedoing enemy submarines.

The immediacy of the audience experience, in turn, enables Maxwell Anderson and the *This Is War!* series in strongest terms to alert listeners to the importance of the Navy and the war effort. For example, after the sound effect of large guns being shot at sea, the narrator (Fredric March) says:

That's it. That's how it sounds. The big guns of the fleet speaking in the name of our freedom-loving nations. As of tonight they hold the straits and sea lanes, making impossible the conquest of the earth by Hitler and his Japanese associates. That's why we look towards our Navy nowadays, and hope so much from it, and listen for news of it in a hush of held breath and thumping hearts. (49)

Listeners are thus not merely educated but also pointedly cued as to how they should feel. Finally, in the concluding moments of *Your Navy,* the civilians become the family that the paternal figures, the men of the Navy, are protecting, and the broadcast listeners are enjoined to take the war seriously, do their part zealously, and fight the good battle on the home front:

> FAIRBANKS. Every time they make port they consider it a battle won. But, go about their work as callously as they may, they have a sense of importance to the world that gives a new sharpness to the eye, a new conviction to the spirit. They know that they are the men in the house of civilization. They defend that house.
>
> MARCH. I hope you heard that, you boys out there, you boys on the blue water. We know we can depend on you, and we want you to know that you can depend on us. . . . We know that our existence as a nation and as citizens depends on doing our jobs at home as relentlessly, as tirelessly, as efficiently, as courageously as you do yours at sea.
>
> We know that we must face the production struggle with the same resolution which you show at your battle stations when the enemy line looms up over the horizon. We pledge you, men of the Navy, your nation will not let you down. (66–67)

Ultimately, a broadcast such as *Your Navy* uses dramatic art to create a stunning oxymoron of morale: a "feel good" spirit in the midst of national crisis.

By contrast, *Your Army*, Stephen Vincent Benét's contribution to the *This Is War!* series, is rambling and unfocused, speaking of armies in past American wars; chiding politicians who presume to know better than the military strategists, and Americans who are not 100 percent behind the war effort; and vaunting the sacrifices the fighting men of the army will make in the cause of duty, honor, and country.

Ranald MacDougall's *Your Air Forces* gains some special weight and authority for being narrated by Jimmy Stewart, himself a Lieutenant in the Army Air Forces. MacDougall's play recaptures some of Maxwell Anderson's momentum but also strikes out in an appropriately new direction. Radio audiences knew full well what the Army and Navy do and how they function, but air power—and consequently the Air Forces—was still coming into its own in 1942. Like Moss Hart's stage play *Winged Victory*, *Your Air Forces* has a heuristic objective: to teach civilians about the importance, needs, and manpower of the Air Forces:

> All over the world, American planes are carrying the fight to the enemy. And with them are American crews, to assemble the planes and to instruct foreign crews in their operation. . . . That takes time. That takes planning. And it takes a lot of help from home. Not somebody to yelp— . . . But somebody to *help*. You take the airplane industry, for instance. A few years ago, there wasn't much to it. A few planes for airlines here and there. Some attempt at making a cheap, mass-production flivver plane. No money to spend for research—or expansion. Then—wham! . . . Things are

different now. I guess it's no military secret that America is more than 90% ahead in aircraft production since December 7th, and our production before Pearl Harbor wasn't so bad either. All over the country, aircraft factories are really putting on the heat. (179–180)

The feel of American air strength and a sense of what it is like to fly a plane in the war is, further, made immediately manifest by MacDougall through the aural power of simple radio sound effects.

In *Your Air Forces,* there is, as in many of the plays that make up the *This Is War!* programs, a dominant leitmotif that enjoins Americans at home to participate on the home front in the fight: "help, not yelp." This is the message of *You're on Your Own* (aired 21 March 1942), a drama by another well-known writer contributing to this series, Philip Wylie. *This Is War!* is a whole made up of disparate and uneven parts, some more effective than others. But the rhythms of Norman Corwin always rescue the series when it seems to border on the jejune. His *The Enemy, Concerning Axis Propaganda,* and *To the Young* have some of the rousing jingoistic rhetoric of *We Hold These Truths* and *This Is War!* though in softer tones. *The Enemy* has its narrator, Clifton Fadiman, recount Nazi and Japanese harrowing atrocities against conquered people and then, in Fadiman's characteristic measured tones, explain that these things are not random but part of a master plan:

> Behind every monstrous action is a double purpose. First, to help the Axis win the war; second, to build the kind of world the Axis wants: a world where every people, *including us Americans,* will be the helpless and hopeless slaves of the Nazis and Japan. Even the Germans and the Japs, except for the élite, would be slaves. The only difference between them and us— well—*we* would be the *slaves of slaves.* (207)

Using the voice of Donald Crisp, the villainy of Axis propaganda, especially on radio broadcasts, is the subject of *Concerning Axis Propaganda,* a drama that never articulates but clearly implies the difference between Corwin's own truth telling—"All incidents cited in this program are based upon actual occurrences" (216)—and the lies sent across the airwaves from Berlin and Tokyo. Finally, in *To the Young,* Corwin takes the paradigm of many wartime plays and films— the unity of men from across the United States coming together to fight a common foe—and eloquently expands it to the unity of freedom-loving people across the globe, writing: "There are no longer a dozen big powers in the world, there are only two: *good* and *evil*" (272). With its near-captive weekly audience, *This Is War!* attests to the power of the drama and, in this case, radio drama in particular as a major weapon in the American wartime armory.

Around the same time that the *This Is War!* series was launched, the U.S. Treasury Department launched its own series of syndicated programs, *The Treasury Star Parade.*[23] These were fifteen-minute shows appearing at various times and on various stations. Some were musical and variety, others dramatic. They starred important celebrities who volunteered their talents for the war effort. In a preface to the published collection of representative scripts from *The Treasury Star Parade,* Henry Morgenthau, Jr., Roosevelt's Secretary of the Treasury, writes, "I am glad, above all, that this achievement grew spontaneously out of patriotic teamwork between the Treasury and the broadcasters, between Government and its free citizens" (xii).[24] As with *We Hold These Truths* and the *This Is War!* programs, the real connection between government and radio at the time was turbid and murky. Were these programs, as Morgenthau suggests, a happy cooperation between the government and the radio networks, or was pressure brought to bear by Washington on the networks? Whatever the answer, the radio scripts that resulted in *The Treasury Star Parade* show the effective use of dramatic art for morale-building wartime radio programming. Unlike the palpably propagandistic play scripts issued by the Treasury Department for use in schools and by community groups, the radio dramas aired on *The Treasury Star Parade* were more of a soft sell. They were all patriotic, and although some of them unabashedly pushed the purchase of War Bonds and War Stamps, others did not. What they did do, however, is keep the immediacy of the war and the importance of support for the war in the minds and hearts of the millions of American radio listeners who tuned in regularly to *The Treasury Star Parade.*

Among the more popular plays in the series were a threesome called *Education for Death* by Gregor Ziemer, and *Education for Life* and *Education for Victory* by Violet Atkins. The first was based on an account by Gregor Ziemer that had been published in *Reader's Digest.* It presents the brainwashing of the German people and especially the children so that they lose their humanity and blindly follow the orders of Hitler. The narrator, actor Henry Hull, exclaims that the world of Hitler "is a world sinking toward death! These are not children anymore—they are machines! They are like robots, wound with one thought—one great, terrible, ghastly idea—the wish to die!" (52). He then ends the program by exhorting the listeners:

> And there you have it—that is the challenge of Hitlerism to America. What are we going to do about it? *He* is making fanatics—*we* must make believers. [*Orchestra into last eight bars of "America" softly*] Our democracy is *worth* getting excited about. We must recognize the gifts we have—but also the obligations that go with them. "Let me die for Hitler!" cried the little German boy. Then our slogan must be: "Let me live for America!" [*Orchestra up to full finish*]. (53)

Violet Atkins's *Education for Life* (whose cast included Sidney Lumet and Dickie Van Patten) is a rejoinder to *Education for Death.* It is about tolerance, about youngsters doing their part in the war effort, and about love of America.[25] It ends with an affirmation to country, parents, self, and "to that Strong, Gentle, Humane Man in the White House" (70), and the cast closes the play with the

Pledge of Allegiance. *Education for Victory* tells of the bravery of the children of Russia and concludes, "Our aim is to defeat Nazism. Hitler is the enemy not only of Russian children, but of English and American children. Polish—Chinese—Greek—all are his victims. In fighting him, we are not only defending their children—but ours as well" (86). These scripts are indicative of many heard on *The Treasury Star Parade.*

There are others overtly about War Bonds. Among these are John Latouche's *Mrs. Murroyd's Dime* (narrated by Robert Montgomery) and Joseph Ruscoll and Noel Huston's *The Modern Scrooge* (starring Lionel Barrymore, who was renowned for playing Scrooge every year, from 1934 to 1954, in the Orson Welles Mercury Theatre Group radio production of Dickens's *A Christmas Carol*).[26] In Norman Rosten's *Miss Liberty Goes to Town* (starring Alfred Lunt and Lynn Fontanne), the Statue of Liberty, which looks out onto New York Harbor, wants to see what is going on behind her back.[27] Accompanied by Ulysses S. Grant from Grant's Tomb, she sees that all is well with New York and America: people are pitching in to win the war and they are buying War Bonds. Perhaps the most well known of *The Treasury Star Parade* programs is the one called *Chicago, Germany,* written by one of the greats of radio scriptwriting, Arch Oboler. It featured Joan Blondell and Hans Conried. Oboler, whose forte was science fiction and horror, and who developed the long-running *Lights Out* and *Inner Sanctum* series, wrote *Chicago, Germany,* a ghastly scenario fictively presaging what would happen in America if the Germans won the war. Using a full range of sound effects, the play chills the radio audience as they hear that, with the war won by the Germans, the citizens of Chicago are killed, placed in forced labor camps, and classified into Aryans and non-Aryans. The broadcast then concludes with the stern imperative, "This has been a play about an America that must never happen—that *will* never happen—NEVER!" (328).

The Treasury Star Parade programs are impressive because in the space of a fifteen-minute time slot, they couple the art of the drama with audio technology to produce highly charged infusions of national pride, support for the war, a determination to combat fascism, and a motivation for buying War Bonds. In an article announcing that the series was now being heard on 759 radio stations, the *New York Times* aptly said of William Bacher, the director of the series, "Mr. Bacher tackles his work with the conviction that Americans, though slow to wrath, 'come through like no other guys when they know the facts and understand the issues.' "[28] Eschewing the fanfare of *This Is War!* or *We Hold These Truths, The Treasury Star Parade* made its quiet but nonetheless significant impact, often airing its programs on off-network stations and at odd hours. As one columnist wrote, "there are many attractive aspects of the *Treasury Star Parade.* One of them, and it is surely gratifying to a lot of listeners, is the privilege of enjoying good radio at hours when the airwaves are not usually overburdened with quality and on stations which normally do not present such talent-laden programs as these."[29]

A year after the initiation of the *This Is War!* and *The Treasury Star Parade* series, another important radio drama series, *Free World Theatre*, was launched on 21 February 1943 (and ran until 27 June of that year). By this time, World War II was no longer a novelty but a grim reality for the American people now embroiled in the depths of battle across two oceans. Significantly, then, the tone of the *Free World Theatre* radio plays in 1943 is markedly different from that of other plays produced the previous year. Both *This Is War!* and *The Treasury Star Parade* stressed the need for American patriotic support of the war effort and the determination of America to subdue the demonic evil of the Axis powers. *Free World Theatre*, however, while recognizing that war was raging and as yet was unresolved, nonetheless directed listeners to a future imbued with world peace, blessed by the work of the (not yet officially founded) United Nations, and in which the United States played a major role in a new and pacific, Augustan world order. The very title of the series suggests that it is directed as much to the listening audience of a free world as it is to just Americans. In his preface to the published scripts of *Free World Theatre*, Arch Oboler asserts, "beyond the battles themselves, there was the winning of understanding in men so that the peace would be a lasting one" (xiii).[30]

Employing the art of drama in very pointed ways, many of the nineteen *Free World Theatre* productions clearly seek to alter radically the image and self-image of the U.S. from that of a country edged with isolationism, one that had been reluctant to enter both the war and the international political arena, and one that had voted down the League of Nations after World War I, to a nation dedicated to playing a major (possibly *the* major) role in the international community and to maintaining the projected post–World War II peace. *Free World Theatre* was produced and directed for the NBC Blue Network (which would that year become the American Broadcasting Company) by the very capable and talented Arch Oboler. Again, it came about through another fuzzy combination of governmental and private resources: the office of War Information, the Blue Network, the Hollywood Victory Committee, and the Hollywood Writers Mobilization. As was also true of the prior radio series, talented writers and actors were enlisted in the making of the *Free World Theatre* programs. Each script, moreover, was inspired by some statement made by a famous person: for example, Vice President Henry A. Wallace, Thomas Mann, President Manuel Quezon of the Philippines, William Allen White, Secretary of State Cordell Hull, and General H. H. Arnold.

Some of the pieces in *Free World Theatre* are excellent and forceful in themselves, but far more significant is the way the whole series—with more than a soupçon of governmental involvement at work—reflects a turning point in American national self-concept, endorsing the image of the United States as an international peacekeeper, an image that continued after the war and into the present. The tone of the series was clearly set from its very beginning, with Arch Oboler's *The People March*, starring the renowned Russian-born actress Alla Nazimova. Oboler's play begins with the words, "The Hollywood Writers' Mobilization present The Free World Theatre—dedicated to you, the fighting men and women of the United Nations!" (3). The focus on the United Nations rather than the United States and on an audience listening beyond American shores becomes the prelude to a radio drama affirming that victory and the subsequent peace will be an international undertaking but one spearheaded by the United States.[31]

The People March oscillates tellingly between the present tense of wartime and the future tense of peacetime. The play begins with a man in the U.S. reacting skeptically as he listens to a speaker on the air talking about what should happen at the close of the war. The speaker on the radio asserts, "We must use our power at the peace table to build an economic peace that is just, charitable and enduring," to which the man responds, "I ask what the devil's the use talking about what's going to be after the war's over, when the war's still going on?" (5). Oboler here sets up a straw man who might well represent a doubting listener tuned in to *Free World Theatre* in 1943, while the war is raging. The remainder of the play proves the importance of both the broadcast within the broadcast and of American dedication to a meaningful postwar peace, a dedication not easily made during the precarious period of 1943, with its long casualty lists and military setbacks.

In occupied Holland, where *The People March* begins, young men hear the broadcast from the United States telling them, "We cannot now blueprint all the details of the world after victory is won, but we can and must begin now to think about it" (6). The men are inspired to print these words in their underground newspaper not merely because they are words of hope but because those words come from America. In occupied Norway, men have been waiting to hear word from America, and they are inspired to ford the foggy North Sea and escape to England when they hear the Americans tell them over the airwaves, "I believe the United States also has learned her lesson and that she is willing to assume responsibility among the United Nations proportionate to her strength" (8). The broadcast asserts the connection between God and the United States: "The idea of freedom—the freedom that we in the United States know and love so well—is derived from the Bible, with its extraordinary emphasis on the dignity of the individual" (10). When the men in the Warsaw Ghetto hear these words, they find the courage to face the worst from the Nazis. In Russia, the response to the radio broadcast is curiously one of eschewing vengeance when the enemy is defeated. When the radio says that after the war the diabolical work of Hitler and the Japanese warlords must be punished, Oboler's Russian character says that when the people of the enemy nations are contrite, "I will pity them—and I will help them—once they know their defeat and their shame" (14). Finally, hospitalized, wounded American soldiers hear the broadcast suggesting wartime full employment can become peacetime full employment, and one soldier tells his skeptical friend in the next hospital bed, "They [the ordinary people], and we, have got to *learn* something out of this war!"

(16). The speaker on the broadcast predicts a new era that will include not only the U.S. and England, not only India, Russia, China, and Latin America, but also Germany, Italy, and Japan. Yet the new era is more than international:

> Some have spoken of the "American Century." Yes, perhaps it will be America's opportunity to suggest the freedom and duties by which the common man must live. But I say that the century on which we are entering—the century which will come out of this war—can be and must be—the *Century of the Common Man*. (18)

As a work of drama, *The People March* is lackluster. What is impressive, however, is how in fifteen minutes the play layers a peace plan on top of the ongoing warfare, suggests God is on America's side, preaches postwar prosperity and forgiveness, highlights the centrality of the U.S. in the war and in the future peace, and projects a future that is international and for the common man. In many ways and significantly, *The People March* takes the ideas found in the leftist plays of the Depression era and refashions them in such a way that they become mainstream and part of the American democratic leadership for a new postwar age.

The second drama in the *Free World Theatre* series, Budd Schulberg and Jerome Lawrence's *Tomorrow*, continues some of the themes initiated in *The People March*. Schulberg had recently attained fame as the author of the Hollywood novel *What Makes Sammy Run?* (1941). Jerome Lawrence was just beginning his career and was soon to found Armed Forces Radio with Robert E. Lee, with whom he was in later years to co-author *Inherit the Wind* (1955), *Auntie Mame* (1956), and *The Night Thoreau Spent in Jail* (1970). *Tomorrow* starred John Garfield, Beulah Bondi, and Ray Collins and tells of a soldier who returns home when the war has ended to find that his father believes the victory to have been an exclusively American one. The father, moreover, wishes as well to return to the isolationist America of 1941. The son, Jack, who is a voice of a new generation and a new American world mission, exclaims:

> you don't have to wear a swastika on your arm to make the world run backwards. You can do it by sitting home in your dining room and cooking up a lot of hate and distrust. You can do it by yapping about England and Russia like you just did! You can do it sitting in a window marked "Business as Usual" and thumbing your nose at the rest of the world! There you're just as much of an anachronism as Hitler was! (29)

He adds later, "*Join hands around the world—and don't let go!*" (33). Impressive here, in 1943, is not only the castigation of those who stayed home and carried on "business as usual," but more especially the call for men bonding together for universal peace. These are the very themes that were to play a prominent role some years later, when the war was actually won, in plays such as Arthur

Miller's *All My Sons*, Robert Sherwood's *The Rugged Path*, and Howard Lindsay and Russel Crouse's *State of the Union*.

Other notable plays in the *Free World Series* include *China to America* by Nobel laureate Pearl Buck, Irving Ravetch's *The Second Battle of Warsaw*, and *White House Kitchen* by Bernard C. Schoenfeld. The cast of the Pearl Buck piece included Lee J. Cobb, Mercedes McCambridge, and Hans Conried and projected a radio contact between American pilots and the citizens of a village in Buck's second homeland, China. In keeping with the thrust of the *Free World Theatre* agenda, *China to America* stresses three main issues: offering Americans insight into life in wartime China, affirming the similarity between Americans and Chinese despite their geographic and cultural distance, and driving home the idea that after the war has been won, the U.S. and China will be partners in the same peacetime global community. There is, as well, an undercurrent that suggests the survival of China and the future well-being of the world is largely in American hands. The Chinese radio operator says:

> Our life is very hard. Every day now the enemy bombs come down. We live like in prison. That is, we have very little food now, and money is no better than dust. . . . China is cut off and our people feel alone. We are like shipwrecked men upon an island who search the skies for help. But I who hear your voices coming over the winds, I know we are not alone. America, are you there? (142)

And the village silk merchant adds, "Yes, we are the same, Chinese and American. We love our sons, but we send them out to fight this enemy. I know your sons are fighting, too" (142–143).

The discussion moves from China and Chinese-American points of congruence to the need for internationalism. A local high school teacher, speaking didactically, avers, "We teachers here in China, we are saying, it is not enough any more to teach children only about their own country. It is because teachers in Japan have taught that their country alone is good and their people better than all others that today we have this enemy ruining and robbing us" (145). The town magistrate goes one step further, asserting, "We believe in freedom— not only our own but we believe in the freedom of all people under heaven" (149). Here Pearl Buck shrewdly subverts a traditional American complacent sense of national superiority by implicitly equating it with Japanese arrogance. She then urges her fellow Americans to fight not solely for the freedoms guaranteed by the Constitution to American citizens but to fight so that those same freedoms will be granted to all citizens on the planet.

Irving Ravetch and Bernard Schoenfeld were two talented young men in their twenties who were soon to carve out careers as successful Hollywood screenwriters.[32] Whereas Pearl Buck's *China to America* depicts the ongoing courage of the Chinese people in the face of the Japanese oppressor, Ravetch's *The Second Battle of Warsaw* feelingly dramatizes the courage of a family in the Jewish ghetto who, knowing they will die in the process, fight valiantly against the Nazis in the name of freedom.[33] The finest of all the *Free World Theatre* programs, however, is Schoenfeld's excellent and moving *White House Kitchen*, which envisions, from backstairs at the White House, the American political world as it will be when the war is over. The president's domestic staff, who represent the common people, some with sons and husbands who have fought and died in World War II, wait anxiously in the kitchen as the president and senators decide the future course for America.

The largely unspoken idea behind the whole *Free World Theatre* series is that after World War I, the U.S. made a great error by rejecting entry into the League of Nations. Woodrow Wilson's speeches and rhetoric were unable to move the American public to join the international community of nations. Oboler and his playwrights, however, replace Wilson's speeches with the political power of drama, a power they witnessed in the agitprop plays of the 1930s. Their aim is to reach the emotions of their listeners, convincing them to think generously and globally rather than solipsistically and nationally.

In the kitchen, there is a confrontation between the White House domestic staff and the chauffeur of a reactionary "America first" senator. In an interchange between Foster, the presidential butler, and Scott, Senator Gray's chauffeur, the defeat of Wilson is remembered:

> FOSTER. I stayed up late the night Woodrow Wilson sat in his study with the Senators and told them the future depended on how they voted the next week. I hear Mr. Wilson spoke like a prophet out of the Bible that night. . . .
>
> SCOTT. Yeah, and Wilson got beaten.
>
> FOSTER. We all were beaten. [*With quiet intensity*] But tonight we're going to win. (69)

Wilson here becomes an archetype of the biblical prophet unheeded by a stiff-necked people who are brought to disaster by their failure to heed his prophetic words. Wilson's idea is born again at the envisioned end of another world war, but this time the idea springs not from the president but from the common people around the world, the common people very much like the White House servants, the common people very much like the radio listeners:

> It's not his idea, Catherine. The tailor at the corner had the idea. The butcher in London had the idea. The farmer in Russia had the idea. The coolies in China had the idea. It doesn't belong to him or to any party. It's in the air. You might as well stop breathing as stop it from being born. (70–71)

Above stairs, however, Senator Gray is trying to quash the idea, arguing American isolationism and greed once more: "Commendable as this world plan is, it's purely visionary. I say, follow the old dollar and cents viewpoint" (73).

White House Kitchen ends with dramatic and rhetorical flair, as one of the servants reports the president's words, a powerful amalgam of vision, commitment, and sentimentality:

> "Gentlemen, Senator Gray's argument is a sound one—on the basis of dollars and cents. . . . Why give up some of our money and some of our trade and some of our power so that all the world can be more prosperous and happier? . . . But, gentlemen, I ask you—is that the *new* brand of American horse-sense? Yes, the new American horse-sense that came out of the blood, and the sacrifice, and the tears of millions of American men, women and children. The new common sense which says isn't it better to sacrifice a little national power and forget a little of our dollars and cents values in return for the security of a world without the hatreds which build to another war?" And then he stopped speaking and looked out the window at the rain and then he spoke so quickly I could hardly hear him. He said: "Gentlemen, that rain is soaking into the graves of many men out there in Arlington who died for this moment. I think they expect us to do something fine with the freedom they won back for us." And then the President turned and he just looked at the other men, and Senator Harrison, whose son *is* buried out there, was crying, and he held out his hand to the President, and then all of them were around the President. (76–77)

Brilliantly, Schoenfeld uses dramatic essentialism to create a struggle between internationalism and isolationism, protagonist and antagonist, and in doing so sways a wartime audience recently shaken from an era of isolationism to assent to a political agenda that will be very different once the war has been won. Indeed, what one see here once again is how, using drama, the playwrights could take what were the leftist socialist and communist ideas of the 1930s and bring them into the mainstream, making them part of a new centrist political agenda. "Workers of the World, Unite" becomes domesticated into an internationalism hailed by the common man and implemented by the politicians. Clearly one can see how, rather transparently, in both *White House Kitchen* and the *Free World Theatre* series more generally, the playwrights fashion the war so that it becomes a catalyst of immense importance, pushing for major social and political changes in America.

Although many established writers—Norman Corwin, Maxwell Anderson, Stephen Vincent Benét, Archibald MacLeish, Pearl Buck—wrote impressive radio scripts during the war, the medium also provided an apprenticeship for young writers. Some, such as Schoenfeld and Ravetch, went on to Hollywood. Others moved to Broadway. Morton Wishengrad, who was later to write *The*

Rope Dancers (1957), for example, wrote *The Battle of the Warsaw Ghetto* for NBC a few months after the armed resistance in the Warsaw Ghetto.[34] It was part of a move by the Jewish Theology Seminary to use radio dramas as a means of demystifying Judaism for the American public and, very likely, of bringing to the attention of listeners the plight of the Jews in Europe. It also targeted a specifically Jewish audience as well by airing the play on 8 October 1943, the eve of Yom Kippur (the Day of Atonement). Like Ravetch's *The Second Battle of Warsaw,* Wishengrad's script presents a human interest story of Jews who had been deported to the Warsaw Ghetto and then fight off the Germans, but juxtaposes its poignant fictional characters against a historical context.

Still another bright, young, extremely talented, but then relatively unknown playwright who contributed to the radio drama of the war years is Arthur Laurents. He was then an enlisted serviceman writing for the Army's radio broadcasts called *Assignment Home.*[35] Arguably his radio plays—in particular *The Last Day of the War* and *The Face*—are the finger exercises that enabled him to write his renowned Broadway hit *Home of the Brave* (1945) immediately after the war. Read nowadays, after decades of plays and films about disabled and wounded soldiers, these plays seem predictable. But read in the context of 1943 to 1945, when thousands of men were returning from the front maimed for life, *The Last Day of the War* and *The Face* are small gems. Both plays could have been simplistic, but both show the unerring touch of an emerging master.

The Last Day of the War tells of Mickey Ryan, a worker in the Toledo freight yards before the war, who is badly wounded when an enemy shell explodes next to him. Laurents shrewdly realizes that visually the sight of the injured Ryan would be more than an audience could bear, but that by rendering it orally, he can safely bring his audience to the scene of the action: "two company aidmen from the medics belly out over the screaming ground to the bloody, floppy body. . . . They apply tourniquets to stop the Ohio blood, to save Mickey Ryan from hemorrhages. They give him morphine to stop the fifty million pains. They put sulfa on his wounds and dress them" (93).[36] Most radio playwrights employ a narrator to set the stage for the listening audience, and Laurents is no exception. Laurents, however, takes that device and uses it in order to convey the fact that Mickey Ryan's is no special story, and that what the audience is about to hear is—and is going to be—a typical story for as long as the war lasts and for some years thereafter.

Laurents homes in on the protagonist, his nurse, and the trauma of dealing with an amputated left leg and then an amputated right leg as well. With sensitivity, *The Last Day of the War* renders Ryan's painful physical comeback and his more difficult psychological recovery. The play also conveys the role played by his nurse-therapist and by his very young wife, whom he had married a month before entering the military. In thirty short minutes, the audience identifies with Mickey Ryan's painful recuperation as his body heals from the wounds and his stumps are fitted for prosthetic limbs. But more important, *The Last*

Day of the War likewise enables listeners to identify with Mickey's terrible, despairing sense of his disability as a double amputee:

> I haven't got any legs. I got two pieces of wood and a pair of canes. You say walk. So I walk. But like what? Like a guy with no legs on a pair of stilts! . . . You know what I need? A board with wheels on it. Yeah, and a tin cup . . . Want to buy an apple? How about a pencil? Shoelaces? Chewing gum? Yeah—that's what I'm good for! (109)

The play allows the audience, moreover, to understand the disabled Mickey's concerns for his wife: "A month after I met Margie, we got married. And a month later, I went overseas. . . . the way I figure it," he says, "just because of two months, there's no reason she should be stuck with a—well, me. . . . Ah, she's better off if she never sees me again" (99). When Margie and Mickey do finally meet again, Laurents sensitively conveys her emotions as well as the dynamics between maimed husband and young wife. Using Miss Piper, Mickey's combination physical therapist and psychotherapist, Laurents rather boldly even touches on the underlying sexual issue: "You just feel too sorry for yourself. You see your wife and you go to pieces. You get afraid that you won't be able to hold her!" (107).

When, at the close of *The Last Day of the War*, Mickey takes his first steps and reaches out, manually and emotionally, to his wife, the music swells and the eyes of the radio audience fill with tears. But this is much more than cheap sentimentality, for Laurents's aim is to educate. Fatal casualties are a terrible fact of war, and we grieve for them. But they are dead and a closed chapter. But what, Laurents posits, of the physically and psychologically wounded who do not die, but return home disabled to continue their lives? *The Last Day of the War* stunningly enables radio listeners to begin understanding these men, to admire them, and to prepare to accept them into civilian life in their now compromised conditions.

Laurents's *The Face*, which aired near the war's end during the spring of 1945, is similar to *The Last Day of the War* but still more intense. It charts a soldier whose face is horrifically burned during a battle at Casablanca Harbor. Paradoxically, the moment is *graphically* rendered through narrative and sound and is perhaps all the more moving because the image a listener will conjure up in the mind's eye is likely to be worse than any stage representation or photographic image:

> NARRATOR. There were some who didn't die but who wished they had. Like T/5 Harold Ingalls. He was in the Transportation Corps . . . unloading gasoline from supply ships.
>
> MUSIC. [*Out*]

NARRATOR. They strafed him while he was unloading that gasoline and a ten gallon can he was holding burst into flame.

INGALLS. [*A horrible scream*]

[*Pause*]

NARRATOR. No; T/5 Harold Ingalls didn't die. But he lost his ears, his nose, and the upper part of his face. Casablanca. (83)[37]

Ingalls's face must, over many months, be reconstructed with plastic surgery. When the script was chosen for an award, it was aptly said, "This is a tough script. It is tough to read it or hear it on the air and not be profoundly moved."[38] Exploiting the radio medium to the fullest, Laurents allows the audience to visualize the different stages of the reconstructive plastic surgery without actually seeing them. As a radio playwright, Laurents is simply a master of the mind's eye.

Laurents poignantly presents the psychological anxieties and anger of the maimed Ingalls as he faces life without his face, and then with a new face under construction. The portrait is such that, as in *The Last Day of the War*, the radio audience is being prepared to face, and not turn their faces from, the many men like Ingalls whom they will see in increasing numbers when the war is over. Further, *The Face* nicely imbricates Ingalls's improving visage and morale with news bulletins that mark the winning of the war in Europe, thereby linking the international struggle with a personal one and suggesting that Ingalls and those like him are as heroic as those who continue to fight the enemy on the battlefields. Unlike many of his fellow radio playwrights, moreover, Laurents does not focus on patriotism, demonizing the enemy, or the role of America in both the world war and the international community. Instead, he urges listeners to honor and accept the GIs who served their country heroically and well but who will be returning home disabled.

Not long after writing his radio plays, Arthur Laurents made his splash on Broadway with *Home of the Brave*. Looking back, one can see how in that play the psychological damage of one character and the physical damage of another originate in *The Last Day of the War* and *The Face*. Similarly, another famous Arthur, Arthur Miller, serves his apprenticeship in wartime radio drama. When Miller's *All My Sons* opened in 1947, he was essentially an unknown. During the war, however, he had steadily been at work not merely preparing *Situation Normal, Focus*, and *The Man Who Had All the Luck* but also earning his keep writing radio scripts, primarily for the prestigious NBC *Cavalcade of America* series.[39] Despite Miller's eventual fame and his emergence as arguably *the* great American playwright—rivaled only by Eugene O'Neill and perhaps Tennessee Williams—almost none of his several radio plays has to date been published. In his autobiography, *Timebends*, Miller is himself noticeably reticent about his radio days, and only one critic, Gerald Weales, has discussed them at any length.[40] Miller's radio scripts, however, reveal the playwright learning his trade and developing his insights. As with any young radio writer who has not yet achieved the clout and independence that fame brings, one must remember that the scripts are undoubtedly a hybrid of what Miller wanted to write and what he was commissioned to write.

The first of Miller's radio plays after Pearl Harbor is *The Battle of the Ovens* (22 June 1942).[41] Written for the *Cavalcade of America*, which focused on American history and historical figures, it is the story of Christopher Ludwick, the Philadelphian who served as Baker General of the United States and provided the much-needed bread for George Washington's army. The dramatization starred Jean Hersholt as Ludwick. In Miller's hands, the story of Ludwick becomes a moral tale about the ethics of businessmen garnering personal profit instead of aiding their country during wartime. In *The Battle of the Ovens*, then, the embryo of the moral dilemma in Miller's first Broadway success, *All My Sons* (1947), can be clearly seen. Ludwick has sent his apprentice, Jerry, to bake bread for the Revolutionary troops. Each soldier is given a ration of a pound of flour for a loaf of bread, but since only half a pound is needed for a loaf, Jerry keeps the remaining flour and drives to Philadelphia to sell it to Ludwick. The outraged Christopher Ludwick accuses Jerry of stealing, but Jerry, not unlike many American businessmen during World War II and not unlike Joe Keller in *All My Sons*, argues that wartime is an optimal time for personal gain:

> CHRIS. All these weeks I sit watching the boys go off to the war and I curse my bones for being so old, and the only thing that brightens my life is that I know I taught a man how to bake an honest loaf of bread and he is baking for the army. And now you come to sell me stolen flour! You common thief!
>
> JERRY. Me and about five hundred others. All the bakers are doing it in every regiment.
>
> CHRIS. You vandal! You are a disgrace to every honest baker in the world! Get out!
>
> JERRY. I guess you're just the same old fool. You don't even know there's a war on. What's war for except to make money? (5–6)

The elderly Ludwick, casting aside personal risk and undergoing financial loss, convinces Washington to make him head of baking operations. It is, Miller's radio play suggests, through common men (like modern-day Ludwicks) doing their part in the World War II effort that the war can be won, or as Ludwick reports, quoting General Washington, "He said he could not have won the war unless the bakers and the shoemakers and all the people like us got so mad they could not rest until they won" (28).

In part, the producers of *The Cavalcade of America*, which was sponsored by the DuPont Corporation, commissioned *The Battle of the Ovens* as a tribute to an uncelebrated American hero. At the same time, the play served as a lead-in for a DuPont commercial about their product, Mycoban, a preservative used to retard the formation of mold in bread and, therefore, useful to the Army and Navy. With these two constraints likely confining his playwriting, Miller nevertheless manages to raise an essential issue of the war and of dramatic writing during the war: the need for every citizen, regardless of age and trade, to get behind the war effort and support the American troops. He introduces as well— as early as 1942—a recurrent theme of postwar drama: the selfish and unethical practices of businessmen who lined their pockets during the war, ultimately at the expense of the servicemen who were putting their lives on the line for American freedoms.

Three months later, as part of the same *Cavalcade* series and in much the same vein, Miller's *Thunder from the Hills* (28 September 1942) airs.[42] This drama celebrates the career of Benito Juarez, the liberator of Mexico, and stars Orson Welles as Juarez. Throughout *Thunder from the Hills,* Juarez is portrayed by Miller as the Mexican Lincoln, but rather than fighting against slavery, Juarez fights against the oppression of the common people by the dictators of Mexico, first Santa Ana and then Emperor Maximilian, both of whom, one realizes, are prototypical fascists. Without connecting the dots, Miller suggests to the listening audience that Santa Ana and Maximilian are images of Hitler and Mussolini. When, moreover, Maximilian is defeated and captured, Juarez argues against clemency and in favor of execution: "Maximilian must die not for the sorrow he caused nor the blood he spilled. That would call only for revenge. . . . [But] for a democratic state to pardon a would-be tyrant is to make a mockery of that state and its whole people." Thus even in 1942, Miller used his drama not only to champion the principles of liberty and democracy over tyranny, but to look ahead to the end of the war and argue against pardoning Hitler and Mussolini.

Gerald Weales, with some justification, calls Miller's next radio play, *I Was Married in Bataan* (5 October 1942), "a very weak script."[43] Miller very likely had but little wiggle room in writing this drama, for it was a dramatization of a published account. As the announcer explains:

> Bataan, Corregidor—today these names stand out like banners of our defiance for the stature of American manhood was measured on Corregidor and found tall and unafraid. But American women too passed through that Philippine ordeal, and it is their heroic story—and a true story—that Cavalcade tells tonight. Lt. Dorothea Daley Engel, United States Army Nurse Corps has set down her experiences in an article written for the October American Magazine under the title "I Was Married In Battle" (1).[44]

Miller's play, we are told, is "based on Lieutenant Engel's own record of events" (1). The play is a romantic story of Dorothea English, played by Madeleine Carroll, an Army nurse who finds her true love during the battle in Bataan but loses him in the course of the disastrous events. The real point of the program is not Miller's play but Madeleine Carroll's post-performance address to the radio listeners:

> Thank you. A play is usually finished with its last line. But not our play of tonight. The story of American nurses will go on through this night and all the days of war that await us. The immediate need for trained and experienced nurses who will serve with either the Army or Navy is acute.
>
> If you are a graduate registered nurse, single and under forty years of age, won't you enroll for service with the armed forces, and inscribe your name on this roll of honor. Your Red Cross chapter can give you details. In the name of those heroes of Corregidor, offer your services now. [APPLAUSE] (32)

The weakness of the play surely stems from Miller's being compelled to write in the service of dramatic ends other than his own.

A month later, Miller is more the master of his material in his next *Cavalcade* script, *Toward a Farther Star* (2 November 1942), which again stars Madeleine Carroll, this time as Amelia Earhart.[45] In this case, Miller's play about Earhart's struggles is framed by a preface that is a tribute to women working in aeronautics as part of the war effort, and by a postscript spoken by a woman pilot who urges American women to seek employment in aeronautics.

Whether Miller penned the preface to *Toward a Farther Star* is unclear, but his radio drama about Earhart italicizes the program's combination of patriotic and feminist messages. Those messages are there from the very outset, when the announcer introduces the drama:

> As these words are spoken twenty-two hundred women are now piloting Civil Air Patrol planes. Others are ferrying bombers to distant places. Thousands of American women are pouring through the gates of factories, shipyards and airplane plants, after a hard day's work. Today we know that there is hardly a job that a woman cannot do. And if there is one woman who proved that fact, once and forever, it is America's greatest woman flyer whose thrilling story we tell this evening. (1)

The boldest colors in Miller's portrait of Earhart are those that render her uphill struggle as one of a woman gate-crashing the male preserve of aviation. She argues with the owner of an airline who refuses to employ her because of her gender:

> What are you telling me? To go home and scrub pots? Isn't it time to unlock the kitchen and let women out into the free air? . . . Yes, indeed, look at the world. And think, try to imagine how much richer it would

be now if half its population, if all its women were freed to do their part of the worlds [sic] work. The world has been walking on one foot, working with one hand when it has two; blinding two of its eyes, stifling half its brain—yes, and flying with only one of its wings. Do look at the world, Mr. Brown, and hold your breath. Because it's changing . . . right now! (9, 10)

Again when a male friend questions whether Earhart's flying will allow her to be a traditional woman and make a marriage work, Earhart pointedly retorts:

I'm going to be his wife, and I'm going to fly. It's got to work because it must be true that a woman can live out her personal dreams and still be a wife. I mean, women must have a right to lead the way once in a while, to search for new things, instead of sitting home, waiting for men to do the work of the world. Isn't that true? (15)

Impressive here is the vehemence and force of *Toward a Farther Star*'s feminist agenda and its eloquent testimony to the connection between the war and the expanding of gender roles for women. It is impressive, too, that the text comes from Miller, who has more than once been accused of not creating plays with strong women.

The postscript to *Toward a Farther Star* brings the dramatized history of Amelia Earhart into the present tense as Madeleine Carroll steps out of her role as Earhart to introduce a modern woman doing her share for her country through aviation:

CARROLL. Mrs. D. A. McNeill, of Ellington Field, Texas,—the first woman air crew chief in the world. Women like Mrs. McNeill are working day and night in flying fields stationed all over America. . . . These are the women who keep the planes in the air! (24A)

McNEILL. As a pioneer, Amelia Earhart foresaw woman's place in aviation. There are many branches of that field open to women today. I want to make an appeal to you tonight—go to your post office, secure the information regarding women needed in various branches of this one great service. Women are needed in machine shops, as lathe workers, and workers on delicate precision instruments. . . . We women can keep our men and our planes flying by doing the ground work! (24B)

To what extent Miller's play was written with a prescribed point of view is unknown, but what is palpably present in *Toward a Farther Star* is the ability of this young apprentice playwright to convey with power significant wartime women's issues.

Miller's two subsequent radio plays, *The Eagle's Nest* (28 December 1942) and

Listen for the Sound of Wings (19 April 1943), depart from *Cavalcade*'s usual agenda of presenting famous Americans, presenting instead three courageous Europeans—Italian patriots Giuseppe Garibaldi and Alberto Liguri and Pastor Martin Niemoeller of Berlin—who come, in Miller's dramas, to embody American democratic values.[46] *The Eagle's Nest* is a straightforward but rather mechanical play in which Paul Muni plays the roles of Garibaldi and Liguri. In part, the play seems addressed to Italians, Italian Americans, and admirers of Mussolini, reminding them of the more admirable Italian passion for freedom and democracy, a passion expressed by Garibaldi, who wrote a letter to the American people:

> On November 13th, 1866 Garibaldi sat in Caprera and wrote this to Americans. The sympathy which comes to me from free men, citizens of a great nation, like yourselves, gives me courage for my task in the cause of liberty and progress. I regard the American people as the sole arbiter of questions of humanity amid the universal thraldom of the soul and intellect. Please express these, my sentiments to your countrymen, and believe me, Yours for life, Giuseppe Garibaldi.
>
> So you see, America has the right to speak to Italy. Garibaldi bequeathed to us that privilege. Tonight the voice of Garibaldi speaks to lovers of liberty everywhere. No Nazi government will tell this story but we will tell it. (2)

The play proceeds to be a brief record of Garibaldi's fight for a unified and democratic Italy, as well as Liguri's contemporary and heroic resistance to the Nazis. The remarkable disparity between the Italian zeal for liberty under Garibaldi and the Italian devotion to Mussolini Fascism seventy years later is carefully and pointedly presented in *The Eagle's Nest*. Miller, furthermore, effectively forges the connection between the 1860s and the 1940s by employing the easy transitions radio allows and by writing the lines of Garibaldi and Liguri for the same actor (in this case, Muni). Looking at *The Eagle's Nest* in terms of Miller's later career, what one sees is the beginnings of Miller's abiding interest in Italy and in conflicted Italian feelings about a desire for freedom versus a desire for rules, a theme that will come to the fore a few years later in *The Hook* (1950), the filmscript he wrote with Elia Kazan, and to fruition in *A View from the Bridge* (1955).[47]

One of Miller's finest radio scripts is surely *Listen for the Sound of Wings*, in which he charts the trials and resistance of the modern martyr Reverend Martin Niemoeller (whose name Miller consistently spells Niemüller). Playing Niemüller is Paul Lukas, a perfect choice, for two years earlier, Lukas had achieved Broadway fame as another heroic anti-Nazi German martyr, Kurt Müller, in Lillian Hellman's *Watch on the Rhine*. When *Listen for the Sound of Wings* begins, it announces its alleged theme: "A right of American citizenship, the right to worship. But in Nazi Germany this right no longer exists." This may have been the theme *Cavalcade of America* and its sponsor, the Du Pont Company, requested, but Miller writes instead a moving drama about resistance to Nazi oppression and will. Initially accepting the word of Hitler that he is not against religion but that "The atheism we preach sometimes is purely a tactic," Niemüller publicly endorses the German *Führer* only to discover that Hitler's words have been a prevarication. When the son of one of his parishioners is shot in the street for making a speech against Hitler, Niemüller ruefully says, "Murderer. Cold-blooded murderer. I made a covenant with a murderer." Miller cleverly shifts the play here from the issue of religious freedom to that of free speech and resistance to the Nazi regime.

When Niemüller himself changes from acceptance of evil to outspoken defiance in his sermons, he is harassed by the Gestapo, to whom he angrily shouts, "Tell Herr Hitler as long as I have a tongue in my head, I will damn him and all his works." And to his Berlin congregation he says, "To serve him is to obey the very spirit and essence of evil. To obey him is a crime before God." Eventually Niemüller is thrown into a concentration camp, where he undergoes a series of hair-raising tortures to make him recant his anti-dictatorship views and sign a paper declaring his allegiance to Hitler and the Third Reich. Miller's radio play is especially effective because the physical violence is powerfully delivered through sound and because Niemüller's personal strength in the face of his oppressors offers a frightening picture of Nazi brutality and renders Niemüller a modern martyr. In the personal trials of conscience and body that Niemüller undergoes in *Listen for the Sound of Wings*, Miller lays the groundwork for his portrait, ten years later, of John Proctor in *The Crucible*.

Miller seems to have taken a break for a year from writing radio plays after *Listen for the Sound of Wings*, probably to work on his first Broadway play, *The Man Who Had All the Luck*, which did not fare well. In 1945, he returned to radio with a weak play about a lonely soldier who is helped by the Red Cross to make contact with his wife: *Bernadine, I Love You* (5 March 1945), starring William Bendix.[48] Miller followed this lackluster play, however, three weeks later with one of his best, an effective, heart-swelling, sentimental radio drama, *Grandpa and the Statue* (26 March 1945), which is one of the only two published Miller radio plays.[49] With the war clearly drawing to a close, Miller wrote a warmhearted play about Grandpa Monaghan (acted by Charles Laughton), who refused to contribute to the funds to erect the base for the Statue of Liberty, a statue that he thinks is nonsense. When his grandson takes him to Bedloe's Island (as Liberty Island was then called), however, he meets a soldier who tells him, "This statue kinda looks like what we believe" (280). Miller uses *Grandpa and the Statue* to endorse his audience's national pride and to applaud their belief in America and in the liberties for which World War II was fought. At the same time, he subversively reminds his audience that the famous Emma Lazarus poem inscribed on the base of the statue—"Give me your tired, your poor, your huddled masses yearning to breathe free"—was no longer true in light of the U.S.'s stringent immigration laws, laws that had denied entry to many who were, consequently, killed during the war. Miller is quoted in Erik Barnouw's introduction to the published script, "I will not deny though that I had a desire to make people realize that the Statue of Liberty was erected to signify America's former open-door policy. If people get the idea from the show that Jew, Irish, Italian or what not, we were all welcome here once, that will be a great satisfaction to me" (268). In short, *Grandpa and the Statue* in a way marks the transition in drama from wartime patriotic to postwar critical views of American participation during the course of World War II.

A month later, in *The Philippines Never Surrendered* (30 April 1945), Miller sounded an unequivocally celebratory note in his dramatization of a *Saturday Evening Post* article about Edward Kuder (portrayed by Edward G. Robinson), the superintendent of schools on the Philippine island of Mindanao.[50] As the Japanese invade the Philippines, Kuder urges the Moros inhabitants of Mindanao to resist and then later to strike against the Japanese so as to keep the Philippines free. Miller's drama works effectively and simultaneously in different ways for his American audience. It demonizes the Japanese as cruel and tyrannical invaders and creates a scenario whereby the American teacher, Kuder, moves out of the schoolroom to instruct the Moros and their leader, Pandangaman (and by extension the radio listeners), on the importance of repulsing the Japanese.

The conflict in *The Philippines Never Surrendered* endorses an American concept of colonialism, for the choice the Moros have, as Miller posits it, is subjugation by the Japanese or an American paternalism, embodied by Kuder, that will lead to Philippine pride and eventual independence. The teacherly Kuder first tells the Moros:

> I'm not trying to tell you what you should do. But you *must* choose between . . . resistance . . . or possibly a lifetime of slavery under the Japanese . . . [SLIGHT MURMUR UP] If you decide to resist . . . you must not repair the road this morning. Resistance should begin in ways like that . . . not working . . . wrecking trucks . . . blowing up bridges. (10)

As the conflict with the Japanese intensifies, Kuder eventually tells Pandangaman that sabotage is not enough:

> It's your freedom too, Pandangaman . . . and I've come to this conclusion. Sabotage is not enough. It's time for the Moros to kill Japs. . . . Well, soon every Moro must decide, no matter what you their leader may think— that to have their own country . . . to be free. . . . They have to fight. (13–14)

Instilling the spirit of the American Revolution into the Filipinos and their leader, Kuder transforms them into patriots, and with strains of triumphant music in the background, he tells the audience, "From that night on the Japanese on Mindanao died in many ways. By bullet, by stone, by knife and by rope. The Japs had swallowed up the Philippines, and the feast had killed them. [Music: up and out]" (20).

At the close of *The Philippines Never Surrendered,* Miller swings the action into the present. Although V-J Day is still three and a half months away, the play prepares the American audience for victory and celebrates not so much the courage of the Filipinos but the fulfillment of General MacArthur's famous "I shall return" Corregidor promise. And Kuder, who narrates the play, has presumably, like the Moros he has instructed, gone from civilian to fighter, for at its conclusion in 1945, the play finds him in a military hospital:

> KUDER. On that black day of May, 1942, they listened in Seattle and the radio was dead in Corregidor. But in February 1945 I lay in a New York hospital, and beside me the radio was tuned to the same wave band. The voice had returned to Corregidor; to Manila and to those islands the speech of free men had returned and it soared like strong birds across the long Pacific. . . . soared in the voice of General MacArthur. . . . [Sound: static in: clears]

> MacArthur. [As on short wave] President Osmena, my country has kept the faith. On her behalf I now solemnly declare the full powers and responsibilities under the Constitution restored to the Philippine Commonwealth. We come here as an army of free men, dedicated with your people to the cause of human liberty. Manila has regained her rightful place as a living and heroic symbol of democracy. [Sound: static segue into] [Music: under]

> KUDER. The level voice of Douglas MacArthur rose out of the sea, and the silence of the sea was rolled away. And I knew then what I had stayed behind to prove. . . . The Philippines never surrendered [Music: up to finish]. (22–23)

Miller here emerges as someone whose apprenticeship in radio drama has taught him to be a savvy radio dramatist, able to exploit the advantages of the medium. *The Philippines Never Surrendered* is arguably Miller's most masterful work for radio in part because the music and the smooth segues work so well with Miller's use of the actual sound recording, complete with static, of MacArthur's speech. It was also Miller's last radio play performed during the war, for with the war's end, he turned to the stage and the work that catapulted him to fame: *All My Sons.*

His radio plays from 1942 to 1945 show much more than an Arthur Miller serving his playwriting apprenticeship and doing finger exercises. In a larger sense, his plays and those of others provide an insight into the ways in which wartime playwrights used radio and how wartime radio used playwrights. Radio theatre during World War II, in fact, seems to emerge from the dynamics created by an unruly troika, each member of which has different ends: the playwright hopes to be untrammeled to create dramatic art, the government (especially the Office of War Information) wishes to set the play's agenda, and the radio networks and their corporate sponsors seek large audiences for the program and many prospective buyers for their products. Nowhere is this more keenly demonstrated than in the case of *The Story of Gus,* the only Arthur Miller radio play, beside *Grandpa and the Statue,* ever to be printed.[51] *The Story of Gus* was never aired. Joseph Liss, a radio writer who worked during the war for the Office of War Information (OWI), had helped get Miller a commission to write a script for OWI's Domestic Radio Bureau. Miller was supposed to write a radio play about the merchant marines with the aim of recruiting experienced sailors for the war effort.

After the war, Liss published a collection of radio plays that included Miller's *The Story of Gus.* In his introduction to the Miller script, Liss relates that when Miller submitted his script, a nameless vice president of one of the radio networks vetoed it because "It was 'radical' " and because there was " 'too much character in the stories' " (305). Miller's play is about Gus, a seaman whose feelings for the sea and for his country lead him back into service together with his young stepson. Gerald Weales correctly calls the script "innocuous," but one might speculate that it did not pass muster because Gus had slept with his wife for many years before their marriage, or because his wife runs a bar, or because his wife works hard to keep Gus and her son from engagement with the war.[52]

Whatever the specific reason the network executive might have had for keeping Miller's script off the air, the rejection evoked an important and strong reaction from Miller, who must have been brought face-to-face with the reality that radio was not merely an artistic but also a commercial medium. At its best during World War II, radio married art and technology to deliver stirring plays to literally millions of listeners across the land, and masters of radio art such as Norman Corwin shrewdly knew just how to use the medium to its best effect and while pleasing both government officials in Washington and network executives in New York.[53] Miller, however, who has never been heralded for his diplomacy and who has always been admirably outspoken, lashed out when *The Story of Gus* was rejected for broadcast. His diatribe is important because it brings to light the pitfalls and limitations of writing forcefully and freely for radio. In Joseph Liss's preface to Miller's play, he reports that Miller writes acerbically:

> No medium of expression can fulfill itself if its forms and content are prescribed beforehand. There is so much you can't say on the radio that for a serious writer it presents a blank wall. The answer is freedom, which is tightly circumscribed in the present setup. I mean not only freedom of speech, but freedom to write a radio play without a format. . . . Radio today is in the hands of people most of whom have no taste, no will, no

nothing but the primitive ability to spot a script that does not conform to the format. Give the medium to the artists and something might happen. As it is—[it is] death in the afternoon and into the night. (306)

In short, although wartime radio's union of government, commerce, and art can be viewed as the medium's greatest asset, it can also be seen, as Miller affirms, as its greatest liability.

Wartime radio drama was a fertile proving ground for emerging playwrights such as Laurents, Miller, Schoenfeld, and Ravetch. It was also a rich medium for established masters such as Archibald MacLeish, Stephen Vincent Benét, Arch Oboler, and Norman Corwin. Although these writers contributed to network series such as *Free World Theatre, The Treasury Star Parade, This Is War!* and others, they also created series of their own and wrote radio plays that were not part of specific series. MacLeish, for example, followed up his radio masterpieces, *Air Raid* and *Fall of the City*, with his epic ten-script *The American Story*, which aired on NBC from February through April 1944.[54] Although not specifically about the war, MacLeish's scripts celebrate the discovery and founding of the Americas and instill pride among the radio audience for being part of the citizenry populating and defending the New World. Far more pointedly about war issues are some of the radio plays collected in Benét's volume *We Stand United.*[55]

Benét is certainly writing at top form in his six-part series *Dear Adolf*, which was prepared for the Council on Democracy and aired on successive Sundays on the NBC Red Network from 21 June to 2 August 1944. Each program—written partly in verse and partly in prose—is a letter directed to Adolf Hitler by an American farmer, businessman, workingman, housewife and mother, soldier, and foreign-born American. These were narrated, respectively, by Raymond Massey, Melvyn Douglas, James Cagney, Helen Hayes, William Holden, and Joseph Schildkraut. Using his or her own vernacular, each character relates a personal antagonism to Hitler and Fascism as well as an individualized affirmation of American values and way of life. For example, the farmer writes:

> Every bushel of wheat in this country is against you. Every furrow we plowed this spring, we plowed against you.
>
> Against you and all your works, because we don't like you and can't stand you and we're bound and determined to get rid of you, whatever it costs us all.
>
> Ever think what that means,—to rouse up a free people, Adolf? Guess not.
>
> . . .
>
> Our government's found that out and you're going to find it out, too.
> We're labor and capital—both. We've got everything to lose, if you win. And we know it. (12,13)

In the course of *We Stand United*, Benét metonymically uses Adolf for all the Axis powers, so he has the farmer write, "But we've got Pearl Harbor written down on our hearts. Pearl Harbor and Wake Island and the names of the dead" (18).

Of course, the letters to Adolf are really directed to the American listening public, as may be seen in the businessman's pointed statement:

> Sure—we kick about a lot of things here. We kick about taxes and we kick about red tape. We kick about rules and regulations and we kick about government interference. We kick about questionnaires and we kick about the New Deal. We can kick—we're free men. Your fellows can't kick—or they're shot.
>
> It's curious, Adolf. Not one American businessman has yet been shot by our government because he didn't agree with our government's policies. It's curious with all that, we're making a production record now that we never made in our lives. (25–26)

And one can imagine the slangy, defiant patriotism in the voice of Jimmy Cagney, who, as the American laborer, snarls at Hitler:

> Then don't talk to us, mister. We aren't softies and we aren't pampered. We're working stiffs and we're tough.
>
> That's where you made your mistake about us, Adolf. . . . Well, we're thinking now and we're thinking about this war. (33)

Another laborer makes a pitch specifically directed to the workingmen listening to the program as he voices the government's need for Americans to purchase War Bonds, "I have been buying war bonds with every spare dollar. . . . I intend to go on doing that because I know that never again will I have overtime pay or a shop committee or the right to change my job—if Hitler wins" (35). Finally, the most passionate of Benét's scripts is the last, the one from a foreign-born American, for Benét seems to realize that even more than native-born citizens, who grow up taking American democracy for granted, it is the immigrants, those who have experienced oppression overseas, who cherish more than anyone the freedom and guarantees that spell America. In short, Benét's *Dear Adolf* series uses the radio format to reach Americans in many walks of vocational life, uniting them in antagonism to the Axis and in praise of their country and their country's role in the war.

Focusing as it often does on voice, sound, and rhythm, radio drama is a gold mine for poets and verse dramatists such as MacLeish and Benét. MacLeish especially exploits its possibilities to the fullest. These poets bring out the best in radio, and radio seems to bring out the best in them. But radio also bred poets of its own, indigenous practitioners who did not arrive as colonists from another genre but who were homegrown, born and raised on radio's rich audio soil, which they tilled with ardor and made to bear lush dramatic fruit that would bolster American morale during the war years. These poets did not write in verse, but many of their works were poetry of another kind, the poetry of radio writing, which forges its poetic essence from speech, sound, and the combined imaginations of artist and audience. Best exemplifying the poets of radio drama are the two artistic talents that radio brought to the fore and delivered to millions of wartime listeners: Arch Oboler and Norman Corwin.

Oboler's special gift was writing what could variously be called altered reality, the fantastic, the phantasmagoric, and science fiction. Although Oboler is now largely remembered by the cult of OTR (old time radio) fans as the major writer for the *Inner Sanctum* and *Lights Out* series, his creative genius reached its zenith during the war years, when his penchant for altered reality became married to his anti-fascist zeal, as it did in *Chicago, Germany* (aired on NBC, 24 April 1942). Even before American entry into the war, Oboler's *Bathysphere* (18 November 1939), written, as he says, "in the midst of neutrality talk," nicely shows the beginnings of his unique amalgam of travel to another reality with the psychological, science fiction, and the political.[56] It also foreshadows a recurrent Oboler theme: a victim of fascism has a person-to-person confrontation with the oppressor during which opposing ideologies are juxtaposed. In *Bathysphere*, Eric, a young technician, takes the tyrant, simply called Leader, of an unspecified dictatorship to the bottom of the sea in a supposed demonstration of a new bathysphere. There Eric plans to let the tyrannical Leader die, sacrificing himself in the process. As Eckhard Breitinger points out, "Gemeint ist mit diesem Stück offensichtlich der eurpäische Faschismus" [Obviously what is represented in this piece is European Fascism].[57] When Eric reveals his plans, the Leader is incredulous. He knows Eric has been brainwashed with official ideology in the schools and that to date has had an unblemished record of loyalty to Leader and the state. But Eric tells him:

> you didn't condition me quite well enough—should have started with the embryo, for somewhere along the line a little humanity got inside of me that cried out against what you were doing! It grew and grew until it said you had to die. . . . And you *will* die—yes! Here in the black under the sea. They won't roll drums for you—march for you—ended here [*sic*]! (71)[58]

In what seems to be the last minutes of their lives, the two confront each other politically and psychologically. In a twist ending, Leader outflanks Eric psychologically, argues that another leader will merely take his place, and leads Eric to take the bathysphere back to the surface. In the last lines of the play, Leader admits that he has revealed too much of himself, "And since you, of necessity, heard what I said—when we get up there I will probably have you shot. . . . The victim sentences his murderer. . . . It will be most amusing" (76).

In the course of *Bathysphere*, oppressed and oppressor as well as opposing ideologies confront one another. The play is not merely symbolic but a science fiction in which the events are played out in another world, in a space outside reality, in this case the floor of the sea. At the same time, Oboler skillfully uses the technology of radio to make his play an intense experience for his listeners. At the beginning and later in the background, he uses the music of *The Sea* by Finnish composer Selim Palmgren, adding to it the sounds of the shore: "*Music: Palmgren's 'The Sea'—down on cue, segue into: Wind sighs—splash of water—all painting the scene of shipboard down and continuing behind*" (57). Later he blurs the sound of the actors' voices to suggest their enclosure in the bathysphere: "*slight metallic ring to voice to give impression of being inside of small hollow steel hemisphere*" (61). Throughout, the psychological and political essence of the play is sharply heightened by the thoughtful use of radio technology. Oboler shows himself the master of his medium.

Bathysphere, written as it is for the radio audience two years before Pearl Harbor, is, consequently, allegorical and relatively tame, a mere pencil sketch for what was to come. After America enters the war, Oboler takes off his gloves to write fierce anti-fascist radio scripts, making the most of the intense atmospheres that states of altered realities are able to conjure up. In 1942, Oboler initiated a series of radio plays under the rubric *Plays for Americans*, and it is in these that he shows to best advantage that confluence of the psychological, fantastic, and political that is the signature of so much of his work.[59] *Chicago, Germany* appears as part of *Plays for Americans*, but several of the others in the collection are also worthy of note for the points of view they present, the stylistic devices Oboler employs to underscore his views, and their particularly effective use of the radio medium.

One such play—and one that reflects the intensification of Oboler's hostility to the now official enemy—is *Hate* (aired 3 March 1942).[60] Set in Norway, *Hate* describes the effects of the Nazi invasion of that country. Believing that God does all things for the best and that retribution should be left to heaven, the kindly, pacifist Pastor Halversun preaches nonviolence and nonresistance to his flock. The credulous Halversun is pitted against a ruthless Nazi commanding officer assigned to the region, Major Berkoff. For his part, Berkoff encourages Halversun, for the pastor helps defuse rebellion among the local Norwegian populace, whom the Nazis consider slave labor for the Reich. Even when Halversun's son is murdered by the Nazis, the pastor remains true to his idea of forgiving and nonviolent Christianity, exclaiming to his parishioners and to God that his son died "in error, for he shut his heart to Thy word of peace and forbearance—violence was in his act and violence was in his death" (35). But as Halversun says these words, the Nazis enter, intending to shoot six men because a sniper has killed one German soldier. When the pastor intercedes with Major Berkoff, he is promised that the men will not be shot, only to learn that the Nazis care little about the spirit of the promise and trick the pastor by hanging the men instead of shooting them.

It is then that the two main characters face off against each other, and Halversun learns to his shock—as does, of course, Oboler's radio audience—what the Nazi attitudes and agendas truly are:

> Do you think we are fools! Do you think we give our precious blood to build a great German world only to have that world fall apart through revolution and sabotage and peasants' uprisings? . . . We come with *science!* Yes, we have *won* with science, with our Stuka bombers, and our great Panzer divisions, and we will make our victory *secure* with *science!* . . . We are going to exterminate you—yes—throughout the world! Exterminate every possible source of non-Germanic intellectualism! Every man, every woman, every teacher, every student, yes, even every child who has within him even the germ of an idea contrary to the plan of a German world will be liquidated! . . . and all your peace-bringers, and your freedom lovers, and your faith fools will be dead and buried and there will be *one* race in the world, our *master* race, and the rest will be servants and slaves! (39–40)

Oboler shrewdly paces the program so that the audience is all along made to be more realistic and one or more steps ahead of the naïve pastor. With each event of ruthless Nazi brutality toward the peace-loving Norwegians and their spiritual leader, the audience's gorge rises higher and higher until Oboler creates a release, first in sound and then in speech. As the pastor acts out what the audience has been feeling, the audio directions read:

> [*Words are choked off as the other man's hands are suddenly around his neck— we hear the* COMMANDANT'S *strangled cries—the heavy breathing of his murderer in close*] [*All blotted out by: Music—harsh, discordant; this segues into the "Goose Step" motif—then the "Sibelius" chords as at beginning of the play— tension music continuing behind.*] (40)

The pastor takes a positive stand and slays the oppressor who would leave mankind "*Without hope for the future.*" And the script ends with the rhetorical question, "Almighty God, I have killed a man! [*Militantly*] *Must I ask your forgiveness?*" (41).

The debate or confrontation between oppressed and tyrant is iterated in *Hate*, in which, in comparison to *Bathysphere* three years earlier, Oboler displays a stepped-up anger, pugnacity, and endorsement of violence toward the enemy. Most important, however, is the way Oboler uses *Hate* to cue his large listening audience that they, too, must shed their prewar isolationism and desire for neutrality, that they must get tough and hate the fascists. He implies that, for the United States, this war is Armageddon, a war not merely against *an* enemy but a war in which the battle is against the modern incarnation of Satan's legions, who wish nothing less than the annihilation of men and women of good will, Christians, and all those who are not purely Satanic (or Germanic, which amounts to the same thing). Oboler, in fact, is quite explicit and eloquent about his intentions. He recalls addressing the participants at a conference about radio held at Ohio State University after *Hate* was aired and at which the play was criticized for its animus:

> I then began to talk of hate, the hatred of evil and the hatred of an enemy that the fighting man, properly educated in war, must know.
>
> I said that we at home needed a little of this hatred of evil in us; with nothing but defeat after defeat behind us at this point in the war, and with the certainty of sudden death ahead for thousands of our men, too many of us back here at home were concerned only with "getting the war over with by any means" and, particularly in academic circles, with the pleasant mental calisthenics of aimless postwar planning in a war that had hardly begun.
>
> The time had come for us to begin to hate a little, I went on. . . . And we at home needed the anger and the determination and the hate to enable us to endure the coming death of our sons and our fathers and our husbands. (192)[61]

For Oboler, then, his radio audience should, like Pastor Halversun, be moved by the script to hate the Germans enough to kill them and rejoice at their demise.

Hate, powerful as it is, nevertheless lacks the best ingredient in the usual Oboler formula: altered reality. His excellent *Adolf and Mrs. Runyon,* which aired on 21 June 1942 starring Bette Davis and Hans Conried, added the missing ingredient. In Oboler's script, Mary Runyon is high-strung because she has said farewell to her husband, who has just departed on a train en route to an army camp. She drives off in her car, cursing Hitler for disrupting her newlywed life, vowing: "That Hitler! Dear God, if I only had him here!" (132). In her nervous state, she stops at a gas station, realizing that she has run out of gas. Her husband is the one who always kept the gas tank filled. This use of realistic detail tricks the audience into accepting the verity of the narrative, even as Edgar Allen Poe often overwhelms his readers with specific detail before plunging them headlong into the fantastic. As Mary leaves the gas station, sound effects place the audience inside the moving car with Mary, who stops to pick up a hitch-hiking soldier because, like her husband, he is a man in uniform. But, when the hitchhiker enters the automobile, the play suddenly moves from conventional to altered reality, for the soldier proves to be none other than Hitler himself, speaking German, believing himself to be in Germany, and on his way back to his headquarters in Berchtesgaden. Suddenly, therefore, Mary's wish, "if I only had him here," becomes reality.

Certainly one of the strong points of *Adolf and Mrs. Runyon* is Oboler's decision to highlight and empathize with the feelings of the many women whose lives were being drastically affected by the war, whose husbands and loved ones were joining up or being conscripted, perhaps never to return, and who suddenly found themselves, like Mary Runyon, responsible for the large and little things (like filling the gas tank of the automobile) for which they had relied on men. In its way, *Adolf and Mrs. Runyon* legitimizes the anger felt by American women and lets women listeners know that their anger is shared by great numbers across the nation. Indeed, what they would say and do to Hitler if they had him alone was likely something about which many people fantasized. Oboler's making it happen in his play is, consequently, fantastic but believable, and, importantly, *Adolf and Mrs. Runyon* allows that scenario to play out to a reasonable conclusion. As Hitler and Mary Runyon discuss the state of the world, Oboler once more allows for the confrontation of two ideologies while he simultaneously inculcates, early in the war, American hatred of Germany while praising American domestic fortitude.

As much as Mary Runyon finds it difficult to believe that Adolf Hitler is a hitchhiker in the passenger seat of her car, Hitler is incredulous at being in America. The moment allows Mary to tell Hitler not only where he is but who he is:

> MARY. Look—look at the car you're driving in! Can't you see it's American? And me—look at me? Can't you see I'm an American?
>
> ADOLF. [*Slowly*] It—it cannot be . . . [*Building*] No! America? *I*—the Fuehrer in *America?* It cannot be!
>
> MARY. [*Quietly*] Is that any more impossible than—than the fact that almost all the people of Europe, in just a few months, have become slaves? . . . And is it any more impossible than—than an ignorant Austrian house-painter . . . *you* . . . has become their slaver? (138)

She then proceeds to tell him that the United States has not entered the war against the Third Reich too late, that Americans in factories are working overtime to defeat him, and that "Yes, you forgot one thing! You and your generals and your planning boards! One thing! That Americans are people who don't get going until they're angry—as all America *is* angry now!" (141). She informs him, furthermore, as she speeds up the car, that she is going to kill him. With this, Hitler attempts blandishments of the sort with which, the play makes clear, he seduced Quisling and tricked Chamberlain. These Mary, who becomes increasingly the voice of America, flatly rejects. Speaking at once for herself and for all Americans, she retorts angrily and proudly, when Hitler says she will not wish to die in the car in order to kill him:

> You're positive I won't die to kill you? Well, you're wrong, as wrong as you've always been about America and Americans! I'll die to kill you—gladly! Anyone of us would die to put an end to *you!* (146)

These lines permit Oboler's listeners to know almost viscerally that if their loved ones die in this war, they are doing so for a right and just cause. Finally, Mary does slam the car at eighty miles per hour into a concrete retaining wall. The vehicle is demolished, and the crash would be fatal. When the police arrive, there is no Hitler inside, but Mary miraculously emerges from the wreck without a scratch. The symbolism seems clear: World War II and the drive to eliminate Hitler and Hitlerism will eventually seem like a great car wreck, from which America, like Mary Runyon, will walk out less naïve but essentially unscathed.

Oboler's *Memo to Berchtesgaden* (which aired on 15 February 1942 and whose cast included Raymond Massey, Lou Merrill, and Mercedes McCambridge) shares some similarities with *Adolf and Mrs. Runyon*, though it is lighter in tone. In *Memo to Berchtesgaden*, Karl Smeckler, a Nazi operative in the U.S., types a memo to Hitler. Karl, while driving to Canada, has found himself unexpectedly stranded in a small Vermont town. There he encounters Sam Troe, the town's leading citizen. Misjudging Troe, who has strong family values, a string of successful businesses, and political power, Smeckler feels he has serendipitously discovered the perfect candidate to become the American Quisling. He suggests Troe align himself with the Nazis, the voice of the future, "the voice which says that America is a melting pot—a dirty melting pot that must be emptied so that men like you can come to their full power" (125). To his surprise, Troe turns around and socks him in the eye, saying that he reviles the Nazis and their agenda. In a few words, he counters with what Oboler posits as the American agenda:

> I'm a human being! Do you hear that? Can you understand that? A human being—a man who knows in his heart when he does wrong and is ashamed of it! Listen to the word, you Nazi—*ashamed*—ashamed in the sight of his neighbors, and his children, and his wife—and his God! (127)

The play ends on an amusingly wry note when Smeckler reveals that he is writing his memo to Hitler because he has been captured, placed in the county jail, and is in need of Nazis troops to come to Vermont and rescue him from incarceration. *Memo to Berchtesgaden* begs comparison with Sinclair Lewis's 1936 *It Can't Happen Here*, which is set in the same sort of New England town. Whereas Lewis saw the flaws in American society and showed how American values could be skewed to become fascist, Oboler's broadcast gives his audience pride in America, for he emphasizes American values and trust in God as a bulwark against fascism.

On a more surrealistic note, Oboler's *Execution* (which aired 10 May 1942 and starred Elisabeth Bergner) makes an appeal of a different kind to his listeners. Set in wartime France, *Execution* tells the story, similar to the one in *Hate*, of a Nazi captain's attempt to execute fifty French women because one French female sniper has wounded a German officer. As each woman is executed, she reviles the Nazis for their atrocities in a succession of countries. But each woman proves to be the same woman. The Nazis become frightened by the unnatural turn of events. The American radio audience, however, hears in the speech of the woman a moving account of what the Third Reich has done. Even America is included in her list of those who have felt the evil of the Germans:

> WOMAN. [*Slight echo*] Spain—Poland—Belgium—Holland—Norway—Greece—Yugoslavia—Russia, Britain—America—I tell you, Nazi, no matter what the politicians try to do at the peace tables. The peoples will not forget their vengeance—they will not forget their dead children and their dead wives and their dead sons and their dead mothers and their dead sisters and their dead brothers and their dead lovers and their dead hopes and their dead wasted years! They will not stop at the borders of your Germany this time—they will march *into* it, into your Germany, the people, and their vengeance will be on every one of you who traded the cross for the swastika, and the great God of humanity for the little man who thought he was God! (226)

Using the rhetorical device of *enumeratio,* Oboler arouses the anger of his audience through the account of countries damaged and crimes committed by the Nazis. He goes on to fan the flames of hatred and vengeance among his listeners, as he further demonizes the Nazis for their satanic opposition to God. In the brilliant conclusion to *Execution,* the several French women who have gone to the scaffold all prove to be the same woman who suddenly strikes the air with thunder and lightening. The scaffold is burned to the ground and the woman disappears, but not before the Germans learn who these identical French women are. The Nazi captain writes his report to Hitler, and it is read aloud by Himmler:

> Can you imagine such a report, mein Fuehrer. A woman who grows up into the sky! Of course the man will be shot!—Wait a minute!—there seems to be an addition to the report! It says, "Note—the Frenchwoman said she could be found at latitude 41° N. and a longitude 74° W. Investigation indicates this is a place in the Western Hemisphere known as Bedloe's Island. Further investigation indicates that there is only one Frenchwoman on this island. She is called—" [*he hesitates, then:*] "The Statue of Liberty." (227–228)

The mixture of the confrontation with the Nazis, anger, a call for hatred, comedy, and the surreal is what Oboler's wartime plays are about. And his strange, heady, and powerful dramatic brew went out over the airwaves, reaching and influencing millions each week.

Oboler's radio dramas were, at the beginning of the war, meant to rouse the

American public to action and hate. Clearly he feels that Americans are slow to become angry, and he knows that the American entry into the war came only after the traumatic events at Pearl Harbor pushed many people who strongly supported isolationism or neutrality into not always enthusiastic acceptance of Roosevelt's declaration of war. Oboler's *Plays for Americans* contains radio dramas meant to rouse Americans to hate and anger and to give them fortitude for the years that lay ahead in a war that would be no overnight victory. Three years later, when victory was in the air, it was not Oboler but Norman Corwin who taught Americans how to celebrate it. Corwin, the master of radio dramaturgy and rhetoric, whose brilliant *We Hold These Truths* had rallied sixty million listeners eight days after Pearl Harbor, became, appropriately, the same master who guided Americans on V-E Day. It is appropriate, too, that a discussion of radio drama during World War II should conclude with Corwin's towering *On a Note of Triumph*, which aired across the country on V-E Day, 8 May 1945.

With the war drawing to a close and with Allied victory in sight, Corwin began writing *On a Note of Triumph* several months before V-E Day. When the great day came, therefore, his script was ready and he could use radio drama to provide a review of the war and a celebration of its conclusion to a national audience very likely as large as the one that had heard *We Hold These Truths* nearly two and a half years earlier, in December 1941. It was Corwin's radio drama, then, as much or more than any speech or newscast on that momentous day, that gave the American nation a voice of closure for the years of war in Europe. Consequently, it is hardly surprising that Corwin was immediately swamped with congratulatory phone calls as soon as the program ended and inundated with fan mail for days thereafter.[62]

Literally beginning with brass winds sounding notes of triumph, *On a Note of Triumph* is a fast-paced, remarkably stirring piece that artfully combines pride in the Allied victory and an anatomy of Hitler's villainy.[63] Narrated by Martin Gabel, with other actors playing small parts, *On a Note of Triumph* is riveting dramatic verse perhaps more than it is drama. One commentator goes so far as to call it "a choral poem of remarkable intensity."[64] Its language is surely a form of poetry, and a poetry much inspired by Walt Whitman.[65] Yet it is dramatic and theatrical to the hilt. Corwin's writing consists of short sentences, replete with masculine colloquialism and slang, rhetorical rhymes, and the sort of allusions an average listener would recognize. It is at once patriotically American but takes pains always to include the role of the Allies. It is a paean to those who fought in the war for liberty, and it is an acerbic condemnation of the enemy. An eloquent and brilliantly apt description of *On a Note of Triumph* is given by the narrator of Philip Roth's novel *I Married a Communist:*

> The form of Corwin's play was loose, plotless—"experimental." . . . It was
> written in the high colloquial, alliterative style that may have derived in
> part from Clifford Odets and in part from Maxwell Anderson, from the
> effort by American playwrights of the twenties and thirties to forge a

recognizable native idiom for the stage, naturalistic yet with lyrical coloration and serious undertones, a poeticized vernacular that, in Norman Corwin's case, combined the rhythms of ordinary speech with a faint literary stiltedness. . . . Whitman claimed America for the roughs, Norman Corwin claimed it for the little man—who turned out to be nothing less than Americans themselves! Corwin's "little guy" was American for "proletariat," and . . . the revolution fought and won by America's working class was, in fact, World War II, the something large that we were all, however small, a part of, the revolution confirmed the reality of the myth of a national character to be partaken of by all. (38)[66]

Roth's narrator exclaims ecstatically, "The power of that broadcast! There, amazingly, was *soul* coming out of a radio" (41).

Both power and soul are what exploded from *On a Note of Triumph* from the moment it began. After a jubilant blast of brass that announces the play, the text opens dramatically in a way that reveals Corwin's powerful rhetorical and poetic devices, as Corwin's narrator intones:

> So they've given up.
> They're finally done in, and the rat is dead in an alley back of the
>   Wilhelmstrasse.
> Take a bow, GI,
> Take a bow, little guy.
> The superman of tomorrow lies at the feet of you common men of this
>   afternoon.
> This is It, kid, this is The Day, all the way from Newburyport to
>   Vladivostock.
> You had what it took and you gave it, and each of you has a hunk of
>   rainbow round your helmet.
> Seems like free men have done it again.
> Is Victory a sweet dish or isn't it?
> And how do you think those lights look in Europe after five years of
>   blackout, going on to six? (9–10)

One can see here the glorification of Allied troops with "a hunk of rainbow" versus the vermin Hitler, the dead rat. There is the rhyme of GI and "little guy," the ring of D-Day in "The Day," the inclusion of Vladivostock along with Newburyport, the deprecatory reference to the Nazi ideal of the Nietzschean superman, colloquialisms such as "This is It, kid" and "take a bow," and perhaps the oblique reference to "The lamps are going out all over Europe," proclaimed by Viscount Grey of Falloden on the eve of World War I.

Effectively punctuating and defusing the sometimes bombastic prose of *On a Note of Triumph* is a refrain that recurs throughout the program, "Round and Round Hitler's Grave." It has the ring of a folk song but has original lyrics composed by noted folksingers Woody Guthrie, Pete Seeger, and Millard Lampell.[67] For the most part, though, Corwin's play is a large aural canvas, a sweeping mural celebrating allied victory and German defeat. The main sections of *On a Note of Triumph* are organized around the pressing questions posed by a private first class:

> *If you don't mind, there are some things we guys would like to know!*
> *First of all, who did we beat?*
> *How much did it cost to beat him?*
> *What have we learned? What do we know now that we didn't know before?*
> *What do we DO now?*
> *Is it all going to happen again?* (21)

What these questions or topics do is allow Corwin to capture and present to his audience of millions what he deems as the main issues both of the war and of the ensuant peace.

When he addresses the first question, Corwin compels his audience to remember and concentrate primarily on the human aspect, the sheer wickedness of the Germans vented on innocent citizens. He takes the audience directly into scenes and moments of Nazi turpitude:

> *Tear his beard out by the roots! If his face comes off with it, all the*
> *   better. . . .*
> The fat and hairy fist against the fragile mouth:
> *Now spit out your teeth, pretty one, and tell us—who else was in your trade*
> *   union?*
> The conscript of children: putrescence in the classroom: scum injected
> *   in the growing arm:*
> *My father last night said to my mother that he hates Der Fuehrer.*
> *Good boy. Where do you live, Hans?* (26, 27)

Having gripped his vast radio audience with these outrages and aggressions toward individuals, Corwin deftly moves to the outrages and aggressions enacted upon the peoples of other nations. The sardonic and ironic tone, whereby the theatre of Nazi operations becomes conflated with the theatre itself, cuts like a sharp steel blade into the consciousness of those listening to *On a Note of Triumph:*

> Extra: double feature: Austria and Anschluss.
> And the corpses of the suicides of gay Vienna are sanitarily disposed of.
> Darkness rising: pageants and parades: drapes and flags and search lights
> and the goose-step:
> Next week, umbrella dance at Munich—Salomé bearing the head of
> John, the Czech.

> And coming soon, too soon, Lavish Spectacle: Millions in the Cast:
>   Curtain Going Up:
>   POLAND DEVOURED
>   BY LIGHTNING AND LOCUSTS
>   IN 18 DAYS! (29–30)

Corwin's script is far more than a celebration of V-E Day's having come at last and a rejoicing that American boys will return home triumphant. It is a call to remember the terrible dimensions of the evils wrought by an enemy who has now been defeated.

In raising the issue of the cost of the war, Corwin shrewdly uses an old rhetorical gambit. He enumerates some of the monetary costs—"Well the gun, the half-track and the fuselage come to a figure resembling mileages between two stars" (39)—but after listing them shunts them aside to stress the cost in human lives, to lament the boy who died for whom "There is no fixed price, and no amount of taxes can restore him to his mother" (39). He addresses his audience, asking them the rhetorical question, "Have *you* paid something of the cost?" and then, amid the jubilation of the day, reminds them:

> Well, you're not through paying and the bill's not settled,
> For in this way and that, for the rest of your days,
> The cost will appear—it will present itself in the form of deductions
>   from the paycheck;
> In a surplus of widows and fatherless children;
> In the remembering eyes of the sweetheart;
> In babies never to be conceived on lovebeds never lain in;
> In the tubercular lung of the stunted girl;
> In the stammering speech of the shellshocked boy. (44)[68]

The insistence here, as throughout *On a Note of Triumph*, is on the human element of the war. Clearly Corwin's agenda is to keep the American listening public from distancing themselves from the war now that it is over. He does not want the war and its events to become reduced to the dry data of economics and politics. He knows that the personal, the human interest aspect, is what will keep the important issues of the war and of the consequent peace active in the minds and visceral in the sentiments of Americans.

In *On a Note of Triumph*'s "what have we learned" section, Corwin makes his strongest political pitch. He is at pains to ensure that the country will not make the same mistakes twice, that the exultation of victory will not obscure the important political and social lessons of the war. He remembers American pre-war isolationism and wants to be certain that it will never return. Corwin reminds Americans, too, that the future will be one of internationalism. He does this in the published text with bold uppercase letters, and on the air he has Martin Gabel intone the words with special emphasis:

WE'VE LEARNED THAT OUR EAST COAST IS THE WEST BANK OF THE RHINE, AND THAT THE DEFENSES OF SEATTLE BEGIN IN SHANGHAI. (48)
WE'VE LEARNED THE VALUE OF ALLIES IN A WORLD WHERE ANY WAR IS SOONER OR LATER A WORLD WAR. (50)

He points his finger accusingly at fascist journalism in America:

WE'VE LEARNED THAT A NEWSPAPER RIGHT AT HOME CAN LIE WITH A STRAIGHT FACE SEVEN DAYS A WEEK, AND BE AS FILTHY AND FASCIST AS A HANDOUT IN BERLIN. (49)

He reminds his listeners of the change the war has wrought in gender roles, and that women will never return to their prewar subaltern positions:

WE'VE LEARNED THAT WOMEN CAN WORK AND FIGHT, AS WELL AS LOOK PRETTY AND COOK. (50)

Finally, Corwin vigorously supports maintaining postwar vigilance, insisting that world events have taught the nation that freedom cannot be taken for granted but must be constantly cultivated:

WE'VE LEARNED THAT FREEDOM ISN'T SOMETHING TO BE WON AND THEN FORGOTTEN. IT MUST BE RENEWED, LIKE SOIL AFTER YIELDING GOOD CROPS; MUST BE RE-WOUND, LIKE A FAITHFUL CLOCK; EXERCISED, LIKE A HEALTHY MUSCLE. (51)

He goes on to remind his audience as well that V-E Day is not the end of the war, that there is still "unfinished business in Asia" (54). Corwin is, moreover, eerily and unwittingly prophetic in his prediction for Japan:

The Japs in conference tonight may well consider the latest news from
     Europe,
And while they're at it, please to note the weather forecast for
     tomorrow:
Dawn coming up like thunder. (60)

In ways Corwin likely did not anticipate, the dawn would indeed soon come up like thunder in Hiroshima and Nagasaki. But the great lesson of the war and of the victory that *On a Note of Triumph* preaches is "To win is great: to learn from winning, greater: but to put the lessons learnt from winning, hard to work, that is the neatest trick of all" (64).
     The great achievement of *On a Note of Triumph* is that it employs drama and

dramatic poetry to celebrate victory, the end of hostilities in Europe, the achievement of the Allies and their soldiers, and the death of fascism and the Third Reich. But along with the fanfare, exultation, and high spirits natural on a day of triumph must come a lasting memory of the servicemen killed, the innocents brutally slaughtered, the atrocities enacted, and the freedoms nearly lost. *On a Note of Triumph* concludes not with huzzahs, cheers, and self-congratulations, but, like a solemn religious service, with a request for God's benediction, His blessing for the future of mankind and civilization, as Corwin's narrator implores the Almighty to

> Appear now among the parliaments of conquerors and give instruction to their schemes:
>
> Measure out new liberties so none shall suffer for his father's color or the credo of his choice:
>
> Post proofs that brotherhood is not so wild a dream as those who profit by postponing it pretend:
>
> Sit at the treaty table and convoy the hopes of little peoples through expected straits,
>
> And press into the final seal a sign that peace will come for longer than posterities can see ahead,
>
> That man unto his fellow man shall be a friend forever. (71)

Infused into the last words of the play here are the beginnings of a new postwar agenda that prognosticates what would become the civil rights movement, and that promulgates a new respect for minorities at home and a commitment internationally to the United Nations and the protection of smaller nations (such as Holland, Belgium, Czechoslovakia, Poland, and Norway) from aggression. What Corwin does in his radio drama that was heard by millions across the country on V-E Day is to employ his power as a playwright to inject, amid the joyous horns and firecrackers of that day's victory celebrations, his own more serious notes of triumph, which sound the music for a future of peace and brotherhood.

The use of American radio drama during World War II deserves a full-length study. The works discussed here merely touch some of the high points. During the war years, the marriage of playwriting, radio, and government was not always a perfect or pacific union, but artists like Norman Corwin, Arthur Miller, Archibald MacLeish, Stephen Vincent Benét, Arthur Laurents, Robert Sherwood, Maxwell Anderson, and Arch Oboler found in radio a medium for dramatizing and broadcasting the issues of the war. They found in radio, too, an audience infinitely greater than that any playhouse could seat, even during the longest run of a Broadway success. The theatre of radio proved itself, alongside stage plays, to be among the most powerful weapons in America's wartime armory.

FIVE

The Aftermath

I

After the V-E (8 May 1945) and V-J Day (14 August 1945) surrenders, the actual combat of World War II concluded and the time for recovery, reconciliation, and remembrance began. With a postwar perspective, Americans could look with new eyes at the issues over which the war was fought, the sacrifices that were made on the battlefront and home front, the behavior of servicemen and civilians during the war years, and the legacy of the war for individuals and for American society as a whole. Once again, the drama during the years immediately following the war not only reflected these concerns but helped Americans to face them. And that drama both revisited the war years and used the war to contextualize the present. The plays written after the war could examine how the war had been managed by those in command of the troops and those in command in Washington, and the way the war at home had moved the American economy from prewar depression to wartime prosperity.

When the United States entered World War II, the major topics of interest for Americans were fascist versus democratic ideologies and the wanton takeover of geographies and populations by the Axis powers. As the war progressed and reports leaked out, Americans became increasingly aware of what was transpiring in Nazi concentration camps. Then, as they encountered at war's end the liberated victims of those camps and saw the photographic evidence of gas chambers and human remains, the horror and issue of the war increasingly became the terrible acts carried out in the name of racial superiority. Indeed, nowadays for most Americans World War II conjures up far fewer feelings about the fascist threat to democracy than it does about concentration camps, piles of bones, families annihilated, and the terrible acts carried out in the name of racial superiority. But America's own record on this last issue was itself not an admirably clean one. Certainly anti-Semitic prejudices and quotas existed in the United States, and ethnic stereotyping of all kinds was common. Racial segregation was enforced by the Armed forces themselves during the war, and black servicemen served exclusively in black units. In many ways the wartime castigation of the racial and ethnic prejudices promulgated by Nazi ideology, prejudices strongly dramatized by wartime theatre, eventually spurred American society to scrutinize more carefully its own prejudices. During the war, in plays like *Tomorrow the World* or *The Common Ground*, the subject of American anti-Semitism had been raised. In *Foxhole in the Parlor*, which includes a Negro domestic who serves in that position because he could not find a place in the business world, and in *Decision*, the subject of American treatment of African Americans had also been raised. After the war (with the exceptions of Arthur Laurents's *Home of the Brave* and Don Appell's *This, Too, Shall Pass*), American anti-Semitic prejudice seemed to drop from view in the theatre. But this country's segregationist practices, whether enforced by law in the South or by custom in the North, became an increasing concern of the drama. In Arnaud d'Usseau and James Gow's *Deep Are the Roots*, Maxine Woods's *On Whitman Avenue*, and even Rodgers and Hammerstein's musical *South Pacific*, American racial and ethnic prejudices are at issue.

With so many men serving in military units both abroad and at home during the war, a large-scale, all-male, homosocial world came into being, an unusual world, largely devoid not only of women, children, and parents but of diurnal family responsibilities. For many, that world offered a simplicity—even perhaps a fraternal fantasy come true—of unalloyed male bonding. It provided a homosocial experience that, despite or maybe because of the context of combat, injuries, and the abiding threat of death, created something gratifying, something to cherish. The almost pleasurable power of such male bonding during combat is well evoked in a play produced just a few months after V-J Day, *A Sound of Hunting*. After the war was well over, plays such as *Command Decision, Mister Roberts, Teahouse of the August Moon, No Time for Sergeants,* and *The Caine Mutiny Court-Martial* seem redolent of nostalgia for the male bonding of wartime.

Revisionist historians like Allan Bérubé and Charles Kaiser have sought to chart the homosexual edge of World War II's all-male experience, but that edge, not surprisingly, is essentially unexplored in the wartime and immediately postwar drama, though perhaps it can occasionally be glimpsed by speculative implication.[1]

Opening at the Belasco Theatre on 27 December 1945, just four and a half months after the Japanese surrender, Arthur Laurents's compelling drama *Home of the Brave* is a play that deftly brings together a range of important postwar issues. On one level, *Home of the Brave* follows in the footsteps of Elsa Shelley's

Foxhole in the Parlor to explore the psychological injuries suffered by servicemen during combat.[2] Like Dennis Patterson in Shelley's drama, Pvt. First Class Peter "Coney" Coen has been traumatized by seeing his best friend, Finch, killed by the enemy, and the psychological shock has caused amnesia and paralysis. Whereas *Foxhole in the Parlor*, produced just half a year before the Laurents play, clearly meant to help civilians prepare for the return of the psychologically bruised and to help those men restore themselves to equilibrium, *Home of the Brave* demystifies the processes of psychological restoration. In a scene that will nowadays seem simplistic, when the army doctor is asked whether Coney will recover, the doctor replies, "I'm a psychiatrist, Major, not a clairvoyant. The boy suffered a traumatic shock. Now he has paralysis. Amnesia. Physical manifestations. They're curable—sometimes" (6).[3] He goes on to explain his treatment: "Narcosynthesis. You administer a drug [sodium pentothal] that acts as a release for the patient. Usually, he will relive the experiences immediately preceding the shock if the doctor leads him. Usually one or two injections are enough for him to recover physically. . . . It's not perfect. It was started about fifteen years ago. We're still learning. But we've learned a great deal using it in the war. See? War has its uses" (7, 8). The narcosynthesis of course engenders the play's flashbacks, but more important, the audience is made to applaud psychiatric treatment as a welcome by-product of the war, even as the play will help them understand and accept the postwar neuroses of demobilized soldiers like Coney.

Coney's breakdown takes place while he and four others are on a special mission to explore and draw a map of a critical Pacific island occupied by Japanese forces. The situation provides an excellent opportunity for Laurents to transport his audience to the Pacific war zone, to show American soldiers working together during a dangerous mission, and to display the terrible results of Japanese torture methods. At the same time, *Home of the Brave* implicitly applauds the heroism of soldiers, like those in the play, who put their lives on the line to ensure American victory. As his Major later tells Coney, "[The island] was invaded four days ago, And everything went off 100 per cent perfect—thanks to our maps" (128). Laurents, moreover, makes clear that in reckoning the cost of winning the war, human lives and human injury, both physical and mental, must be taken into account. At the conclusion of *Home of the Brave*, not only is Finch dead and Coney the victim of traumatic shock, but enemy bullets result in the amputation of their comrade T/Sgt. Mingo's arm.

The psychological causes of Coney's amnesia and paralysis are various, but one main cause is the anti-Semitism he has encountered growing up and continues to encounter in the Army. "Scarred by years of anti-Semitism," writes Ellen Schiff in an introduction to *Home of the Brave*, "he [Coen] has accepted his tormenters' image of himself as different from everybody else, and less worthy."[4] The Jew-baiting antagonist in Coney's unit is the feckless, insecure Corporal T. J. Everitt, whose relentless and denigrating references to Coney and his kind are a twisted way to assert his own racial and social superiority. This is recognized by all, except Coen, the object of T.J.'s racial scorn. For Coney, T.J.'s remarks are a replication of what Jews are compelled to learn in American society, as Coney tells of his childhood and loss of innocence:

> I heard something in the middle of the night once. Some drunken bum across the hall from my aunt's yelling: Throw out the dirty sheenies! . . . That was us. But I just turned over and went back to sleep. I was used to it by then. What the hell! I was ten. That's old for a Jew. When I was six, my first week in school, I stayed out for the Jewish New Year. The next day a bunch of kids got around me and said: "Were you in school yesterday?" I smiled and said, "No." They wiped the smile off my face. They beat the hell out of me. I had to get beat up a coupla more times before I learned that if you're a Jew, you stink. You're not like the other guys. You're—you're alone. You're—you're something—strange, different. [*Suddenly furious*] Well, goddamit, you make us different, you dirty bastards! What the hell do you want us to do? (55)

Coney's feelings of otherness and of persecution by T.J. and those like him is the paradigm of the anti-Semitism Jews encountered from Nazis, the very Nazis and the very racism Americans had fought in Europe. Avoiding what would be the heavy-handedness of setting *Home of the Brave* in the European theatre of the war, Laurents craftily sets his drama in the Pacific. But his point is well taken: ethnic prejudice and othering (in this case of Jews) remain a part of the fabric of American life, even as they had been part of the fabric of German life. In *Home of the Brave*, Laurents furthermore astutely links negative attitudes toward ethnicity with those toward disability, suggesting that T.J.'s anti-Semitism is of a piece with his unkind remarks about the mentally bruised and physically handicapped. The destructive nature of prejudice is at the heart of *Home of the Brave*, but so is an image of a new, prejudice-free America as Coen and a one-armed Mingo leave at the play's conclusion to go into business together.

In part, the anti-Semitic substance of *Home of the Brave* may well come from Arthur Laurents's own Jewish background. But surely he invokes anti-Semitism as one specific example so as to make an indictment of American racism more generally. Indeed, when *Home of the Brave* was released as a film in 1949, the character of the Jewish Peter Coen was excised and replaced by that of Peter Moss, a 1940s Negro played by the African-American actor James Edwards. Interchanging black for Jewish, the film relinquishes none of the power of the original play. Furthermore, Laurents was not only Jewish but, for his day, fairly open about his gay sexuality. The intense homosocial texture of *Home of the Brave*, with its unusually strong bonding between Coen and Finch, carries overtones of homosexuality. It may be that the anti-Jewish theme of the play and the anti-black theme of the film are the acceptable stand-ins for a play whose underlying theme is really about homophobia. Indeed, in his memoir, Laurents writes ambivalently, "Finch and Coney's relationship is homosexual; the portrayal is psychologically accurate but unconscious on the author's part. Had I realized that the friendship could be construed that way, I would have worked overtime to clean it out."[5] In terms of its stand on prejudice, *Home of the Brave* is finally not about Jews, blacks, homosexuals, or even the handicapped but about the irony of pronounced prejudices in a country that has just waged war against prejudice, that prides itself on being "the land of the free and the home of the brave."

Home of the Brave raises still another wartime and postwar issue, the one revealed to be at the core of Coney's psychosomatic mental and physical condition. In a moment of stress on the island, Coney's trusted buddy, Finch, thinks he has lost the maps he's drawn and wants to go back into the bush to find them. Coney exclaims, "You'll get us both killed! You dumb Arizona bastard!" And under the pressure of the moment, Finch replies, "I'm not asking you to stay, you lousy yellow—[*He cuts off. They both stand dead still, staring at each other*]—jerk! (64). But both men know Finch was about to say "Jew." Moments later Finch goes into the bush and is captured, tortured, and eventually killed by the Japanese. It is at this point that Coen goes to pieces. And he does so as an act of self-punishment and denial because his horror and grief at Finch's death are alloyed with a terrible guilt. He has felt a momentary pleasure that derives from two disparate and unequal underlying causes. In small part, there is a sense that Finch has been punished for nearly uttering his racist comment. In much larger part, however, Coney feels momentary gladness that he has escaped Finch's fate. In his autobiographical memoir, *Original Story By*, Laurents writes redundantly:

> What *Home of the Brave* was about was simple. Underneath, we are all the imperfect same. I dramatized this by showing that any soldier who sees the man next to him get shot instantly thinks: I'm glad it wasn't me. . . . For dramatic conflict, I needed a reason for my soldier hero to feel guilty that he'd been glad it wasn't he who'd been shot. And so he became a Jew named Coney who thought his buddy Finch was about to call him a "yellow Jew boy" just before Finch was shot. A valid reason to make Coney feel glad Finch was shot, and then feel guilty that he had felt glad.[6]

Quite apart from its exploration of anti-Semitism and prejudice, then, an important contribution of *Home of the Brave* is the way it openly puts on the table and addresses the postwar guilt of those who survived the war and combat, the nagging and guilt-ridden question that haunts all survivors of trauma: Why was I spared and they were not?

But it is Laurents's anti-Semitism theme that stands out in *Home of the Brave*. It is a theme also evoked both more centrally and more far more melodramatically in Don Appell's *This, Too, Shall Pass*, which opened at the Belasco Theatre on 30 April 1946, ran for thirty performances, and starred Sam Wanamaker and Jan Sterling. This play, which Burns Mantle calls "a near success," concerns the situation that occurs when two army pals, Buddy Alexander and Mac Sorrell, are demobilized and return to Buddy's small Midwestern town, where Mac will finally meet Buddy's sister, Janet, whom he has not met but with whom he has been exchanging meaningful letters.[7] When It becomes clear that Mac is Jewish, Mrs. Alexander recoils and tries to prevent the love relationship between her daughter, Janet, and Mac. The play points an accusing finger at indigenous American anti-Semitism, but Appell writes an unsatisfying melodramatic ending with which even he is apparently uneasy. In the extant play script, a sensitive Mac, undone by the anti-Semitism directed his way, drives off, crashes the car, and dies. As Burns Mantle and Bordman summarize the Broadway production, however, Janet and Mac drive off but accidentally kill brother Buddy as he chases after them.[8] In either case, the ending is contrived. What is important, however, is the subject matter of American prejudice in the wake of a war that was fought in part over the very issue of prejudice.

Laurents's secondary theme of "Why was I spared when others were not, and what is my responsibility as a survivor?" is one that in an essential and primary way informs another major postwar play, *All My Sons*, which catapulted the hitherto relatively unknown Arthur Miller to his first moment of Broadway fame. Opening at the Coronet Theatre in New York on 29 January 1947 and directed by Elia Kazan, *All My Sons* starred Ed Begley and Arthur Kennedy as Joe and Chris Keller and featured Karl Malden as George Deever. In Miller's play, Chris Keller returns to Ohio from having commanded a company of young men during the war. He enters his father's prosperous business and sees before him a future of relative affluence in a peacetime America. His situation is not unlike that of many men who returned to their hometowns when they were demobilized. But unlike his father, Joe Keller, who is focused on the success of his business and the security it can provide for his family, Chris has experienced combat and in a direct way known a communal enterprise. Chris is irrevocably scarred by having lost most of the men under his command in battle, but that has also now, after the war, made him feel both an uneasiness and a social responsibility that comes from having escaped the death that befell his comrades and, by sheer grace, surviving into a bright future complete with thriving family business as well as probable marriage and children. For Chris, the war has been more than some aberrant interruption in his life between schooling and entering his father's business. Just what the war has meant is something that he and the audience come to understand in the course of *All My Sons*.

Chris, serving as Miller's mouthpiece, recognizes that his having been spared when others were not demands from him a social responsibility and imbues him with a moral imperative. He is shocked, moreover, that those who had remained safely on the home front and were spared battle and death do not share his feelings. Quite the contrary, they have quickly come to regard the war as some momentary aberration, as a "bus accident":

[The men in my company] didn't die; they killed themselves for each other. I mean that exactly; a little more selfish and they'd've been here

today. And I got an idea—watching them go down. . . . it seemed to me
that one new thing was made. A kind of . . . responsibility. Man for man.
. . . And then I came home and it was incredible. I . . . there was no meaning in it here; the whole thing to them was a kind of a—bus accident. I
went to work with Dad, and that rat-race again. I felt . . . what you said
. . . ashamed somehow. Because nobody was changed at all. (35–36)[9]

What Chris does not yet know is how to act on his feelings of responsibility in
a society that seems to have returned to prewar business as usual and that appears
unchanged by what transpired during four years of combat, casualty, and challenge to human decency. What Miller's play finally and so brilliantly offers both
Chris and the audience is a way of putting the lessons of war into practice for
a renewed, better America and for an ennobling vision of mankind:

> I felt wrong to be alive, to open the bank-book, to drive the new car, to
> see the new refrigerator. I mean you can take those things out of a war,
> but when you drive that car you've got to know that it came out of the
> love a man can have for a man, you've got to be a little better because of
> that. Otherwise what you have is really loot, and there's blood on it. (36)

Chris's impassioned rhetoric helps Miller's audience answer with refined understanding, What have we accomplished by our sacrifices and victory in this hard-
fought world war?

The issues of values and morality that inform Chris's speech fan out to the
specifics of the play's tragic action. Whereas Greek tragedies take place in front
of the House of Atreus or the House of Thebes, the set (designed by Mordecai
Gorelik) of *All My Sons* is not the front of the House of Keller but aptly the
backyard, for Miller intends to reveal the life and values that lie behind the
neighborly facade of self-made man Joe Keller, the play's tragic protagonist. In
so doing, Miller also throws a dramatic spotlight behind the scenes on the
tainted wartime behavior of Americans who placed personal gain over patriotism, love of self over love of country. In his introduction to the 1957 volume of
his collected plays, Miller explains his aim in writing *All My Sons:*

> I think now that the straightforwardness of the *All My Sons* form was in
> some part due to the relatively sharp definition of the social aspects of the
> problem it dealt with. It was conceived in wartime and begun in wartime;
> the spectacle of human sacrifice in contrast with aggrandizement is a sharp
> and heartbreaking one. At a time when all public voices were announcing
> the arrival of that great day when industry and labor were one, my personal
> experience was daily demonstrating that beneath the slogans very little had
> changed. In this sense the play was a response to what I felt "in the air."
> It was an unveiling of what I believed everybody knew and nobody publicly

said. At the same time, however, I believed I was bringing news, and it was news which I half expected would be denied as truth.[10]

Focusing his larger social vision onto an individual man, Joe Keller, and his family, Miller can explore what has been his career-long interest, casting the common man as tragic figure rather than following the Aristotelian precepts that demand a protagonist of aristocratic and heroic stature. In *All My Sons*, the very ordinariness of Joe Keller enables the playwright both to admire and condemn his protagonist and the many average Americans who, like him, share a workaday pragmatism. The stage directions mark Joe as "*A man among men*" (6), but the action renders him as a man flawed by his failure to recognize a responsibility to mankind that should go beyond the immediate welfare of his nuclear family. Indeed, who better than the "average Joe" Keller to exemplify misguided self-preservation in a business-driven America, which from its very inception has endorsed the rights of the individual living in a society composed of common men who are all created equal?

A play that owes much to Ibsen's *The Pillars of Society*, *All My Sons* appears to have two separate plots: one about whether Larry Keller, Joe's older son, is dead or missing in action, the other about whether Joe Keller, together with his now convicted and imprisoned partner, Steve Deever, has had a role in shipping out cracked cylinder heads that ultimately caused the deaths of twenty-one Air Force pilots. As the tragedy moves with increasing momentum to its inevitable and disastrous conclusion, the two plots converge and prove to be parts of a single, unified dramatic organism and a play that interrogates American wartime profiteering and moral values. From the play's outset, Joe, as the self-made American success, exhibits his priorities as he holds a newspaper in his hands and asserts, "I don't read the news part any more. It's more interesting in the want ads" (6). This comment in its lighthearted way touches the serious core of the play: that for Americans business and personal gain, both in wartime and peacetime, seem to take priority over humanitarian and political issues.

As *All My Sons* unfolds, it becomes clear that the idealistic, patriotic young men who have served in the armed forces or given their lives for their ideals and their country have been the losers while those who remained behind and were focused on their own welfare profited (financially and otherwise) from doing so. Joe Keller has become rich by turning his plant into a military supplier. Frank Lubey, a young man who stayed home from the war, is now a prosperous husband and father, while the young men who fought in the war are either dead or still unsettled. Joe's wife, Kate, articulates this thinking to George Deever, the splenetic son of Joe's former partner. George, a veteran of the war, has lost the bloom of his youth and is still single. With an admixture of pragmatism and cynicism, she points to Frank Lubey, who has married George's old sweetheart, Lydia. While George was inspired by idealism and off fighting the war, Frank stayed home, has a family, and now resides next door to the Kellers in their upscale neighborhood. To George's situation and to that of her sons—the war-scarred Chris and Larry, who is still missing in action and is memorialized by an onstage tree—Kate compares Frank Lubey's success:

> I told you to marry that girl and stay out of the war! . . . While you were getting mad about fascism Frank was getting into her bed. . . . You had big principles. Eagle Scouts the three of you; so now I got a tree, and this one, [*Indicating* CHRIS] when the weather gets bad he can't stand on his feet; and that big dope [*Pointing to* LYDIA's *house*] next door who never reads anything but Andy Gump has three children and his house paid off. Stop being a philosopher, and look after yourself. (61)

Applied solipsism is Kate's prescription for modern success and survival.

Joe Keller's formula is essentially Kate's, but much enlarged and extended, so that its consequences will be dire and tragic. What Joe does is understandable, ultimately no more than many another businessman did during the war, and perhaps, therefore, forgivable. As Joe recalls the dilemma when a hairline fracture was discovered in the cylinder heads his company was manufacturing, he pleads for his son and his partner's daughter (as well as the audience) to see the situation as *human*:

> Listen, you gotta appreciate what was doin' in that shop in the war. The both of you! It was a madhouse. Every half hour the Major callin' for cylinder heads, they were whippin' us with the telephone. The trucks were hauling them away hot, damn near. I mean just try to see it human, see it human. All of a sudden a batch comes out with a crack. That happens. That's the business. (32)

What eventually becomes clear in one of the play's climactic moments, however, is that Joe acted pragmatically and with egocentric self-preservation when he enjoined his partner to ship out the faulty parts. Those flawed cylinder heads, moreover, are not only the cause of twenty-one deaths among airmen depending on the reliability of those parts. They are also the physical manifestation of the moral flaws that compromise Joe as a responsible human being functioning within society.

By logical extension of his philosophy of self-preservation, Joe not only winks at the cracked cylinder heads but allows his partner to ship them and later take the blame and be incarcerated for the misdeed, while he, Keller, goes free and prospers. He justifies his actions, furthermore, by claiming that he acted as a practical businessman and good paterfamilias should, preserving his source of income and the welfare of his family:

> What could I do! I'm in business, a man is in business; a hundred and twenty cracked, you're out of business; you got a process, the process don't work, you're out of business; you don't know how to operate, your stuff is

no good; they close you up, they tear up your contracts, what the hell's it to them? You lay forty years into a business and they knock you out in five minutes, what could I do, let them take my life away? I never thought they'd install them. I swear to God. I thought they'd stop 'em before anybody took off. (69)

In his impassioned plea here, Keller unwittingly reveals that his business and his life are identical; allowing the authorities to close his plant is to let "them take my life away." Finally, he rationalizes that what he did was actually selfless, an action taken for the survival and well-being of his family, "Chris . . . Chris, I did it for you, it was a chance and I took it for you. . . . For you, a business for you!" (70).

Joe's confession and self-exoneration, followed by the horrified response of his son Chris, allow Miller to offer a spirited and furious rejoinder to Joe's arguments. But what Miller offers in Chris's speech is also a vision of what wartime morality should have been and, more importantly, how the experiences and scars of the war can now serve to impel citizens to make the U.S. a more moral, better nation. As an answer to Joe's urgent plea to "see it human," Chris sees his father as not merely inhuman but even less than an animal:

For me! Where do you live, where have you come from? For me!—I was dying every day and you were killing my boys and you did it for me? What the hell do you think I was thinking of, the Goddam business? Is that as far as your mind can see, the business? What is that, the world—the business? What the hell do you mean, you did it for me? Don't you have a country? Don't you live in the world? What the hell are you? You're not even an animal, no animal kills his own, what are you? (70)

But the answer to Chris's question of whether the world and the business are the same thing is affirmative, because for Joe, the business and the world are, and always have been, one and the same thing. Joe, in fact, shows himself the apt disciple of President Calvin Coolidge, who, in his 17 January 1925 speech, spoke the famous lines: "The chief business of the American people is business." *All My Sons,* however, shows that when the laws of business rule life, then life becomes an animalistic, dog-eat-dog existence. What Chris has learned—what Americans should have learned from the war—is a concept that far transcends the one espoused by Joe or Calvin Coolidge: that success and riches of a higher kind are gained, as they were in military units, when men worked together for the common good of their country and a just cause. In an important way, those many plays of the war years depicting a diversity of men living in barracks and supporting one another in battle provide a way for Miller to envision how the camaraderie and cooperation that existed under wartime stress might be harnessed in the postwar era to achieve an America that lives up to the highest principles of democracy and humanitarianism.

In the final moments of *All My Sons,* the energies of what have appeared to be two separate plots converge to form a dramatic juggernaut that is at once tragic and visionary. First, Chris Keller expresses with intensity his disillusionment and disgust, not merely with his father's opprobrious act but with the universal acceptance of his father's way of thinking as he exclaims, "This is the land of the great big dogs, you don't love a man here, you eat him! That's the principle; the only one we live by—it just happened to kill a few people this time, that's all. The world's that way.... This is a zoo, a zoo!" (81). At this point, the play's other plot concerning Larry, the son missing in action, is collapsed into the drama's tragic thrust as Joe and Kate learn from a letter written by Larry that he is not missing in action but has committed suicide in response to the news of his father's complicity in shipping out cracked cylinder heads: "How could he have done that? Every day three or four men never come back and he sits there doing business.... I don't know how to tell you what I feel ... I can't face anybody ... I'm going out on a mission in a few minutes. They'll probably report me missing" (83). Joe at last derives from this a glimmer of enlightenment as he sees that his concentration on his family was misguided, for those fighting men "were all my sons" (83). Finally, in answer to his mother's question, "What more can we be!" the Christlike Chris passionately replies, "You can be better! Once and for all you can know there's a universe of people outside and you're responsible to it, and unless you know that you threw away your son because that's why he died" (84). In the last seconds of the play, Joe, Miller's protagonist, takes his own life and in doing so suggests the tragic outcome of a life dominated by business first. At the same time and more important, the last word spoken in the play is Kate's imperative, "Live," affirming her endorsement of Chris's and Miller's sense that the lesson of World War II for every American should be that "there's a universe of people outside and you're responsible to it."

It is instructive to compare the magnitude of *All My Sons* and its lasting success to Edward Mabley and Leonard Mins's *Temper the Wind,* which opened on 27 December 1946, just a month before *All My Sons,* and which closed just four days before Miller's play opened. Like *All My Sons, Temper the Wind* concerns itself with business morality during and immediately after the war. Quite apart from lacking the sheer verbal power and playwriting talent of Miller, *Temper the Wind* likely suffers by centering on a German industrialist's moral character. Although the morality of Americans comes into play, it is only in a secondary way, and it seems a truth of wartime and postwar dramas that to be successful they must be about Americans.

Set in Germany immediately after the war, Mabley and Mins's drama presents Hugo Beckendorff, a German industrialist, who in his devotion to business success and the survival of his own affluence presents a European counterpart to Joe Keller, though one far more ruthless and sinister than Joe could ever dream of being. With the war concluded, Beckendorff wants desperately to get his factory, which had produced the materiel of warfare for the Nazis, into production once again. A pragmatic businessman with no regard for morals, he had worked with the Nazis and compelled his daughter, Lissy, to marry a sleazy Nazi officer, Erich Jaeger, because the alliance would keep his factory going, especially after the scandal that ensued when his son, Kurt, was hanged for anti-Nazi activities.

With the war over, Beckendorff is now in league with Theodore Bruce, an American businessman who has no moral qualms about what the Nazis stood for only months earlier. Another believer in the Coolidge credo of "The chief business of the American people is business," he is not interested in what Germany did in the war but simply wants Beckendorff's factory to be part of an international cartel. With the arrival of Lt. Col. Richard Woodruff, a former university friend of Beckendorff's dead anti-Nazi son and now the American officer in charge of postwar reform in the town, a moral voice not unlike Chris Keller's is introduced into the play. Woodruff soon learns that Nazi party members still hold important positions and that many Germans, like Beckendorff, are not reformed but are merely playing along with the Americans to keep their jobs and positions.

Worse even than the duplicitous and immoral Beckendorff is Bruce, the American businessmen who is ready to disregard World War II, the lives lost in combat, the principles motivating the U.S. and the Allies, and the promised democratic world order that the end of the war should initiate. Instead, Bruce represents the American businessmen *Temper the Wind* demonizes, the businessmen eager to look the other way as long as they can line their own pockets and put themselves in an advantageous position for World War III. The moral issues of the play come to a head at its conclusion, when the American officer, Woodruff, engineers the expulsion of his sleazy compatriot Bruce:

> WOODRUFF. I'm going to have your travel permit revoked.
>
> BRUCE. I see. . . . Isn't this a bit high-handed, ordering an American citizen out of here? I admit I was wrong—in this particular case.
>
> WOODRUFF. Mr. Bruce, I accept your apology, and I believe you mean well. But it was *you* who started Beckendorff off at ninety miles an hour.
>
> BRUCE. And what about you? Your bullheadedness has ruined a normally decent, hard-working man—
>
> WOODRUFF. —Who supported the Nazis to protect his business interests.
>
> BRUCE. How else could he protect them? Business is business.
>
> WOODRUFF. Not any more, Mr. Bruce. "Business is business" has just laid the most colossal egg in history.
>
> BRUCE. Woodruff, you're a fool! It's time you started thinking about the *next* war—and what will happen to us if we ruin German industry. . . .

WOODRUFF. Mr. Bruce, you don't scare me. You've never known the people who count. There are a hundred and forty million of them, and they're not going to be fooled. (3-2-21, 22)[11]

Like Miller, Mabley and Mins demonize those who have failed to learn from the war and continue to place acquisitiveness over patriotism and national security. The main attention of their play, however, is given to the German industrialist, who, less than two years after the war, is almost bound to be a villain. The immoral position of Bruce the American is far more stimulating and serious for a postwar audience, but he receives only peripheral attention from the playwrights. Nonetheless, Bruce's "business is business" is given the same moral drubbing as Joe Keller's "What could I do! I'm in business." Both *All My Sons* and *Temper the Wind* seek, in the climate after the war, to draw American eyes away from income and toward ideals.

All My Sons and *Temper the Wind* do not stand alone in their condemnation of a business before morality attitude. That view had already been recorded, though not as incisively and with less dramatic force, fourteen months prior to the opening of *All My Sons* when Robert Sherwood's *The Rugged Path*, starring Spencer Tracy, premiered at the Plymouth Theatre (10 November 1945) not long after V-J Day. Whereas Miller was a new voice in American theatre, Sherwood by then was already the distinguished and respected author of *The Petrified Forest* (1935), *Idiot's Delight* (1936), *Abe Lincoln in Illinois* (1939), and *There Shall Be No Night* (1941). During World War II, moreover, Sherwood had served as a speechwriter for President Roosevelt, special assistant to the Secretary of War and to the Secretary of the Navy, and head of the overseas branch of the Office of War Information. Perhaps by 1945, after his varied Pentagon experiences and his intimacy with the inner workings of the Roosevelt administration, Sherwood had too many conflicting claims on his creative imagination, saw too many sides to every question, to produce a compact, unified, and forceful drama. Or conversely, it may be, as Walter Meserve argues, "that Sherwood's four years of writing propaganda had seriously impaired his ability to see shadings in life or complexities in issues."[12] Whatever the underlying reason, Sherwood's drama did not measure up to his prewar standard, and *The Rugged Path*, despite the appearance of Spencer Tracy, was a great success neither with audiences nor critics. There are, nonetheless, a number of instances when Sherwood's talent shines through to produce some moments of remarkable dramatic and intellectual power.

The Rugged Path is lamentably divided into two acts so extraordinarily distinct in time, setting, and tone that Burns Mantle's assertion that the play was originally two discrete plays is surely true. Given the unevenness of *The Rugged Path*, it is hardly surprising that Spencer Tracy vacillated about appearing in *The Rugged Path* both before and then throughout its pre-Broadway run. When the play closed after just eighty-one performances, Tracy escaped to Hollywood, never again to return to the stage.[13] It is telling, too, that despite Sherwood's stature as a leading American playwright, the full text of *The Rugged Path* was never published. The only extant versions are the abridged text printed in Burns Mantle's volume and the original full-length typescript.[14]

In his postwar play, Sherwood sets his first act in the prewar year of 1940 and his second act during the height of the war in 1944 and then just after V-E Day in 1945. As in *Abe Lincoln in Illinois* and *There Shall Be No Night*, Sherwood writes a drama in which minor figures revolve around a strong central character. In this case it is Morey Vinton, a charismatic newspaper editor who resides in a "medium-sized American city" worthy of the setting for a Sinclair Lewis novel. There he is stifled by the political, moral, social, and commercial conservatism of the city as represented by George Bowsmith, his brother-in-law and the paper's publisher, and Leggatt Burt, the paper's advertising manager, two conservative Republicans, members of the country club, businessmen, and isolationists. Sherwood's topic in *The Rugged Path*, as it had been in *Abe Lincoln* and *There Shall Be No Night*, is once more American prewar isolationism and closedmindedness. But this time Sherwood points his finger at American business self-interest as the generator and promoter of that isolationism.

Curiously, Sherwood and Miller write about two sides of the same coin. For Sherwood, business interests obstruct prewar commitment to the political good. For Miller, those same business interests after the war stifle the implementation of the hard lessons of brotherhood learned from wartime experience. Gil Hartnick, who works with Vinton, is an excellent reporter, extremely intelligent, Jewish, and a former Rhodes scholar (no mean feat for a Jew in the 1930s). He recognizes the need for American intervention in the 1930s European political situation, but he and Vinton both also know the editorial they plan to publish espousing America's engagement in the war against fascism will be considered radical and incendiary by the town's businessmen and, consequently, by Bowsmith and Burt, who have made a free press subservient to business interests:

> GIL. We've expressed polite sympathy for the British in their hour of agony. But now, the big chips are really down. We could point out that if Hitler conquers Russia, his empire extends to the Pacific—to the Aleutian Islands. We can use those old weasel words about "enlightened self-interest," if you insist.
>
> MOREY. So you feel that we should send our American goods to the Bolsheviks—give them the products of our American toil and sweat? Take the butter out of the ice-boxes of American housewives and give it to the enemies of religion? That's a fine, popular platform for us to stand on. That's a fine way to make friends with the National Association of Manufacturers.
>
> GIL. Sure Morey—that's why we've got to speak out before they do. You know what the isolationists will be saying. They'll be screaming for the

President to send Lend-Lease to Hitler to stop the Red Menace. It won't only be America First. It will be all the silver shirts and the Christian mobilizers—all of our native Fascists. If we come out now—and show some guts in forcing the real issues—then we'll be performing the real mission of a newspaper. Whereas—if we wait to hear the views of the opposition—well—you know as well as I do what will happen. We'll be hesitating and shilly-shallying—and we'll be under-writing another tragedy of too little and too late. (1.3.23)

Indeed Hartnick does lose his position with the paper, and his being Jewish makes it all the more easy for Bowsmith, the paper's publisher, to let him go. Not unlike Arthur Laurents's postwar presentation of anti-Semitism in *Home of the Brave* or the anti-Semitism that is the main subject of Laura Hobson's 1947 novel, *Gentlemen's Agreement,* Sherwood here turns his own momentary postwar gaze at anti-Semitism in the business community of an America that, ironically, has just fought a war in which anti-Semitism was an issue, an America that knows anti-Semitism can lead to Jews butchered in Nazi concentration camps. But Hartnick is a peripheral character. Vinton is not, and he, despite his age, leaves the town, the paper, and his lackluster wife to join the Navy as a cook.

The second act of *The Rugged Path,* a jarring break from the first act, charts Vinton's time in the Navy during the war and presents some well-written moments conveying what it must have been like on a ship during a skirmish with the enemy in the Pacific. But more important, before he dies bravely fighting against the Japanese in the Philippines, Vinton makes a pre-battle speech to his Filipino comrades in which he makes clear to the audience how the war has evoked and made manifest the moral superiority of America and its allies. He says, in short, what Miller's Chris Keller alludes to but is unable to articulate:

There's one piece of equipment we've got for this fight—and it wasn't manufactured yesterday and it won't be destroyed tomorrow—and that one piece of equipment is faith. It's the faith of the people—the devotion of the people to the God who created man in His own image. That faith is our weapon and our hope. You people here on this island—you have proved the power of that weapon and you know what you've got to fight for, and that gives you dignity. It makes you unconquerable. . . . We'll carry this one off not because we're great fighting men but because we've got to do it. There's been a very narrow margin between victory and defeat in this war—it was no wider than the English Channel, no wider than one street in Stalingrad—it may be no wider than Banana Beach. But God has decreed that it must be wide enough—and we shall be obedient to that decree. (2.11.48)

Vinton's belief in the power of faith, God, and the higher principles of human brotherhood becomes an eloquent second-act reply to the self-serving principles espoused by the businessmen of the first act. The references, moreover, to the English Channel, Stalingrad, and Banana Beach place American ideals within an international frame of reference. What Sherwood suggests through *The Rugged Path*'s two disparate acts is that the knowledge gained from combat will seriously change America after the war from the isolationist, business-driven nation it was before Pearl Harbor, and that that isolationism will be replaced by a new postwar internationalism. Although *The Rugged Path* was not a Broadway success, the issues it raises are important ones that were to be echoed in other dramas.

One such echo is Bella and Sam Spewack's *Woman Bites Dog*, which opened on 17 April 1946 at the Belasco Theatre. Even as Sherwood found that Spencer Tracy and the good reviews he received were not enough to make a hit of *The Rugged Path*, so, too, the Spewacks learned that an excellent cast of actors does not always ensure success. Although *Woman Bites Dog* starred Kirk Douglas, Frank Lovejoy, E. G. Marshall, and Mercedes McCambridge, it was, nonetheless, an overnight flop.

The Spewacks' comedy is, however, of some interest because it poses two postwar issues. The action centers around a hoax played by Lt. "Hoppie" Hopkins (Kirk Douglas) on the egocentric, megalomaniac, rabidly reactionary newspaper publisher, Commander Southworth. When asked why he has created a ruse to make a fool of the politically ambitious, vain Southworth, Hopkins points an accusing finger at wartime journalists, retorting:

> Every soldier had his own post-war plan. This was mine. . . . I read your papers overseas. . . . Do you realize what you were saying to me? Here were the Krauts splashing hunks of hot lead in my general direction. And you were saying the enemy wasn't in Berlin. The enemy was in Moscow. The enemy was in London. The enemy was—so help me—in Washington. You even tried to tell me I was fighting the wrong war. That's very annoying to a man in a fox-hole. . . . wasn't worrying you. You were worried about T-bone steaks, nylons, gas and the northern branch of the Democratic Party. (100–101)[15]

This acerbic outburst, reminiscent of the point of view expressed in *The Rugged Path*, once more indicts not merely those who blurred war issues to sell newspapers but all of those stateside who were finally more concerned for their own welfare and profits than for the democratic ideals about which the war was fought or for the servicemen who sacrificed their lives for those ideals. Unfortunately, the Spewacks were unable in their madcap and overblown comedy to address this issue appropriately. It took the focus and high tragic seriousness of Miller's *All My Sons* later in the year to do so.

The hoax played on newspaper publisher Southworth in *Woman Bites Dog*, whatever one might think of the play's artistic flaws, is a most revealing one. Southworth is mercilessly satirized because he believes the U.S. is being infiltrated by communists, and Hopkins tells the xenophobic and paranoid Southworth what he all-too-readily believes: that the town of Danville, a typically conservative and Republican American small town, has been overrun by Reds who are turning private enterprise into communist collectives. The Spewacks mean this as satirical farce. But it is clearly farce and satire at the wrong moment of American history, for even a year after the conclusion of World War II, the odor of Joseph McCarthy was already in the air. And no doubt to their regret, the Spewacks, rather than producing a postwar Jonsonian comedy that could make audiences laugh at their own fears and folly, paid the price of bad timing and saw their comedy killed by the first chilling blasts of the Cold War. It was, after all, only a year after *Woman Bites Dog* that the House Un-American Activities launched its first attack on suspected communists in Hollywood and among the theatre community.

II

From Pearl Harbor to V-J Day, there was a paucity of powerful stage plays about American troops at war. In part this seems due to the physical limitations of the stage, which has never been a strong vehicle for presenting armies at war. Even Shakespeare's combat scenes usually seem stilted in performance. It is film and radio that succeed in presenting armies, the one by using footage of actual combat or by employing scores of actors for just a few scenes, the other through the artful use of sound effects. But in part the near absence of World War II combat onstage may be attributed to a reluctance on the part of playwrights to confront audiences with the immediacy of bloodshed, wounds, and deaths. The movie screen keeps the audience at one remove from reality and radio tells without showing, but for a wartime audience to witness the real bodies of stage actors being maimed on the battlefield or in the throes of death may be too much to bear. Perhaps this is why it is not until after the war, when lives were no longer at stake or being lost, that American theatre could stage meaningful and successful plays about troops on active duty, the psychological stress experienced by men under fire, and the personal dynamics within military units. Indeed, the scenes of skirmish staged in *Home of the Brave* and *The Rugged Path*, presented after the war, seem more graphic and moving than any occurring in American plays produced while the war was in progress.

Perhaps the most powerful postwar play depicting American troops during combat is Harry Brown's *A Sound of Hunting*. John Mason Brown was perfectly on target when, in his essay "Bellona's Bridegroom," he wrote of *A Sound of Hunting* that it is "by all odds the best war play about combat America has so far produced since Mr. Anderson and Mr. Stallings first collaborated [on the 1924 war play *What Price Glory?*]."[16] He goes on to say, "Our theatre has not seen a warmer or more warming statement of the strange, irrational compulsions of this feeling [binding fellowship] which exists among men who face death and have survived dangers jointly" (303). On 20 November 1945, three months after V-J Day and the end of World War II, Harry Brown's first-rate play—perhaps

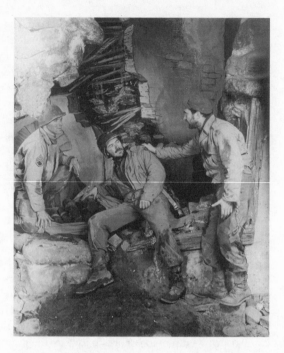

19. *A Sound of Hunting* (1945).
(Left to right) Burt Lancaster,
Frank Lovejoy, Sam Levene.
Courtesy of the New York Pub-
lic Library and the Museum of
the City of New York.

the only excellent play about World War II combat—*A Sound of Hunting* opened
at the Lyceum Theatre in New York. Among its cast were Frank Lovejoy, Sam
Levene, and a young acrobat and trapeze artist making his stage debut in a
serious role: Burton Lancaster.[17] Technically, *A Sound of Hunting*, a postwar play
that clearly must have been written while the war was still being waged, is surely
one of Broadway's beautiful losers. Although a nominee for the 1945 New York
Drama Critics' Circle Award, it ran for only twenty-three performances and
then fell into obscurity, whereas, as John Mason Brown astutely recognized, it
deserves to be prized as a classic of the American stage.

Set in a ruined house in Cassino, Italy, where a group of American GIs are
holed up stemming the gunfire of German troops, *A Sound of Hunting* has only
a minimal plot, which is precisely its great strength.[18] Basically, the American
soldiers, who come from various walks of life and have seen battle together, have
become a fraternal unit, a makeshift family looking out for one another. Although war-weary, reduced to K-rations, and bespattered with the mud of a
rain-soaked Italian countryside, the men, on the verge of being moved out at
last, are unwilling to abandon Small, one of their comrades who has been
trapped in a shelter during an engagement with the Germans. This is not much
of a story line, but the power of the play resides elsewhere: in its realistic presentation of persevering soldiers, their dialogue with one another (minus exple-
tives), and their commitment to each other.

Brown shows an affection and camaraderie that crosses the lines between   ·

officers and enlisted men. Most important, he shows a commitment to country and cause through the actions of the men trying to save their trapped friend while bantering about enduring difficult conditions and surviving constant attacks from German snipers. There is never, furthermore, amid the understatement of *A Sound of Hunting,* to be found the sort of bald, grandstanding patriotic speeches featured in *The Eve of St. Mark, Storm Operation,* and *Cry Havoc.* In fact, it seems to be Harry Brown's aim to challenge what he regards as the hollow rhetoric of other writers who would make Olympian heroes of honest American soldiers doing their jobs.

Injected into *A Sound of Hunting* is Finley, is an American wartime journalist who travels to the warfronts and has built a career writing human interest stories which are designed to elevate fighting men into verbal war memorial statuary. The aptly named Small is a small and charmingly accident-prone soldier who never appears onstage and who is eventually killed by the Germans as he tries to escape the abandoned structure where he is trapped by enemy fire. In the interchange between Finley and the soldiers that ensues over Small, Brown's mordant satire is leveled at the eager journalist trying to create a newspaper epic from the grim realities of day-to-day combat and to win some authorial fame for himself in the process:

FINLEY. Here today and gone tomorrow, that's me. It's a pretty big war, you know.

SHAPIRO. So they tell me.

FINLEY. I certainly don't envy you fellows the time you spent up here.

COLLUCCI. Oh, think nothing of it. Don't mention it. Any time.

FINLEY. I mean it. You're the men who are really fighting the war—you and fellows like Small. You're the men that people want to hear about. They don't care about the generals and people like that. They want to know what's going on in the line.

SHAPIRO. I can tell 'em. A lot of noise is going on in the line. Tell 'em we got real guns up here.

FINLEY. Oh, come, on, they know all that. People don't realize the little things that go on—things like Small being caught out there on the day you're moving out, and the fact that you have to move out and leave him behind. Things like that make up the real tragedies of war.

COLLUCCI. The real tragedy of this war is that they even let a guy like Small into the army. A cross-eyed WAC could do better. Hey Shapiro, throw me something to eat. (110–111)

In the tension between Finley's overstatement and Shapiro and Collucci's understatement, Brown adeptly evokes an implicit picture of the courageous perseverance of American fighting men. At the same time, Finley is Brown's stand-in for writers and playwrights greedily exploiting the war and simultaneously feeding the American public glorified portraits of combat soldiers in the form of reprehensibly false rhetorical poster art:

> FINLEY. This is where I want to be. This is where the stories are. I told you that before.
>
> CARTER. We don't want you up here. You don't belong, I'm telling you that now. . . . You sit twenty miles behind the lines, guzzling all the Scotch you can get your hands on, then you come up here to pick up enough money to pay for it. This little trip ought to be worth a couple of thousand to you. . . . And you can spend it all at Twenty-One, sitting around on your tail and telling the pretty girls how brave you are and what you said to the general. Well, you tell 'em that one day you ran into a buck sergeant who thought you were a sanctimonious slob with about as much ethics as a tomcat.
>
> FINLEY. By god, you can't talk to me like that. No man alive can talk to me like that.
>
> CARTER. I can talk to you like that. And I'll tell you why. Because I know you, Finley. You go up in the line for two minutes and you tell some poor doughfeet how wonderful they are, and you squeeze something out of them. Then you write it up as though it were the Twenty-third Psalm and take all the credit for the war. I've read your junk. It makes me sick. [*He puts on his ammo belt and picks up his gun, preparatory to going out.*]
>   . . .
>
> CARTER. I'm just fed up with people like you.
>
> FINLEY. I told you I had a job to do. I'm paid to do it.
>
> CARTER. And you can hardly wait to get out of here to make a martyr out of Small. You'd probably like him to get knocked off, so you'd have a really good story. . . . A good corpse is worth an extra thousand to you. (119–121)

Brown is here obviously lambasting an exploitative writer and his unctuous journalism (to whom and to which he tacitly posits himself and this play as laudable contrasts).

Kate Buford describes the stage decor of *A Sound of Hunting,* saying, "The bombed-out stage set banked in mud looked like a piece of the wartime battlefield shipped home."[19] Into that realistic set Brown places mud-spattered, battle-worn, straight-talking soldiers often speaking very believable one-liners, including those by Pvt. Dino Collucci, played by comic Sam Levene, who had already made his mark in Kaufman and Hart's *Three Men on a Horse* and who was eventually to become famous as the original Nathan Detroit in Frank Loesser's *Guys and Dolls*. The brilliance of *A Sound of Hunting* lies partly in the power of its all-male ensemble production, but also partly in the way it eschews showing actual battle but nevertheless poignantly conveys the stresses and bonding among men under fire. Brown's drama comes remarkably close to a genuine representation of men in battle. Unfortunately, despite favorable reviews, *A Sound of Hunting* had only a short run. Possibly *A Sound of Hunting* appeared too soon after the war was over, at a time when audiences wished to look ahead to a nation at peace rather than back to a nation in combat.

It was not until two years after *A Sound of Hunting* and more than two years after V-E and V-J Days that the first commercially successful drama depicting American servicemen at war was mounted. Produced by Kermit Bloomgarden, William Wister Haines's *Command Decision* opened at the Fulton Theatre on 1 October 1947. Furthermore, although *Command Decision* is about the critical bombing of German airplane factories, it takes place entirely in England at the American headquarters and landing strip where the Allied fighter planes are located and where the bombing orders are issued. The planes, the pilots on their missions, and the German targets are never shown. Although ostensibly a drama about combat, it is actually one of executive decision making.

Gerald Bordman reminds us, "no one hailed it as a great play," but *Command Decision* did run successfully for nearly a full year.[20] Although no theatrical masterpiece, *Command Decision* is a centrally important text for seeing how, in the postwar period, the opposing wartime energies of personal gain versus winning the war are repeatedly examined, interrogated, and dramatized. While World War II was being waged, a playwright who criticized the management of the war would be viewed as impolitic, if not culpably treasonous. The captiousness of Lillian Hellman's *The Searching Wind* and Irwin Shaw's *Sons and Soldiers*, for example, possibly subverted the reputation of those playwrights and almost certainly helped ensure the failure of those plays. But after the war had been won, playwrights could afford to be more critical as they looked back, perceiving wartime weaknesses and suggesting that these must be addressed now, before any future national crisis could occur. Consequently, in *All My Sons, The Rugged Path,* and *Woman Bites Dog*, the playwrights seem free to explore, as they would not have been during the war years, the ways in which profit-driven business interests (including those of the allegedly free press) were too often at odds with the war effort, the armed forces, and the fighting men who were sacrificing their lives for a democratic, American way of life.

Command Decision also engages the conflict between the drive for personal gain versus working for the greater good, but it does so by setting the play within the military establishment itself and by playing out the conflict within the context of crucial decisions that could affect the outcome of the war and its duration. At the play's center is Brigadier General K. C. "Casey" Dennis, a strong-willed commander and tactician who is sending scores of pilots out on bombing missions to destroy three German factories dedicated to producing

20. *Command Decision* (1947).
Robert Pike and Paul McGrath.
Used by permission.

planes so advanced in design that they will likely soon be able to make short
work of Allied air power. Sending American bomber planes into Germany, however, necessarily means that a significant number of planes will be shot down
and their pilots killed as they try to attack the German aeronautics plants. Is
Dennis's determination to destroy the German targets at the cost of a significant
number of lives and planes rash and ruthless, or is it the unpleasant decision
that must be made in the short run to avoid deaths in far greater numbers in
the long run and even possibly losing the war itself? Haines's drama does take
its stand on this question, but does not do so before making the audience aware
of the conflicting issues and the players involved.[21]

Casey Dennis, who has devised Operation Stitch (. . . in time saves nine) to
obliterate the German factories in the (fictitious) cities of Posenleben, Schwein-
hafen, and Fendelhorst, seems a hardened warrior with ice-water coursing
through his veins, and initially the description of him by a newspaperman as a
"Fascist megalomaniac" (5) seems well taken.[22] His mind and actions seem entirely preoccupied with the objective of demolishing the factories that produce
deadly German aircraft. He is, for example, unfazed by the sexual misconduct
of men under his command. When a charge of rape of her daughter is leveled
by the mother of an English girl who lives near the airbase, Dennis can flippantly
remark, "I've told you: when these boys tomcat they're to go in pairs. How can
you expect one man, flying missions, to keep the whole family happy?" (14).
Nowadays for such a comment, condoning not merely sexism but rape, Dennis

would be roundly condemned and demonized. For a 1947 audience, however, it is merely an example of Dennis's callous insensitivity to anything other than his missions and the welfare of the men who must fly them. Likewise, when Dennis becomes annoyed with an atheist pilot who dropped a bomb on a church, it is the waste of a bomb that could have struck a military target that irks Dennis, not the destruction of the church, the attack on religion, or the possible civilian injury. Most important, Dennis is not averse to discreet withholding or adjusting of information so that his missions are not canceled by his superiors. In short, *Command Decision* begins with an imperious, insensitive main character whose one-track focus on his missions seems impervious to the loss of pilots' lives and the wisdom of his superiors.

Quickly this judgment, voiced by other characters and felt by the audience, is reversed as it is measured against the attitudes and deeds of decision makers who are themselves far removed from the site of combat or, worse yet, who see the war as an opportunity for personal advancement. *Command Decision* never turns the hard-edged Dennis into a suddenly lovable commander, but Dennis's unwavering determination to trounce the enemy and his sorrowful willingness to sacrifice the lives of several pilots in the short run in order to save many lives and his country in the long run emerges as increasingly heroic, especially when he is compared to a gallery of acidly satirized characters who would, the play suggests, throw Allied victory off course if left to their own devices. Most broadly lambasted is a Southern congressman, Representative Malcolm, who visits the air base in order to create photo opportunities for himself. Malcolm hopes to score a public relations triumph by making a hero of a rather cowardly young soldier who happens to hail from Malcolm's home state. And, still more reprehensible, Malcolm hopes to put himself in the political limelight by criticizing the military. As Malcolm and Dennis cross swords, the play sounds the familiar postwar note of the conflict between those who fought the war and those who lined their pockets—in this case, political pockets—at home:

MALCOLM. General Dennis, I want to know why you, puhsonally, are the only single one oveh heah that sen's his Division beyon' fighteh coveh, every time Gennel Kane got his back turned! Every otheh Division consis'en'ly increases sorties an' tonnages of bombs dropped every month. The only solitary thing you increase is losses!

DENNIS. Sorties and tonnages are meaningless except on the right targets, Mr. Malcolm. If you want statistics, the training command in America fly more sorties than we do—except the ones in your state.

MALCOLM. What you sayin' about mah state?

DENNIS. That every airfield in it is under a foot of water half the year and twelve thousand feet of fog for nine months. But when we asked permission to move to where we could operate efficiently the recommendation was blocked by your committee. (115–116)

Malcolm's pejorative and comically overstated Southern accent helps playwright Haines underscore his pointed accusation against legislative, self-serving pork-barreling that, during a war, is nearly tantamount to treason. Although Malcolm is not a central character and is spoofed by being a stereotypical pompous and self-righteous Southern legislator, his pragmatism and actions ultimately put him under the same umbrella as Arthur Miller's Joe Keller.

Dennis's forthrightness will almost certainly cause him the loss of his command, and he is likely to be replaced by the politically shrewd Brigadier General Clifton Garnett, who is well aware of how to rise in rank. The satire of Garnett is delivered by his brother-in-law, a seasoned fighter pilot and Dennis's closest friend:

> MARTIN. Clifton has flown some of the hottest desks in Washington.
>
> DENNIS. We needed those guys—to get planes for hoodlums like you and me.
>
> MARTIN. Casey, no record after this war will be worth a damn without Command in it. Cliff knows this is still the best Command in the Air Forces. Any Brigadier alive would give his next star for your job. (57)

Although far less broadly satirized than Congressman Malcolm, Garnett does not escape the scourge of Haines's satire, for Garnett, while sensitive to the need of advancing the war effort, is nonetheless an opportunist equally sensitive to advancing his own military career.

A more complex figure in the constellation of portraits that surrounds Dennis is his superior officer, Major General Kane, an older career soldier who fought vigorously for American air power in the years between World War I and World War II. With a note of sadness and cynicism, he relates what happened during the interwar years: "We were promised fifty thousand planes—and our boys were never going to fight in foreign wars—so the country went back to sleep and we were called back from stables and rifle ranges to make a modern air force—out of promises—and what was left over after they gave our planes and instructors to every goddamned ambassador in Washington. . . . we'd just begun to get the tools to get started when we were in it ourselves—with a double war—and a fifty thousand plane paper air force that didn't add up to fifty serviceable bombers" (86–87). The scoundrels are the government and the military bureaucrats whose small-mindedness and failure to understand issues beyond their office doors constitute the weakness of the United States. Kane, for his part, has taken on the role of go-between, trying to help American combat troops by appeasing and lobbying the men who occupy the desks at the Pentagon and in Washington's legislative offices. The result is that the well-meaning Kane has become ineffectual, can be easily duped, and spends too much time hosting the likes of Congressman Malcolm on visits to military installations. When Dennis's pilots hit the wrong enemy target and Dennis must give Kane the photos of what the pilots have demolished, we hear, "These pictures will keep Kane happy for twenty-four hours. He doesn't know a strike photo from a gonorrhea smear" (70). In short, the "business" interests of government and military officials have rendered a once-feisty Kane laughably inept.

With the figure of Elmer Brockhurst, an influential war correspondent highly critical of Dennis and Dennis's tactics, Haines creates his most interesting character, moving the target of his satire from government and the military to the fourth estate. As in Sherwood's *The Rugged Path* and the Spewacks' *Woman Bites Dog*, it is the business interests, in this case the headline grabbing and scandal seeking of journalists, that compromise the war effort. In one of several sallies on Brockhurst, Dennis attacks the newspaperman:

> DENNIS. Press and public be goddamned! Your magazine would crucify us for one headline.
>
> BROCKHURST. When did we *ever . . . ?*
>
> DENNIS. After Bremfurt. We needed a second attack to finish there. But by the time you got done with our losses and Washington got done with your insinuations, we were told it was politically impossible to attack there again. *Politically impossible!* Today boys were killed with cannon made at Bremfurt since that attack. (47)

But that very newspaperman who initially called Dennis a "Fascist megalomaniac" comes, in the course of *Command Decision*, to admire Dennis's tenacity, to recognize the danger inherent in the shallowness of opportunists like Malcolm and Garnett, and to understand the importance of Dennis's determination to quash the enemy. Indeed, Brockhurst becomes the play's spokesperson for cuing the audience not merely to alter their views of Dennis but to revile publicity-seeking politicians, rank-seeking professional soldiers, and headline-seeking journalists.

With the foes across the Atlantic and Pacific subdued and already becoming a part of history, with the wartime motto Loose lips sink ships no longer necessary, Americans and American drama could now turn their attention to the foes at home, who had been protected by a ring of secrecy while World War II was being fought. As the spate of plays written immediately after the war so clearly documents, it was open season on the opportunists who had profited during the war. With its focus on domestic matters, the eye of drama seemed to move increasingly away from the locations of combat. The battlefront scenes of *A Sound of Hunting* and *The Rugged Path* in late 1945 are succeeded in 1947 by a space more remote from combat, the air base of *Command Decision*, from which pilots are dispatched but are never seen in action.[23] And by 1948, Thomas Heggen and Joshua Logan's *Mister Roberts* takes place during the summer of 1945, between V-E and V-J Days, on a supply ship in the Pacific that has never seen and presumably never will see battle action.

21. *Mister Roberts* (1948). Henry Fonda (center). Courtesy of the New York Public Library. John Swope/Timepix.

Thomas Heggen's 1946 novel (or what amounts to a series of linked vignettes) *Mister Roberts* was first written while the author was aboard a naval vessel in the Pacific, sending his stories to his famous cousin, writer Wallace Stegner, who encouraged Heggen to publish them.[24] The novel was a success, but *Mister Roberts* became even more successful as the Broadway play (written by Heggen and Joshua Logan) that starred Henry Fonda in one of his most memorable performances.[25] Opening at the Alvin Theatre on 18 February 1948, *Mister Roberts* was a smash success, running for nearly three years and closing on 6 January 1951 after 1157 performances. It was then made into the equally successful 1955 film with Fonda reprising his Broadway role, and with James Cagney, William Powell, and Jack Lemmon now cast in, respectively, the major supporting roles of the Captain, Doc, and Ensign Pulver. The play and film in turn spawned a comic film sequel, *Ensign Pulver* (1964), as well as a 1965 television series based on that film. A 1984 television revival of the play starred Robert Hays in the title role, with Charles Durning as the Captain and Kevin Bacon as Ensign Pulver.

What accounts for the unusual success of *Mister Roberts*? An answer might be that, in 1948, it struck just the right note about the war. It is comic, even at times slapstick, but it also projects an undertone of seriousness. And it moves an important step away from combat with the foes of America, for Heggen and Logan's play is not about opposition to the Japanese enemy. Rather it is almost entirely about the "war" between the sailors on *The Reluctant*, a supply ship in the Pacific, and their despotic Captain. World War II itself has not disappeared, but it is very much on the periphery of the play's action. The news that the foe in Europe has been conquered does get broadcast in the middle of the play, and there is a palpable awareness that the U.S. is in the last weeks of its war with Japan. To be sure, too, the Japanese are still out there, and in the last moment of the play a stunned audience learns by letter that Mister Roberts, transferred to a battleship in the vicinity of Okinawa, has been killed by Japanese kamikaze pilots. But those moments provide the barest flicker of warfare in a play that is largely a series of comic incidents aboard a supply ship well removed, in both geography and spirit, from the war zone. The enemy in *Mister Roberts* is selfish ambition of which the Captain is the dramatic avatar.

In a tense moment, the ruthless Captain pulls out a gold braided cap, the symbol of his willingness to sacrifice the welfare of the men under his command to his own lust for advancement, and he smugly tells Mister Roberts, whose career he has single-handedly blocked, "You see that? That's the cap of a full-commander. I'm gonna wear that cap some day and you're going to help me. . . . There's nothing gonna stand between me and that hat—certainly not you" (85). To this Roberts pointedly replies, "How did you get in the navy? How did you get on our side? You're what I joined to fight *against*. You ignorant, arrogant, ambitious . . . jackass! Keeping a hundred and sixty-seven men in prison because you got a palm tree for the work *they* did" (86). Later, a radio broadcast following the announcement of V-E Day proclaims:

> Our boys won this victory today. But the rest is up to you. You and you alone must recognize our enemies: the forces of ambition, cruelty, arrogance and stupidity. You must recognize them, you must destroy them, you must tear them out as you would a malignant growth! And cast them from the surface of the earth! (133–134)

In short, this generalization serves to use the revulsion of the audience toward those foreign foes—Hitler, Mussolini, and Hirohito—to indict as well the domestic foes—such as the Captain—who are likewise characterized by personal ambition and arrogance. Yet, as the battlefronts of the war fade into the background in *Mister Roberts* so too does much of the vitriol toward personal advancement evidenced in the military plays that precede it. Heggen and Logan's Captain is more the butt of comedy than the villain of the piece.

A year later, when James B. Allardice's *At War with the Army* opens on 8 March 1949, no drop of vitriol remains.[26] It has disappeared along with any reference at all to battle. Allardice's play is pure farce, and though it takes place during the war, it is appropriately set at an army camp in Kentucky, far from European and Asian theatres of the war. Neither the war nor its social and political issues are mentioned. As Allardice's title makes clear, his play is not about the war against the Axis powers but against army life. The Army—and not the war—simply provides a convenient backdrop for a series of comical mishaps. In its own way, following the pattern of other postwar plays, *At War with the Army* points its finger at a domestic antagonist, but that finger is purely a comic one, and the antagonist—if one can make a stretch and call it that—is the complications and bureaucratic regulations of the military.

In short, postwar military drama begins in 1945 with the immediacy of the battlefront and with death and injuries in *A Sound of Hunting*. By 1947, in *Command Decision*, the setting is removed from the front lines to an air force command base in England, where the air battles over Germany are reported but not depicted. A year later in 1948, in *Mister Roberts*, the war is there but only in the remote background, making an epistolary impact only in the last seconds of the play. Finally in *At War with the Army* in 1949, the war and its battles have completely vanished, leaving only the high jinx at the stateside army base. One feels, in these plays about servicemen, a gradual fading from view of the war, of battles, and of wartime issues.

III

As the bloodshed and hardships of World War II begin to evaporate from the drama, a warm nostalgia seems concomitantly to develop for the male bonding, remarkable friendships, comical exploits, and unusual experiences in foreign places that the war brought about. This comes to flower in World War II plays of the 1950s like *Teahouse of the August Moon* and *Stalag 17*, but it is clearly already present in the camaraderie of *Mister Roberts* and perhaps even more so in Norman Krasna's *John Loves Mary*, which opened on 4 February 1947 at the Booth Theatre. Produced by Rodgers and Hammerstein and staged by Joshua Logan, who a year later was to stage *Mister Roberts*, Krasna clearly hoped to recapture, in the immediately postwar period, the success of his long-running wartime comedy, *Dear Ruth*. Krasna calculated well and Rodgers and Hammerstein made a wise investment, and although *John Loves Mary* did not quite equal *Dear Ruth*'s box office success, it did fill the house with 423 performances. *John Loves Mary* benefited, moreover, from the performances of actress Nina Foch, who made her Broadway debut in Krasna's comedy, and of a hitherto relatively unknown character actor, Tom Ewell.

Like *Dear Ruth*, *John Loves Mary* is a trivial but charming comedy of errors based on information withheld from the female lead and her family. Part of that charm has its origins in the friendship of John Lawrence and Fred Taylor (Tom Ewell), a powerful friendship born out of wartime sacrifices. Indeed, underlying the froth of *John Loves Mary*—as is also true in other postwar comedies—there is a sense that civilians can never completely understand the homosocial chemistry and dynamics generated among army buddies uniquely bonded by the isolation and dangers of war. In the case of Krasna's play, John narrates how Fred saved his life:

> I'd like to tell you about it, though, as it really happened. It's important that you get the right picture. Fred here—and I—were side by side when I got hit. Shells were flying all around. It was worth a man's life to stand up [*He gets down on one knee, really acting it out*] Fred looked at me. I looked at him. I knew what was going through his mind. If he kept his head down, he was safe. But here was his friend—me—bleeding—what was he to do? . . . He made up his mind like that! [*He stands up, struggling with his imaginary burden*] He picked me up in his arms as you do a baby, and carried me not fifty yards, not a hundred yards—but two hundred yards! He brought me in! He saved my life! (25–26)[27]

Perhaps exemplary of American postwar sensibility more largely, this poignant and warmly nostalgic moment gives birth not to serious reflection but to farce. The special bond of comradeship between John and Fred, forged by Fred's self-sacrifice for John, has led John to make a self-sacrifice of another kind for Fred. During the war, Fred had fallen in love with Lilly, an exotic dancer in London, but when Fred was sent overseas, Lilly disappeared, leaving him heartbroken. Returning to London after V-E Day, John rediscovers Lilly and marries her so he can legally bring her back to the States, quickly divorce her, deliver her to Fred, and then proceed to marry his own fiancée, Mary (Nina Foch). The comedy ensues when John learns the demobilized Fred has forgotten Lilly, married someone else, and is now an expectant father. *John Loves Mary* touches, though lightly, on the difficulties of resuming relationships interrupted by the war. During their years of service, men in the armed forces met other women and were reshaped by what they had seen and done under fire. In short, for *John Loves Mary* the war and its effects, particularly on the men who served, provide a thin but noticeable crust for what otherwise is pure dramatic meringue.

One is tempted to say that the strain of national self-absorption or solipsism in American culture also affected American postwar drama. During the war years, those American dramas about the war that were not about America and Americans did not fare well. Janet and Philip Stevenson's *Counterattack*, about two Russian soldiers guarding some German soldiers, ran for only two months and was likely held afloat by the box office draw of its principal actors: Morris Carnovsky, Karl Malden, and Richard Basehart. Dan James's *Winter Soldiers*, about Eastern European civilians resisting the German military, though the recipient of the Playwrights Company's Sidney Howard Memorial Award, staged by Erwin Piscator, and praised by Burns Mantle, never left its off-Broadway location and was never published. Immediately after the war, plays not about America or Americans were likewise unsuccessful. The cases in point are Irwin Shaw's *The Assassin* and Joseph Fields and Jerome Chodorov's *The French Touch*.

The Assassin, written while Shaw was stationed in Europe, was first staged in London, where it enjoyed some success. The New York production that followed featured the talented Karl Malden. The team of Fields and Chodorov (brother of playwright Edward Chodorov) already had two big hits under its belt—*My Sister Eileen* and *Junior Miss*—and *The French Touch* also benefited from the considerable talents of French director René Clair, already famous for his films *À Nous la Liberté*, *The Ghost Goes West*, and *I Married a Witch*. Starring in *The French Touch* were Brian Aherne, whose performance in *The Barretts of Wimpole Street* had marked him as an important Broadway star, and Arlene Francis, who had enjoyed particular stage success in Fields's *Doughgirls*. One might assert that, by sheer coincidence, none of these wartime and postwar plays with settings abroad was well-written or well-produced, but in light of the quality of the writers, stars, and directors that seems too pat a dismissal. The truth likely lies somewhere between the flaws of the script and the relative lack of interest on the part of American audiences in seeing aspects of World War II that did not feature Americans or American issues. Whatever the case may be, *The Assassin* and *The French Touch* did raise some important issues about the European resistance to the war, even if those issues fell on deaf American ears.

Irwin Shaw's *The Assassin* opened at New York's National Theatre on 17 October 1945 and closed ten days later after thirteen performances. The failure of his drama prompted a bitter preface from its author when the play was published. A bruised Shaw wrote:

> Four days before *The Assassin* opened in New York City, I was discharged from the Army. After reading the reviews the morning after the opening, I was not certain I hadn't made a mistake in allowing the Adjutant-General to relieve me from duty.
>
> The critics, it developed, had done me more harm than the German Army. It is true that the Germans had tried to kill me, but they, at least, had missed. The critics had not missed. As a tribute to their marksmanship, *The Assassin* closed ten days later. (vii)[28]

He goes on to attack the critics for damning works that deal with serious matters and that, as his play does, create characters who are not paragons of perfection and idealism. He lambastes the critics for preferring Lillian Hellman's *Watch on the Rhine* with its flawless Kurt Muller and Norman Krasna's frothy *Dear Ruth* to *The Assassin*, with its panorama of flawed but patriotic Frenchmen victimized by French Nazis. Indeed, after the failure of *The Assassin*, Shaw licked his wounds and turned his attention almost entirely to fiction. But Shaw's vituperation is misdirected. It is not that critics and audiences prefer the extremes of good and evil or mindless comedy to probing drama, but that *The Assassin* presents a spectrum of political attitudes not readily understandable to most Americans.

The assassination of Admiral Marcel Vespery in Shaw's play is roughly based on the real case of Admiral Jean François Darlan, who served as prime minister of France under the Vichy government until his assassination in 1942.[29] The characters whom Vespery terrorizes include French communists, Jews, anti-Vichy partisans, and the foppish Robert de Mauny (Karl Malden) who eventually kills him. For Shaw, who had been living in London and Paris while writing *The Assassin,* the spectrum of characters was familiar, as it likely was to the London audiences who saw the play. To Americans, however, the assortment of French political attitudes was surely unfamiliar, and it is unlikely that more than a handful in Shaw's New York audience would have been familiar with or cared very much about Darlan's treachery and assassination.[30]

Less than two months after the failure of Shaw's *The Assassin,* Joseph Fields and Jerome Chodorov's comedy *The French Touch* opened at the Cort Theatre (8 December 1945). Also set in Vichy, France, during the war and featuring an assassination of a Nazi officer, *The French Touch* is nonetheless a classic meta-theatrical comedy about theatre people preparing to put on a new play. The playwrights also endow the script with more than a soupçon of Noel Coward's *Private Lives* to provide persiflage and wit. Director, actor, and playwright Roublard (Brian Aherne), impoverished by the ravages of the war and the Nazi regime in Paris, is suddenly commanded to stage a play about Franco-German amity. In his youth, Nazi commander Felix von Brenner had seen Roublard's troupe and fallen in love with their skill and more especially with their lead actress, Jacqueline Carlier (Arlene Francis), who had been lothario Roublard's first wife. Brenner demands that Jacqueline now star in the new play, which will also feature Roublard's second wife and his present third wife. For the most part, *The French Touch* spotlights the Coward-like banter among the three wives and Roublard, but it is also about French resistance and their hatred for their German invaders. At first, Roublard considers accepting deportation to a Polish concentration camp rather than write and stage the Nazi-sympathetic play Brenner prescribes, but instead he writes a play that the Nazi censors will approve but that will contain a last scene that turns the whole play into a resistance statement. In the meantime, the indigent Roublard, his wives, and his troupe live and eat well on the food the Nazis provide for them during the rehearsal period.

Fields and Chodorov's comedy has some of the makings of *The Producers* but falls short by concentrating on Roublard's squabbling wives and by never showing the anti-Nazi subversive play with its proudly resistant final scene. Indeed, we never really know what sort of final scene it will be. And in a last comic moment, Brenner is shot dead almost by accident and the curtain comes down as the actors leave to take their places onstage for a performance that will be their proud slap in the face to the Nazis in the audience. Fields and Chodorov thus end *The French Touch* with an awkward transition from the smiles and laughter that accompany the death of the Nazi commander to the realization that the Parisian players' act of resistance will likely land them in forced labor camps.

Noteworthy in *The French Touch* is that behind its comic wit and badinage is a tribute to Gallic wartime resistance, and the comic tone itself conveys the joy and relief Frenchmen felt in the months following V-E Day. In the figure of Brenner, the German comic heavy, Fields and Chodorov introduce what was to become a familiar American stage and film stereotype: the Nazi buffoon, comical for his lack of humor, insistence on authoritarian order, heavy German accent, intellectual denseness, and inability to appreciate any art or culture other than that approved by the Third Reich. During and just prior to World War II, fascist Germans were characterized as brutal, monomaniacal, diabolical racists for whom "tomorrow the world" was a driving principle and who were prepared to use torture, imprisonment, concentration camps, and murder to achieve their territorial and racial objectives. Clare Boothe's *Margin for Error*, Elmer Rice's *Flight to the West*, James Gow and Arnaud d'Usseau's *Tomorrow the World*, and the Army training play *This Is Your Enemy* provide notable examples of the stage Nazi during and just prior to the war. When, however, the war ends in an Allied victory and the defeated Germans no longer pose a threat, the sinister image of the pernicious, ruthless Nazis begins to give way to a new "Kraut" stereotype: the comically bungling, heavily accented, shouting but still deep-seatedly cruel German oaf, like Fields and Chodorov's Brenner, whose Teutonic obsession with rules and order deprives him of all subtlety. It is this comical but still dangerous stage and film stereotype that some years later *Stalag 17* would play to a fare-thee-well.

I V

Not surprisingly, most of the plays written during the aftermath of World War II reflect back on the war years; however, some plays begin, importantly, to look ahead to America's future and the ways that future might be shaped by what was experienced and learned during the bitter years between Pearl Harbor and V-J Day. Although the gaze of Miller's *All My Sons* is directed primarily to the past and to the sins of the adults during the war, the play's last words are "Live, live" as it makes a gesture toward the future, enjoining the play's young people to create a more moral America for the next generation. The bellwether play of the period is, perhaps appropriately, a comedy, and like most comedies it presents an agenda for sending its main character or characters into a bright future after they have successfully overcome a series of obstacles. That play is Howard Lindsay and Russel Crouse's *State of the Union*, which opened at the Hudson Theatre on 14 November 1945, just months after the conclusion of World War II.

Lindsay and Crouse's title is a clever pun that suggests not merely the president's annual message to the nation or the national condition of the United States but also the endangered marital union between Grant Matthews, a presidential hopeful, and his wife, Mary. Consequently, the spirit of this comedy means to propel into an enlightened future both the country itself and its political main characters. Given the issues for which the United States was fighting a war only a few months before, neither America nor Americans should revert, the playwrights warn, to the politics of selfishness, acquisitiveness, ethnic separation, and general divisiveness that characterized prewar America. *State of the Union* centers on the choices facing Grant Matthews, a presumptive Republican presidential candidate. These choices echo the ones projected in *All My Sons* and again in the first act of Sherwood's *The Rugged Path:* does a person choose what is morally right or what is politically or personally expedient? What is significantly different about Lindsay and Crouse's play from Miller's and Sherwood's is that the dilemma in *State of the Union* is faced not when the country is at war, when moral choices are relatively black and white, but in peacetime, when choices take on a noticeably grayer hue.

Performed as it was just weeks after V-J Day, *State of the Union* touches on essential decisions that will shape a new postwar American order and give meaning to the country's postwar political agenda. Lindsay and Crouse deftly touch on the set of dilemmas and issues that the conclusion of the war initiated, and they see, moreover, how the end of wartime political solidarity rekindled the old scramble for power among American party politicians. Americans had put aside much of the usual pugnacity between Republicans and Democrats to stand behind the Roosevelt administration during the war years. But with the war over, *State of the Union*, in its comic way, sounds the starting bell for the renewal of the old Republican versus Democrat boxing match, a match that, the play satirically posits, is about the election of candidates and not about the welfare of the country. Taking a stand against the squabbling of ambitious politicians and their scramble for political ascendancy, *State of the Union* asks its audience to look to the future, reminding them that the present moment in politics is a crucial one, for it will set the United States on its postwar course and put in place both the values and the fate of the next generation.

If the country is pulled in different directions by its two political parties, on a more domestic plane, *State of the Union*'s main character, Grant Matthews, is caught between two women. His wife, Mary, tries to keep Grant's mind on the essential values in his life and in American life, deflating her husband with sarcastic jibes when his rhetoric swells to bombast and his ego to self-congratulation. Grant's vanity, however, has sent him into the arms and wiles of Kay Thorndyke, the wealthy owner of a string of newspapers, who sees Grant as the fulfillment of her ambitions for the Republican Party. Willing to use her newspapers to market Grant Matthews as the next American president, Kay lures Grant into sacrificing his ideals when they might compromise his party or stand in the way of his being nominated for the presidency. As he is thrust by Kay into the hands of James Conover, a political kingmaker, and Spike Macmanus, a political reporter and candidate handler, Grant loses his ability to be a spokesman for new directions in American postwar thinking and increasingly becomes commodified, a political product whose ideals must be held in check so that he can be successfully marketed and sold to the electorate.

At the beginning of *State of the Union*, Grant Matthews declaims with feeling

22. *State of the Union* (1945).
(Left to right) Ralph Bellamy,
Herbert Hayes, Edith Atwater.
Courtesy of Billy Rose Theatre
Collection, The New York Pub-
lic Library for the Performing
Arts, Astor, Lenox and Tilden
Foundations.

his (and presumably Lindsay and Crouse's) strong sense of what the United States must do in the aftermath of the war. What Grant has said in a forthright speech given in Cleveland does not suit Conover, who is eager to ruffle no voter feathers. Conover's concern is for the welfare of his party and not the country, and he hopes for a platform that is thoroughly bland and unobjectionable. Grant replies spiritedly:

> When I made that speech in Cleveland I was trying to put both parties on the spot. I wasn't speaking as a Republican. I was speaking as a citizen. I'm worried about what's happening in this country. We're splitting apart. Business, labor, farmers, cattlemen, lumbermen—they're all trying to get the biggest bite of the apple. We talk about the war being over—well, we've got a war on here at home now—a civil war—an economic war. . . . you politicians are trying to make capital out of that situation—you appeal to each one of these pressure groups just to get their votes. But let me tell you something. I don't think that's good politics. Of course I will admit that the business men liked best what I said about labor, and the unions said I was absolutely right about big business, and the farmers were pretty pleased with what I said about everybody but the farmers. But they all knew what I was talking about. They know we've all got to work in harness, if we're going to take our place in this world. And if we don't there won't be any world. We may be kidding ourselves that our party is going

to win in '48—that the people here will want a change the way they did in England—but if our party does win, whoever is President has to have guts enough to pull us together and keep us together. (9–10)[31]

Here *State of the Union* immediately sets forth its oppositions: the self-serving tactics of ambitious politicians versus the good of the country, and the fostering of ethnic, labor, and economic fractiousness versus pulling the country together "to work in harness." And Mary Matthews echoes her husband's views, neatly capturing the American postwar situation when she exclaims, "I can't read the newspapers any more! While the war was on we were a united country—we were fighting Germany and Japan. Now we're just fighting each other" (50–51). The newspapers Mary can no longer read are precisely those controlled by her rival, Kay. When Grant tells Mary about his feelings, the conflict in the play becomes more pointed and specific: "If I can make the people see the choice they've got to make—the choice between their own interests and the interests of the country as a whole—damn it, I think the American people are sound. I think they can be unselfish" (64).

The choices here are those of Miller's *All My Sons*. But Joe Keller's choice in wartime is replaced in *State of the Union* not merely by Grant Matthews's choice but by the direction the country as a whole must choose in peacetime. At the heart of Grant Matthews's vision is reconversion, converting wartime industries and procedures back once more to peacetime uses. The partisan politicians such as Conover and Kay have only one vision: electing a Republican president no matter what it takes to do so. The conflict becomes clear as Grant tells of what he will say in his speech in Detroit:

> GRANT. I'm going to tell them they did a great job in war production— and they did! . . . They had their engineering brains, and plenty of manpower to do the work.
>
> CONOVER. All right. Why don't you let it go at that?
>
> GRANT. Oh, no! I've got to tell them that now they're up against the test. Now they're on their own. They talk about how they want to save the private-enterprise system. . . . They're not going to do it by lowering production so they can raise prices. And they're not going to save it by closing down plants to cut down competition. . . . And those babies who are stirring up war veterans to fight labor—I'm going to take their hide off!
>
> CONOVER. Grant, you can't do that!
>
> GRANT. Jim, you know reconversion goes deeper than re-tooling our plants. We need a moral reconversion. . . . What's behind most of the opposition to full employment—behind opposing the whole idea of the Government supplying work. To give private enterprise the chance to supply the employment? Nuts! It's to keep prices up on everything but labor. Let

labor starve for a while! Jim, there isn't going to be a free-enterprise system if it means that men are free to starve!

CONOVER. Grant, you can't say those things now, and you can't say them here! This town is one of my best sources for silent money! (129–130)

Not merely does Conover attempt to douse Grant's fire, but he concludes with a bottom line matter of trimming one's ideals to suit those who finance party politics under the table. And in his anger at Grant's honesty, he reveals his hand completely, admitting, "The people have damn little to say about the nomination. . . . You're not nominated by the people—you're nominated by the politicians! Why? Because the voters are too damned lazy to vote in the primaries!" (130–131).

As the political kingmakers, Conover and Kay, make their impact on Grant's ideas, he begins to pull in his horns. Mary plays the role of Grant's moral conscience, but her influence is increasingly diminished by the vision of the presidency temptingly held forth by the party power brokers, who never hesitate to replace ethics with expedience. When Grant decides he will take "silent money," Mary warns, "If you take money, you have to pay it back some way." As Grant protests he's not for sale, Mary sharply tells him, "You've arranged that very neatly in your mind, Grant. All they have to do is buy Conover! I warned you the Presidency was a great temptation!" (137). As Grant tries to decide whether to replace his fiery Detroit speech with a bland one that will pander to the selfish interests in the audience, the stage directions pinpoint his struggle and that within the play more generally: "MARY *realizes* GRANT *is torn between ambition and integrity*" (139). After consulting with Kay before entering the hall to deliver his speech, Grant abandons his zeal and chooses ambition, soft-pedaling his platform about reconversion.

At a reception for key politicians and deep-pocket donors, Grant listens tamely to those who would pit one ethnicity against another, not flinch at this American form of fascism, support business over labor, and capitalize on the new American fears of Russia. These political pragmatists are more than willing to use the postwar peace talks for their own political advantage. Kay blithely tells Grant, "We know that every nation is going to feel the peace terms have done them an injustice. We can make a perfectly honest appeal for justice, and if that gets us some votes—I don't think we should quibble." To which Grant disenchantedly responds, "Which are you thinking of first, the votes or the justice?" (216–217). Lindsay and Crouse leave the final salvo for Mary, allowing her not merely to annihilate "the other woman" but, more important, to speak movingly for a postwar America laudably acting on what is right rather than what is merely personally or politically expedient. She makes it clear that the issue at hand should be what happens to America, not who is elected president:

I've sat here listening to you making plans for Grant to trade away the peace of the world to get a few votes! Now that we're in the United

Nations let's use it—use it to get Italian votes and Polish votes—let's use it to get the votes of those who hate the Russians and those who hate the British! How long is it going to be before you ask us to forgive the Germans to get the German vote? . . . Look at Sam [a conservative friend who supports big business over labor]—he wants to leave a fortune to Bobby. What kind of world is he going to leave Bobby? The kind he wants isn't good enough for my children. Don't you know what's happened in the world? Are you willing to trust the people you brought here tonight with atomic power? . . . Nobody represented the American people! They don't even represent the Republican Party. You represent what's dead in the Republican Party . . . and what's dead in the Democratic Party! . . . What have you got faith in? The people? You're afraid to let them know what Grant really thinks. Don't you believe in democracy? . . . Everybody here tonight was thinking of the next election. Well, it's time somebody began thinking of the next generation! (217–219)

Mary's rejoinder to the smooth politicians who would sacrifice the nation to elect their candidate and her call to Americans to vote not for the good of their party but for that of their country and the next generation will, if delivered effectively, bring a lump to the throat of every audience member. Her exhortation brings her husband to his senses, and as the play ends, the marital union of Grant and Mary is reestablished, foreshadowing the reunification of the nation's fragmented, fractious interest groups. *State of the Union* is a rededication of the central couple and of the audience with renewed spirit to forge the nation's bright future.

What *State of the Union* does is to set out in generalities some of the problems the nation must address in light of the war that has just taken place. Other postwar plays locate problems more specifically. One of those problems is racial prejudice and segregation. The Civil War and the Thirteenth Amendment to the Constitution have freed the slaves, but they did little to free America of its racist attitudes toward African Americans, to eliminate the violence toward blacks, or to affect the Jim Crow laws in the South. One side of American racism can be seen in the very fact that, as late as World War II, black troops were still placed in segregated units. Another side is evidenced in the minstrel show scripts disseminated to white troops by the USO. *South Pacific* (1943), Dorothy Heyward and Howard Rigsby's unsuccessful melodrama about an African-American soldier scarred by racism, and Edward Chodorov's poignant drama *Decision* (1944), about prejudice toward African Americans working in wartime industries, point to the anger that a decade later would boil over into both peaceful and violent civil rights demonstrations. The unjust and oppressive life to which African Americans were relegated became increasingly clear and problematic after a war during which many of them had served so loyally and valiantly. They had seen combat, moreover, in a war that, ironically, was fought over issues of racism and for the preservation of liberty and justice for all.

As American troops were demobilized and returned home from the battle-fields of Europe and the Pacific, the problem of domestic racism was refocused against the backdrop of African-American participation in World War II. Far stronger than Chodorov's *Decision* are three important plays staged just after the war ended: James Gow and Arnaud d'Usseau's *Deep Are the Roots,* which was directed by Elia Kazan and opened on 26 September 1945 at the Fulton Theatre in New York; Robert Ardrey's *Jeb,* which opened at the Martin Beck on 21 February 1946 and featured Ossie Davis in his stage debut and Ruby Dee (whom Davis married soon thereafter); and Maxine Woods's excellent but now-adays scarcely remembered *On Whitman Avenue,* directed by Margo Jones and produced by and starring Canada Lee at the Cort Theatre in New York on 8 May 1946.[32] All three plays center on the return home of educated African-American soldiers, who have fought side by side patriotically with whites in World War II and who have been decorated for bravery.[33]

In *Deep Are the Roots,* Lt. Brett Charles returns to his home in the Deep South only to find his prewar second-class citizenship absolutely unaltered. Like-wise, in Ardrey's *Jeb,* the title character, who has earned a Silver Star and a Purple Heart and has been trained by the army to operate a cash register, causes strife in his Louisiana town when he seeks a position as a cash register operator, a job held by whites. In *On Whitman Avenue,* David Bennett (portrayed by the play's producer, Canada Lee) is a returning black soldier who has also won a Purple Heart, has nearly died in the Pacific in the service of his country, and is now registering for college, looking forward to new opportunities as a veteran in peacetime America. He returns to an unnamed Northern city to find that the white working-class families on Whitman Avenue, where he has rented a flat, are outraged by his family's presence among them and have, therefore, organized to drive him and his black family from their all-white neighborhood.

Gow and d'Usseau, who during the war also co-authored *Tomorrow the World,* had a postwar agenda in mind when they wrote *Deep Are the Roots.* They write in their preface to *Deep Are the Roots,* "We're entering a period of peace. The war is over, and the artist, no longer in the immediate service of the state, must again face his full individual responsibility" (xx).[34] They go on to say that in American literature blacks have been depicted either as Uncle Toms or Bigger Thomases, but never (or not very often) realistically:

> There are in America today thousands upon thousands of Negro university graduates, they are schoolteachers and lawyers, businessmen and artists; in the Army they were sergeants and lieutenants and majors. That such peo-ple rarely or never appear as important characters in our literature is in itself as an indication of the backward social scene in which we live, a commentary upon the implicit prejudice with which we have all been infected. Both by sheer inertia and, in many cases, conscious determina-tion, we preserve the role of the Negro as a second-class citizen. (xxiv)

23. *Deep Are the Roots* (1945).
Gordon Heath and Barbara Bel
Geddes. Courtesy of the New
York Public Library.

In *Deep Are the Roots*, there are several speeches and lines reminiscent of Chodorov's *Decision*. One of the white Southerners complains, "You take this problem of our colored people. They aren't what they used to be with all these war factories springing up in the most unlikely places. Of course, it's good for business, but after all, you know, it's practically impossible any more to get decent servants" (22).

Gow and d'Usseau create a central black character who has felt a freedom in the Army he never knew in the South. He returns home a decorated lieutenant, unable to slip unthinkingly back into his former role as the abject beneficiary and object of white paternalism. Lt. Brett tells his mother, "It's very difficult to be a Negro in the Army—even a Negro officer. And yet in the Army I was able to see things—do things. The Army gave me privileges I never had before" (34). And when Brett attempts to assert his new manhood and independence, to challenge the Jim Crow laws of the South, Langdon, the Southern senator in whose house he was raised, falsely accuses Brett of theft and tries to have him lynched.

Senator Langdon is *Deep Are the Roots*'s heavy, the archetypal dramatic Southern racist who harks back to the racist governor of Edward Sheldon's 1911 melodrama, *The Nigger*. More interesting are Langdon's daughters, Alice and Genevra. Alice is the image of a Southern Lady Bountiful, who over the years has been Brett's patroness, his seeming friend and a would-be image of a liberal

Southern lady. She is even engaged to a cynical, liberal Northern journalist who despises the racist attitudes of his fiancée's white Southern family and friends as well, and finds repellant the servile deference he receives from the town blacks. When the allegedly progressive Alice feels Brett challenging the thrall of her patronage and when she senses there may be feelings of sexual attraction between Brett and her younger sister, Genevra, her white privilege is threatened and her progressive views are put to the test—a test she fails. Reverting to Southern stereotype, Alice calls the police to have the transgressive Brett arrested for theft. She does this knowing full well Brett is likely to be lynched and that she herself will alienate the affections of her progressive Northern fiancé. But for her, the racist order of life below the Mason-Dixon Line must take precedence even over her own her sense of truth or her marriage plans.

Deep Are the Roots recognizes that black soldiers who fought to eliminate racism in Europe return home to find racism still in full force in this country. The play raises strong issues and uses the power of drama—and d'Usseau and Gow are masters of both the highly dramatic and the melodramatic—to challenge and awaken its audience, providing neither a simple solution nor a happy ending. The senator is humiliated and exposed as out of step with the times. His young relative, a pragmatic political hopeful in the postwar South, tells the old senator, "You don't realize the winds that are blowing" (106). But the younger Southerner reveals that his own willingness to soften the lines of segregation originates purely from political expedience and not from any genuine commitment to American democracy. Although Lt. Brett's stereotypical Southern servant mother (styled after Hattie McDaniel in the film version of *Gone with the Wind*) breaks free of her servility and finally gives the white senator a piece of her mind, her black son and the senator's white younger daughter are nevertheless forced to flee the Southern town and seek an uncertain future as a mixed-race couple in the North. The point of the drama, however, is to throw American race problems into the lap of the audience. *Deep Are the Roots* implicitly asks the audience questions but provides no pat answers. The playwrights in their preface lay down their challenge:

> What you, as a reader, will find in this play, since it presents you no happy answer, will depend largely upon you yourself—whether, upon thinking it over, you prefer a world of racial superiority with the cruelties and dishonesties which such a world ultimately imposes, or whether maybe you'd like some changes made. (xxv)

Race prejudice is not a new issue in twentieth-century American drama, but it clearly takes the issues of World War II and the role of black men in the armed forces to empower the theatre after the war to be a weapon for change and to challenge the conscience of playgoers.

As dramatically and melodramatically powerful as it is, *Deep Are the Roots* is compromised by the fact that it appeals to the clichéd worst images of the South held by presumably Northern theatre audiences. The racist Southern senator is too easy a target. The image of the new Southern politician and of the would-be liberal Southern gentlewoman are tougher targets, but even so, d'Usseau and Gow load the theatrical dice with their stereotypical presentation of a post– World War II Tara. What is important, however, is the way the playwrights shrewdly factor in the wartime experience of the young black lieutenant, juxtaposing it to the unchanged ways of a South that continues to believe that its black citizens are every bit as second class, as subaltern, as they were before the war. In the Southern town of *Deep Are the Roots,* the implicit assumptions that informed the USO minstrel shows still very much persist, but d'Usseau and Gow point the way to change.

Sir John Vanbrugh, at the turn of the eighteenth century, is one of the few playwrights to distinguish himself in two totally disparate fields, playwriting and architecture. Robert Ardrey was the modern-day Vanbrugh. He wrote stimulating plays such as *Thunder Rock* (1939), *Jeb* (1946), and *Sing Me No Lullaby* (1954). But he also became a distinguished anthropologist, writing such seminal and monumental studies as *African Genesis* (1961) and *The Territorial Imperative* (1966). In his preface to his collection of plays that includes *Jeb,* Ardrey explains, "Inasmuch as I had been born on the edge of Chicago's Black Belt, I never attended any but integrated schools."[35] Perhaps this background, as he suggests, led him to feel the injustice of white American attitudes toward blacks. *Jeb* was a civil rights play ten to twenty years ahead of its time.

Produced and directed by Howard Shumlin, and starring Ruby Dee and Ossie Davis, *Jeb* eschewed the miscegenation red herring of *Deep Are the Roots* to produce a powerful dramatic statement that, nevertheless, closed in a few days.[36] Ardrey is probably right in attributing the play's Broadway failure to its being ahead of its time. Like *Deep Are the Roots, Jeb* centers on a black soldier who has won a Purple Heart and a Silver Star for bravery in the Pacific and who has lost his leg serving his country. Jeb is filled with pride and with love of country, because in the army he has learned a trade: "Why, by heck, I'm just about the best old adding-machine man in the U.S. Army. . . . Uncle Sam learn me to run the adding machine" (110). He soon learns that his vocational training will be his undoing, for his skill threatens to upset the conflation of racial and vocational segregation in his Louisiana town, where blacks work in the sugar cane fields and whites work in the sugar refinery offices.

Before sending Jeb to his Louisiana hometown, Ardrey very astutely sets an initial scene in a Northern city, where white attitudes are shown to be dismissive of Jeb's military record and, in their own way, as brutal as the ones in the South. Ardrey also suggests that part of the racial problem is black exploitation of blacks, as an innocent Jeb is rolled in a bar by a black prostitute and a black con man. Here Ardrey puts his finger on the same problem Lorraine Hansberry will put forth thirteen years later in *A Raisin in the Sun,* when a black con man absconds with the trusting Walter Lee Younger's money. The dramatic mission of *Jeb,* however, lies elsewhere, pointing out that racial segregation is driven by economics.

In Louisiana, Jeb's war record counts for very little, and his adding machine skills are likely to cause a race riot because they threaten the race-based socio-economic structure of the South. As the white manager of the sugar mill asserts:

> We use the poor white trash to keep the niggers in their place, and we use the niggers to keep the white trash in *their* place. It's a fine system, it's a good system. We don't have to pay the niggers any money, and we don't have to pay the trash any money. . . . There's been a war, Charlie. They took our boys away. Now they're coming home. If you think Jeb's the only colored boy that's learning something, then you're very wrong.— The world's caught up with us, man. We'll never keep them in their place the old way, never again. (133–134)

When the drunken, "white trash" adding machine operator realizes that his job is at stake and may be given to Jeb, he concocts a quickly believed story that he has seen Jeb making sexual advances toward a white woman. This sets the whole town agog. Neither the banker nor the clergyman, who know of Jeb's innocence, lift a finger. They allow a white citizens' group to beat Jeb within an inch of his life, and they do so because they wish to maintain the racial and economic ways of the South.

The sugar mill manager, who wishes to employ Jeb and is consequently labeled a "nigger lover," is clearly Ardrey's mouthpiece as he explains the miscegenation issue to Jeb:

> When we say a nigra wants a white man's girl, what we mean it's a nigra wants a white man's job. I got you into this, Jeb. I should have knocked you down the day you first asked me [for a job working an adding machine]. I didn't. I calculated it was just possible if colored folks had learned something fighting a war, white folks had learned something too. We haven't. I'm sorry. . . . I pity you, Jeb. You're a hero. You expect other folks to behave like yourself. (149–150)

Ardrey moves a most important step beyond *Deep Are the Roots* by taking that play's purely melodramatic miscegenation issue and using it to show that the sexual coding of the black-white race issue is merely a convenient and effective tool for keeping an exploitative economic system in place.

At the close of the play, Jeb, who has fled North, as has his beloved Libby, tells Libby that he must return home and fight for what will, more than a decade later, eventually be called civil rights:

JEB. I got to go back down South. . . .

LIBBY. They run you out already, they beat you up—

JEB. What else I do? Stay here? Forget all about my friends, my mama? Rachel—she going to grow up like you, all scared and twisted? Libe and Jefferson—my little brothers—all they ever going to have it's bow down and scrape and take that the white folks leave them? I can't! I can't stay here. . . .

LIBBY. They kill you.

JEB. Well—I might of got killed in that old war too, but I went. Ain't much different. No, sugar, I won't get killed. Ask the white folks, am I going to get killed? They know. They're scareder than me.

LIBBY. Will I ever see you again?

JEB. Wish I knew, sugar—When all this here it's over, I reckon, and you can come home too. (167)

As the bitter civil rights struggle that would ensue some years later in the South would show, Jeb's assertion, "I won't get killed," may be naïve. At the same time, it is essential to see that World War II is shown to have made a man of Jeb, who in the South, despite his medals and artificial leg, is never called anything but "boy." The military discipline Jeb learned in the Army and the bravery he demonstrated in the Pacific, however, will now serve him well in the new, domestic war he proposes to fight. And his leave-taking of Libby echoes the leave-taking heard so often a few years earlier when soldiers left wives and sweethearts to go into battle. Indeed, *Jeb* shows how the participation of African Americans in World War II and the occupational training they received in the armed forces prepare them in the postwar period to dress for battle in a new war to end racial discrimination and oppression at home. This is heady and unsettling stuff in 1946 for Broadway audiences and for a society trying to return to prewar "normalcy" and to put returning white soldiers back into the work force. It is no small wonder that *Jeb*, with its incisive unveiling of racism's economic underpinnings and with its militant ending, closed after six performances.

Somewhere there must be a heaven for excellent plays that didn't make it, perhaps because they were too far ahead of their time. If so, not only Robert Ardrey's *Jeb* but also Maxine Wood's *On Whitman Avenue* (despite its 150 performances) can be found there. Less melodramatic than *Deep Are the Roots, On Whitman Avenue* is a hard-hitting and realistic play in which Toni Tilden, as an idealistic nineteen-year-old white girl, rents the vacant flat in her parents' two-family house to David Bennett and his family while her parents are out of town. Bennett has shared the same foxhole in the Pacific with the Tildens' son and has won a Purple Heart. But the Bennetts are black. When the Tildens return from their trip and realize what their daughter has done, Toni must face the distress of her conservative mother and argue with her more progressive father, whose feelings are in the right place but who lacks backbone to act on them:

> TONI. Dad, you've always said it's a damn shame that Negroes can't vote in their own country.
>
> ED. I know what I've done and what I've said. Don't keep throwing it back at me.
>
> TONI. I'm not throwing it back. I just want to prove that this isn't so different. If you believe in economic and political rights for the Negro, you can't draw the line at social rights, can you? (20–21)[37]

The answer to Toni's rhetorical question, however, proves to be "yes." The time of the play is 1945 and the white community pulls together, exclaiming (now that the war has been won), "They shouldn't have put Negroes in uniform in the first place" (40). The white neighborhood association of Whitman Avenue does not want the negative publicity of dispossessing a decorated veteran's family, so, in ways foreshadowing Lorraine Hansberry's *Raisin in the Sun,* they try to buy the black family out.[38] As Mr. Tilden, who is encouraged by his neighbors to terminate the Bennetts' lease, realizes, "I don't know a nice way of saying you can fight for your country, but you can't live in it" (56).

In *On Whitman Avenue,* which is obviously "On White Man Avenue," the Northern species of de facto racism also affects the life of Bennetts' young black son, Owen, ostracized by the white boys, who replicate the prejudice and attitudes of their parents and bar Owen from their baseball games. In a poignant line, Owen tells the white boys, "You're scared to have me on your team. Just like in professional ball. They're scared to have Negro players. Scared they'll make all the home runs" (48). These lines were spoken on the stage of the Cort Theatre eleven months before Jackie Robinson first stepped onto Ebbets Field. The most moving speech of the play, however, belongs to David Bennett, when he faces the homeowners committee:

> Live a healthy normal life. They told me that when I left the [army] hospital. Good advice. Hard to follow if your skin is black. . . . I tried to register at the university today. So sorry, our quota of Negroes is filled. Now you say it is not safe to live among you. That hurts, ladies and gentlemen. Hurts more than shrapnel tearing through the flesh. In war, you expect that. You know the enemy, the common enemy. But here at home— . . . But you have to keep the nigger in his place. Let's be honest, at least. Call this meeting by its right name. A lynching bee, Northern style. No bloodhounds, no tar and feathers, no shriveled fruit on a lonely tree, but the fruit's the same, ladies and gentlemen. The fruit's the same. (42–43)

24. *On Whitman Avenue* (1946). (Center, left to right) Perry Wilson, Canada Lee, Will Geer. Courtesy of the New York Public Library.

By the play's end, there is considerable guilt and remorse on the part of the Tildens and some other neighbors. But this is 1946, and the forces of conservatism do win the day, though not at all triumphantly. In the final moving moment of the play, there is no happy ending. Bennett is not welcomed into the neighborhood by an educated and reformed white citizenry who now warmly embrace him and his exemplary black family. Instead Bennett submits to his lot, removes his family from Whitman Avenue, and returns the house key to the Tildens.

The best assessment of *On Whitman Avenue* may have been the one by the reviewer in the *New York Post* who wrote, "There might be some criticism that the playwright has not solved her problem, but who has solved this particular problem? What Miss Wood has done, though, is to bring her problem out in the open and to discuss it boldly, candidly and intelligently. That in itself is an achievement."[39] The drama can be at once a register of national attitudes but also a force for shaping those attitudes.[40] In the half-decade during which the U.S. entered World War II and then saw the troops return home, attitudes toward at least one minority, African Americans, were beginning to show signs of change, and in the midst of the change were white American playwrights such as Chodorov, d'Usseau, Gow, and Wood. It was only a matter of a short time before Jackie Robinson became a Dodger, housing and schools integrated, and quotas lifted. It was likewise only a short time before African-American playwrights like Lorraine Hansberry, LeRoi Jones, Lonnie Elder, and Ed Bullins were empowered so that they could, from the point of view of the oppressed, expose to both black and white playgoers the deep scars produced by generations of white privilege.

Read nowadays, *Deep Are the Roots* and *On Whitman Avenue* are plays with courage, moral fiber, and great dramatic power. In them, it is possible to see an often eloquent challenge to the assumptions behind American racist attitudes. Nonetheless, neither of these plays was successful. They did not revolutionize the thoughts of a nation. *Deep Are the Roots* and *On Whitman Avenue* are almost totally unknown today. It is appropriate here to mention the cautious attempt to deal with race relations made by Rodgers and Hammerstein in their 1949 musical *South Pacific*. Against a backdrop of a World War II military engagement in the Pacific, Army nurse Nellie Forbush from Arkansas (Mary Martin) and Marine Corps Lieutenant Joe Cable (William Tabbert) from Philadelphia sing of American ingrained racial prejudice in their duet "You've Got to Be Taught." But the racial prejudice issue is not at the heart of the Rodgers and Hammerstein musical, and besides, the people of color are not African American but Tonkinese, even though the audience knew full well what was meant and even though the dominant Tonkinese character, Bloody Mary, was portrayed by African-American singer Juanita Hall. Rodgers and Hammerstein knew how to raise the issue and make their point without ruffling the audience.[41] *Deep Are the Roots* and *On Whitman Avenue* are, however, the stage plays in which the first chinks in the American monolith of postwar whiteness become visible. Visible, too, are the ways wartime experience helped to create those chinks. Americans did eventually come to accept the ideas articulated in those plays. The terrible truth, however, is that there is a span of fifteen years between David Bennett's impassioned speech to the white citizens meeting in *On Whitman Avenue* and Martin Luther King's similarly impassioned "I Have a Dream" speech at the Lincoln Memorial in Washington.

Change of another (and in some ways related) kind is indicated in a postwar play that one does not immediately think of as war-related: Tennessee Williams's *A Streetcar Named Desire*, which opened on 3 December 1947 at the Barrymore Theatre and was directed by Elia Kazan. During the war, the presence in small towns of large numbers of young soldiers from around the country now stationed there for military training often radically changed the life of those towns. Local women were courted by the soldiers, and both sexual affairs and marriages occurred.

Likewise, servicemen stationed in large (usually port) cities also formed liaisons with local women and then settled in those cities when the war was over. Writing after the war, Tennessee Williams sees, in *A Streetcar Named Desire*, some of the larger implications of the wartime demographic dislocations.

At one level, the agon in Williams's tragedy is the struggle between the old and the new South. The former is embodied by Blanche DuBois, Williams's drawling, exaggerated recollection of Scarlett O'Hara, as she was portrayed by Vivien Leigh in the film version of *Gone with the Wind*. Indeed, it is hardly surprising that when Kazan came to direct *Streetcar* for Hollywood in 1951, he cast Vivien Leigh as Blanche. The new South is embodied by Stanley Kowalski. Although residing in New Orleans, Stanley has no Southern accent and no Southern roots. Williams never reveals Stanley Kowalski's regional origins, but his Polish surname could suggest he was raised amid the large Polish community in the Chicago metropolitan area or in some similar Polish-American neighborhood. Certainly Stanley is no Southerner. How then did he come to New Orleans? Given the date of the play and the fact that his wife, Stella, met him presumably in New Orleans while he was "A Master Sergeant in the Engineers' Corps" (24), it seems likely that Stanley was one of the many Northern-born soldiers who were stationed at camps in the South, married local women, and remained in the South after the war.[42] Williams sees, too, how the sexual self-punishing orgies of Blanche DuBois after her young husband's suicide are facilitated by the fact that randy U.S. Army troops are stationed in the neighborhood of Belle Reve, the DuBois family estate.

One facet of *A Streetcar Named Desire* makes clear the takeover of the American South, with its fading and effeminate antebellum genteel charm, by the likes of a new, coarse but virile and potent breed, of which Stanley is at once the impressive and the hateful representative. The fulcrum of *A Streetcar Named Desire* is Stella. And the struggle between Blanche and Stanley, in part, centers on which one of them will possess Stella. But it is Stanley who has won the love of Stella DuBois, whom he has transformed into Stella Kowalski, even as he has helped transform the traditional old South into the new, post–World War II industrial South. He exults, "When we first met, me and you, you thought I was common. How right you was, baby. I was common as dirt. You showed me a snapshot of the place with the columns. I pulled you down off them columns and how you loved it" (132). Williams here shrewdly suggests the war's role in forging a new Southern demography and style. The network of established Southern aristocratic families is replaced by the new social network of Stanley and his buddies from the Engineering Corps.

The clock in *A Streetcar Named Desire* is Stella's pregnancy, her increasing size, and the imminent delivery of a child who will necessarily displace Blanche from the Kowalski tenement. It is no accident that the day the Kowalski baby—the postwar hybrid of Stanley and Stella—is born is also the day that the representative of the antebellum South, Blanche, is defeated, raped, and destroyed. Williams casts something of a cold eye on the triumph of a new (postwar) South peopled by brutish and insensitive Stanley Kowalskis and their progeny. At the same time, however, he seems to foresee and even applaud the ethnic diversity that characterizes the new South, which replaces the decadent old white and racist Southern aristocracy with the ethnically mixed denizens of Elysian Fields, where whites, African Americans, and Hispanics mingle freely and unaffectedly.

An ethnic postwar issue of another kind concerned the Jews. This issue had several disparate aspects stemming from or related to the Holocaust and the shocking revelation of the extermination of six million Jews in Nazi concentration camps. The first revelations of what was transpiring in those camps came as brief mentions in the *New York Times* on 30 June and 2 July 1942. And on November 1942, relegated to page 10 of the *Times,* came the dramatic assertion from renowned Rabbi Stephen Wise that two million Jews had been exterminated by the Nazis. But the war, as it was seen by Americans and portrayed onstage, was for the most part about defending the United States from fascism and upholding the democratic principles for which the country stands. It was not about rescuing Jews from genocide. This is not surprising, since it was not until the concentration camps were liberated at the end of the war and the public encountered horrific proof of the "the final solution" in photographs and reports from those camps that the magnitude of what had happened could be conceived.[43] Nowadays the images of the skeletal concentration camp prisoners in their striped uniforms, the clothes with the yellow *Judenstern* sewn onto them, the gas chambers, the fatal showers, the piles of corpses or human hair or shoes or bones are synonymous with World War II. But the contemporary preoccupation with the horrific dimensions of the Holocaust—and even the term *Holocaust* itself—only seems to begin in the mid-1950s, ten years after the war.

In the waning months of World War II and in the years immediately after war's end, the situation of the Jews both in Europe and at home became an issue. In Arthur Laurents's *Home of the Brave* or Laura Z. Hobson's novel *Gentleman's Agreement* (1947) it becomes clear that in the United States the germs of anti-Semitism also flourish, the very germs that had with such virulence helped to bring about Auschwitz, Treblinka, Dachau, Theresienstadt, Sobibor, and Buchenwald.

Ancillary to this recognition was a growing realization that the United States and its Allies, even while fighting fascism, had not done right by the Jews. Domestic anti-Semitism is, of course, a central theme in Laurents's *Home of the Brave,* but after the war, Americans also began to ponder the U.S. stance toward the Jews of Europe, who had endured so much during the war and prewar years. On the American postwar stage this idea was dramatized by Jan de Hartog in *Skipper Next to God,* though whether de Hartog or *Skipper Next to God* should be considered American is debatable. Although he lived for many years in the United States and wrote in English, de Hartog was a native of Holland, and *Skipper Next to God* premiered on 27 November 1945 in London at the Embassy Theatre before opening in New York more than two years later, on 13 January 1948, at the Playhouse Theater. In London the lead role of Captain Joris Kuiper was played by de Hartog himself. The role was played in New York by John Garfield in his return from Hollywood to the Broadway stage. Regardless of its technical legitimacy as an American drama, *Skipper Next to God* provides a useful intervention in the discussion of American behavior toward the Jews.

De Hartog's play concerns Captain Kuiper, the commander of the Dutch ship

The Young Nelly, who in 1938 is transporting oppressed Jews to Colombia, where they are not permitted to disembark. He then heads for the United States, where he encounters fierce government opposition. Both the American government and the Dutch consul order him to return the Jews to Europe, where it is clear they will face persecution and probable death. Although *Skipper Next to God* focuses on the psyche of Captain Kuiper, it is clearly a fictionalized retelling of the tragic account of the *St. Louis*. On 13 May 1937, Captain Gustav Schroeder sailed from Hamburg for Havana with approximately 950 Jewish passengers hoping to escape the anti-Semitism running rampant in the Third Reich. With a *J* for *Jude* (Jew) stamped in their passports, Schroeder's Jews were denied entry into Cuba. When he then tried to unload his passengers at a series of U.S. ports, Schroeder found the doors closed to his desperate refugees. Ultimately he was forced by what has been seen as the heartlessness of the Roosevelt administration to return his Jews to Europe, where more than half of them met their end in concentration camps.

In de Hartog's drama, the conflict is not unlike the one faced by Sophocles' Antigone, who is caught between the dictates of her individual conscience, governed by what is right in the eyes of the gods, and the civil laws of the state. Captain Kuiper is a devout Christian, and for him, saving the Jews is following the dictates of Christ. He is, consequently, unable to submit to the rules and regulations of the United States and Holland, to return to Europe, and to abandon his Jewish passengers to the dire fate that awaits them there. The American naval officer who warns Kuiper that he cannot land his Jews in an American harbor, something Kuiper has already tried three times to do, says:

> My dear man, we've gone through all this before, so no need to tell you again what the attitude of the United States authorities is towards you and your unlucky bunch of Hebes. You know we all sympathize with you a lot, and that's the main reason why we've let you get away with it three times now, without taking our gloves off. (29–30; 113)[44]

In sculpting Kuiper as a modern Christian martyr, *Skipper Next to God* points an accusing finger at an unfeeling prewar America whose actions were, de Hartog implies, tinged with anti-Semitism.

Far more outspoken and shamelessly sentimental is Ben Hecht's agitprop performance vehicle *A Flag Is Born*, which tackles the postwar dilemma of displaced persons released from Nazi concentration camps only to face political roadblocks when they wish to immigrate to Palestine. Rebuilding a war-torn Europe was, in general, a concern of great importance in the years following V-E Day, but perhaps a more pressing problem was a human one: what to do with the masses of D.P.s (displaced persons) released from concentration camps and emerging from hiding. They could not return to the homes or towns from which they had been driven and had no place to which they might immigrate. One obvious possibility for Jews in this situation was immigration to Palestine, the Jewish homeland. The obstacle to this, however, was that Great Britain, with its mandate over Palestine, was determined to close the doors to D.P.s and new immigrants. As the foreword to *A Flag Is Born* (written by journalist, novelist, and Vice Chairman of the governing board of the American League for a Free Palestine, Konrad Bercovici) unambiguously states, "It was written and presented to bring to the attention of the world in a dramatic form the plight of the Hebrews now behind barbed wire in and out of Palestine."[45]

The Balfour Declaration of 1917 established England's commitment to the creation of a Jewish homeland in Palestine. In 1922, the League of Nations upheld the Balfour Declaration and, in 1924, granted England a mandate over Palestine. Subsequent years saw several waves of Jewish immigration to Palestine. Those years also saw protests, culminating in a 1936 general strike by non-Jewish Palestinians over Jewish immigration and the bestowal of land to Jews. In 1939, the British issued a new white paper severely limiting Jewish immigration to Palestine (15,000 per year for five years) and proposing the establishment of Palestine as an independent state in 1946. The result was armed and bitter conflict of Zionist groups in Palestine with British and Palestinian Arab forces. During the years of World War II and immediately thereafter, anti-British activities organized by the militant Zionist organizations Haganah, Stern, and Irgun increased steadily. In the 1930s and early 1940s, Palestine was a favored destination for those fleeing Nazi-occupied Europe, especially for those who had no relations or friends to facilitate their immigration to such places as the U.S., Canada, South Africa, South America, and Australia. At the close of World War II, with no place to go for large numbers of displaced persons, the Jewish homeland in Palestine (Eretz Yisrael) offered a logical solution to the problem. There was only one immense stumbling block: the British seemed relentless in their determination to continue, as far as possible, to maintain their policy of restricting Jewish immigration to Palestine and maintaining the 1939 limit of a mere 15,000 persons a year. Since an Anglo-American commission, which arrived in Palestine in March 1946 to resolve the problem, accomplished little, the conflict continued to escalate, sometimes into armed confrontation in Palestine between the British and Jewish militant groups.

It is in this context that in 1946, Ben Hecht, who during the war had written the enormously successful propaganda play *We Shall Survive*, wrote *A Flag Is Born*, a second, powerful propaganda play designed to move audiences and governments to favor opening Palestine to Jewish immigration and establishing a new nation, the state of Israel. The purpose of *A Flag Is Born* was, furthermore, not merely to raise consciousness but also to raise funds for the resistance groups. Sponsored by the American League for a Free Palestine, *A Flag Is Born* opened at the Alvin Theatre on 5 September and marshaled the talents of more than just Ben Hecht.[46] The music was written by Kurt Weill (himself a German-Jewish refugee) and the play was staged by Luther Adler. The narrator of *A Flag Is Born* was revered journalist–news commentator Quentin Reynolds.[47] Paul Muni played one of the two leading male roles, and the female lead was per-

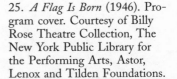

AMERICAN LEAGUE FOR A FREE PALESTINE

presents

A Flag is Born

by BEN HECHT

.... *Souvenir Program*

25. *A Flag Is Born* (1946). Program cover. Courtesy of Billy Rose Theatre Collection, The New York Public Library for the Performing Arts, Astor, Lenox and Tilden Foundations.

formed by famed Yiddish theatre actress Celia Adler (half-sister of Luther and Stella Adler, daughter of Yiddish actor Jacob Adler). Playing the other leading male role was a relative newcomer to Broadway, a talented twenty-two-year-old (non-Jewish) actor whose strong sympathies lay with the founding of Israel: Marlon Brando.[48]

A Flag Is Born is not meant to be subtle. It unabashedly pulls out all the stops and is awash in Jewish sentimentality. Casting Celia Adler, a queen of the Yiddish melodramatic stage, as Zelda and using the character of Tevya (played by Paul Muni), an archetypal shtetl figure modeled directly on Sholem Aleichem's Tevya the milkman, deliver the audience adroitly and directly into familiar sentimental Yiddish literary territory. At the same time, the audience is relentlessly stunned into awareness by blow after blow of Hecht's agitprop punches.[49] The effective combination of heartwarming *Yiddishkeit* with the consciousness-raising style of John Howard Lawson and Clifford Odets opened the purses of spectators bathed in tears of sorrow and of rage. Pledge cards were inserted into the programs of *A Flag Is Born*, a timely bit of fund-raising, since many in the audience were preparing to fill out similar annual pledge cards in their synagogues four weeks after the opening performance, on Yom Kippur. Originally meant to play for four weeks, *A Flag Is Born* instead played for 120 performances in New York and then moved to other cities (where Muni's role was assumed sometimes by Luther Adler, other times by Jacob Ben-Ami, and Brando's role by Sidney Lumet). According to Atay Citron, *A Flag Is Born* netted a quarter of a million dollars for D.P. relocation within just eight weeks of its premiere, and Hecht himself claimed it ultimately netted nearly a million.[50]

The content of Hecht's propaganda piece is starkly presented. It begins with the Narrator (Quentin Reynolds) intoning an elegy for the death of the Jewish people and of Jewish life in Europe. At the same time and very significantly, Hecht uses the Narrator to refocus the audience's view of the war, which had always been seen as a war against fascism and a war to ensure the principles of (American) democracy. For what is the first time in an American stage play, the audience is asked to see that World War II will be only secondarily remembered as a war for democracy. Rather, it will be remembered primarily for the six million murdered Jews and for those who stood by in silence and let it happen:

> Out of his burning houses, out of his crematoriums and lime pits, the Jew of Europe looked on a murderer called the German. But beyond this murder face of the German were other nation-faces to be seen—dim and watchful faces whose silence was a brother of murder. . . . But all this is known. There is no need to dwell on the whys and wherefores of it. History will sum up the tale someday. And people will read it plainly. History will say, "of all the things that happened in that time—our time—the slaughter of the Jews of Europe was the only thing that counted forever in the annals of man. The proud orations of heroes and conquerors will be a footnote in history beside the great silence that watched this slaughter." (1–2)

To a large degree the prediction is correct, but in 1946 it represents a rather radical and revisionist view of the war, one ahead of its time.

The action of *A Flag Is Born* centers on Tevya and Zelda, frail Old World Jews who have emerged from Treblinka death camp weak and decrepit. Having lost all their children in the Holocaust, they are now feebly and abortively seeking their way to Palestine and Jerusalem, *Eretz Yisrael* and *Yirushalayim*, "the two words left in the dark night" (3). The context of their journey is described in Hecht's lyrical purple prose, which very obviously forces the American audience to face its worst mental images of concentration camps, violent death, and human carrion. It evokes the sentimental images of grandparents and babies butchered in the camps. It recalls as well the archetype of the wandering Jew, now recontextualized in a ravaged post-Holocaust Europe:

> Europe is a gallows and a lime pit to these two who wander southward in the dark. There is no doorstep in Europe on which to sit. Out of every window of Europe looks a murderer. There are dead people under every road of Europe—dead Jews—moaning to Jewish feet, "Fly, fly." There are Jewish infants and grandmothers wailing out of all the brooks and rivers

of Europe, "Fly. Fly." The word Europe falls like a whip on the shoulders of the two who move in the night—and a voice still echoes out of the seven years of dying—Begone—begone." (4)

Read in the present, speeches like these seem shamelessly overwritten, but their effect was surely powerful on a largely Jewish New York audience which, a year after the conclusion of the war, was facing not merely the staggering statistics of the Holocaust but possibly their personal sorrows over their own murdered relatives. Very likely they were also encountering the faces of the death camp survivors now coming to American shores with nightmarish recollections, arms branded with numbers, bearing the mental and bodily cicatrices of their suffering.

On the road, Tevya and Zelda encounter a cynical, embittered young man, David (Marlon Brando), who had also been incarcerated in Treblinka. David, too, seeks the Promised Land and sees that Europe is not that land, for it equates Jews with disposable trash equally fit for either incineration at a garbage dump or in concentration camp ovens. The only place for Jews, therefore, he fervently argues, is Palestine:

> Tevya, we have been praying in the wrong countries. . . . My father taught me that I belonged in the land where I was born. Then, one day, all the Jews in that land were gathered together like a pile of garbage and burned up. Now the English say to me, "Come, go back to your father's village— and start over again and breed another garbage pile for Europe." And I answered them, "A curse on all the lands and villages of Europe. I go to find a corner of the earth where Jews do not turn into garbage—where Jews can die on a battlefield—instead of in a crematorium. On their own battlefield, for a change. I go to Palestine." (9)

Even as he justifies the significance and appropriateness of Palestine for Jews displaced and homeless in a Europe that rewarded their presence there with grief and with the structures dedicated to Hitler's "final solution," David directs his venom at the Jews themselves, especially the American and British Jews, who averted their gaze from the slaughter of their brethren, and who now stand mutely by as England bars Jews from settling in Palestine. Hecht here glosses over the general wartime ignorance of what was transpiring in the camps, but he is a master of writing dialogue that arouses audience guilt:

> Where were you—Jews? Where were you when the killing was going on? When the six million were being burned and buried alive in the lime pits, where were you? Where was your voice crying out against the slaughter? We didn't hear any voice. There was no voice. You Jews of America! You Jews of England! Strong Jews, rich Jews, high-up Jews; Jews of power and genius! Where was your cry of rage that could have filled the world and

stopped the fires? Nowhere! Because you were ashamed to cry out as Jews.
You would rather die than speak out as Jews! A curse on your silence!
That frightened silence of Jews that made the Germans laugh as they
slaughtered. You with your Jewish hearts hidden in your American boots!
You—with your Jewish hearts hidden behind English accents—you let the
six million die—rather than make the faux-pas of seeming a Jew. We
heard—your silence—in the gas chambers. (20–21)

With such accusations rubbing the sores of audience guilt, Hecht's agitprop
dramatic technique opened the mouths of Jews to speak out against British
policy in Palestine and opened their purses to bankroll the Irgun.

After encountering David and listening to his cynical negativism and bitter
accusations, Tevya is encouraged by encountering the phantasms of Palestine's
strong biblical rulers of old—Kings Saul, David, and Solomon—who push him
to press on, tackle his enemies, and find Palestine. Tevya tells them, "The name
of my enemy is the WORLD" (27). But suddenly he finds himself transported
from the biblical kings to the modern seat of rule, the Council of the Mighty,
Hecht's parody of the U.N. Security Council. Here Tevya pleads for opening
the gates of Palestine to Jewish immigration and addresses the resistance of the
character allegorically named English Statesman. Tevya suggests that the contemporary tyranny of the English in Palestine is analogous to the tyranny that
fostered the American Revolution. Hecht thus uses his drama to support two
radical attitudes. First, just a year after the conclusion of World War II, he
stigmatizes one of the Allies, the British, as tyrants nearly as evil as the Germans.
Second, he endorses militant and military action, a revolution to cast off the
British oppressors. The young David has already spoken of a homeland where
a Jew can die on the battlefield instead of in a crematorium. Here, addressing
the Council of the Mighty, Tevya invokes the American Revolution, arguing,
"Look Englishmen, look how nice it would have been if you had acted a little
different toward America long ago. If you had not hired German Hessians to
go to fight the young Americans as you are hiring Arabs to go fight the Jews
now," and he accuses the British of acting dishonorably only to get their clutches
on Middle East oil (39).

Tevya pleads eloquently for the rights of postwar Jews to find a haven in
Palestine, and the Council of the Mighty—even English Statesman—vote to
open the doors of Palestine to the Jews. This seeming success is countered by
the bureaucratic assertion and dodge that before this can occur, there must be
more meetings and conferences to determine how it can take place. This delaying tactic is highlighted and castigated by Zelda's death and Tevya's soon
thereafter. Clearly, for Hecht, the councils of the U.N. and other diplomatic
resources will drag on forever and, with the best of stated intentions, will consciously work to delay the establishment of a Jewish homeland for generations.
Hecht's radical script calls for an end to talk and for immediate military action,
as is made manifest when three soldiers from "the Hebrew army of Palestine"

come onstage to fetch the young David and draw him into battle for the establishment of Israel: "Don't you hear our guns, David? We battle the English—the sly and powerful English. We speak to them in a new Jewish language, the language of guns. We fling no more prayers or tears at the world. We fling bullets. We fling barrages" (46).

The concluding and very powerful moment of *A Flag Is Born* shows David moving across a bridge to the Promised Land, thus symbolically moving from the European old world of death camps to the new world of a future in Palestine. He moves as well from Judaism to Zionism, from religion to patriotism. With the mixed sounds of "Hatikva" (the Israeli national anthem) and the sounds of guns in the background, David dramatically cuts the fringes from Tevya's tallith, his prayer shawl. He then takes a blue Star of David from his pocket and places it on what is left of the talis, thereby fashioning a makeshift version of what will become the flag of the state of Israel. It is with the corner fringes of the talis that Jews touch the holy Torah scrolls, and by cutting off those fringes, Hecht transmogrifies the talis into a flag, a radical gesture that dramatically replaces the primacy of religion with the primacy of achieving a Jewish homeland. Hecht's audience could hardly help itself from being profoundly moved by the combined power of Jews taking a proud stand, the raising of a new flag, the strains of "Hatikva," and the image of Brando himself, of whom one biographer recalls, "Dressed in a black turtleneck sweater and rope-belted trousers, he was breathtakingly handsome—a figure of charismatic, mythic beauty."[51]

A Flag Is Born is thus, in several ways, a significant dramatic document. With the abandonment of restraint common to agitprop drama, it lays bare, as no American drama had done before, the horrors of the Holocaust. It underscores as well the questionable silence of America and American Jews while their fellow Jews were being massacred in Europe. It lashes out in strongest terms against America's ally, the British. In the face of postwar peacetime, it endorses new battles in Palestine. And it suggests that the Jewish religion be revised to become simply a background for the founding of a Jewish state. Not surprisingly, many conservative Jewish organizations demonstrated against the performances of *A Flag Is Born,* but the success of Hecht's piece prevailed. In its own way, *A Flag Is Born* made an important contribution, both in zeal and dollars, to the end of British rule in Palestine and, just twenty months after its opening, to the establishment of the state of Israel on 14 May 1948. *A Flag Is Born* is surely among the minority of American dramas in which stage action became almost immediately translated into realized political action.

Despite its potent if broken-record references to crematoria, lime pits, and Jews who are seen as human garbage, *A Flag Is Born* is something of an anomaly. For years after the war, the American stage is nearly silent about the Shoah and its atrocities, and it will be decades before it again speaks with the vehemence of *A Flag Is Born.*[52] Rather, World War II becomes, as historian Michael Adams details, "the best war ever; the Armageddon war that pitted good American Democracy against evil Fascism."[53] Indeed, the first American Holocaust play after *A Flag Is Born* does not appear until ten years after the war and nine years after Ben Hecht's agitprop. It is Frances Goodrich and Albert Hackett's *The Diary of Anne Frank,* based on the original diary first published in English in 1952. Goodrich and Hackett's play, which opened at the Cort Theatre on 5 October 1955, ran in New York for 717 performances before traveling throughout the U.S. and Europe. In its unexpected and unprecedented success, *The Diary of Anne Frank* garnered theatre's triple crown: the 1956 Pulitzer Prize for best drama, the Tony, and the Critics' Circle Award. What became clear is that Goodrich and Hackett had, consciously or unconsciously, found an effective instrument for addressing a national need: to domesticate and palliate the unfathomable reality of the Holocaust.

In many ways, *The Diary of Anne Frank* is a far cry from Anne Frank's original text. As many critics have been quick to point out, the Goodrich and Hackett play converts the Frank text into a saccharine piece that obfuscates the Shoah in order to extol American values and to express optimism about humanity and human resilience hardly appropriate to the butchery that the Nazis enacted on millions. Although the characters in the play do celebrate Hanukkah, the Jewishness of the Franks and those in hiding with them is strongly and noticeably downplayed in order to make Anne Frank a typical (American) teenager caught in a perilous and compromising dilemma.[54] In the hands of Goodrich and Hackett, Anne Frank becomes the metonymic martyr of the Holocaust. She becomes, paradoxically, a gallant Jewish saint. But the paradox is barely felt, for there is little Jewish about Anne, and the issue of anti-Semitism is obscured by Anne as a universalized icon of optimism prevailing in the midst of disaster. As Alan Mintz and Alvin H. Rosenfeld each points out:

> Anne's diary entries in fact unambiguously affirm her identity as a member of the Jewish people and display an acute awareness of her situation as a Jew in Nazi Germany in relationship to historical anti-Semitism. In the play, however, her Jewishness is not hidden but made to seem inessential; her identity is folded into the generality of victims of fanaticism and even into the larger class of the unjust sufferers of the world. (Mintz, 18)

> In brief, the Anne Frank who emerged from this play was fashioned to evoke the most conventional of responses about "man's inhumanity to man," the "triumph of goodness over evil," the eternal verities of "the human spirit," and other such banalities. The harshness of history was left behind, and in its place softer, more acceptable images of a young girl's gaiety and moral gallantry come to the fore. (Rosenfeld, 254)

The resounding phrase in *The Diary of Anne Frank* is "In spite of everything, I still believe that people are really good at heart" (143, 146).[55] The comments of the critics are well taken, especially if Goodrich and Hackett's mission was to translate Anne Frank's story with fidelity onto the stage. But those harsh com-

26. *Diary of Anne Frank* (1955). (Left to right) David Levin, Susan Strasberg, Eva Rubinstein, Joseph Schildkraut, Lou Jacobi. Used by permission.

ments must fall away if *The Diary of Anne Frank* is meant to enable audiences to make a kind of peace with the wartime atrocities from which they had understandably been averting their eyes. Sometimes bromidic phrases are a necessary first step for encouraging a fuller understanding of things so horrific and unspeakable in their dimensions that they boggle the mind and reduce one to stunned silence.

What specific sections of Anne Frank's diary Goodrich and Hackett omit or spotlight in their play should be of less concern than the way *The Diary of Anne Frank* enables its American (and international) audience to avert its gaze from the terrible acts committed in the name of anti-Semitism. The persecution of the Jews, the lime pits, and crematoria that *A Flag Is Born* constantly invokes are absent. *The Diary of Anne Frank* instead allows the audience to mourn six million dead but to do so without directly witnessing or even hearing very much about the atrocities. The confinement of the Franks in their attic is, moreover, not symbolic of what the Third Reich enacted. Rather it symbolizes what Americans feared for themselves and what valorized the American participation in the war, namely, that fascism would abrogate the inalienable rights to life, liberty, and pursuit of happiness. When Anne says, "Look, Peter, the sky. What a lovely, lovely day! . . . You know what I do when it seems as if I couldn't stand being cooped up for one more minute? I *think* myself out" (141), she touches on the larger idea of liberty that, from Patrick Henry to the present, has become synonymous with what the American way of life embodies.

In the years following the war, Americans were faced with assessing the terrible years from which they had just emerged. What did so many deaths among both soldiers and civilians mean? How could they be justified? What did those many corpses say about the nature of humankind and society? The answers offered by *The Diary of Anne Frank* are for some at once naïve, maudlin, and bathetic. The unprecedented success of Goodrich and Hackett's play, however, suggests that for the vast majority it provided a much desired and needed optimism, an optimism imbued, moreover, with religious faith:

> We're not the only people that've had to suffer. There've always been people that had to . . . sometimes one race . . . sometimes another. . . . I know it's terrible, trying to have any faith . . . when people are doing such horrible . . . But you know what I sometimes think? I think the world may be going through a phase, the way I was with Mother. It'll pass, maybe not for hundreds of years, but some day . . . I still believe, in spite of everything, that people are really good at heart. (142–143)

The Golgotha of World War II is contracted, diminished, and domesticated into some global teenage mood swing, "a phase." Anti-Semitism and the death of six million become just something that "sometimes one race . . . sometimes another" is forced to endure. Nevertheless, what stands out here is how *The Diary of Anne Frank* enabled individual Americans to temper their reactions to the Holocaust as they formulated their own spiritual and internal peace with the war and its atrocities. V-E and V-J Days officially ushered in peace for the nation and the world, but inner peace for those who had lived through the war was not so easily won. True to the original text or not, Goodrich and Hackett designed their play to salve the doubts and wounds of a nation. And perhaps that salve was particularly timely, for when *The Diary of Anne Frank* opened, the U.S. was reacting to still another embroilment and more loss of life from the Korean War.

V

In the wake of V-E and V-J Days and with the playwright's airbrush skillfully applied to remove carnage and suffering, several popular plays presented the public with nostalgic snapshots of the war. In each of these primarily male productions, World War II becomes merely a backdrop for both a sometimes affectionate, sometimes ruefully nostalgic look at the war years. These plays begin with *Mister Roberts* in 1948 and include Rodgers and Hammerstein's *South Pacific* (1949), Donald Bevan and Edmund Trzcinski's *Stalag 17* (1951), John

Patrick's *Teahouse of the August Moon* (1953), Herman Wouk's dramatic version of his novel *The Caine Mutiny* (1954), and Ira Levin's *No Time for Sergeants* (1955).[56]

With the war safely won, playwrights were free to write about the war in terms other than the demonization of the enemy or the patriotic affirmation of American democracy. In *South Pacific*, for example, Rodgers and Hammerstein, drawing loosely on James Mitchener's *Tales of the South Pacific* (1947), make a claim for racial tolerance, but their musical illuminates far more than that. Using Ensign Nellie Forbush and Marine Lt. Joseph Cable, two of the musical's protagonists, Rodgers and Hammerstein lucidly exemplify the ways in which the dislocating experiences of wartime had their powerful effect on regionally and socially provincial Americans, unexpectedly transforming them into citizens of the world. Nellie characterizes herself as a "Little Rock fugitive" as she cringes over the clipping her mother has sent from the local newspaper with the headline "Ensign Nellie Forbush, Arkansas' own Florence Nightingale" (275). Stationed in a U.S. Army hospital on a Pacific island that is in danger of possible Japanese incursion, Nellie falls in love with a French political expatriate planter some years her senior who has two half-caste children from his deceased common-law islander wife. Nothing could be more different from what she was led to expect from her provincial Arkansas upbringing. The physical geography of palm trees and sandy beaches surrounding her is hardly that of Little Rock. More important still is her encounter with a new social geography, replete with what would be a constellation of taboos in Arkansas. Far away from the U.S., in a new climate and hemisphere, she is led to consider marriage with an older man, who is not only a French-speaking foreigner, but also a fugitive who has killed a tyrannical political bully. He is, furthermore, a father raising dark-skinned children of mixed race whose mother was probably not legally his wife. Any one of these would raise scandalized eyebrows or be outright taboo in a then still segregated Arkansas. One remembers, too, that in 1957, eight years after *South Pacific*, Little Rock was the scene of extraordinary racial tension as segregationist Governor Orval Faubus tried to block the integration of Little Rock Central High School. Indeed, Nellie Forbush's behavior is transgressive in the extreme. It is softened and made acceptable, however, by the good feelings that go with musical comedy atmosphere, the palm trees, a racial issue that is defused by being Tonkinese rather than African American, and, most of all, by *South Pacific*'s memorable songs and production numbers.

To drive their point home, Rodgers and Hammerstein echo the experience of the innocent Nellie with that of the more sophisticated and urbane Lt. Cable, as an officer and a gentlemanly Princeton graduate with a (presumably socially prominent) girlfriend in Philadelphia. He, too, feels the allure of Bali Ha'i, the tropics, and a native Tonkinese girl, all a far cry from what his Princeton education might have led him to expect. Rodgers and Hammerstein wrote pointedly and affably of Cable's situation in the song "My Girl Back Home," which was originally written for *South Pacific,* dropped from the show in the interest of saving time, but recorded by Mary Martin. In that song, Cable, to the delight of his family, is engaged to a girl back home, but the song explains:

> And he was told by his uncle and dad
> That if he were clever and able,
> They'd make him part of a partnership
> In Cable, Cable, Cable & Cable.
>
> How far away
> Philadelphia, Pa.,
> Princeton, N.J.
> How far are they
> From coconut palms and banyan trees,
> And coral sands and Tonkinese.[57]

But Nellie's and Cable's experiences in a war zone thousands of miles from their country and upbringing offers them both a new, much widened tolerance and understanding. Rodgers and Hammerstein suggest this was true for many Americans who served overseas, and that a broadened tolerance for racial and ethnic others can also become available to the civilian audience as they watch and are affected by the sounds and sentiments of *South Pacific.*

While Rodgers and Hammerstein's musical posits dangerous Japanese troops offstage, onstage sailors are bonding together in camaraderie, singing "There Is Nothing Like a Dame" and staging a jolly Christmas show. The war is thereby marginalized in favor of a warm nostalgia for the good times shared by virile sailors. Giving only a nod to the seriousness of engagement with the enemy, *South Pacific* looks back nostalgically, as do other postwar plays, on the time in the military as a kind of stag party. Certainly this is likewise the case in *Mister Roberts,* which, with the jokes and pranks perpetrated on the ship's captain by Ensign Pulver, also seems to recall the war with the sort of sentimental nostalgia common to high school reunions.

Looking back to the war period as a time of male bonding is an essential part of Donald Bevan and Edmund Trzcinski's hit play *Stalag 17,* which opened at the 48th Street Theatre on 8 May 1951, exactly a year after *South Pacific,* and ran for 472 performances before closing on 21 June 1952. Featuring an all-male cast, *Stalag 17* honors an often forgotten group of servicemen, prisoners of war. Reminiscent of Cpl. Kurt S. Kasznar's one-acter, *First Cousins, Stalag 17* is a suspenseful drama based on a group of P.O.W.s who try to find the traitor in their midst. Among the men captured by the Germans and being held in stalag 17, one is a Nazi spy who endangers the welfare of all. When the men fall into dissension over the identity of the alleged traitor and when they quarrel over matters of social class and ethnicity, deaths and disaster ensue. Not until they close ranks and act in a united way is the German operative revealed and two

27. *Stalag 17* (1951). Courtesy of Billy Rose Theatre Collection, The New York Public Library for the Performing Arts, Astor, Lenox and Tilden Foundations.

prisoners are able to escape. Indeed, the issue of bonding is raised to a sociopolitical level when Sefton, who has emerged from the slums of Boston and who has the classic underclass hatred of the rich, gains a sense of brotherhood and becomes the one to help Dunbar, a scion of a Boston Brahmin family, escape from the prisoner of war camp. Sefton wittily but pointedly quips, "Only in a democracy can a poor guy get his ass shot off with a rich guy" (70). That comment is immediately juxtaposed to the pleas of Price, the German spy, who begs in vain that his fellow Germans not shoot him, "*Kameraden! Kameraden! Schiesst nicht! Schiesst nicht!*" (71).

Stalag 17's focus is squarely on the interpersonal relationships among its group of American P.O.W.s. Their antagonist is not so much the Third Reich as it is the stereotypical Corporal Schultz, who becomes the butt of the Americans' humor and whose unctuous and smarmy bearing do not conceal his innate sadism and brutality. The events of the war itself are only present in a peripheral way, when the men tune in to the U.S. troop reports on their hidden radio. This is representative of what appears to happen in the war-related drama after V-J Day: the actual events and issues of the war move from center stage to become a backdrop—sometimes only a decorative backdrop—for plays that spotlight other matters.

Certainly the war is only background material for John Patrick's *Teahouse of the August Moon*, though how and why it is in the background is revealing. As in *South Pacific*, the widening of American foreign cultural experience courtesy of the war is a major theme of *Teahouse*. Here American military occupation personnel at war's end are assigned to bring democracy and American ways to the inhabitants of Tobiki, a rural village on Okinawa. In the course of the East-meets-West comedy, Patrick stages a significant comic reversal, so that it is the Americans who learn the ways and values of the Okinawans. Patrick's earlier play, *The Hasty Heart* (1945), had been a great success, but *Teahouse*, which opened at the Martin Beck Theatre on 15 October 1953, was a record-breaking smash, running for 1027 performances and lasting nearly two and a half years. The unusual éclat of this lightweight comedy provides some insight into American nostalgia about the war and about seeing the war period with rose-tinted glasses.

In the years after the war, the need to give unilateral support to the military chain of command was no longer a necessity, and it was permissible to look back, expose, and satirize commanding officers and military bureaucracy. Ranking officers were sometimes characterized as sadistic, psychologically disturbed martinets (e.g., *Mister Roberts* or *The Caine Mutiny Court-Martial*), or more often they were simply butts of comedy caricatured as bumbling, insensitive fools (e.g., *No Time for Sergeants* and *At War with the Army*). *Teahouse* falls into the latter category, gently satirizing its commanding officer, Colonel Wainwright Purdy III, who is not so much a bully as a representative of the military's risible attempt to cover all contingencies with prescribed formulas composed by Washington bureaucrats who have no concept of real situations. *Teahouse* thus provides the audience with a postwar opportunity to laugh safely at the authority figures and government it would have been near treason to mock only a few years earlier while the battles across the Pacific and Atlantic were being waged.

But *Teahouse* is much more than a comic military version of labor versus management. It is also a modern version of Roman comedy and commedia dell'arte, in which the naïve young man (Capt. Fisby) is initiated into Okinawan ways by his lovable Asian "witty servant" (Sakini). The play generates love and respect for the Okinawans among both the play's American characters and its spectators. At the same time, the Okinawans benefit materially from American economic know-how. Their poverty is rapidly transformed into prosperity when the Americans teach them the economic benefits of marketing their potent sweet potato brandy to the occupation troops. On the surface, then, *Teahouse* provides a comic rapprochement, whereby the Americans become Orientalized and the Orientals become Americanized.

It is important to see, however, that what *Teahouse of the August Moon* entirely omits, and thus denies, is the grim reality of what took place during the war on Okinawa and what sort of horrors the allegedly innocent Okinawans lived through. In April 1945, a major invasion of Okinawa by American troops took place. The Okinawans had been instructed by the Japanese authorities to commit

28. *Teahouse of the August Moon* (1953). (Left to right) Mariko Niki, David Wayne, John Forsythe. Used by permission.

suicide rather than surrender. The battle of Okinawa proved to be a long and bloody one, during which "ninety-five thousand civilians had been killed by enemy fire, by Japanese soldiers, by loved ones and trusted acquaintants, and by their own hands."[58] The rose-tinted glow with which *Teahouse* is suffused allows no glimpse of Okinawa as blood-stained soil or the populace as one that has suffered recent human tragedy of enormous dimension. Rather, *Teahouse* is the fiction of happy relations between East and West that Americans desired after the war and that they applauded into existence at each performance of *Teahouse* and then in the subsequent 1956 Glenn Ford and Marlon Brando film.

Two other disparate features of *Teahouse of the August Moon* are also noteworthy. First, its embrace of Asian ways is underscored not merely by the play's setting in postwar occupied Japan but also by the fact that when the play was staged, the U.S. was emerging from another Asian engagement not far from Okinawa, in Korea. Second, the play's embrace of East Asia opened the Broadway doors to Asian-American actors. In the plays of the war years and immediately thereafter, the Japanese enemy was almost always lurking in the bushes or in the distance but never seen onstage. Whether in internment camps or simply unacceptable, Asian-American actors were markedly absent from the Broadway stage during the 1940s. *Teahouse of the August Moon* seems to be the first major Broadway production to cast Asian Americans. Nevertheless, the major Asian role, that of Sakini the artful servant, was played by white actor David Wayne (and by Marlon Brando in the film version).

In a curious way, *Teahouse of the August Moon* bears a resemblance in spirit to *The Diary of Anne Frank*. The latter was one of the only plays in the postwar decade to bring the Holocaust to the stage, yet it sugarcoated the terrible and tragic truth with inappropriate optimism. Similarly, *Teahouse* sweeps the recent bloodstained Okinawan history under the rug, putting in its place its own optimistic fiction about well-meaning Americans and friendly, if primitive and naïve, Japanese. The spectacular success of both plays gives considerable credence to the idea that the fictions of these plays addressed an American desire to avoid confronting the carnage and atrocities of the war. At the same time, these plays were perhaps a necessary first step for the more probing and honest examinations that would come during subsequent years of the events that had taken place in Europe and the Pacific.

The realities, atrocities, and events of World War II recede into the distance once more in still another popular postwar offering, Herman Wouk's dramatic rendering of his novel *The Caine Mutiny Court-Martial*, which opened at the Plymouth Theatre on 20 January 1954 and closed a year later after playing 415 performances. A classic courtroom drama directed by Charles Laughton and starring Henry Fonda, John Hodiak, and Lloyd Nolan, *The Caine Mutiny Court-Martial* follows in the footsteps of *Mister Roberts* by positing a rebellion against a neurotic, despotic ship's captain.[59] It likewise reflects the postwar license to criticize senior officers whose severity sometimes crossed the line into abusiveness. Although the action of the play is set in February 1945 while the war was still raging, little is said of the war itself. What Wouk, in the play's denouement, does argue, however, is that the mutiny enacted against the tyrannical Capt. Queeg may be justified from one point of view, but it is not from another. Using Greenwald, the defense attorney, as his mouthpiece, Wouk suggests that Queeg's crew could successfully have worked with Queeg. Instead officers have been taken away from the Pacific, where they might be subduing the Japanese, in order instead to subdue their captain in a courtroom. Moreover, it is dedicated career officers like Queeg who led the battles that saved lives in Europe and the Far East. With visions of how the Nazis would have turned his Jewish mother into soap, Greenwald, having brought down Queeg and exonerated his client, laments:

> If you hadn't filled Steve Maryk's [the leader of the mutiny] thick head full of paranoia and Article 184, why he'd have got Queeg to come north, or he'd have helped the poor bastard come through to the south, and the *Caine* wouldn't have been yanked out of action in the hottest part of the war. . . . Queeg deserved better at my hands. I owed him a favor, don't you see? He stopped Hermann Goering from washing his fat behind with my mother. (102)

But other than these remarks, the action of *The Caine Mutiny* could just as easily be set at any time up to the present.

Ira Levin's runaway hit *No Time for Sergeants* goes still a step further. A comic vehicle for Andy Griffith, *No Time for Sergeants* pits Will Stockdale, the laughably literal-minded, undereducated, amiable backwoods Georgia draftee, against the educated army's top brass.[60] Although the comedy is written in the period after World War II and after the Korean War, no war or specific year is mentioned. War issues are gone altogether, and what is left is, as in *At War with the Army,* only slapstick comedy in military dress. Thus, in the decade after the war, the seriousness of the World War II issues, the loss of lives both military and civilian, the threat of fascism, and the affirmation of American democratic values eventually dwindle into near nothingness. These are replaced by a nostalgia for army buddies and friendships, accusations leveled at those who sat behind desks stateside and made profits while servicemen endured losses, and conflicts (both serious and comic) within the military bureaucracy between labor and management. The bloodbaths of armed combat and the wholesale slaughters of Jews, dissidents, and undesirables in concentration camps are rendered nearly invisible. What so often happens after trauma is that participants need to domesticate that trauma so that they can come to grips with it and begin to recover. If that is what happened in the years when men came home from World War II and the country returned to life under peacetime conditions, then the American theatre served as an important means for allowing them to do so. It provided the scripts not merely for actors but for a nation.

NOTES

INTRODUCTION

1. Clayton R. Koppes and Gregory D. Black, *Hollywood Goes to War: How Politics, Profits and Propaganda Shaped World War II Movies* (Berkeley and Los Angeles: University of California Press, 1987); Colin Shindler, *Hollywood Goes to War: Films and American Society, 1939–1952* (London and Boston: Routledge and Kegan Paul, 1979).

1. GETTING INVOLVED

1. Dates for plays giving day, month, and year indicate opening night dates.
2. Wendy Smith, *Real Life Drama: The Group Theatre and America, 1931–1940* (New York: Alfred A. Knopf, 1990); Harold Clurman, *The Fervent Years* (New York: Alfred A. Knopf, 1945); Sam Smiley, *The Drama of Attack: Didactic Plays of the American Depression* (Columbia: University of Missouri Press, 1972); Morgan Y. Himelstein, *Drama Was a Weapon: The Left-Wing Theatre in New York, 1929–1941* (New Brunswick, N.J.: Rutgers University Press, 1963); Gerald Rabkin, *Drama and Commitment: Politics in the American Theatre of the Thirties* (Bloomington: Indiana University Press, 1964); and Malcolm Goldstein, *The Political Stage: American Drama and the Theater of the Great Depression* (New York: Oxford University Press, 1974).
3. In his autobiography, Rice makes clear his interest in the Dimitrov trial. See Elmer Rice, *Minority Report: An Autobiography* (London: Heinemann, 1963), pp. 334–335.
4. Elmer Rice, *Judgment Day: A Melodrama in Three Acts* (New York: Coward-McCann, 1934).
5. Robert Hogan argues as well that *Judgment Day* was unfairly criticized because its opinions "were delivered in late 1934 when the threat of war was scarcely one which Americans wished to face," and that the play was warmly received abroad, where its truths were more immediate and better understood. See Robert Hogan, *The Independence of Elmer Rice* (Carbondale and Edwardsville: Southern Illinois University Press, 1965), pp. 71–72.
6. Gerald Bordman, *American Theatre: A Chronicle of Comedy and Drama, 1930–1969* (New York and Oxford: Oxford University Press, 1996), p. 110.
7. The concentration camps of 1934 were not yet the death camps of a few years

‹

later. One must remember, too, that it was not until 25 November 1942, eight years after *Rain from Heaven,* that the *New York Times* revealed the first hint of mass Jewish extermination and the nature of the death camps.

8. S. N. Behrman, *Rain from Heaven,* in *Four Plays by S. N. Behrman* (New York: Random House, 1952).

9. John C. Moffitt was a minor film writer who wrote the script for the 1936 Bing Crosby and Frances Farmer musical film, *Rhythm on the Range,* and co-wrote both the 1937 Boris Karloff horror film *Night Key* and the 1944 Humphrey Bogart film *Passage to Marseilles.*

10. Tony Buttitta and Barry Witham, *Uncle Sam Presents: A Memoir of the Federal Theatre, 1935–1939* (Philadelphia: University of Pennsylvania Press, 1982), pp. 79, 81–82. See also John O'Connor and Lorraine Brown, *Free, Adult, Uncensored: The Living History of the Federal Theatre Project* (Washington, D.C.: New Republic Books, 1978), p. 59.

11. The script for the 1936 version of *It Can't Happen Here* is unpublished, but the manuscript is part of the Federal Theatre Project collection held by the New York Public Library. All references here refer to the 1938 published version, John C. Moffitt and Sinclair Lewis, *It Can't Happen Here* (New York: Dramatists Play Service, 1938).

12. The poster of the Federal Theatre's Detroit production of *It Can't Happen Here,* featuring a caricature of Hitler, suggests that productions targeted Hitler rather than Long (O'Connor and Brown, *Free, Adult, Uncensored,* p. 67).

13. Gerald Weales, *Clifford Odets, Playwright* (New York: Bobbs-Merrill, 1971), p. 87; Rabkin, *Drama and Commitment,* p. 178.

14. Clifford Odets, *Till the Day I Die,* in *Six Plays of Clifford Odets* (New York: Grove Press, 1979).

15. Weales, *Clifford Odets, Playwright,* 85–86.

16. Oliver H. P. Garrett, *Waltz in Goose-Step* (unpublished, 1938). The play exists only in one typescript held by the New York Public Library's theatre collection. There is no regular pagination, but each page is marked with the act number followed by the page of that act.

17. Jacques Deval, *Lorelei* (unpublished, 1938). The play exists only in one typescript held by the New York Public Library's theatre collection. There is no regular pagination, but each page is marked with the act number followed by the page of that act.

18. Robert E. Sherwood, *Idiot's Delight* (New York: Charles Scribner's Sons, 1936).

19. Brenda Murphy, *American Realism and American Drama, 1880–1940* (Cambridge: Cambridge University Press, 1987), p. 173.

20. Sidney Howard, *The Ghost of Yankee Doodle: A Tragedy* (New York: Charles Scribner's Sons, 1938).

21. A useful overview of the play and its production is given in Malcolm Goldstein, *George S. Kaufman: His Life, His Theater* (New York and Oxford: Oxford University Press, 1979), pp. 311–319.

22. George S. Kaufman and Moss Hart, *The American Way* (New York: Random House, 1939).

23. See Burns Mantle, *The Best Plays of 1938–1939* (New York: Dodd, Mead and Co., 1939), pp. 145–146.

24. Steven Bach, *Dazzler: The Life and Times of Moss Hart* (New York: Alfred A. Knopf, 2001), p. 185.

25. Again, Steven Bach takes a rather dim view of *The American Way*, complaining, "It was all just chauvinistic hokum, perhaps, but playing to the largest possible audience and the lowest common denominator approached pandering" (ibid., p. 186). Bach seems here to forget that Kaufman and Hart's aim was to move the American public to take an active stand against fascism, and that they were clearly willing to pull out all the dramatic stops to achieve that end. See also Eberhard Brüning, *Das amerikanische Drama der dreißiger Jahre* (Berlin: Rütten and Loening, 1966), pp. 250–251.

26. See Bach, *Dazzler*, p. 181.

27. Thornton Wilder, *Our Town* (1938; reprint, New York: Harper and Row, 1957).

28. Goldstein, *The Political Stage*, p. 359; Brooks Atkinson, review of *The Time of Your Life*, by William Saroyan, *New York Times*, 26 October 1939, reprinted in Bernard Beckerman and Howard Siegman, *On Stage: Selected Theatre Reviews from "The New York Times," 1920–1970* (New York: Arno Press and Quadrangle, 1973), p. 214.

29. William Saroyan, *The Time of Your Life* (New York: Harcourt, Brace and Company, 1939).

30. Robert E. Sherwood, *Abe Lincoln in Illinois* (New York: Charles Scribner's Sons, 1937).

31. As R. Baird Shuman writes in *Robert Emmet Sherwood* (New York: Twayne Publishers, 1954), p. 86, "But few people seeing it in 1938 and 1939 could fail to draw conclusions regarding the similarity between Lincoln's plight in 1861 and that facing the free world just prior to World War II." See also Walter J. Meserve, *Robert Sherwood: Reluctant Moralist* (New York: Pegasus, 1970), pp. 141–142, and Thomas P. Adler, *Mirror on the Stage* (West Lafayette, Ind.: Purdue University Press, 1987), p. 91.

32. Robert E. Sherwood, preface to *There Shall Be No Night* (New York: Charles Scribner's Sons, 1941).

33. See also Shuman, *Robert Emmet Sherwood*, p. 95.

34. The antiwar reaction to Sherwood's play is well described in Jared Brown, *The Fabulous Lunts* (New York: Atheneum, 1986), pp. 291–294.

35. Montgomery Clift played the role of the Valkonen's idealistic son Erik, and in her biography of Clift, Patricia Bosworth adds an interesting footnote to this play, "The tour for *There Shall Be No Night* ended just after Pearl Harbor; President Roosevelt phoned Robert Sherwood to tell him *Night* was much too controversial politically to run in wartime. The show closed abruptly on the road." See Patricia Bosworth, *Montgomery Clift: A Biography* (New York: Harcourt, Brace, 1978), p. 83. See also Brown, *The Fabulous Lunts*, p. 296.

36. Rice, *Minority Report*, p. 393.

37. Elmer Rice, *Flight to the West* (New York: Coward-McCann, 1940).

38. Lillian Hellman, *Watch on the Rhine*, in *Six Plays by Lillian Hellman* (New York: Vintage Books, 1979).

39. Richard Moody, *Lillian Hellman: Playwright* (New York: Bobbs-Merrill Co., 1972), p. 130.

40. Clare Boothe, *Margin for Error* (New York: Random House, 1940).

41. A brief discussion of the humorous side of *Margin for Error* appears in Sam Smiley, *The Drama of Attack*, pp. 191–192.

42. Maxwell Anderson, *Key Largo*, in *Eleven Verse Plays, 1929–1939* (New York: Harcourt, Brace, 1939). The plays in this volume are separately paginated as they are in the single editions published by Anderson House.

43. For a more recent reflection on Anderson's strengths and weaknesses as a playwright, see Mervyn Rothstein, "Q. Where's Maxwell Anderson?" *New York Times,* 29 September 1988, pp. C21 and C25.

44. Maxwell Anderson, preface to *Journey to Jerusalem* (Washington, D.C.: Anderson House, 1940), pp. v, vi.

45. Lynn Fontanne lamented that *Candle in the Wind* could have been a successful play had Anderson been able to make the ameliorations Alfred Lunt suggested. See Brown, *The Fabulous Lunts,* p. 295 n. 8.

46. Burns Mantle, *The Best Plays of 1941–42* (New York: Dodd, Mead and Co., 1942). See also Bordman, *American Theatre,* p. 206.

47. Maxwell Anderson, *Candle in the Wind* (Washington, D.C.: Anderson House, 1941).

48. Anderson suggests the folly of the American averted gaze by creating two American women who seek to elude the reality of the Nazis by limiting themselves to searching for the past in the closed gardens of Versailles. "Because they can't touch us here in the gardens of the past. And so we have eluded them, haven't we?" says one of them (ibid., 101).

49. Frederick Hazlitt Brennan, *The Wookey* (New York: Alfred A. Knopf, 1941).

50. Philip Barry, *Liberty Jones: A Play with Music for City Children* (New York: Coward-McCann, 1941).

51. Ellis St. Joseph, *A Passenger to Bali* (Boston: Little Brown, 1940). Not surprisingly, this heavy-handed allegory, although it starred Walter Huston, ran for only four performances. See Bordman, *American Theatre,* p. 189.

52. Edmond M. Gagey, *Revolution in American Drama* (New York: Columbia University Press, 1947), p. 154; Michael Shnayerson, *Irwin Shaw: A Biography* (New York: G. P. Putnam's Sons, 1989), p. 85; Goldstein, *The Political Stage,* pp. 325–327.

53. Irwin Shaw, *The Gentle People* (New York: Random House, 1939), [v].

54. Brüning, *Das amerikanische Drama,* p. 251, translation mine. See also the discussion of the play in James R. Giles, *Irwin Shaw* (Boston: Twayne Publishers, 1983), pp. 17–24.

55. See Rabkin, *Drama and Commitment,* p. 88.

56. Robert Ardrey, *Thunder Rock* (New York: Dramatists Play Service, 1939). A somewhat different version of the play appears in Robert Ardrey, *Plays of Three Decades* (New York: Atheneum, 1968). Quotations are taken from the 1939 version.

57. One cannot, of course, rule out the possibility that Ardrey may have been bending to the wishes of his editor or publisher to provide something more politically acceptable.

58. Malcolm Goldstein provides an incisive discussion of this interpolated passage (*The Political Stage,* p. 331).

59. For a detailed and sensitive discussion of MacLeish as a radio playwright, *Fall of the City,* and *Air Raid,* see Mary E. McGann, "Voices in the Dark: A Study of the Radio Achievement of Norman Corwin, Archibald MacLeish, Louis MacNeice, Dylan Thomas, and Samuel Beckett" (Ph.D. diss., Indiana University, 1979), pp. 58–90.

60. Archibald MacLeish, foreword to *The Fall of the City* (New York: Farrar and Rinehart, 1937).

61. For an informative discussion of the presentation and historical context of *The Fall of the City* and *Air Raid,* see Howard Blue, *Words at War: World War II Era Radio Drama and the Postwar Broadcasting Industry Blacklist* (Lanham, Md., and Oxford: Scarecrow Press, 2002).

62. Archibald MacLeish, *Air Raid* (New York: Harcourt, Brace and Co., 1938). All references are to this edition.

2. THE DRAMA OF THE WAR YEARS

1. See, for example, John Patrick Diggins, *The Proud Decades: America in War and Peace, 1941–1960* (New York: W. W. Norton, 1989), pp. 25–27.

2. Maxwell Anderson, *The Eve of St. Mark* (Washington, D.C.: Anderson House, 1942).

3. Maxwell Anderson, *Storm Operation* (Washington, D.C.: Anderson House, 1944).

4. Anderson's biographer, Alfred Shivers, relates that the original text, censored by the War Department, had the second unmarried nurse as being pregnant. Alfred S. Shivers, *The Life of Maxwell Anderson* (New York: Stein and Day, 1983), pp. 215–216. See also Shivers's critical study, *Maxwell Anderson* (Boston: Twayne Publishers, 1976), p. 63.

5. Burns Mantle, *The Best Plays of 1943–44* (New York: Dodd, Mead and Co., 1944), p. 277; Shivers, *The Life of Maxwell Anderson*, pp. 207–214.

6. Burns Mantle, *The Best Plays of 1942–43* (New York: Dodd, Mead, 1943), pp. 24–25.

7. Allan R. Kenward, *Cry Havoc* (New York and Los Angeles: Samuel French, 1943).

8. Kaier Curtin in *"We Can Always Call Them Bulgarians": The Emergence of Lesbians and Gay Men on the American Stage* (Boston: Alyson Publications, 1987), p. 253, suggests that Lee Shubert, who produced Kenward's drama, probably never read the script and had no idea it was about lesbianism in the military.

9. See Allan Bérubé, *Coming Out under Fire: The History of Gay Men and Women in World War II* (New York: Penguin Books, 1990), pp. 98–127 passim.

10. Janet Stevenson and Philip Stevenson, *Counterattack: A Play in Three Acts* (typescript, revised edition, 1944). There is a copy of the original version in the New York Public Library. Copies of the revised version are held by the UCLA Library and the Minneapolis Public Library. There is no regular pagination, but each page is marked with the act number followed by the page of that act. The parentheses after the quotation reflect this pagination from the Minneapolis typescript. According to Burns Mantle, *Counterattack* is based on a Russian play called *Probyeda*. See Mantle, *The Best Plays of 1942–43*, p. 9.

11. Dan James, *Winter Soldiers* (unpublished, 1942), 1.3.26–27. (Numeration indicates act, scene, and page number in the typescript.) The piece exists only in one typescript held by the New York Public Library's theatre collection.

12. Mantle, *Best Plays of 1942–43*, pp. 9 and 143–179.

13. Paul Osborn, *A Bell for Adano* (New York: Alfred A. Knopf, 1945).

14. John Mason Brown, "Tintanabulation, Indeed!" in *Seeing Things* (New York and London: McGraw-Hill, 1946).

15. John Patrick, *The Hasty Heart* (New York: Random House, 1945).

16. Sidney Kingsley, preface to *The Patriots*, in *Five Prizewinning Plays*, ed. Nena Couch (Columbus: Ohio State University Press, 1995); Sidney Kingsley, *The Patriots* (New York: Random House, 1943). Quotations from the text of the play will be followed by parentheses indicating first the page numbers in the Couch collection and then the page numbers from the 1943 edition of the play.

17. Kingsley, preface to *The Patriots*, in *Five Prizewinning Plays*, p. xxiii.

18. Of course Kingsley is using the historical material for his own purposes. There are many who would argue that had Jefferson's ideas really been followed, the U.S. would have been based on a predominantly agricultural model, and that it is perhaps Madison who set the country on the course to become a strong international power.

19. Florence Ryerson and Colin Clements, *Harriet* (New York: Charles Scribner's Sons, 1943)

20. Malcolm Goldstein, *The Art of Thornton Wilder* (Lincoln, Nebr.: University of Nebraska Press, 1965), p. 117; Linda Simon, *Thornton Wilder: His World* (Garden City, N.Y.: Doubleday, 1979), p. 164.

21. Thornton Wilder, preface to *Three Plays* (New York: Harper and Brothers, 1957), p. xiv.

22. Tallulah Bankhead, however, felt Kazan was incompetent and tried to have him removed. See Patricia Bosworth, *Montgomery Clift: A Biography* (New York: Harcourt, Brace, 1978), p. 94.

23. Thornton Wilder, *The Skin of Our Teeth* (New York and London: Harper and Brothers, 1942).

24. Donald Haberman, *The Plays of Thornton Wilder: A Critical Study* (Middletown, Conn.: Wesleyan University Press, 1967), p. 71, and Rex Burbank, *Thornton Wilder* (New York: Twayne Publishers, 1961), p. 102.

25. Karl Malden, *When Do I Start? A Memoir* (New York: Simon and Schuster, 1997), pp. 127–128; Michael Shnayerson, *Irwin Shaw: A Biography* (New York: G. P. Putnam's Sons, 1989), pp. 120–121.

26. Irwin Shaw, *Sons and Soldiers* (New York: Random House, 1944).

27. Lillian Hellman, *The Searching Wind* (New York: Viking Press, 1944).

28. Burns Mantle, *Best Plays of 1941–42* (New York: Dodd, Mead, 1942), pp. 212–243.

29. Fritz Rotter and Allen Vincent, *Letters to Lucerne* (New York: Samuel French, n.d. [1943?]).

30. John Anderson, review of *Tomorrow the World*, by James Gow and Arnaud d'Usseau, *New York Journal-American*, 15 April 1943.

31. James Gow and Arnaud d'Usseau, *Tomorrow the World* (New York: Charles Scribner's Sons, 1943).

32. A similar portrait of indoctrinated Nazi youth surfaces again a year later in *This Is Your Enemy* (Governors Island, N.Y.: Military Training Division, Second Service Command, 1944), a play issued by the American military for use in training soldiers.

33. See Peter Novick, *The Holocaust in American Life* (Boston: Houghton Mifflin, 1999), pp. 24–29.

34. "1,000,000 Jews Slain by Nazis, Report Says," *New York Times*, 29 June 1942, p. 7.

35. James MacDonald, "Himmler Program Kills Polish Jews," *New York Times*, 26 November 1942, p. 10.

36. For a full discussion of how the brutalities of the death camps leaked into public notice, see Deborah E. Lipstadt, *Beyond Belief: The American Press and the Coming of the Holocaust, 1933–1945* (New York and London: The Free Press, 1986), chapter 8.

37. A full description of the genesis and production of *We Shall Never Die* is given in Stephen J. Whitfield, "The Politics of Pageantry, 1936–1946," *American Jewish History* 84 (1996): 234–244. See also Atay Citron, "Ben Hecht's Pageant Drama: *A Flag Is Born*," in *Staging the Holocaust: The Shoah in Drama and Performance*, ed. Claude Schumacher

(Cambridge: Cambridge University Press, 1998), pp. 75–77; Ben Hecht, *A Child of the Century* (New York: Simon and Schuster, 1954), pp. 553–558; and William MacAdams, *Ben Hecht: The Man behind the Legend* (New York: Charles Scribner's Sons, 1990), pp. 229–230.

38. Ben Hecht, *We Will Never Die* (unpublished, 1943). The piece exists only in one typescript held by the New York Public Library's theatre collection.

39. Edward Chodorov, *Common Ground* (New York: Samuel French, 1945 and 1946).

40. Dorothy Heyward and Howard Rigsby, *South Pacific* (working title, *New Georgia*), unpublished. This play exists only in a typescript held by the New York Public Library's theatre collection.

41. Mantle, *The Best Plays of 1943–44*, pp. 133–163.

42. Lewis Nichols, review of *Decision*, by Edward Chodorov, *New York Times*, 3 February 1944, p. 23; Robert Garland, review of *Decision*, by Edward Chodorov, *New York Journal-American*, 3 February 1944.

43. Edward Chodorov, *Decision* (New York: Samuel French, 1943).

44. Burton Rascoe, review of *Decision*, by Edward Chodorov, *New York World-Telegram*, 3 February 1944.

45. *Janie* was made into a film in 1944 and starred Edward Arnold as Mr. Colburn (renamed Conway in the film) and humorist-writer Robert Benchley as John Van Brunt. Two years later, these same actors appeared in a film sequel, *Janie Gets Married*.

46. Gerald Bordman, *American Theatre: A Chronicle of Comedy and Drama, 1930–1969* (New York and Oxford: Oxford University Press, 1996), p. 215; John Anderson, review of *Junior Miss*, by Joseph Fields and Jerome Chodorov, *New York Journal-American*, 11 September 1942.

47. Josephine Bentham and Herschel Williams, *Janie: A Comedy in Three Acts* (New York: Samuel French, 1943).

48. Bordman, *American Theatre*, p. 216.

49. Howard Lindsay and Russel Crouse, *Strip for Action* (New York: Random House, 1942).

50. The 1944 Warner Bros. film version of the play marketed for a national audience does, however, posit one of the couples to be on their honeymoon.

51. Natalia Chodorov's surname is a Broadway in-joke, for it is a reference to Fields's frequent co-author, Jerome Chodorov, who had been drafted. See Malcolm Goldstein, *George S. Kaufman: His Life, His Theater* (New York and Oxford: Oxford University Press, 1979), pp. 364–365.

52. As Goldstein notes (*George S. Kaufman*, p. 365), some audience members and reviewers did object to *The Doughgirls*'s rather liberal sexual morality, but that obviously made no dent in the comedy's extraordinary success.

53. Joseph Fields, *The Doughgirls* (New York: Random House, 1943).

54. The Ephrons went on to write the screenplays for *Carousel, Desk Set, What Price Glory? Daddy Long Legs, There's No Business Like Show Business*, and *Captain Newman, M.D.* They are also the parents of writer-screenwriters Nora, Delia, Hallie, and Amy Ephron.

55. Phoebe Ephron and Henry Ephron, *Three's a Family* (New York and Los Angeles: Samuel French, [1944?]).

56. Edward Chodorov, *Those Endearing Young Charms* (New York: Samuel French, 1943).

57. Some of the reviewers objected to Hank the ruthless roué's rather sudden and

sentimental reform. Lewis Nichols in his *New York Times* review (17 September 1943) wrote, "Finally, the ending destroyed the whole point of the story, which was whether a girl should have an affair with the young man she loves before he goes away."

58. Even as American-born T. S. Eliot is considered British, Van Druten, though British born, can be considered an American playwright, since he wrote largely for the American stage. *The Voice of the Turtle*, moreover, is set in New York and all its characters are American.

59. Wilella Waldorf, *New York Post*, 9 December 1943.

60. John Van Druten, *The Voice of the Turtle* (New York: Random House, 1944).

61. Bruce Weber, "A Play outside the Mainstream of Its Time and Ours," *New York Times*, 14 September 2001. *The Voice of the Turtle* was also successfully revived in 1995 at the Shaw Festival in Niagara-on-the-Lake, Canada.

62. Whereas the Bernstein-Comden musical is about three sailors on shore leave in New York, four months later Luther Davis's comedy *Kiss Them for Me*, about three sailors on shore leave in San Francisco, opened at the Belasco Theatre (20 March 1945).

63. Indeed, Kaufman wrote to Moss Hart about *Over 21*, commenting, "Our little charade is an unbelievable smash, considering that it ain't much of a play." See Goldstein, *George S. Kaufman*, p. 376.

64. Goldstein suggests that Max may be inspired by Thornton Wilder, and that the entire comedy is something of a *drama à clef*. See ibid., p. 375.

65. Ruth Gordon, *Over 21* (New York: Dramatists Play Service, 1945).

66. One notable exception is Ann Margaret Fox, "Open Houses: American Women Playwrights, Broadway Success, and Media Culture, 1906–1944" (Ph.D. diss., Indiana University, 1998), pp. 175–189.

67. Rose Franken, *Soldier's Wife* (New York: Samuel French, 1944).

68. Fox, "Open Houses," pp. 188–189.

69. Arthur Miller, *That They May Win*, in *The Best One-Act Plays of 1944*, ed. Margaret Mayorga (New York: Dodd, Mead and Co., 1945).

70. Nelson had had roles in both the original and revival productions of Sherwood's *There Shall Be No Night* and had written *Mail Call* for the Army-sponsored production of one-acters, *The Army Play by Play*. After the war, Nelson had a rich Hollywood acting, directing and producing career.

71. Ralph Nelson, *The Wind Is Ninety* (Chicago: Dramatic Publishing Co., 1946).

72. Elsa Shelley, *Foxhole in the Parlor* (New York: Dramatists Play Service, 1946). This is the only published version of the play but is a revised edition and incorrectly gives the opening date as 27 May 1945. It also contains references (p. 13) not only to the Yalta and San Francisco conferences but also to the Potsdam conference, which actually took place two months after *Foxhole in the Parlor* closed.

3. THE DRAMATIC ART OF UNCLE SAM

1. *The Army Play by Play: Five One-Act Plays* (New York: Random House, 1943).

2. *Where E'er We Go* was directed by Cpl. Paul Tripp, who also acted in the play. In later years, Tripp was to write the popular children's book *Tubby the Tuba* and to play the title role in the CBS children's television show, *Mr. I Imagination*.

3. Ralph Nelson had done some acting in Los Angeles, had been married briefly to actress Celeste Holm before the war, and had been cast in a small role in the original production of Robert Sherwood's *There Shall Be No Night*. *Mail Call* is his first play, but

in June 1945, his play *The Wind Is Ninety* was produced at the Booth Theatre in New York. The cast included Wendell Corey and Kirk Douglas. Nelson went on to become a distinguished film actor, director, and producer (including *Lilies of the Field, Once a Thief, Top Gun, The Burbs, As Good As It Gets, The Karate Kid,* and *9 to 5*) and a television director (including the *I Remember Mama* series and *Requiem for a Heavyweight*).

4. Margaret Mayorga, ed., *The Best One-Act Plays of 1943* (New York: Dodd, Mead and Co., 1944), pp. 57–74.

5. Not surprisingly, Kasznar (1913–79) is, along with Ralph Nelson, one of the two playwrights among the five whose plays were chosen for *The Army Play by Play* who had a theatre background and who would continue after the war in a theatre, film, and television career. Kasznar, sometimes Kasner, was born in Vienna as Kurt Serwischer (sometimes Serwicher). Before immigrating to the United States, he had trained as an actor in Vienna with Max Reinhardt and then played small parts in New York prior to entering the army, where he wrote and acted in *First Cousins*. He did not write other plays but after the war had an active stage career, regularly acting in New York and in regional theatres. He appeared in the original Broadway productions of *Waiting for Godot* (Pozzo), *Barefoot in the Park* (Victor Velasco), and *The Sound of Music* (Max Detweiler). He also played Tevye in several productions of *Fiddler on the Roof* and the Director in *Six Characters in Search of an Author*. He appeared as well in over thirty films and in several television productions. One wonders whether Russel Crouse, who was one of the judges picking the scripts for *The Army Play by Play*, remembered Kasznar years later when the cast was chosen for *The Sound of Music*, for which Crouse provided the script.

6. Steven Bach, however, claims that "Arnold later admitted he had never heard of Moss Hart." Steven Bach, *Dazzler: The Life and Times of Moss Hart* (New York: Alfred A. Knopf, 2001), p. 239.

7. Burns Mantle, *The Best Plays of 1943–44* (New York: Dodd, Mead and Co., 1944), pp. 32–33; Bach, *Dazzler*, pp. 239–240; Rosamond Gilder, "The Fabulous Hart," *Theatre Arts* 28 (February 1944): 98.

8. "*Winged Victory* in Production," *Theatre Arts* 28 (February 1944): 93–96. This four-page inset on how *Winged Victory* came to be is graced with comic drawings by Sgt. Harry Horner, who had recently been the scene designer for Hart's *Lady in the Dark*.

9. See Gerald Bordman, *American Theatre: A Chronicle of Comedy and Drama, 1930–1969* (New York and Oxford: Oxford University Press, 1996), pp. 226–227. Bach records a cast of 210, orchestra of 45, and choral group of 50, as well as a stage crew of 70.

10. See Bach, *Dazzler*, pp. 243–244.

11. Mantle, *The Best Plays of 1943–44*, pp. 32–33.

12. Moss Hart, *Winged Victory: The Air Force Play* (New York: Random House, 1943). Numbers in parentheses following quotations refer to this edition.

13. Bordman, *American Theatre*, p. 227.

14. Bach, *Dazzler*, p. 243.

15. Karl Malden, *When Do I Start? A Memoir* (New York: Simon and Schuster, 1997), p. 137.

16. See, for example, *Soldier Shows* (Washington, D.C.: Special Services Division, Army Service Forces, U.S. GPO, 1944) (W109.102: So4); *Soldier Shows* (Washington, D.C.: War Department, U.S. GPO, 1945) (W1.43: 28–15c); and *Soldier Shows* (Washington, D.C.: Special Services Division, Army Service Forces [Entertainment Section], U.S. GPO, 1945) (W109.116: 28). The last contains, among other materials, copies of John Patrick's *The Hasty Heart* and George S. Kaufman's *Freedom of the Air*.

17. Bob Stuart McKnight, "Original Army Shows," *Theatre Arts* 27 (July 1943): 427.

18. The Writers and Material Committee of Camp Shows, eds., *"At Ease,"* vol. 1, *Comedy Sketches* (New York: USO–Camp Shows, 1942).

19. An incisive account of gay men and government-sponsored theatre in the armed forces is given in Allan Bérubé, *Coming Out under Fire: The History of Gay Men and Women in World War Two* (New York: Penguin Books, 1990), pp. 67–97. See also Arthur Laurents, *Original Story By* (New York: Alfred A. Knopf, 2000), pp. 25–26, and Charles Kaiser, *The Gay Metropolis, 1940–1996* (Boston and New York: Houghton Mifflin, 1997), pp. 37–38.

20. The Writers and Material Committee of Camp Shows, eds., *"At Ease,"* vol. 2, *Minstrel Shows* (New York: USO–Camp Shows, 1942). Page references given in parentheses are to this edition.

21. Frank Loesser et al., *About Face!* (Washington, D.C.: Army Service Forces, Special Services Division, n.d. [c. 1943–44]); *Hi, Yank* (Washington, D.C.: Army Service Forces, Special Services Division, n.d. [c. 1943–44]); *P.F.C. Mary Brown: A WAC Musical Revue* (Washington, D.C.: Army Service Forces, Special Services Division, n.d. [c. 1944]).

22. Susan Loesser, *A Most Remarkable Fella: Frank Loesser and the Guys and Dolls in His Life* (New York: D. I. Fine, 1993).

23. The scripts have no dates, but *About Face!* presumably predates *Hi, Yank,* since it is advertised on the inside front cover of the latter.

24. *P.F.C. Mary Brown* follows after *About Face!* and *Hi, Yank,* since these shows are advertised on the back page of the *P.F.C. Mary Brown* volume. There seem to be no records revealing the identity of Capt. Ruby Jane Douglass, but Arthur Altman had already written the music for a pop tune "All or Nothing at All" (1940), recorded by Billie Holiday and in later years (1956?) recorded again by Frank Sinatra. After the war, he also wrote the music for "American Beauty Rose," recorded by Sinatra (1950), and "I Wish I Had a Record of the Promises You Made," recorded by Perry Como (1949).

25. An exception here is Allan R. Kenward's *Cry Havoc,* sometimes staged as *Proof through the Night* (1943).

26. Mary Percy Schenck was later recognized with a 1948 Tony Award for her costume designs for *The Heiress.*

27. Clearly the published plays discussed here were just a few of those produced. For mention of some others, see Bob Stuart McKnight, "Original Army Shows," 426–433.

28. *Death without Battle* (Governors Island, N.Y.: Military Training Division Headquarters, Second Service Command, 1944).

29. *Stripes* (Governors Island, N.Y.: Army Service Forces, Second Service Command, 1944); *The Eternal Weapon* (Governors Island, N.Y.: Army Service Forces, Second Service Command, 1944).

30. *Ghost Column* (Governors Island, N.Y.: Military Training Division Headquarters, Second Service Command, 1944).

31. *This Is Your Enemy* (Governors Island, N.Y.: Military Training Division, Second Service Command, 1944).

32. Aileen L. Fisher, *The Squanderbug's Mother Goose* (Washington, D.C.: Education Section, War Finance Div., U.S. Treasury, U.S. GPO, 1944), (T66.2: Sq 20).

33. Sally Miller Brash, *The Magic Bond: A Short Timely Play for Children of Nine to Twelve Years of Age,* in *Plays for Schools-at-War* (Washington, D.C.: U.S. Treasury Department, U.S. GPO, 1944) (T66.2: P69/4).

34. Mildred Hank and Noel McQueen, *We Will Do Our Share,* in *War Savings Pro-*

grams: A Handbook of Dramatic Material (Washington, D.C.: Treasury Department, Education Division, U.S. GPO, 1943) (T66.6: P94), pp. 61–69.

35. Ibid., pp. 70–76.

36. Sally Miller Brash, *Star for a Day: A Musical Play for High School Students,* in *Plays for Schools-at-War* (Washington, D.C.: Education Section, War Finance Division, Treasury Department, U.S. GPO, 1944) (T66.2: P 69/5).

37. Walter Hackett, *For the Duration: A Play for Junior and Senior High Schools,* in *Plays for Schools-at-War* (Washington, D.C.: Treasury Department, U.S. GPO, 1944) (T66.2: P69/2); and Howard Tooley and Carolyn Wood, *A Letter from Bob: A War Savings Play for Junior and Senior High Schools,* in *Plays for Schools-at-War* (Washington, D.C.: Treasury Department, U.S. GPO, 1945) (T66.2: P69/3 1945).

38. *War Savings Programs.*

39. Ibid.; Bernard J. Reins, *Message from Bataan,* pp. 38–52, and *Letter to Private Smith,* pp. 77–85.

40. *War Bond Plays and Other Dramatic Material for Use in Connection with War Finance Promotion* (Washington, D.C.: Treasury Department, U.S. GPO, 1943) (T66.2: P69).

41. A useful sketch of Bella and Sam Spewack's careers is given in Jean Gould, *Modern American Playwrights* (New York: Dodd, Mead and Co., 1966), pp. 135–140.

42. William McBrien, *Cole Porter: A Biography* (New York: Alfred A. Knopf, 1998), pp. 303–309

43. Representative scripts appear in William A. Bacher, ed., *The Treasury Star Parade* (New York and Toronto: Farrar and Rinehart, 1942); James Boyd, ed., *The Freedom Company Presents . . .* (Dodd, Mead and Co., 1941); and Norman Corwin et al., *This Is War! A Collection of Plays about America on the March* (New York: Dodd, Mead and Co., 1942).

44. Morgan Y. Himelstein, *Drama Was a Weapon: The Left-Wing Theatre in New York, 1929–1941* (New Brunswick, N.J.: Rutgers University Press, 1963).

4. AIRING THE WAR

1. Arch Oboler, "The Art of Radio Drama," in Arch Oboler, *Fourteen Radio Plays* (New York: Random House, 1940), p. xv.

2. Soon after the National Broadcasting Company (NBC) was established in 1926 as the first commercial broadcasting network in the world, it produced two networks, the Blue and the Red. The Blue was sold in 1943 and became the American Broadcasting Company (ABC).

3. Arch Oboler and Stephen Longstreet, eds., *Free World Theatre: Nineteen New Radio Plays* (New York: Random House, 1944).

4. For an extensive and informative history of American wartime radio drama, see Howard Blue, *Words at War: World War II Era Radio Drama and the Postwar Broadcasting Industry Blacklist* (Lanham, Md., and Oxford: Scarecrow Press, 2002).

5. *This Is War! A Collection of Plays about America on the March* (New York: Dodd, Mead and Co., 1942).

6. "The tone of the pieces [in *This Is War!*] is strident and strongly anti-Fascist," comments Mary E. McGann in her chapter on Corwin. Mary E. McGann, "Voices in the Dark: A Study of the Radio Achievement of Norman Corwin, Archibald MacLeish,

Louis MacNeice, Dylan Thomas, and Samuel Beckett" (Ph.D. diss., Indiana University, 1979), p. 29.

7. R. LeRoy Bannerman, *On a Note of Triumph: Norman Corwin and the Golden Years of Radio* (New York: Carol Publishing Group, 1986), p. 100. The *New York Times* also reported that "the series is being extensively short-waved": *New York Times*, 22 February 1942, sect. 8, p. 12.

8. Boyd's papers and correspondence are held by the University of North Carolina Library (inventory no. 3610). Many of them relate to the Free Company.

9. James Boyd, ed., *The Free Company Presents . . . : A Collection of Plays about the Meaning of America* (New York: Dodd, Mead and Co., 1941).

10. See Blue, *Words at War*, pp. 89–95, for a history of The Free Company.

11. As quoted in Boyd, ed., *The Free Company Presents*, p. 1.

12. William Saroyan, *The People with Light Coming out of Them*, in Boyd, ed., *The Free Company Presents*.

13. Marc Connelly, *The Mole on Lincoln's Cheek*, in Boyd, ed., *The Free Company Presents*.

14. Sherwood Anderson, *Above Suspicion*, in Boyd, ed., *The Free Company Presents*.

15. Orson Welles, *His Honor, the Mayor*, in Boyd, ed., *The Free Company Presents*.

16. The full and romantic story of how *We Hold These Truths* came to be written and its success is colorfully told by Bannerman, *On a Note of Triumph*, pp. 73–88. See also Blue, *Words at War*, pp. 103–107.

17. Norman Corwin, *More by Corwin: 16 Radio Dramas by Norman Corwin* (New York: Henry Holt and Co., 1944), p. 55; and Bannerman, *On a Note of Triumph*, p. 84.

18. In addition to the published script of the play in *More by Corwin*, the original production (complete with Lionel Barrymore's introduction and President Roosevelt's speech) exists on sound recording: Norman Corwin, *We Hold These Truths*, recorded 15 December 1941, audio cassette CORW007 and compact disc CORW027 (LodeStone, n.d.).

19. Bannerman, *On a Note of Triumph*, p. 84.

20. *New York Times*, 16 December 1941, p. 30.

21. A brief history of *This Is War!* can be found in Blue, *Words at War*, pp. 107–115.

22. "White House Accepts Radio Chain Series," *New York Times*, 1 February 1942, p. 33.

23. See Blue, *Words at War*, pp. 100–103.

24. William A. Bacher, ed., *The Treasury Star Parade* (New York and Toronto: Farrar and Rinehart, 1942).

25. Violet Atkins was a prolific radio (and later television) scriptwriter. Her papers, including many of her radio scripts, are in the special collections library of California State University at Northridge.

26. John Latouche was primarily a lyricist best known for writing some of the lyrics for Leonard Bernstein's *Candide* (1956) and the libretto for Douglas Moore's opera *The Ballad of Baby Doe* (1956).

27. Norman Rosten was a Brooklyn poet and writer, who later became a close friend of Marilyn Monroe and co-wrote a memoir about her.

28. Edward Jenks, "759 Stations and Going Strong," *New York Times*, 5 August 1942, p. 10.

29. John K. Hutchens, "The 'Parade' Goes On," *New York Times*, 22 November 1942, p. 12.

30. Oboler, *Free World Theatre*.

31. The expression "United Nations" came into being with Franklin D. Roosevelt's address the "Declaration by United Nations" (1 January 1942), on the occasion when representatives of twenty-six countries pledged to continue their fight against the Axis.

32. Among Schoenfeld's screenplays are *Phantom Lady* (1944), *The Dark Corner* (1946), and *Caged* (1950), for which he received an Academy Award nomination. Among Irving Ravetch's screenplays are *The Long Hot Summer* (1957), *Hud* (1963), *Hombre* (1967), *The Reivers* (1969), and *Norma Rae* (1979).

33. See Blue, *Words at War*, pp. 314–315.

34. Morton Wishengrad, *The Battle of the Warsaw Ghetto*, in Erik Barnouw, *Radio Drama in Action*, pp. 31–45. See also Blue, p. 315.

35. See Arthur Laurents, *Original Story By* (New York: Alfred A. Knopf, 2000), pp. 28–29.

36. Arthur Laurents, *The Last Day of the War*, in *Radio Drama in Action*, pp. 91–110.

37. Arthur Laurents, *The Face*, in Joseph Liss, ed., *Radio's Best Plays* (New York: Greenberg, 1947).

38. These words are attributed to Robert Landry of the Writers' War Board and are quoted by Joseph Liss, the editor of the collection of radio plays in which the published version of *The Face* appears. *Radio's Best Plays*, p. 81.

39. A brief but useful description of *Cavalcade of America* is given in John Dunning, *Tune in Yesterday* (Englewood Cliffs, N.J.: Prentice-Hall, 1976), pp. 117–119.

40. Gerald Weales, "Arthur Miller Takes the Air," *American Drama* 5 (Fall 1995): 1–15.

41. Arthur Miller, *The Battle of the Ovens*, typescript. (E. I. Du Pont Nemours and Co., 1942). The copy owned by the University of Colorado at Boulder seems to be the only extant copy of this radio play.

42. *Thunder from the Hills* seems to exist only in the form of a recorded broadcast. The recording is held by the Museum of Radio and Television (New York and Los Angeles), call number R88:0159.

43. Weales, "Arthur Miller Takes the Air," 11.

44. Arthur Miller, *I Was Married in Bataan*, typescript. (E. I. Du Pont Nemours and Co., 1942). The only extant copies of this radio play seem to be those at the New York Public Library's Center for the Performing Arts and the Harry Ransom Center at the University of Texas.

45. Arthur Miller, *Toward a Farther Star*, typescript. (E. I. Du Pont Nemours and Co., 1942). The only extant copies of this radio play seem to be those at the New York Public Library's Center for the Performing Arts and the Harry Ransom Center at the University of Texas.

46. Arthur Miller, *The Eagle's Nest*, typescript. (E. I. Du Pont Nemours and Co., 1942). The only extant copy of this radio play seems to be that at the New York Public Library's Center for the Performing Arts. Arthur Miller, *Listen for the Sound of Wings* (E. I. Du Pont Nemours and Co., 1943). This text exists only as a recording held by the Museum of Radio and Television (New York and Los Angeles), call number R82:0055. The only extant typescript seems to be that held by the Harry Ransom Center at the University of Texas.

47. For a discussion of the unpublished filmscript and its relation to *A View from the Bridge*, see Albert Wertheim, *"A View from the Bridge,"* in *The Cambridge Companion to*

Arthur Miller, ed. Christopher Bigsby (Cambridge and New York: Cambridge University Press, 1997), pp. 101–114.

48. Arthur Miller, *Bernadine, I Love You,* typescript. (E. I. Du Pont Nemours and Co., 1942). The only extant copy of this radio play seems to be that at the New York Public Library's Center for the Performing Arts.

49. Arthur Miller, *Grandpa and the Statue,* in *Radio Drama in Action,* ed. Barnouw, pp. 267–281. It is printed as well in *Plays from Radio,* ed. A. H. Lass, Earle L. McGill, and Donald Axelrod (Cambridge, Mass.: Houghton Mifflin Co., 1948), pp. 235–252. Quotations refer to the Barnouw edition.

50. Arthur Miller, *The Philippines Never Surrendered,* typescript. (E. I. Du Pont Nemours and Co., 1945). The only extant copies of this radio play seem to be those at the New York Public Library's Center for the Performing Arts and the Harry Ransom Center at the University of Texas.

51. Arthur Miller, *The Story of Gus,* in *Radio's Best Plays,* pp. 303–319.

52. Weales, "Arthur Miller Takes the Air," 13–14.

53. In the preface he provides for Liss's anthology, Corwin specifically discusses the problems of art versus commerce in radio dramatic writing (*Radio's Best Plays,* pp. iii–vi).

54. Archibald MacLeish, *The American Story* (New York: Duell, Sloan and Pearce, 1944).

55. Stephen Vincent Benét, *"We Stand United" and Other Radio Scripts* (New York and Toronto: Farrar and Rinehart, 1944).

56. Oboler, *Fourteen Radio Plays,* p. 56.

57. Eckhard Breitinger, *Rundfunk und Hörspiel in den USA, 1930–1950* (Trier: Wissenschaflicher Verlag, 1987), p. 255. Translation mine.

58. Stephen Vincent Benét, *"We Stand United" and Other Radio Scripts.*

59. Arch Oboler, *Plays for Americans: Thirteen New Non-royalty Radio Plays* (New York and Toronto: Farrar and Rinehart, 1942).

60. See Blue, *Words at War,* pp. 207–208.

61. Arch Oboler, *Oboler Omnibus: Radio Plays and Personalities* (New York: Duell, Sloan and Pearce, 1945).

62. Bannerman, *On a Note of Triumph,* p. 158.

63. Happily, as with *We Hold These Truths,* there is a sound recording of the original broadcast: Norman Corwin, *On a Note of Triumph,* recorded 8 May 1945, audio cassette CORW001 (LodeStone, n.d.). The published script does not indicate sound effects and other stage directions: Norman Corwin, *On a Note of Triumph* (New York: Simon and Schuster, 1945). A script with stage directions has been published by LodeStone Audio Theatre, CORW002 (Bloomington, Ind., n.d.). Parentheses following references indicate page numbers in the 1945 edition.

64. McGann, "Voices in the Dark," p. 33. See her astute discussion of *On a Note of Triumph,* pp. 33–41.

65. The published script contains an epigraph from Whitman; and Bannerman, *On a Note of Triumph,* p. 144, mentions that Corwin had been reading Whitman at that time and was inspired by him as he wrote *On a Note of Triumph.*

66. Philip Roth, *I Married a Communist* (New York: Vintage Books, 1999).

67. The music is actually that of the folk song "Old Joe Clark," and the "Round and Round Hitler's Grave" song was used earlier in the first play in Corwin's *This Is War!* series. See Corwin, *This Is War!* pp. 20–21.

68. The last two lines were cut from the actual production.

5. THE AFTERMATH

1. Allan Bérubé, *Coming Out under Fire: The History of Gay Men and Women in World War II* (New York: Penguin Books, 1990), and Charles Kaiser, *The Gay Metropolis, 1940–1996* (Boston and New York: Houghton Mifflin, 1997), chapter 1.

2. Worthy of mention is another play that opened a month prior to *Home of the Brave* and which also treats wartime psychological damage though to a civilian. Robert Turney's *The Secret Room* opened at the Royale Theatre on 7 November 1945 and ran for only twenty-one performances. It is a suspense play centering on an Italian woman who was raped by the Nazis and whose child was taken from her to be raised by a Nazi family. Psychologically injured, she is hired by an American family whose children she attempts to possess and whose mother she attempts to destroy. This play exists only in a typescript held by the New York Public Library's Theatre Collection.

3. Arthur Laurents, *Home of the Brave* (New York: Random House, 1946).

4. Ellen Schiff, *Awake and Singing: 7 Classic Plays from the American Jewish Repertoire* (New York: Mentor Books, 1995), p. 375.

5. Arthur Laurents, *Original Story By: A Memoir of Broadway and Hollywood* (New York: Alfred A. Knopf, 2000), p. 53.

6. Ibid., pp. 49–50.

7. Burns Mantle, *The Best Plays of 1945–46* (New York: Dodd, Mead and Co., 1946), pp. 12–13.

8. The extant copy of the play exists only as a microfilm of a typescript: Don Appell, *This, Too, Shall Pass* (New York: Microfilm Corporation, 1963). Mantle, *The Best Plays of 1945–46*, p. 439; Gerald Bordman, *American Theatre: A Chronicle of Comedy and Drama, 1930–1969* (New York: Oxford University Press, 1996), p. 257.

9. Arthur Miller, *All My Sons* (New York: Penguin Books, 1947).

10. Arthur Miller, introduction to *Arthur Miller's Collected Plays* (New York: Viking Press, 1957), p. 22.

11. Edward Mabley and Leonard Mins, *Temper the Wind* (1947). This play exists only in a typescript held by the New York Public Library's Theatre Collection. Pagination in the typescript is given by act, scene, and page number of that particular act. My parentheses after the quotation reflect act, scene, and page numbers from the New York Public Library typescript.

12. Walter J. Meserve, *Robert E. Sherwood: Reluctant Moralist* (New York: Pegasus, 1970), p. 188.

13. Mantle, *The Best Plays of 1945–46*, pp. 308–309; Meserve, *Robert E. Sherwood*, p. 189.

14. Mantle, *The Best Plays of 1945–46*, pp. 309–344. A complete text of *The Rugged Path* exists only in a typescript in the New York Public Library's Theatre Collection. Pagination in the typescript is given by act, scene, and page number of that particular act. My parentheses after quotations reflect act, scene, and page numbers from the New York Public Library typescript.

15. Bella Spewack and Sam Spewack, *Woman Bites Man* (New York: Dramatists Play Service, 1947).

16. John Mason Brown, "Bellona's Bridegroom," in *Seeing Things* (New York and London: McGraw-Hill, 1946), pp. 300–306. Another version of this essay prefaces Harry Brown, *A Sound of Hunting* (New York: Alfred A. Knopf, 1946), p. viii.

17. Burt Lancaster was discovered by Hollywood while playing S/Sgt. Mooney in *A*

Sound of Hunting. A year later he appeared in his first film, *The Killers,* based on the Hemingway story of that name, and became an overnight Hollywood star. See Kate Buford, *Burt Lancaster: An American Life* (New York: Alfred A. Knopf, 2000), pp. 60–62.

18. The title and some of the inspiration of the play seem to come from Brown's poem "Incident on a Front Not Far from Castel di Sangro," whose first lines read: "There was a sound of hunting in the mountains, / That came back dark and dangerous to the ears / Of those who crouched among the broken fountains." See Harry Brown, *The Beast in His Hunger* (New York: Alfred A. Knopf, 1949), pp. 80–83.

19. Buford, *Burt Lancaster,* p. 61.

20. Bordman, *American Theatre,* p. 268.

21. For John Mason Brown, the terrible responsibility for knowingly sending men to their death is the essence of *Command Decision.* See John Mason Brown, "Stars That Weigh a Ton," in *Seeing More Things* (New York: McGraw-Hill, 1948), pp. 273–281.

22. William Wister Haines, *Command Decision* (New York: Random House, 1947).

23. John Mason Brown senses some of this when he writes, "Mr. Haines's dialogue cannot claim the pungency of Harry Brown's *A Sound of Hunting*" (*Seeing More Things,* p. 278).

24. Thomas Heggen, *Mister Roberts* (Boston: Houghton Mifflin, 1946).

25. Thomas Heggen and Joshua Logan, *Mister Roberts* (New York: Random House, 1948).

26. James B. Allardice, *At War with the Army* (New York: Samuel French, 1950).

27. Norman Krasna, *John Loves Mary* (New York: Dramatists Play Service, 1947).

28. Irwin Shaw, preface to *The Assassin* (New York: Random House, 1946).

29. James R. Giles, *Irwin Shaw* (Boston: Twayne Publishers, 1983), pp. 24–25.

30. Arthur Miller's *Incident at Vichy* is a drama that bears some comparison with *The Assassin.* Writing *Incident at Vichy* in 1964, Arthur Miller escaped the pitfalls of Shaw's plays by presenting a general cross-section of people, thereby avoiding the specifics of party line politics or of historical analogy.

31. Howard Lindsay and Russel Crouse, *State of the Union* (New York: Random House, 1945).

32. The music for *On Whitman Avenue* was written by composer-novelist Paul Bowles, who had previously written the music for *Liberty Jones, Watch on the Rhine, Jacobowsky and the Colonel,* and *The Glass Menagerie.*

33. Thomas D. Pawley, "Three Views of the Returning Black Veteran," *Black-American Literature Forum* 16 (1982): 163–167, presents the theme of the black soldier returning home together with a précis of *Deep Are the Roots, Jeb,* and *On Whitman Avenue.* Although black soldiers were promoted and began to fight alongside white soldiers during World War II, true integration did not go into effect until President Harry S. Truman's message to Congress, 2 February 1948, and the subsequent Executive Order 9981, Equality of Treatment and Opportunity in the Armed Forces, July 1948. See Albert P. Blaustein and Robert L. Zangrado, eds., *Civil Rights and African Americans* (Evanston, Ill.: Northwestern University Press, 1968), pp. 380–386.

34. Arnaud d'Usseau and James Gow, preface to *Deep Are the Roots* (New York: Charles Scribner's Sons, 1946).

35. Robert Ardrey, preface to *Plays of Three Decades* (New York: Atheneum, 1968), p. 24.

36. In their joint autobiography, Ruby Dee and Ossie Davis give useful behind-the-

scenes glimpses of *Jeb* as well as of their own first meeting in the production of the play: Ossie Davis and Ruby Dee, *With Ossie and Ruby: In This Life Together* (New York: William Morrow, 1998), pp. 151–156.

37. Maxine Wood, *On Whitman Avenue* (New York: Dramatists Play Service, 1948).

38. See Glenda E. Gill, *White Grease Paint on Black Performers: A Study of the Federal Theatre, 1935–1939* (New York: Peter Lang, 1988), p. 46.

39. Vernon Rice, "*On Whitman Avenue* Boldly Faces the Negro Problem," *New York Post*, 9 May 1944.

40. In her chapter on Canada Lee, Glenda Gill offers some unique quotations from her correspondence with Maxine Wood and suggests that one of the play's problems is that it could be construed as " 'race riot' material." See Gill, *White Grease Paint on Black Performers*, pp. 43–47.

41. It was not until 1962 that Rodgers would tackle the American race issue in a direct way. His musical *No Strings* is about a mixed-race romance between an African American (Diahann Carroll) and a white American (Richard Kiley) who meet in Paris. But even in *No Strings,* the couple does not unite because they realize their union would make their lives too difficult and problematic in the United States.

42. Tennessee Williams, *A Streetcar Named Desire* (New York: New Directions, 1947).

43. See Peter Novick, *The Holocaust in American Life* (Boston: Houghton Mifflin, 1999), pp. 24–29.

44. There are two published editions, one American and one British, of the play. The numbers in parenthesis give the pages of the American and British version, respectively. Jan de Hartog, *Skipper Next to God* (New York: Dramatist Play Service, 1949), and Jan de Hartog, *Skipper Next to God,* in *Embassy Successes II, 1945–1946* (London: Sampson Low, Martson and Co., 1946), pp. 85–143.

45. Konrad Bercovici, foreword to *A Flag Is Born,* by Ben Hecht (New York: American League for a Free Palestine, 1946).

46. The political background of the play is carefully enunciated in Atay Citron, "Ben Hecht's Pageant Drama: *A Flag Is Born,*" in *Staging the Holocaust: The Shoah in Drama and Performance,* ed. Claude Schumacher (Cambridge: Cambridge University Press, 1998), pp. 70–93. See also Edna Nahshon, "From Geopathology to Redemption: *A Flag Is Born* on the Broadway Stage," *Kurt Weill Newsletter* 20 (Spring 2002): 5–8; Stephen J. Whitfield, "The Politics of Pageantry, 1936–1946," *American Jewish History* 84 (1996): 234–244; and Doug Fetherling, *The Five Lives of Ben Hecht* (Toronto: Lester and Orpen, 1977), pp. 133–135.

47. For a commentary on Weill's music for *A Flag Is Born,* see Christian Kuhnt, "Approaching the Music for *A Flag Is Born,*" *Kurt Weill Newsletter* 20 (Spring 2002): 8–9.

48. In his autobiography, Marlon Brando provides a sense of *A Flag Is Born* and his role in it. See Marlon Brando with Robert Lindsey, *Brando: Songs My Mother Taught Me* (New York: Random House, 1994), pp. 107–111.

49. Citron, "Ben Hecht's Pageant Drama," in *Staging the Holocaust,* pp. 78–79.

50. Ibid., p. 92, and Ben Hecht, *A Child of the Century* (New York: Simon and Schuster, 1954), p. 614.

51. Gary Carey, *Marlon Brando: The Only Contender* (New York: St. Martin's Press, 1985), p. 34. Another view of Brando in the part of David is given in Jerome Lawrence, *Actor: The Life and Times of Paul Muni* (New York: G. P. Putnam's Sons, 1974), pp. 291–294.

52. One exception is Arthur Goodman's *Seeds in the Wind,* which featured Sidney

Lumet. However, this drama about children hiding in the mountains after the Nazi massacre in Lidice ran for only seven performances and was never published, nor does there seem to be an extant script. See John Chapman, ed., *The Burns Mantle Best Plays of 1947–1948* (New York: Dodd, Mead and Co., 1948), pp. 405–406, and Bordman, *American Theatre,* p. 275. Furthermore, of the sixty-eight full-length, English-language stage plays listed in Alvin Goldfarb's bibliography of Holocaust plays, only four postwar plays predate 1965. See Alvin Goldfarb, "Select Bibliography of Holocaust Plays, 1933–1997," in *Staging the Holocaust,* pp. 298–334.

53. Michael C. C. Adams, *The Best War Ever: America and World War II* (Baltimore: Johns Hopkins University Press, 1994).

54. See Alvin H. Rosenfeld, "Popularization and Memory," in *Lessons and Legacies: The Meaning of the Holocaust in a Changing World,* ed. Peter Hayes (Evanston, Ill.: Northwestern University Press 1991); Alex Sagan, "An Optimistic Icon: Anne Frank's Canonization in Postwar Culture," *German Politics and Society* 13 (Fall 1995): 95–107; Alan Mintz, *Popular Culture and the Shaping of Holocaust Memory in America* (Seattle: University of Washington Press, 2001), pp. 18–19; Lawrence Graver, *An Obsession with Anne Frank* (Berkeley and Los Angeles: University of California Press, 1995); and Ralph Melnick, *The Stolen Legacy of Anne Frank* (New Haven: Yale University Press, 1997).

55. Frances Goodrich and Albert Hackett, *The Diary of Anne Frank* (New York: Random House, 1956).

56. Richard Rodgers and Oscar Hammerstein II, *South Pacific,* in *Six Plays by Rodgers and Hammerstein* (New York: Modern Library, 1959); Donald Bevan and Edmund Trzcinski, *Stalag 17* (New York: Dramatists Play Service, 1951); John Patrick, *Teahouse of the August Moon* (New York: G. P. Putnam's Sons, 1952); Herman Wouk, *The Caine Mutiny Court-Martial* (Garden City, N.Y.: Doubleday, 1954); and Ira Levin, *No Time for Sergeants* (New York: Random House, 1955).

57. "My Girl Back Home" appears as a bonus track on Richard Rodgers and Oscar Hammerstein II, *South Pacific with Original Broadway Cast,* remastered compact disc and audio cassette, Columbia (Sony) SK 60722, 1998.

58. John W. Dower, *War without Mercy: Race and Power in the Pacific War* (New York: Pantheon, 1986), p. 45.

59. *The Caine Mutiny Court-Martial* also occasioned the Broadway debut of actor Jim Bumgarner, later to become famous as James Garner.

60. *No Time for Sergeants* also marked the Broadway debut of Don Knotts.

BIBLIOGRAPHY

PRIMARY TEXTS

Allardice, James B. *At War with the Army.* New York: Samuel French, 1950.

Anderson, Maxwell. *Candle in the Wind.* Washington, D.C.: Anderson House, 1941.

———. *The Eve of St. Mark.* Washington, D.C.: Anderson House, 1942.

———. *Journey to Jerusalem.* Washington, D.C.: Anderson House, 1940.

———. *Key Largo.* In *Eleven Verse Plays, 1929–1939.* New York: Harcourt, Brace, 1939.

———. *Storm Operation.* Washington, D.C.: Anderson House, 1944.

Anderson, Sherwood. *Above Suspicion.* In James Boyd, ed., *The Free Company Presents . . . : A Collection of Plays about the Meaning of America.* New York: Dodd, Mead and Co., 1941.

Appell, Don. *This, Too, Shall Pass.* New York: Microfilm Corporation, 1963.

Ardrey, Robert. *Plays of Three Decades.* New York: Atheneum, 1968.

———. *Thunder Rock.* New York: Dramatists Play Service, 1939.

The Army Play by Play: Five One-Act Plays. New York: Random House, 1943.

Bacher, William A., ed. *The Treasury Star Parade.* New York and Toronto: Farrar and Rinehart, 1942.

Barnouw, Erik, ed. *Radio Drama in Action.* New York and Toronto: Farrar and Rinehart, 1945.

Barry, Philip. *Liberty Jones: A Play with Music for City Children.* New York: Coward-McCann, 1941.

Behrman, S. N. *Four Plays by S. N. Behrman.* New York: Random House, 1952.

Benét, Stephen Vincent. *"We Stand United" and Other Radio Scripts.* New York and Toronto: Farrar and Rinehart, 1944.

Bentham, Josephine, and Herschel Williams. *Janie: A Comedy in Three Acts.* New York: Samuel French, 1943.

Bevan, Donald, and Edmund Trzcinski. *Stalag 17.* New York: Dramatists Play Service, 1951.

Boothe, Clare. *Margin for Error.* New York: Random House, 1940.

Boyd, James, ed. *The Free Company Presents . . . : A Collection of Plays about the Meaning of America.* New York: Dodd, Mead and Co., 1941.

Brash, Sally Miller. *The Magic Bond: A Short Timely Play for Children of Nine to Twelve*

Years of Age. In *Plays for Schools-at-War.* Washington, D.C.: Treasury Department, U.S. GPO, 1944 (T66.2: P69/4).

———. *Star for a Day: A Musical Play for High School Students.* In *Plays for Schools-at-War.* Washington, D.C.: Education Section, War Finance Division, Treasury Department, U.S. GPO, 1944 (T66.2: P69/5).

Brennan, Frederick Hazlitt. *The Wookey.* New York: Alfred A. Knopf, 1941.

Brown, Harry. *The Beast in His Hunger.* New York: Alfred A. Knopf, 1949.

———. *A Sound of Hunting.* New York: Alfred A. Knopf, 1946.

Chodorov, Edward. *Common Ground.* New York: Samuel French, 1945 and 1946.

———. *Decision.* New York: Samuel French, 1943.

———. *Those Endearing Young Charms.* New York: Samuel French, 1943.

Connelly, Marc. *The Mole on Lincoln's Cheek.* In James Boyd, ed., *The Free Company Presents . . . : A Collection of Plays about the Meaning of America.* New York: Dodd, Mead and Co., 1941.

Corwin, Norman. *More by Corwin: 16 Radio Dramas by Norman Corwin.* New York: Henry Holt and Co., 1944.

———. *On a Note of Triumph.* Recorded 8 May 1945, audio cassette CORW001. LodeStone, n.d.

———. *On a Note of Triumph.* New York: Simon and Schuster, 1945.

———. *We Hold These Truths.* Recorded 15 December 1941, audio cassette CORW007 and compact disc CORW027, LodeStone, n.d.

Corwin, Norman, et al. *This is War! A Collection of Plays about America on the March.* New York: Dodd, Mead and Co., 1942.

Death without Battle. Governors Island, N.Y.: Military Training Division Headquarters, Second Service Command, 1944.

Jan de Hartog. *Skipper Next to God.* New York: Dramatist Play Service, 1949.

———. *Skipper Next to God.* In *Embassy Successes II, 1945–1946.* London: Sampson Low, Martson and Co., 1946.

Deval, Jacques. *Lorelei.* Typescript, 1938.

d'Usseau, Arnaud, and James Gow. *Deep Are the Roots.* New York: Charles Scribner's Sons, 1946.

Ephron, Phoebe, and Henry Ephron. *Three's a Family.* New York and Los Angeles: Samuel French, [1944?].

The Eternal Weapon. Governors Island, N.Y.: Army Service Forces, Second Service Command, 1944.

Fields, Joseph. *The Doughgirls.* New York: Random House, 1943.

Fisher, Aileen L. *The Squanderbug's Mother Goose.* Washington, D.C.: Education Section, War Finance Division, Treasury Department, U.S. GPO, 1944 (T66.2: Sq 20).

Franken, Rose. *Soldier's Wife.* New York: Samuel French, 1944.

Garrett, Oliver H. P. *Waltz in Goose-Step.* Typescript, 1938.

Ghost Column. Governors Island, N.Y.: Military Training Division Headquarters, Second Service Command, 1944.

Goodrich, Frances, and Albert Hackett. *The Diary of Anne Frank.* New York: Random House, 1956.

Gordon, Ruth. *Over 21.* New York: Dramatists Play Service, 1945.

Gow, James, and Arnaud d'Usseau. *Tomorrow the World.* New York: Charles Scribner's Sons, 1943.

Hackett, Walter. *For the Duration: A Play for Junior and Senior High Schools.* In *Plays for*

Schools-at-War. Washington, D.C.: Treasury Department, U.S. GPO, 1944 (T66.2: P69/2).

Haines, William Wister. *Command Decision*. New York: Random House, 1947.

Hart, Moss. *Winged Victory: The Air Force Play*. New York: Random House, 1943.

Hecht, Ben. *A Flag Is Born*. New York: American League for a Free Palestine, 1946.

———. *We Will Never Die*. Typescript, 1943.

Heggen, Thomas. *Mister Roberts*. Boston: Houghton Mifflin, 1946.

Heggen, Thomas, and Joshua Logan. *Mister Roberts*. New York: Random House, 1948.

Hellman, Lillian. *The Searching Wind*. New York: Viking Press, 1944.

———. *Six Plays by Lillian Hellman*. New York: Vintage Books, 1979.

Heyward, Dorothy, and Howard Rigsby. *South Pacific* (working title, *New Georgia*). Typescript, 1943.

Howard, Sidney. *The Ghost of Yankee Doodle: A Tragedy*. New York: Charles Scribner's Sons, 1938.

James, Dan. *Winter Soldiers*. Typescript, 1942.

Kaufman, George S., and Moss Hart. *The American Way*. New York: Random House, 1939.

Kenward, Allan R. *Cry Havoc*. New York and Los Angeles: Samuel French, 1943.

Kingsley, Sidney. *Five Prizewinning Plays*. Edited by Nena Couch. Columbus: Ohio State University Press, 1995.

———. *The Patriots*. New York, 1943.

Krasna, Norman. *John Loves Mary*. New York: Dramatists Play Service, 1947.

Lass, A. H., Earle L. McGill, and Donald Axelrod, eds. *Plays from Radio*. Cambridge, Mass.: Houghton Mifflin Co., 1948.

Laurents, Arthur. *The Face*. In *Radio's Best Plays*, edited by Joseph Liss. New York: Greenberg, 1947.

———. *Home of the Brave*. New York: Random House, 1946.

———. *The Last Day of the War*. In *Radio Drama in Action*, edited by Eric Barnouw. New York and Toronto: Farrar and Rinehart, 1945.

Levin, Ira. *No Time for Sergeants*. New York: Random House, 1955.

Lindsay, Howard, and Russel Crouse. *State of the Union*. New York: Random House, 1945.

———. *Strip for Action*. New York: Random House, 1942.

Liss, Joseph, ed. *Radio's Best Plays*. New York: Greenberg, 1947.

Loesser, Frank, et al. *About Face!* Washington, D.C.: Army Service Forces, Special Services Division, [c. 1943–44].

———. *Hi, Yank*. Washington, D.C.: Army Service Forces, Special Services Division, [c. 1943–44].

———. *P.F.C. Mary Brown: A WAC Musical Revue*. Washington, D.C.: Army Service Forces, Special Services Division, [c. 1944].

Mabley, Edward, and Leonard Mins. *Temper the Wind*. Typescript, 1947.

MacLeish, Archibald. *Air Raid*. New York: Harcourt, Brace and Co., 1938.

———. *The American Story*. New York: Duell, Sloan and Pearce, 1944.

———. *The Fall of the City*. New York: Farrar and Rinehart, 1937.

Mayorga, Margaret, ed. *The Best One-Act Plays of 1943*. New York: Dodd, Mead and Co., 1944.

Miller, Arthur. *All My Sons*. New York: Penguin Books, 1947.

———. *Arthur Miller's Collected Plays*. New York: Viking Press, 1957.

————. *The Battle of the Ovens.* Typescript, E. I. Du Pont Nemours and Co., 1942.

————. *Bernadine, I Love You.* Typescript, E. I. Du Pont Nemours and Co., 1942.

————. *The Eagle's Nest.* Typescript, E. I. Du Pont Nemours and Co., 1942.

————. *Grandpa and the Statue.* In *Radio Drama in Action,* edited by Erik Barnouw. New York and Toronto: Farrar and Rinehart, 1945.

————. *Grandpa and the Statue.* In *Plays from Radio,* edited by A. H. Lass, Earle L. McGill, and Donald Axelrod. Cambridge, Mass.: Houghton Mifflin Co., 1948.

————. *I Was Married in Bataan.* Typescript, E. I. Du Pont Nemours and Co., 1942.

————. *Listen for the Sound of Wings.* E. I. Du Pont Nemours and Co., 1943. Sound recording (R82.0055).

————. *The Philippines Never Surrendered.* Typescript, E. I. Du Pont Nemours and Co., 1945.

————. *The Story of Gus.* In *Radio's Best Plays,* edited by Joseph Liss. New York: Greenberg, 1947.

————. *That They May Win.* In *The Best One-Act Plays of 1944,* edited by Margaret Mayorga. New York: Dodd, Mead and Co., 1945.

————. *Thunder from the Hills.* Recorded broadcast. The Museum of Radio and Television (New York and Los Angeles), call number R88:0159.

————. *Toward a Farther Star.* Typescript, E. I. Du Pont Nemours and Co., 1942.

Moffitt, John C., and Sinclair Lewis. *It Can't Happen Here.* New York: Dramatists Play Service, 1938.

Nelson, Ralph. *The Wind Is Ninety.* Chicago: Dramatic Publishing Co., 1946.

Oboler, Arch. *Fourteen Radio Plays.* New York: Random House, 1940.

————. *Oboler Omnibus: Radio Plays and Personalities.* New York: Duell, Sloan and Pearce, 1945.

————. *Plays for Americans: Thirteen New Non-royalty Radio Plays.* New York and Toronto: Farrar and Rinehart, 1942.

Oboler, Arch, and Stephen Longstreet, eds. *Free World Theatre: Nineteen New Radio Plays.* New York: Random House, 1944.

Odets, Clifford. *Six Plays of Clifford Odets.* New York: Grove Press, 1979.

Osborn, Paul. *A Bell for Adano.* New York: Alfred A. Knopf, 1945.

Patrick, John. *The Hasty Heart.* New York: Random House, 1945.

————. *Teahouse of the August Moon.* New York: G. P. Putnam's Sons, 1952.

Reins, Bernard J. *Letter to Private Smith.* In *Plays for Schools-at-War.*

Rice, Elmer. *Flight to the West.* New York: Coward-McCann, 1940.

————. *Judgment Day: A Melodrama in Three Acts.* New York: Coward-McCann, 1934.

Rodgers, Richard, and Oscar Hammerstein II. *South Pacific.* In *Six Plays by Rodgers and Hammerstein.* New York: Modern Library, 1959.

Rotter, Fritz, and Allen Vincent. *Letters to Lucerne.* New York: Samuel French, [1943?].

Ryerson, Florence, and Colin Clements. *Harriet.* New York: Charles Scribner's Sons, 1943.

St. Joseph, Ellis. *A Passenger to Bali.* Boston: Little Brown, 1940.

Saroyan, William. *The People with Light Coming out of Them.* In James Boyd, ed., *The Free Company Presents . . . : A Collection of Plays about the Meaning of America.* New York: Dodd, Mead and Co., 1941.

The Time of Your Life. New York: Harcourt, Brace and Company, 1939.

Schiff, Ellen. *Awake and Singing: 7 Classic Plays from the American Jewish Repertoire.* New York: Mentor Books, 1995.

Shaw, Irwin. *The Assassin.* New York: Random House, 1946.

————. *The Gentle People.* New York: Random House, 1939.

————. *Sons and Soldiers.* New York: Random House, 1944.

Shelley, Elsa. *Foxhole in the Parlor.* New York: Dramatists Play Service, 1946.

Sherwood, Robert E. *Abe Lincoln in Illinois.* New York: Charles Scribner's Sons, 1937.

————. *Idiot's Delight.* New York: Charles Scribner's Sons, 1936.

————. *There Shall Be No Night.* New York: Charles Scribner's Sons, 1941.

Soldier Shows. Washington, D.C.: Special Services Division, Army Service Forces, U.S. GPO, 1944 (W109.102: So4).

Soldier Shows. Washington, D.C.: War Department, U.S. GPO, 1945 (W1.43: 28–15c).

Soldier Shows. Washington, D.C.: Special Services Division, Army Service Forces [Entertainment Section], U.S. GPO, 1945 (W109.116: 28).

Spewack, Bella, and Sam Spewack. *Woman Bites Man.* New York: Dramatists Play Service, 1947.

Stevenson, Janet, and Philip Stevenson. *Counterattack: A Play in Three Acts.* Ts, revised edition, 1944.

Stripes. Governors Island, N.Y.: Army Service Forces, Second Service Command, 1944.

This Is Your Enemy. Governors Island, N.Y.: Military Training Division, Second Service Command, 1944.

Tooley, Howard, and Carolyn Wood. *A Letter from Bob: A War Savings Play for Junior and Senior High Schools.* In *Plays for Schools-at-War.* Washington, D.C.: Treasury Department, U.S. GPO, 1945 (T66.2: P69/3).

Van Druten, John. *The Voice of the Turtle.* New York: Random House, 1944.

Welles, Orson. His Honor, the Mayor. In James Boyd, ed., *The Free Company Presents . . . : A Collection of Plays about the Meaning of America.* New York: Dodd, Mead and Co., 1941.

Wilder, Thornton. *Our Town.* 1938. Reprint, New York: Harper and Row, 1957.

————. *The Skin of Our Teeth.* New York and London: Harper and Brothers, 1942.

————. *Three Plays.* New York: Harper and Brothers, 1957.

Williams, Tennessee. *A Streetcar Named Desire.* New York: New Directions, 1947.

Wishengrad, Morton. *The Battle of the Warsaw Ghetto.* In *Radio Drama in Action,* edited by Erik Barnouw. New York and Toronto: Farrar and Rinehart, 1945.

Wood, Maxine. *On Whitman Avenue.* New York: Dramatists Play Service, 1948.

Wouk, Herman. *The Caine Mutiny Court-Martial.* Garden City, N.Y.: Doubleday, 1954.

The Writers and Material Committee of Camp Shows, eds. *"At Ease."* Vol. 1, *Comedy Sketches.* New York: USO–Camp Shows, 1942.

The Writers and Material Committee of Camp Shows, eds. *"At Ease."* Vol. 2, *Minstrel Shows.* New York: USO–Camp Shows, 1942.

SECONDARY SOURCES

Adams, Michael C. *The Best War Ever: America and World War II.* Baltimore: Johns Hopkins University Press, 1994.

Adler, Thomas P. *Mirror on the Stage.* West Lafayette, Ind.: Purdue University Press, 1987.

Anon. *"Winged Victory* in Production." *Theatre Arts* 28 (February 1944): 93–96.

Bach, Steven. *Dazzler: The Life and Times of Moss Hart.* New York: Alfred A. Knopf, 2001.

Bannerman, R. LeRoy. *On a Note of Triumph: Norman Corwin and the Golden Years of Radio.* New York: Carol Publishing Group, 1986.

Beckerman, Bernard, and Howard Siegman. *On Stage: Selected Theatre Reviews from "The New York Times," 1920–1970.* New York: Arno Press and Quadrangle, 1973.

Bérubé, Allan. *Coming Out under Fire: The History of Gay Men and Women in World War II.* New York: Penguin Books, 1990.

Blaustein, Albert P., and Robert L. Zangrado, eds. *Civil Rights and African Americans.* Evanston, Ill.: Northwestern University Press, 1968.

Blue, Howard. *Words at War: World War II Era Radio Drama and the Postwar Broadcasting Industry Blacklist.* Lanham, Md., and Oxford: Scarecrow Press, 2002.

Bordman, Gerald. *American Theatre: A Chronicle of Comedy and Drama, 1930–1969.* New York and Oxford: Oxford University Press, 1996.

Bosworth, Patricia. *Montgomery Clift: A Biography.* New York: Harcourt, Brace, 1978.

Brando, Marlon, with Robert Lindsey. *Brando: Songs My Mother Taught Me.* New York: Random House, 1994.

Breitinger, Eckhard. *Rundfunk und Hörspiel in den USA, 1930–1950.* Trier: Wissern-schaftlicher Verlag, 1987.

Brown, Jared. *The Fabulous Lunts.* New York: Atheneum, 1986.

Brown, John Mason. *Seeing More Things.* New York: McGraw-Hill, 1948.

———. *Seeing Things.* New York and London: McGraw-Hill, 1946.

Brüning, Eberhard. *Das amerikanische Drama der dreißiger Jahre.* Berlin: Rütten und Loening, 1966.

Buford, Kate. *Burt Lancaster: An American Life.* New York: Alfred A. Knopf, 2000.

Burbank, Rex. *Thornton Wilder.* New York: Twayne Publishers, 1961.

Buttitta, Tony, and Barry Witham. *Uncle Sam Presents: A Memoir of the Federal Theatre, 1935–1939.* Philadelphia: University of Pennsylvania Press, 1982.

Carey, Gary. *Marlon Brando: The Only Contender.* New York: St. Martin's Press, 1985.

Chapman, John, ed. *The Burns Mantle Best Plays of 1947–1948.* New York: Dodd, Mead and Co., 1948.

Citron, Atay. "Ben Hecht's Pageant Drama: *A Flag Is Born.*" In *Staging the Holocaust: The Shoah in Drama and Performance,* edited by Claude Schumacher. Cambridge: Cambridge University Press, 1998.

Clurman, Harold. *The Fervent Years.* New York: Alfred A. Knopf, 1945.

Curtin, Kaier. *"We Can Always Call Them Bulgarians": The Emergence of Lesbians and Gay Men on the American Stage.* Boston: Alyson Publications, 1987.

Davis, Ossie, and Ruby Dee. *With Ossie and Ruby: In This Life Together.* New York: William Morrow, 1998.

Diggins, John Patrick. *The Proud Decades: America in War and Peace, 1941–1960.* New York: W. W. Norton, 1989.

Dower, John W. *War without Mercy: Race and Power in the Pacific War.* New York: Pantheon, 1986.

Dunning, John. *Tune in Yesterday.* Englewood Cliffs, N.J.: Prentice-Hall, 1976.

Fetherling, Doug. *The Five Lives of Ben Hecht.* Toronto: Lester and Orpen, 1977.

Fox, Ann Margaret. "Open Houses: American Women Playwrights, Broadway Success, and Media Culture, 1906–1944." Ph.D. diss., Indiana University, 1998.

Gagey, Edmond M. *Revolution in American Drama*. New York: Columbia University Press, 1947.

Gilder, Rosamond. "The Fabulous Hart." *Theatre Arts* 28 (February 1944): 89–98.

Giles, James R. *Irwin Shaw*. Boston: Twayne Publishers, 1983.

Gill, Glenda E. *White Grease Paint on Black Performers: A Study of the Federal Theatre, 1935–1939*. New York: Peter Lang, 1988.

Goldfarb, Alvin. "Select Bibliography of Holocaust Plays, 1933–1997." In *Staging the Holocaust: The Shoah in Drama and Performance*, edited by Claude Schumacher. Cambridge: Cambridge University Press, 1998.

Goldstein, Malcolm. *The Art of Thornton Wilder*. Lincoln, Nebr.: University of Nebraska Press, 1965.

———. *George S. Kaufman: His Life, His Theater*. New York and Oxford: Oxford University Press, 1979.

———. *The Political Stage: American Drama and the Theater of the Great Depression*. New York: Oxford University Press, 1974.

Gould, Jean. *Modern American Playwrights*. New York: Dodd, Mead and Co., 1966.

Graver, Lawrence. *An Obsession with Anne Frank*. Berkeley and Los Angeles: University of California Press, 1995.

Haberman, Donald. *The Plays of Thornton Wilder: A Critical Study*. Middletown, Conn.: Wesleyan University Press, 1967.

Hecht, Ben. *A Child of the Century*. New York: Simon and Schuster, 1954.

Himelstein, Morgan Y. *Drama Was a Weapon: The Left-Wing Theatre in New York, 1929–1941*. New Brunswick, N.J.: Rutgers University Press, 1963.

Hogan, Robert. *The Independence of Elmer Rice*. Carbondale and Edwardsville: Southern Illinois University Press, 1965.

Hutchens, John K. "The 'Parade' Goes On." *New York Times*, 22 November 1942, p. 12.

Jenks, Edward. "759 Stations and Going Strong." *New York Times*, 5 August 1942, p. 10.

Kaiser, Charles. *The Gay Metropolis, 1940–1996*. Boston and New York: Houghton Mifflin, 1997.

Koppes, Clayton R., and Gregory D. Black. *Hollywood Goes to War: How Politics, Profits and Propaganda Shaped World War II Movies*. Berkeley and Los Angeles: University of California Press, 1987.

Kuhnt, Christian. "Approaching the Music for *A Flag Is Born*." *Kurt Weill Newsletter* 20 (Spring 2002): 8–9.

Laurents, Arthur. *Original Story By*. New York: Alfred A. Knopf, 2000.

Lawrence, Jerome. *Actor: The Life and Times of Paul Muni*. New York: G. P. Putnam's Sons, 1974.

Lipstadt, Deborah E. *Beyond Belief: The American Press and the Coming of the Holocaust, 1933–1945*. New York and London: The Free Press, 1986.

Loesser, Susan. *A Most Remarkable Fella: Frank Loesser and the Guys and Dolls in His Life*. New York: D. I. Fine, 1993.

MacAdams, William. *Ben Hecht: The Man behind the Legend*. New York: Charles Scribner's Sons, 1990.

MacDonald, James. "Himmler Program Kills Polish Jews." *New York Times*, 26 November 1942, p. 10.

Malden, Karl. *When Do I Start? A Memoir*. New York: Simon and Schuster, 1997.

Mantle, Burns. *The Best Plays of 1938–39*. New York: Dodd, Mead, and Co., 1939.

———. *The Best Plays of 1941–42*. New York: Dodd, Mead, and Co., 1942.

———. *The Best Plays of 1942–43.* New York: Dodd, Mead, and Co., 1943.

———. *The Best Plays of 1943–44.* New York: Dodd, Mead and Co., 1944.

———. *The Best Plays of 1945–46.* New York: Dodd, Mead and Co., 1946.

McBrien, William. *Cole Porter: A Biography.* New York: Alfred A. Knopf, 1998.

McGann, Mary E. "Voices in the Dark: A Study of the Radio Achievement of Norman Corwin, Archibald MacLeish, Louis MacNeice, Dylan Thomas, and Samuel Beckett." Ph.D. diss., Indiana University, 1979.

McKnight, Bob Stuart. "Original Army Shows." *Theatre Arts* 27 (July 1943): 426–433.

Melnick, Ralph. *The Stolen Legacy of Anne Frank.* New Haven: Yale University Press, 1997.

Meserve, Walter J. *Robert Sherwood: Reluctant Moralist.* New York: Pegasus, 1970.

Mintz, Alan. *Popular Culture and the Shaping of Holocaust Memory in America.* Seattle: University of Washington Press, 2001.

Moody, Richard. *Lillian Hellman: Playwright.* New York: Bobbs-Merrill Co., 1972.

Murphy, Brenda. *American Realism and American Drama, 1880–1940.* Cambridge: Cambridge University Press, 1987.

Nahshon, Edna. "From Geopathology to Redemption: *A Flag Is Born* on the Broadway Stage." *Kurt Weill Newsletter* 20 (Spring 2002): 5–8.

Novick, Peter. *The Holocaust in American Life.* Boston: Houghton Mifflin, 1999.

O'Connor, John, and Lorraine Brown. *Free, Adult, Uncensored: The Living History of the Federal Theatre Project.* Washington, D.C.: New Republic Books, 1978.

Pawley, Thomas D. "Three Views of the Returning Black Veteran." *Black-American Literature Forum* 16 (1982): 163–167.

Rabkin, Gerald. *Drama and Commitment: Politics in the American Theatre of the Thirties.* Bloomington: Indiana University Press, 1964.

Rice, Elmer. *Minority Report: An Autobiography.* London: Heinemann, 1963.

Rice, Vernon. "*On Whitman Avenue* Boldly Faces the Negro Problem." *New York Post,* 9 May 1944.

Rosenfeld, Alvin H. "Popularization and Memory." In *Lessons and Legacies: The Meaning of the Holocaust in a Changing World,* edited by Peter Hayes. Evanston, Ill.: Northwestern University Press, 1991.

Roth, Philip. *I Married a Communist.* New York: Vintage Books, 1999.

Rothstein, Mervyn. "Q. Where's Maxwell Anderson?" *New York Times,* 29 September 1988, pp. C21 and C25.

Sagan, Alex. "An Optimistic Icon: Anne Frank's Canonization in Postwar Culture." *German Politics and Society* 13 (Fall 1995): 95–107

Shindler, Colin. *Hollywood Goes to War: Films and American Society, 1939–1952.* London and Boston: Routledge and Kegan Paul, 1979.

Shivers, Alfred S. *The Life of Maxwell Anderson.* New York: Stein and Day, 1983.

———. *Maxwell Anderson.* Boston: Twayne Publishers, 1976.

Shnayerson, Michael. *Irwin Shaw: A Biography.* New York: G. P. Putnam's Sons, 1989.

Shuman, R. Baird. *Robert Emmet Sherwood.* New York: Twayne Publishers, 1954.

Simon, Linda. *Thornton Wilder: His World.* Garden City, N.Y.: Doubleday, 1979.

Smiley, Sam. *The Drama of Attack: Didactic Plays of the American Depression.* Columbia, Mo.: University of Missouri Press, 1972.

Smith, Wendy. *Real Life Drama: The Group Theatre and America, 1931–1940.* New York: Alfred A. Knopf, 1990.

War Bond Plays and Other Dramatic Material for Use in Connection with War Finance Promotion Washington, D.C.: Treasury Department, U.S. GPO, 1943 (T66.2: P69).

War Savings Programs: A Handbook of Dramatic Material. Washington, D.C.: Treasury Department, Education Division, U.S. GPO, 1943 (T66.6: P94).

Weales, Gerald. "Arthur Miller Takes the Air." *American Drama* 5 (Fall 1995): 1–15.

———. *Clifford Odets, Playwright.* New York: Bobbs-Merrill, 1971.

Weber, Bruce. "A Play outside the Mainstream of Its Time and Ours." *New York Times,* 14 September 2001, p. E3.

Wertheim, Albert. *"A View from the Bridge."* In *The Cambridge Companion to Arthur Miller,* edited by Christopher Bigsby, pp. 101–114. Cambridge and New York: Cambridge University Press, 1997.

Whitfield, Stephen J. "The Politics of Pageantry, 1936–1946." *American Jewish History* 84.3 (September 1996): 221–251.

INDEX

Page numbers in italics refer to illustrations.

Clift, Montgomery: *Searching Wind,* 82; *Skin of Our Teeth,* 78; *There Shall Be No Night,* 293n35
Coleman, Nancy, *Liberty Jones,* 40
Comden, Betty, *On the Town,* xi, 113
comedy, 103–18
Command Decision (Haines), 245–49
Common Ground (Chodorov), 95–97
communism: desire to exterminate, 85; *Till the Day I Die,* 8–9; *Woman Bites Dog,* 240–41
concentration camps: in *Candle in the Wind,* 37; *Common Ground,* 95–97; as death camps, 90–91; in *Listen for the Sound of Wings,* 206; not in plays, 53; Theresienstadt, xvi; in *Tomorrow the World,* 87, 89; truth of, xiv, 225–26, 272; vs. death camps, 291n7
Concerning Axis Propaganda (Corwin), 189
Connelly, Marc, *Mole on Lincoln's Cheek,* 179–80
conscience, appeal to, 121–22
Constitution, 195; Bill of Rights, 177, 182–85; Thirteenth Amendment, 261
conversion, 3
Corregidor, 203, 208
Corwin, Norman: art vs. commerce, 304n53; *Concerning Axis Propaganda,* 189; *Enemy,* 189; *On a Note of Triumph,* 219–24; *This Is War!,* 176, 185–87, 304n67; *We Hold These Truths,* xiii, 182–85; *To the Young,* 189
Couch, Nina (editor), *Five Prizewinning Plays,* 72
Counterattack (Stevenson), 67, 253
Coward, Noel, *Private Lives,* 255
Crouse, Russel: *Army Play by Play,* 126–27; and Kurt Kasznar, 299n5; *State of the Union,* xiv, 256–61; *Strip for Action,* 106–107
Cry Havoc (Kenward), 63–67, 295n8
Cry Uncle (Bingham), 168
cultural diversity, 128–29, 132–34
Curtin, Kaier, 295n8

D.P.s (displaced persons), 273–74
daily life, importance of, 19
Date With Judy (radio series), 104
Davis, Luther, *Kiss Them for Me,* 298n62
Day's Work for America (Donovan), 170
de Hartog, Jan, *Skipper Next to God,* 272–73
Dear Adolf (Benét), 210–11
Dear Ruth (Krasna), 113, 252, 254
Death without Battle, 152–53
Decision (Chodorov), 100–103, 261
decision makers, 245–49
Deep Are the Roots (Gow and d'Usseau), xiv, 262–65, *263*
democracy, 69–70; superiority of, 71–72
demographic change, 106, 270–71
despair, 35–36
Deval, Jacques, *Lorelei,* 10–11, 292n17

Diary of Anne Frank (Goodrich and Hackett), xiv, 280–82, *281*
dictatorships, 3–4; in *Bell for Adano,* 69–70; in *It Can't Happen Here,* 5–7
Digges, Dudley, *82*
Dimitrov, Georgi, basis for *Judgment Day,* 3, 291n3
displaced persons (D.P.s), 273–74
diversion, 1–2, 3
diversity, 178–79
Donovan, Alice B.: *And We Talk about Sacrifice,* 170–71; *Day's Work for America,* 170
Doughgirls (Fields), 107–108, 296nn50,52
Douglass, Ruby Jane, 149, 300n24
Drama Was a Weapon (Himelstein), 173
DuPont Corporation, 201–202, 206
d'Usseau, Arnaud: *Deep Are the Roots,* xiv, 262–65; *Tomorrow the World,* 83–90, 181
Dyrenforth, Harold, *Flight to the West,* 26

Eagle's Nest (Miller), 204–205
Earhart, Amelia, 203–204
Eastern Front, *Counterattack,* 67
economic policy, 119–20
Education for Death (Ziemer), 190
Education for Life (Atkins), 190–91
Education for Victory (Atkins), 190, 191
Einstein, Albert, on *Flight to the West,* 25
Eldredge, Florence: *American Way,* 16; *Skin of Our Teeth,* 76
end of the world, 76–77
Enemy (Corwin), 189
Ensign Pulver, 250
enumeratio, 218
Ephron, Phoebe and Henry, *Three's a Family,* 108–109
Eretz Yisrael, 274, 276
Eternal Weapon, 153–54
Eve of St. Mark (Anderson), xi, 56–59, 295n4
"Eve of St. Mark" (Keats), 58
Evensen, Isobel, *New Recruit,* 170
evil personified, 78–79
Execution (Oboler), 217–18
extramarital sex: *Doughgirls,* 107–108; *Streetcar Named Desire,* 270–71

fables, *Gentle People,* 42–43
Face (Laurents), 199–200, 303n38
faith, 239–40
Fall of the City (MacLeish), xiii, 47–50
fascism, 4–5; anthropomorphization of, 212–13; attraction of, during Depression, 17–19; desire to embrace, 50; ostracism of, 41
Father Wins the Peace (Bridgman), 169–70
fatherhood, and *Three's a Family,* 108–109
Federal Theatre Project: *It Can't Happen Here,* 5; power of theatre, 2–3
feminism, 61, 106, 110–11, 117–18, 203–204

Albert Wertheim (1940–2003) was Professor of English and of Theatre and Drama at Indiana University. He published widely on modern and classic British and American drama and on postcolonial writing; directed several NEH seminars on politics in the theatre and on new literatures from Africa, the West Indies, and the Pacific; and served on the editorial boards of *American Drama, Theatre Survey, South African Theatre Journal,* and *Westerly.* He authored *The Dramatic Art of Athol Fugard: From South Africa to the World,* also published by Indiana University Press.